iPhoto 6

THE MISSING MANUAL

*The book that
should have been
in the box*

iPhoto 6

THE MISSING MANUAL

David Pogue and Derrick Story

POGUE PRESS™

O'REILLY®

Beijing • Cambridge • Farnham • Köln • Paris • Sebastopol • Taipei • Tokyo

iPhoto 6: The Missing Manual

by David Pogue and Derrick Story

Published by O'Reilly Media, Inc., 1005 Gravenstein Highway North, Sebastopol, CA 95472.

O'Reilly Media books may be purchased for educational, business, or sales promotional use. Online editions are also available for most titles: *safari.oreilly.com*. For more information, contact our corporate/institutional sales department: (800) 998-9938 or *corporate@oreilly.com*.

March 2006:   First edition.

This book uses a durable and flexible lay-flat binding.

ISBN: 0-596-52725-X

Table of Contents

Part Two: iPhoto Basics

The Missing Credits

About the Authors

 David Pogue is the weekly computer columnist for the *New York Times*, an Emmy-winning correspondent for *CBS News Sunday Morning*, and the creator of the Missing Manual series. He's the author or co-author of 38 books, including 17 in this series and six in the "For Dummies" line (including *Macs, Magic, Opera*, and *Classical Music*). In his other life, David is a former Broadway show conductor, a magician, and a pianist. News, photos, links to his columns and weekly videos await at *www.davidpogue.com*.

He welcomes feedback about his books by email at *david@pogueman.com*.

 Derrick Story focuses on digital photography, music, and Mac computing in his teaching and writing. You can keep up with his online articles, weblogs, and books at *www.oreilly.com*. Derrick's also a regular contributor to *Macworld* magazine and speaker at the Macworld Expo. You can listen to his photography podcasts and browse his daily tips and tricks at *www.thedigitalstory.com*.

About the Creative Team

Joseph Schorr (co-author, first two editions), a former *Macworld* contributing editor, began collaborating with David Pogue in 1982—on musical comedies at Yale. Years later, they co-authored six editions of *Macworld Mac Secrets*. Now that Joe is a product manager at Apple, he's technically not supposed to work on books like this. Still, many chapters of this book are based on his original prose.

Rose Cassano (cover illustration) has worked as an independent designer and illustrator for 20 years. Assignments have spanned everything from the nonprofit sector to corporate clientele. She lives in beautiful southern Oregon, grateful for the miracles of modern technology that make living and working there a reality. Email: *cassano@cdsnet.net*. Web: *www.rosecassano.com*.

Dennis Cohen (technical reviewer, previous editions) has served as the technical reviewer for many bestselling Mac books, including several editions of *Macworld Mac Secrets* and most Missing Manual titles. He is the author or co-author of *FileMaker Pro 7 Bible, Mac Digital Photography,* and numerous other books. Email: *drcohen@mac.com*.

Teresa Noelle Roberts (copy editor) is a freelance copy editor and proofreader, as well as a published fiction writer and poet. When she can tear herself away from the computer, she may be found gardening, belly dancing, or enjoying the beautiful beaches of New England.

Phil Simpson (design and layout) works out of his office in Southbury, Connecticut, where he has had his graphic design business since 1982. He is experienced in many facets of graphic design, including corporate identity, publication design, and corporate and medical communications. Email: *pmsimpson@earthlink.net.*

Lesa Snider (production/technical editor and graphics goddess) assists David Pogue on many projects. As Chief Evangelist for iStockphoto.com and a veteran writer for international graphics publications, Lesa is on a mission to teach the world how to create beautiful graphics. You can see more of her work at *TheGraphicReporter.com,* and catch her live at many conferences.

Acknowledgements

In the three years that I've been writing articles about iPhoto and speaking at conferences and user group meetings, I've received many helpful comments from Mac DevCenter readers and enthusiasts who have attended my talks. For those of you who have shared your passion for digital photography with me, I want you to know that your comments, questions, and support are very much a part of this book.

—*Derrick Story*

The Missing Manual series is a joint venture between Pogue Press (the dream team introduced on these pages) and O'Reilly Media (a dream publishing partner). I'm indebted, as always, to Tim O'Reilly, Mark Brokering, Betsy Waliszewski, and the rest of the gang.

I'm also grateful to proofreaders John Cacciatore and Sada Preisch; to Apple's Greg Scanlon; and to David Rogelberg. Above all, thanks to Jennifer, Kelly, Tia, and baby Jeffrey, who make these books—and everything else—possible.

—*David Pogue*

The Missing Manual Series

Missing Manuals are witty, superbly written guides to computer products that don't come with printed manuals (which is just about all of them). Each book features a handcrafted index; cross-references to specific page numbers (not just "see Chapter 14"); and RepKover, a detached-spine binding that lets the book lie perfectly flat without the assistance of weights or cinder blocks.

Recent and upcoming titles include:

- *Mac OS X: The Missing Manual,* Tiger Edition by David Pogue
- *iMovie 6 & iDVD: The Missing Manual* by David Pogue
- *iPod & iTunes: The Missing Manual,* Fourth Edition by J.D. Biersdorfer
- *AppleScript: The Missing Manual* by Adam Goldstein
- *iWork: The Missing Manual* by Jim Elferdink

- *Office 2004 for Macintosh: The Missing Manual* by Mark H. Walker, Franklin Tessler, and Paul Berkowitz

- *FileMaker Pro 8: The Missing Manual* by Geoff Coffey and Susan Prosser

- *Switching to the Mac: The Missing Manual,* Tiger Edition by David Pogue and Adam Goldstein

- *Photoshop Elements 3: The Missing Manual* by Barbara Brundage

- *Google: The Missing Manual* by Sarah Milstein and Rael Dornfest

- *eBay: The Missing Manual* by Nancy Conner

- *Dreamweaver 8: The Missing Manual* by David Sawyer McFarland

- *Flash 8: The Missing Manual* by Emily Moore

- *CSS: The Missing Manual* by David Sawyer McFarland

- *AppleWorks 6: The Missing Manual* by Jim Elferdink and David Reynolds

- *Windows XP Home Edition: The Missing Manual,* 2nd Edition by David Pogue

- *Windows XP Pro: The Missing Manual,* 2nd Edition by David Pogue, Craig Zacker, and Linda Zacker

- *Windows Vista Home Edition: The Missing Manual,* by David Pogue

THE MISSING CREDITS

Introduction

In case you haven't heard, the digital camera market is exploding. By early 2006, a staggering 92 percent of cameras sold were digital cameras. It's taken a few decades— the underlying technology used in most digital cameras was invented in 1969—but film is decidedly on the decline.

And why not? The appeal of digital photography is huge. When you shoot digitally, you never have to pay a cent for film or photo processing. You get instant results, viewing your photos just moments after shooting them, making even Polaroids seem painfully slow by comparison. As a digital photographer, you can even be your own darkroom technician—without the darkroom. You can retouch and enhance photos, make enlargements, and print out greeting cards using your home computer. Sharing your pictures with others is far easier, too, since you can burn them to CD, email them to friends, or post them on the Web. As one fan puts it: "There are no 'negatives' in digital photography."

But there is one problem. When most people try to *do* all this cool stuff, they find themselves drowning in a sea of technical details: JPEG compression, EXIF tags, file format compatibility, image resolutions, FTP clients, and so on. It isn't pretty.

The cold reality is that while digital photography is full of promise, it's also been full of headaches. During the early years of digital cameras, just making the camera-to-computer connection was a nightmare. You had to mess with serial or USB cables; install device drivers; and use proprietary software to transfer, open, and convert camera images into a standard file format. If you handled all these tasks perfectly—and sacrificed a young male goat during the spring equinox—you ended up with good digital pictures.

iPhoto Arrives

Apple recognized this mess and finally decided to do something about it. When Steve Jobs gave his keynote address at Macworld Expo in January 2002, he referred to the "chain of pain" ordinary people experienced when attempting to download, store, edit, and share their digital photos.

He also focused on another growing problem among digital camera users: Once you start shooting free, filmless photos, they pile up quickly. Before you know it, you have 6,000 pictures of your kid playing soccer. Just organizing and keeping track of all these photos is enough to drive you insane.

Apple's answer to all these problems was iPhoto, a simple and uncluttered program designed to organize, edit, and distribute digital photos without the nightmarish hassles. iPhoto 2 through iPhoto 6 carried on the tradition with added features and better speed. (There was no iPhoto 3, however. Keep that in mind if someone tries to sell you a copy on eBay.)

To be sure, iPhoto isn't the most powerful image management software in the world. Like Apple's other iProducts (iMovie, iTunes, iDVD, and so on), its design subscribes to its own little 80/20 rule: 80 percent of us really don't need more than about 20 percent of the features you'd find in a full-blown, $500 digital–asset management program like, say, Apple's own Aperture.

Today, millions of Mac fans use iPhoto. Evidently, there were a lot of digital camera buffs out there, feeling the pain and hoping that iPhoto would provide some much-needed relief.

What's New in iPhoto 6

iPhoto 6 doesn't represent a big overhaul; Apple gave it more nips and tucks than massive surgery. Still, there's quite a bit of juicy stuff in the new version:

- **Speed, glorious speed.** This one's the biggie: iPhoto is dramatically faster than previous versions. Faster opening, faster quitting, faster scrolling. It's fast enough, in fact, that it can manage 250,000 photo at a time—as Apple puts it, enough to handle 1,000 pictures a month for 20 years. All the traditional workarounds and speed tips described in Chapter 14 are far less important now, because a single iPhoto library will keep you coasting for several years.

- **External folder management.** iPhoto can manage your photos even if it doesn't add them to its own library, thus erasing a long-standing grievance of people whose photos were already beautifully organized on the hard drive. The program is perfectly capable of tracking pictures that are outside of its own library.

- **Calendars, cards, and better books.** In addition to the usual professionally published books of your photos and Kodak prints, you can now order custom calendars, postcards, and greeting cards (Chapter 10). And if you do decide to order a book, you'll discover that the printing quality has been upgraded substantially.

- **Full-screen editing.** You can now edit photos in a full-screen, edge-to-edge mode that doesn't eat up space with menus, windows and so on. Movable editing palettes float above the image for your convenience.

- **Photocasting.** Talk about instant gratification! Talk about technophobic grandparents! Now you can "publish" an album full of photos, and your fans or relatives can "subscribe" to it. Whenever you make changes to that album—by adding more pix, for example—your grateful subscribers see the changes reflected automatically.

- **One-click effects.** A new editing palette turns a photo into a sepia-toned, monochrome, desaturated, or saturation-enhanced version.

- **Miscellaneous goodies.** The rest of iPhoto's cornucopia of newness is just garnish. You can trigger a slideshow of the photos you've put into a book layout; in the library, a superimposed label identifies the date or names of the "film rolls" you're scrolling through so you know when to stop; Smart Albums let you search on more kinds of photo data (like shutter speed and aperture size); the program is compatible with the RAW files (page 87) from more camera models, and handles them better; you can embed ColorSync profiles into your pictures; and so on. Oh, and the iPhoto window has been given a 2006 non-brushed-metal makeover.

Apple did very little rejiggering of iPhoto's tool icons, menu commands, and photo techniques. If anything, these elements have grown easier to understand. All of the "stuff you can do with your photos" icons (Slideshow, Email, Order Prints, and so on) now appear at the bottom of the window; you don't have to add them manually, as in iPhoto 5.

About This Book

Don't let the rumors fool you. iPhoto may be simple, but it isn't simplistic. It offers a wide range of tools, shortcuts, and database-like features; a complete arsenal of photo-presentation features; and sophisticated multimedia and Internet hooks. Unfortunately, many of the best techniques aren't covered in the only "manual" you get with iPhoto—its slow, sparse electronic help screens.

This book was born to address two needs. First, it's designed to serve as the iPhoto manual—the book that should have been in the box. It explores each iPhoto feature in depth, offers shortcuts and workarounds, and unearths features that the online help doesn't even mention.

Second, this book provides an invaluable grounding in professional photography. Used together, any good digital camera and iPhoto have all the *technical* tools you need to produce photographic presentations of stunning visual quality. What's missing are the *artistic* factors involved in shooting—composition, lighting, and manual exposure—and how to apply them using the myriad features packed into the modern digital camera. This book gives you all you need to know.

And to make it all go down easier, this book has been printed in full color. Kind of makes sense for a book about photography, doesn't it?

About the Outline

This book is divided into four parts, each containing several chapters:

- Part 1, **Digital Cameras: The Missing Manual,** is the course in photography and digital cameras promised above. These three chapters cover buying, using, and exploiting your digital camera; choosing the proper image resolution settings; and getting the most out of batteries and memory cards. This section of the book creates a bridge between everyday snapshots and the kinds of emotionally powerful shots you see in magazines and newspapers.

- Part 2, **iPhoto Basics,** covers the fundamentals of getting your photos into iPhoto, organizing and filing them, searching them, and editing them to compensate for weak lighting (or weak photography).

- Part 3, **Meet Your Public,** is all about the payoff, the moment you've presumably been waiting for ever since you snapped the shots—showing them off. It covers the many ways iPhoto can present those photos to other people: as a slideshow, as prints you order from the Internet or make yourself, as a professionally published gift book, on a Web page, by email, or as a QuickTime-movie slideshow that you post on the Web or distribute on CD or even DVD. It also covers sharing your iPhoto collection across an office network with other Macs, with other account holders on the same Mac, and with other iPhoto fans across the Internet.

- Part 4, **iPhoto Stunts,** takes you way beyond the basics. It covers a miscellaneous potpourri of additional iPhoto features, including turning photos into screen savers or desktop pictures on your Mac, exporting the photos in various formats, using iPhoto plug-ins and accessory programs, managing (or even switching) Photo Libraries, backing up your photos using iPhoto's Burn to CD command, and even getting photos to and from cameraphones and Palm organizers.

At the end of the book, Appendix A offers troubleshooting guidance, Appendix B goes through iPhoto's menus one by one to make sure that every last feature has been covered, and Appendix C lists some Web sites that will help fuel your growing addiction to digital photography.

About→These→Arrows

Throughout this book, and throughout the Missing Manual series, you'll find sentences like this one: "Open the System folder→Libraries→Fonts folder." That's shorthand for a much longer instruction that directs you to open three nested folders in sequence. That instruction might read: "On your hard drive, you'll find a folder called System. Open it. Inside the System folder window is a folder called Libraries. Open that. Inside *that* folder is yet another one called Fonts. Double-click to open it, too."

Similarly, this kind of arrow shorthand helps to simplify the business of choosing commands in menus, as shown in Figure I-1.

About MissingManuals.com

At *www.missingmanuals.com*, you'll find news, articles, and updates to the books in this series.

But if you click the name of this book and then the Errata link, you'll find a unique resource: a list of corrections and updates that have been made in successive printings of this book. You can mark important corrections right into your own copy of the book, if you like.

In fact, the same page offers an invitation for you to submit such corrections and updates yourself. In an effort to keep the book as up-to-date and accurate as possible, each time we print more copies of this book, we'll make any confirmed corrections you've suggested. Thanks in advance for reporting any glitches you find!

In the meantime, we'd love to hear your suggestions for new books in the Missing Manual line. There's a place for that on the Web site, too, as well as a place to sign up for free email notification of new titles in the series.

Figure I-1:
In this book, arrow notations help to simplify folder and menu instructions. For example, "Choose ■→Dock→Position on Left" is a more compact way of saying, "From the ■ menu, choose Dock; from the submenu that then appears, choose Position on Left."

The Very Basics

You'll find very little jargon or nerd terminology in this book. You will, however, encounter a few terms and concepts that you'll see frequently in your Macintosh life. They include:

- **Clicking.** This book offers three kinds of instructions that require you to use the mouse or trackpad attached to your Mac. To *click* means to point the arrow cursor at something onscreen and then—without moving the cursor at all—press and release the clicker button on the mouse (or laptop trackpad). To *double-click,* of course, means to click twice in rapid succession, again without moving the cursor at all. And to *drag* means to move the cursor while keeping the button continuously pressed.

When you're told to ⌘-*click* something, you click while pressing the ⌘ key (next to the Space bar). Such related procedures as *Shift-clicking, Option-clicking,* and *Control-clicking* work the same way—just click while pressing the corresponding key on the bottom row of your keyboard. (On non-U.S. Mac keyboards, the Option key may be labeled Alt instead.)

Note: On Windows PCs, the mouse has two buttons. The left one is for clicking normally; the right one produces a tiny shortcut menu of useful commands (see the note below). But new Macs come with Apple's Mighty Mouse, a mouse that looks like it has only one button but can actually detect which side of its rounded front you're pressing. If you've turned on the feature in System Preferences, you, too, can right-click things on the screen.

That's why, all through this book, you'll see the phrase, "Control-click the photo (or right-click it)." That's telling you that Control-clicking will do the job—but if you've got a two-button mouse or you've turned on the two-button feature of the Mighty Mouse, right-clicking might be more efficient.

- **Menus.** The *menus* are the words in the lightly striped bar at the top of your screen. You can either click one of these words to open a pull-down menu of commands (and then click again on a command), or click and *hold* the button as you drag down the menu to the desired command (and release the button to activate the command). Either method works fine.

Note: Apple has officially changed what it calls the little menu that pops up when you Control-click (or right-click) something on the screen. It's still a *contextual* menu, in that the menu choices depend on the context of what you click—but it's now called a *shortcut* menu. That term not only matches what it's called in Windows, but it's slightly more descriptive about its function. Shortcut menu is the term you'll find in this book.

- **Keyboard shortcuts.** Every time you take your hand off the keyboard to move the mouse, you lose time and potentially disrupt your creative flow. That's why many experienced Mac fans use keystroke combinations instead of menu commands wherever possible. ⌘-P opens the Print dialog box, for example, and ⌘-M minimizes the current window to the Dock.

When you see a shortcut like ⌘-Q (which closes the current program), it's telling you to hold down the ⌘ key, and, while it's down, type the letter Q, and then release both keys.

If you've mastered this much information, you have all the technical background you need to enjoy *iPhoto 6: The Missing Manual.*

1

Part One:
Digital Cameras:
The Missing Manual

Welcome to Digital Photography

A pple used to have a cute slogan for iPhoto: "Shoot like Ansel; organize like Martha." Today, of course, that slogan would never fly—and the reference to Martha Stewart is only half the problem.

The truth is, iPhoto doesn't help you shoot like Ansel Adams, either. In fact, it does absolutely nothing for your photography skills.

But this book will. The first three chapters cover both the basics and the secrets that the pros use to take consistently good photographs. After all, if you're going to the trouble of mastering a new program, then you should be rewarded with stunning results. Or, put another way: Beautiful pictures in, beautiful pictures out.

Meet Digital Photography

When you use a film camera, your pictures are "memorized" by billions of silver halide crystals suspended on celluloid. Most digital cameras, on the other hand, store your pictures on a memory card.

It's a special kind of memory: *flash* memory. Unlike the RAM in your Macintosh, the contents of flash memory survive even when the machine is turned off. You can erase and reuse a digital camera's memory card over and over again—a key to the great economy of digital photography.

At this millisecond of technology time, most digital cameras are slightly slower than film cameras in almost every regard. Generally speaking, they're slower to turn on, slower to autofocus, and slower to recover from one shot before they're ready to take another.

Once you've captured a picture, however, digital cameras provide almost nothing but advantages over film.

Instant Feedback

You can view a miniature version of the photo on the camera's built-in screen. If there's something about the picture that bothers you—like the telephone pole growing out of your best friend's head—you can simply delete it and try again. Once the shooting session is over, you leave knowing that nothing but good photos are on your camera. By contrast, with traditional film photography, you have no real idea how your pictures turned out until you open that sealed drugstore envelope and flip through the prints. More often than not, there are one or two pictures that you really like, and the rest are wasted money.

Instant feedback becomes a real benefit when you're under pressure to deliver excellent photographs. Imagine the hapless photographer who, having offered to shoot candid photos during a friend's wedding reception, later opens the envelope of prints and discovers that the flash had malfunctioned all evening, resulting in three rolls of shadowy figures in a darkened hotel ballroom. A digital camera would have alerted the photographer to the problem immediately.

In short, digital photographers sleep much better at night. They never worry about how the day's pictures will turn out—they already know!

Cheap Pix

Digital cameras also save you a great deal of money. Needless to say, you don't spend anything on developing. Printing out pictures on a photo printer at home costs money, but few people print every single shot they take. And where are most of your prints now? In a shoebox somewhere?

Printing out 4 x 6 prints at home, using an inkjet photo printer, costs about the same amount as you'd pay at the drugstore. But when you want enlargements, printing your own is vastly less expensive. Even on the glossy $1-per-sheet inkjet photo paper, an 8 x 10 costs about $1.50 or so (ink cartridges are expensive), compared with about $4 ordered online through iPhoto. A poster-sized print from a wide-format photo printer (13 x 19) will cost you about $3.50 at home, compared with $15 from an online photo lab.

Take More Risks

Because you have nothing to lose by taking a shot—and everything to gain—digital photography allows your creative juices to flow. If you don't like that shot of randomly piled shoes on the front porch, then, what the heck, erase it.

With the expense of developing taken out of the equation, you're free to shoot everything that catches your eye and decide later whether to keep it or not. This is how a digital camera can make you a better photographer—by freeing up your creativity. Your risk-taking will lead to more exciting images than you ever dreamed you'd take.

More Fun

Add it all up, and digital photography is more fun than traditional shooting. No more disappointing prints and wasted money. Instead, you enjoy the advantages of instant feedback, flexibility, and creativity.

But that's just the beginning, since now there's iPhoto. Suddenly photography isn't just about producing a stack of 4 x 6 pieces of paper. Thanks to iPhoto, now your photos are infinitely more flexible. At the end of the day, you get to sit down with your Mac and create instant slideshows, screen savers, desktop pictures, professional Web pages, and email attachments. Shoot the most adorable shot ever taken of your daughter, and minutes later it's on its way to Grandma.

Photography doesn't get any better than this.

Buying a Digital Camera

Citizens of the world bought 96 million digital cameras in 2005, and their popularity shows no signs of stopping. Already, digital cameras outsell film cameras—a shift of culture-jarring proportions.

The major players in this market are Sony, Olympus, Nikon, HP, Kodak, and Canon. They're not alone, however. Every company ever associated with electronics or cameras—Panasonic, Casio, Leica, and so on—also has a finger in the pie. Each company offers a variety of models and a wide range of prices, which compete fiercely for your dollars. Some of these companies release new models *every six to twelve months*. And, exactly as in other high-tech industries, each generation offers better features, improved resolution, and lower prices.

If you're in the market for a new digital camera, the rest of this chapter is for you. It's dedicated to helping you find that diamond in the rough: the camera with the features you need at a price you can afford.

Don't worry about the different marketing categories for cameras: entry level, consumer, prosumer, pro, whatever. Just read about the features available in the following pages—presented here roughly in order of importance—and consider how much they're worth to you.

Image Resolution

The first number you probably see in the description of a digital camera is the number of *megapixels* it offers.

A pixel (short for *picture element*) is one tiny colored dot, one of the thousands or millions that compose a single digital photograph. You can't escape learning this term, since pixels are everything in computer graphics.

You need at least one million pixels—that is, one megapixel—for something as simple as a 4 x 6 inch print. Thus the shorthand: Instead of saying that your camera has 4,100,000 pixels, you'd say that it's a 4.1-megapixel camera.

What you're describing is its *resolution*. For instance, a 5-megapixel camera has better resolution than a 3-megapixel camera. (It also costs more.)

So how many pixels do you need?

Pictures on the screen

Many digital photos are destined to be shown solely on a computer screen: to be sent by email, posted on a Web page, pasted into a FileMaker database, turned into a screen saver, or used as a desktop picture.

If this is what you have in mind when you think about digital photography, congratulations. You're about to save a lot of money on a camera, because you can get by with one that has very few megapixels. Even a $100, two-megapixel camera produces graphics files that measure 1600 by 1200 pixels—which is already too big to fit on, for example, the 1024 x 768–pixel screen of an iBook laptop without zooming or scrolling.

Printing out pictures

If you intend to print out your photos, however, it's a very different story.

The typical computer screen is actually a fairly low-resolution device; most pack in somewhere between 72 and 96 pixels per inch. But for the photo to look as smooth as a real photograph, a *printer* must cram the color dots much closer together on the paper—150 pixels per inch or more.

Remember the two-megapixel photo that would spill off the edges of the iBook screen? Its resolution (measured in dots per inch) is adequate only for a 5 x 7 print; any larger, and the dots become distractingly visible and speckled. Everybody in your circle of friends will look like they have some kind of skin disorder.

If you intend to make prints of your photos—and you'll be in very good company—shop for your camera with this table in mind:

Camera Resolution	Max Print Size
0.3 megapixels (some camera phones)	2.25 x 3 inches
1.3 megapixels	4 x 6 inches
2 megapixels	5 x 7 inches
3.3 megapixels	8 x 10 inches
4 megapixels	11 x 14 inches
5 megapixels	12 x 16 inches
6.3 megapixels	14 x 20 inches
8 megapixels	16 x 22 inches

These are extremely rough guidelines, by the way. Many factors contribute to the quality of an 8 x 10 print—lens quality, file compression, exposure, camera shake, paper quality, the number of different color cartridges your printer has, and so on. You may be perfectly happy with larger prints than the sizes listed here. But these figures provide a rough guide to getting the highest quality from your prints.

Memory Capacity

The memory card that came with your camera, if you got one at all, is a joke. It probably holds only about six or eight best-quality pictures. It's nothing more than a cost-saving placeholder, foisted on you by a camera company that knew full well that you'd have to go buy a bigger one.

When you're shopping for a camera, then, it's imperative that you also factor in the cost of a bigger card.

It's impossible to overstate how glorious it is to have a huge memory card in your camera (or several smaller ones in your camera bag). You quit worrying that you're about to run out of storage, so you shoot more freely, increasing the odds that you'll get great pictures. You can go on longer trips without dragging a laptop along, too, because you don't feel the urge to run back to your hotel room every three hours to offload your latest pictures.

You'll have enough worries when it comes to your camera's *battery* life. The last thing you need is another chronic headache in the form of your memory card. Bite the bullet and buy a bigger one.

Here's a table that helps you calculate how much storage you'll need. Find the column that represents the resolution of your camera, in megapixels (MP), and then read down to see how many best-quality JPEG photos each size card will hold.

Camera Resolution	2 MP (1600 x 1200)	3.3 MP (2048 x 1536)	4.1 MP (2272 x 1704)	5 MP (2560 x 1920)
Card Capacity	How many pictures	How many pictures	How many pictures	How many pictures
64 MB	61	35	30	17
128 MB	123	71	61	35
256 MB	246	142	122	70
512 MB	492	284	244	140
1 GB	984	568	488	280

Memory Cards

The *kind* of memory card your camera uses isn't nearly as important as the factors listed earlier in this discussion. But once you've narrowed down your potential purchase to a short list of candidates, it's worth weighing the pros and cons of the cards they use.

- **CompactFlash.** CompactFlash cards are rugged, inexpensive, and easy to handle, which makes them very popular. You can buy them in capacities all the way up to 8 GB. That's a *lot* of pictures—hundreds and hundreds. *Pro:* Readily available; inexpensive; wide selection. *Con:* They're the largest of any memory card format, which dictates a bigger camera. A brand-name 512 MB CompactFlash card costs less than $45.

- **Memory Stick.** Sony created this format as an interchangeable memory card for its cameras, camcorders, and laptops. Memory Sticks are great if you're already knee-deep in Sony equipment, but few other companies use them. *Pro:* Works with most Sony digital gadgets. *Cons:* Works primarily with Sony gear; maximum size is 256 MB. A 128 MB Memory Stick starts at about $35, depending on the brand (Sony's own are the most expensive).

- **Memory Stick Pro.** Sony's latest memory card is the same size as the traditional Memory Stick, but can hold much more. Sony's latest digital cameras accept both the Pro type and the older Memory Stick format, but the Pro cards don't work in older cameras. At this writing you can buy Pro sticks in capacities like 512 MB ($45), 1 GB (about $65), 2 GB ($115), and 4 GB ($300).

- **Secure Digital (SD).** These extremely tiny cards are no bigger than postage stamps, which is why you also find them in Palm organizers and MP3 players. In fact, you can pull this card from your camera and insert it into many palmtops for enhanced viewing. *Pro:* Very small, perfect for subcompact cameras. *Con:* None, really, unless you're prone to losing small objects. 1 GB cards are now around $65 and 2 GB models are in the $100 range.

- **xD-Picture Card.** The latest Fuji camera and Olympus cameras require a new, proprietary format called xD (see Figure 1-1). Its dimensions are so inconveniently small that the manual warns that "they can be accidentally swallowed by small children." *Pro:* Some cool cameras accept them. *Con:* Harder to find and relatively expensive compared to other memory cards (256 MB=$35, 512 MB = $55, 1 GB=$75). Incompatible with cameras from other companies. Also incompatible with the memory card slots in most printers, card readers, television front panels, and so on.

- **Microdrive.** Some CompactFlash cameras can also accommodate the IBM Microdrive—a miniature hard drive that looks like a thick CompactFlash card (in capacities up to 64 GB). For a while, 1 GB drives were popular with pros, but it's slipping in the polls now that you can get CompactFlash cards of up to 8 GB.

Figure 1-1:
The tiny Secure Digital card (middle) is gaining popularity because you can use it in both your digicam and palmtop. The even tinier xD-Picture Card (left) works only with Fuji and Olympus cameras. The larger CompactFlash card is still the most common (especially in larger cameras).

If you already own some memory cards from a previous camera (or even an MP3 player), you have a good incentive to buy a new camera that uses the same format. Otherwise, compare price per megabyte, availability, and what works with your other digital gear.

If all other factors are equal, however, choose a camera that takes CompactFlash cards. They're plentiful, inexpensive, and have huge capacity.

Battery Life

In many ways, digital cameras have arrived. They're not like cell phones, which still drop calls, or wireless palmtops, which are excruciatingly slow connecting to the Internet. Digital cameras are reliable, high quality, and generally extremely rewarding.

Except for battery life.

Thanks to that LCD screen on the back, digital cameras go through batteries like Kleenex. The battery, as it turns out, will probably be the one limiting factor to your photo shoots. When the juice is gone, your session is over.

Here's what you'll find as you shop for various cameras:

- **Proprietary, built-in rechargeable.** Many smaller cameras come with a "brick" battery: a dark gray, lithium-ion rechargeable battery, as shown at top in Figure 1-2. (These subcompact cameras are simply too small to accommodate AA-style batteries, as described next.)

   The problem with proprietary batteries is that you can't replace them when you're on the road. If you're only three hours into your day at Disney World when the battery dies, that's just tough—your shooting session is over. You can't exactly duck into a drugstore to buy a new one.

   Some cameras come with a separate, external charger for this battery. The advantage here is that you can buy a second battery (usually for $50 or so). You can keep one battery in the charger at all times. That way, when the main battery gives up the ghost, you can swap it with the one in the charger, and your day goes on. (Or, in Disney World situations, you can take both batteries with you for the day.)

   All of this is something of a pain, and not nearly as handy as the rechargeable AAs described next.

   But it sure beats any system in which the camera *is* the battery charger. When the battery dies, so does your creative muse. You have no choice but to return home and plug in the camera itself, taking it out of commission for several hours as it recharges the battery.

- **Two or four AA-size batteries**—Some cameras accept AA batteries, and may even come with a set of alkalines to get you started.

   If you learn nothing else from this chapter, however, learn this: *Don't use standard alkaline AAs.* You'll get a better return on your investment by tossing $5 bills out your car window on the highway.

Alkalines may be fine for flashlights and radios, but they're no match for the massive power drain of the modern digital camera—not even "premium" alkalines. A set of four AAs might last 20 minutes in the digital camera, if you're lucky.

So what are you supposed to put in there? Something you may have never even heard of: *rechargeable nickel-metal-hydride (NiMH)* AAs (Figure 1-2, bottom). They last *much* longer than alkalines, and because you can use them over and over again, they're far less expensive.

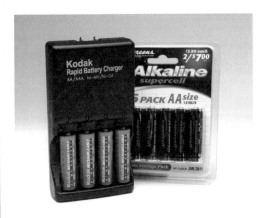

Figure 1-2:
Top: Many digital cameras come with special, proprietary batteries. They're not very big–and neither is their capacity. Invest in a spare. (Quarter not included.)

Bottom: If you find a digicam that accepts AA batteries, use alkalines (right) only for emergency. In the long run, you're better off investing in a couple sets of NiMH rechargeables (left).

You generally won't find NiMHs in department stores, but they're available in national drugstore chains, and they're easy to find online (for example, www.buy.com). A charger and a set of four NiMH AAs cost about $30.

The beauty of digital cameras that accept AAs is that they accommodate so many different kinds of batteries. In addition to rechargeable NiMH batteries, most cameras can also accept something called AA *photo lithium* batteries. They're a lot like alkalines, in that they're disposable and can't be recharged. They're also ideal to carry in the camera case for emergency backup. However, because they last many times longer than regular AAs, they're much more expensive.

The final advantage of this kind of camera is that, in a pinch—yes, in the middle of your Disney World day—you can even hit up a drugstore for a set of standard alkaline AAs. Sure enough, you'll be tossing them in the trash after only about 20 minutes of use in the camera—but in an emergency, 20 minutes is a lot better than nothing.

Tip: Some cameras offer the best of all worlds. Certain Nikon CoolPix cameras, for example, come with a proprietary lithium-ion "brick" and a matching charger—but they *also* accept all kinds of AAs, including alkalines, rechargeables, and the Duracell CRV3 battery (a disposable lithium battery that looks like two AAs fused together at the seam). You should always be able to get juice on the road with *these* babies.

Size and Shape

You could have the best digital camera on the planet, but if it's bulkier than a Volvo, you'll wind up leaving it home and missing lots of good shots.

The trick is to balance the features you need with the package you want; unfortunately, the smaller the camera, the fewer the features you usually get. For example, you'll rarely see a connector for an external flash (a *hotshoe*) or a rotating flip screen on a camera that fits in your shirt pocket.

Once you've balanced features against size, do whatever you can to get your *hands* on your leading candidate. Is it too small to hold comfortably? Does your index finger naturally align with the shutter release? Are you constantly smudging the lens with your other fingers?

Your camera should become a natural extension of your vision. If you're not bonding with it, your pictures will reflect that—or, rather, your *lack* of pictures.

Lens Quality

In the early days of digital photography, cameras had interesting electronics, but only so-so lenses. And if you've ever tried reading fine print through a cheesy magnifying glass, then you have some idea of how the world looks though bad optics—lousy.

Fortunately, the scene is much sharper now. Sony, Olympus, Canon, Leica, and Nikon all take pride in the lenses for their digital cameras and have solid reputations for great glass. (The camera makers not listed here sometimes buy their lenses *from* Olympus, Canon, and Nikon.)

Still, this particular criterion isn't something you'll have much control over. There's no measurement for the quality of a lens, and no way for you to tell how good it is simply by looking. The closest you can come is to read the reviews in photo magazines or the Web sites listed in Appendix C.

Zoom

When you read the specs for a camera—or read the logos painted on its body—you frequently encounter numbers like this: "3X/10X ZOOM!" The number before the slash tells you how many times the camera can magnify a distant image, much like a telescope. That number measures the *optical* zoom, which is the actual amount that the lenses can zoom in (to magnify a subject that's far away).

Note: If you're used to traditional photography, you may need some help converting consumer-cam zoom units (3X, 4X, and so on) into standard focal ranges. It breaks down like this: A typical 3X zoom goes from 6.5mm (wide angle) to 19.5mm (telephoto). That would be about the same as a 38mm to 105mm zoom lens on a 35mm film camera.

Then there's *digital* zoom, the number after the slash. Much as computer owners mistakenly jockey for superiority by comparing the megahertz rating of their computers—little suspecting that higher megahertz ratings don't necessarily make faster computers—camera makers seem to think that what consumers want most in a digital camera is a powerful digital zoom. "7X!" your camera's box may scream. "10X! 20X!"

When a camera uses its *digital* zoom, it simply reinterprets the individual pixels, in effect enlarging them. The image gets bigger, but the image quality deteriorates. In most cases, you're best off avoiding digital zoom altogether.

Base your camera-buying decision on the *optical* zoom range—that's the zoom that counts.

Image Stabilizer (Vibration Reduction)

The hot new feature for 2006-2007 is built-in image stabilization. This feature, available in a flood of new camera models, improve your photos' clarity by ironing out your little hand jiggles.

It's an enormous help in three situations: when you're zoomed in all the way (which magnifies jitters), in low light (meaning that the shutter stays open a long time, increasing the likelihood of blurring), and when your camera doesn't have an eyepiece viewfinder (forcing you to hold the camera at arm's length, decreasing stability).

Flip Screen

Every digital camera has a little LCD screen, but on some specially endowed models, you can flip and swivel the screen around to allow multiple viewing angles (Figure

Figure 1-3:
Flip screens first appeared on camcorders and were soon adapted to digital cameras.

Left: The best ones flip all the way out from the camera, providing multiple viewing angles.

Right: Others allow tilting upward and downward, but remain attached to the camera back.

1-3). These cameras let you hold it any way you want—at your waist, above your head, even at your ankles—and still frame the shot without contorting yourself into a pretzel.

If you're stuck in the middle of a crowd, but want a shot of the parade, then tilt the screen, raise the camera over your head, frame the shot, and shoot. Want to create that low-angle Orson Welles shot for added drama, or snap a terrific baby's-eye-view photo without having to crawl around in the dirt? It's easy with a flip screen.

Optical Viewfinder

Every year, digital camera screens get bigger. That's a welcome trend, because framing your photos and, later, showing them off to other people is a heck of a lot more satisfying when they're bigger than a postage stamp.

These days, though, some screens fill the whole back of the camera—and leave no room for an optical viewfinder (the little glass hole you can peek through). Plenty of people are perfectly happy composing their shots on the screen, but remember that holding a camera up to your face helps to brace it, reducing the likelihood of little jiggles that blur the photo. Without an optical viewfinder, you're forced to hold out the camera nearly at arm's length.

Manual Controls

Cheapo digital cameras are often called *point-and-shoot* models with good reason: You point, you shoot. The camera is stuck in perennial *program mode,* which means it does all the thinking.

More expensive cameras, on the other hand, let you take your camera off autopilot.

Don't assume that all you'll ever need is a point-and-shoot. Read Chapter 3 first. There you'll learn all the amazing, special-situation photos—sports photos, night-

Figure 1-4:
An AF assist light, like the one on the Canon PowerShot series, will greatly improve your percentage of properly focused shots. You might want to put this item near the top of your desirable-features list.

Autofocus assist lamp

time shots, fireworks, indoor portraits, and so on—you can take *only* if your camera offers manual controls.

If you opt for a camera with manual controls, shop for these features:

- *Aperture-priority mode* lets you specify how wide the camera's shutter opens when you take the shot. It's probably the most popular manual control mode, because it's easy to use but offers lots of control. Chapter 3 describes how to use aperture priority to create backgrounds with softly out-of-focus backgrounds, among other great effects.

- *Shutter-priority mode* is particularly handy for freezing or blurring shots. It lets you tell the camera how *fast* the shutter should open and close: fast to freeze sports shots; slow for nighttime shots, or to turn a babbling brook into an abstract, fuzzy blur.

- *Manual mode* allows you to set the aperture and the shutter speed independently. When you hit the right combination, the camera lets you know that you've set the right exposure and can take the picture.

If you're looking for a camera that you can grow with as your photo skills increase, then manual controls are features worth paying for.

Autofocus Assist Light

Even though autofocus technology has been around for years, it's still not a perfect science. There are plenty of lighting conditions, like dark interiors, where your camera will struggle to focus correctly. Autofocus works by looking for patches of *contrast* between light and dark—and if there's no light, there's no focusing.

An autofocus assist light (or *AF assist*) neatly solves the problem (Figure 1-4). In dim light, the camera briefly beams a pattern of light onto the subject, so the camera has enough visual information on which to focus.

Built-In Sliding Lens Cover

Let's face it: Detachable lens covers are a pain. If you tie it to the camera with that little loop of black thread, it bangs against your hand, or the lens, when it's windy. If it's loose, it's destined to fall behind the couch cushions, pop off in your camera bag, or get mixed in with the change in your pocket.

Some cameras, especially compact models, eliminate this madness. They have sliding lens covers that protect the optics. Just sliding the cover open both turns the camera on and makes its zoom lens extend, ready for action. When you're done shooting, the lens retracts and the cover slides back in place.

Unfortunately, built-in lens protectors generally prevent you from adding filters, telephoto lenses, and other attachments. If you're looking for a portable travel mate to take on vacation, the sliding lens cover should be high on your list. On the other hand, if a serious picture-making tool is your focus, then make sure it accepts attachments.

Variable "Film" Speeds

In the old days, when photographers had to walk through ten-foot snow drifts just to get to school (uphill both ways), they also had to carry around different film types for different lighting situations. They would use *400-speed* film in dim lighting, *100-speed* film in bright outdoor light, and so on. You might have heard these film speeds referred to as *ISO settings*.

Even though digital cameras don't need different kinds of film, most still let you "bump up" the speed by pushing a button (Figure 1-5).

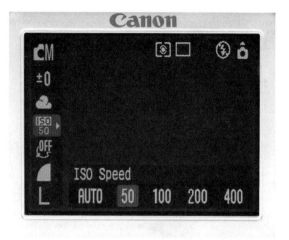

Figure 1-5:
Some cameras provide a menu of film speed options, often under the label "ISO," which is a measurement of light sensitivity familiar to film photographers.

You'll find out more about speeds in Chapters 2 and 3. For now, it's enough to note that a choice of film speeds gives you greater flexibility when shooting indoors or at night outdoors.

Shutter Lag

Shutter lag is the time it takes for the camera to calculate the correct focus and exposure before it actually captures the scene. In many camera models under $700 or so, this interval amounts to an infuriating one-second or half-second delay between the time you press the shutter button and the instant the picture is actually recorded. Unfortunately, that's more than enough time for you to miss the precise moment your daughter blows out the candles on her birthday cake, your son's first step, and that adorable expression on your cat's face. Fractions of a second are a lifetime in photography (Figure 1-7).

You can reduce or minimize shutter lag in either of two ways. First, you can set the camera's focus and exposure manually, as described in the next two chapters. That way, there's no thinking left for the camera to do when you actually squeeze the shutter button.

Most people, though, eventually learn instead to *prefocus*. This trick involves squeezing the shutter button halfway, ahead of time, forcing the camera to do its calculations. Keep your finger halfway down until the moment of truth. Now, when you finally squeeze it down all the way, you get the shot you wanted with very little delay.

Unfortunately, neither of these techniques works in all situations. Manually focusing and prefocusing both take time and eliminate spontaneity.

Figure 1-7:
"Did you get my head spin?" says the break dancer. "Did you get it? Tell me you got that shot! Tell me you got it…" Every digital photographer has a collection of these missed shots, thanks to shutter lag.

Until the electronics of digital cameras improves, the best you can hope for is to buy a model with the smallest shutter lag possible. You won't find this spec in brochures, though; your best bet is to visit one of the camera-review Web sites listed in Appendix C. Many of them list the shutter-lag timings for popular cameras.

Figure 1-6:
Some consumer digital cameras can accommodate accessory lenses and filters using an optional adapter. You can extend the power of this Olympus, for example, by adding telephoto, wide angle, and macro lenses.

Attachments

Digital camera owners usually don't consider attaching filters, telephoto lenses, and external flashes. But if you're coming from a traditional film-camera background, and you're a fairly serious photographer, this may be one of the first features you think about.

In general, most of the big, heavy, traditional-design digital cameras can accept such attachments. Most tiny, capsule-shaped, subcompact pocket cameras can't.

The trick to a happy accessory life is calculating how hard they are to attach. The process often entails fitting the camera with tubular lens adapters (attachable via tiny threads). Nothing is more frustrating than stripping the threads on your camera body because you couldn't get the adapter ring to screw in properly (Figure 1-6).

So after you find a camera that accepts the attachments you want to use, pay attention to *how* they attach. Usually the smaller the adapter and the finer the threads, the more patience you'll need. Your sanity may be at stake here.

Burst Mode (RAM Buffer)

When you press the shutter button on a typical digital camera, the image begins a long tour through the camera's guts. First, the lens projects the image onto an electronic sensor—a *CCD* (Charge-Coupled Device) or *CMOS* (Complementary Metal Oxide Semiconductor). Second, the sensor dumps the image temporarily into the camera's built-in memory (a memory *buffer*). Finally, the camera's circuitry feeds the image from its memory buffer onto the memory card.

You might be wondering about that second step. Why don't digital cameras record the image directly to the memory card?

The answer is simple: Unless your camera has state-of-the-art electronics, it would take forever. You'd only be able to take a new picture every few seconds or so. By stashing shots into a memory buffer as a temporary holding tank (a very fast process) before recording the image on the memory card (a much slower process), the camera frees up its attention so that you can take another photo quickly. The camera catches up later, when you've released the shutter button. (This is one reason why digital cameras aren't as responsive as film cameras, which transfer images directly from lens to film.)

The size of your camera's memory buffer affects your life in a couple of different ways. First, it permits certain cameras to have a *burst mode,* which lets you fire off several shots per second. That's a great feature when you're trying to capture an extremely fleeting scene, such as a great soccer goal, a three-year-old's smile, or Microsoft being humble.

A big memory buffer also permits *movie mode,* described later. It can even help fight shutter lag, because the ability to fire off a burst of five or six frames improves your odds of capturing that perfect moment.

Note: A few expensive cameras can bypass the buffer and save photos directly on the memory card, so that you can keep shooting until the card fills up. This trick usually requires a so-called high-speed memory card–preferably a big one.

As you shop, you probably won't see the amount of memory in a certain camera advertised. But keeping your eye out for cameras with burst mode (and checking out *how many* frames per second it can capture) is good advice.

Panorama Mode

How many times have you showed a travel picture to a friend and remarked, "It looked a lot bigger in real life"? That's because it *was* bigger, and your camera couldn't capture it all. Capturing a vast landscape with a digital camera is like looking at the Grand Canyon through a paper-towel tube.

Figure 1-8:
This image is actually four pictures stitched together using the Panorama mode.

Digital camera makers have created an ingenious solution to widen this narrow view of life: Panorama mode (Figure 1-8). With it, you can stitch together a series of individual images to create a single, beautiful vista, similar to what you saw when you were standing there in real life. The camera's onscreen display helps align the edge of the last shot with the beginning of the next one.

Software Bundle

When reviewing the software bundle included with a camera you're considering, look for Mac OS X compatibility—not for importing and organizing the pictures (you've got iPhoto for that), but for editing them and stitching together panoramas, if your camera offers that feature.

Don't rule out a good camera if the software isn't perfect; for most purposes, iPhoto may be all the software you ever need. But if you're torn between two cameras, favor the one with Mac OS X software in the box.

Tip: You can keep track of all the latest imaging programs for Mac OS X by checking Apple's Web site: *www.apple.com/downloads/macosx/imaging_3d/*.

Noise Reduction

The longer the exposure to record a scene, the more important *noise reduction* becomes. When you shoot nighttime shots, what should be a jet-black sky may exhibit tiny colored specks—*artifacts*—that put a considerable damper on your photo's impact. (The longer the shutter stays open, the more artifacts you'll get, as the camera's sensor gradually heats up.)

A noise reduction feature usually works like this: When you press the shutter, the camera takes *two* shots—the one that you think you're getting, and a second shot with the shutter completely closed. Since the camera's electronics produce the visual noise, both shots theoretically should contain the same colored speckles in the same spots. The camera compares the two shots, concludes that all of the colored specks it finds in the *closed*-shutter shot must be unwanted, and deletes them from the real shot.

Chances are you'll have to dig through the literature or the specs on the manufacturer's Web site to find out whether the camera you're considering has this feature. But if you're a nighttime shooter, it's worth investigating.

Tripod Mount

Nobody *likes* to use a tripod with a digital camera. But there are moments when a tripod is necessary for a beautiful artistic shot, such as streaking car lights across a bridge, or almost anything at night.

So take a moment to turn your camera candidate upside down and inspect the socket. Is it plastic or metal? Metal is better. Where is it positioned? Near the center of the base is better than way off on one side or another.

The location and composition of the tripod mount isn't going to be a deal breaker, but it's certainly worth the short time it takes to examine while the sales clerk is writing up your order.

Movie Mode

Almost every digital camera claims to capture video; some do it better than others.

Cheaper cameras produce movies that are tiny, low-resolution QuickTime flicks. These mini-movies have their novelty value, and are better than nothing when your intention is to email your newborn baby's first cry to eager relatives across the globe.

But more expensive cameras these days can capture QuickTime flicks at a decent size (320 x 240 pixels, full-TV-frame 640 x 480 pixels, or even larger) and smoothness (15, 30, or even more frames per second), usually complete with soundtrack. Better cameras place no limit on the length of your captured movies (except when you run out of memory card space). More on this topic in Chapter 3.

Price

The "P" word is a painful subject in the world of electronic photography. Feature for feature, digital cameras simply cost more than traditional film cameras. Yet whereas a 35mm film camera will probably remain current and serviceable for at least five years, whatever digital camera you buy will probably be discontinued by its manufacturer *in under a year.*

The pace of obsolescence will slow down as the technology levels off. But for now, when you evaluate how much you're willing to spend, keep in mind that this might be a one-year purchase at worst, and a two-year investment at best.

At this writing, a good 4- to 5-megapixel camera costs between $200 and $400. Digital SLR (single-lens-reflex) cameras, like the widely adored Canon Digital Rebel and the Nikon D50, cost about $700. (Of course, you can also find professional models that cost many times more.)

Whatever you do, compare prices before you buy. You'll be astonished at the differences in prices you'll find from store to store. Begin your search at, for example, *www.shopping.com* (Figure 1-9).

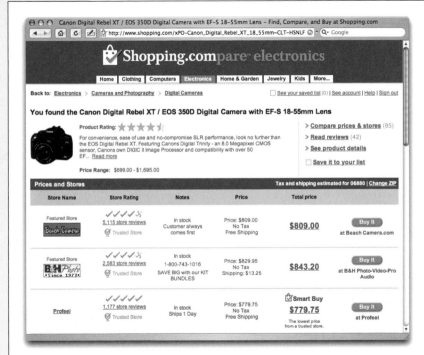

Figure 1-9:
At www.shopping.com *(a price-comparison site), start by searching for the brand, price range, or resolution you want. Then sort the results by the store's customer rating. Buy your camera from a store that has been rated with four stars or more. Watch out for low prices that come with ridiculously inflated "shipping" charges.*

Composing Brilliant Photos

I f your eyes are bleeding from the technical underbrush of Chapter 1—bells, whistles, megabytes—switch on your right brain. This chapter has little to do with electronics and everything to do with the more artful side of photography: composition.

What follows are four tips that photographers have been using for years to create good pictures regardless of the camera type. These time-honored secrets do wonderful things for digital imaging too. Good composition is just as important with a $199 digicam as it is with a $3,000 pro digital SLR—and just as enjoyable.

This chapter offers suggestions that will immediately improve your pictures. But first, a few words about composition itself.

Composition

Composition is the arrangement of your picture, the interplay between foreground and background, the way the subject fills the frame, the way the parts of the picture relate to each other, and so on.

Will the shot be clearer, better, or more interesting if you move closer? What about walking around to the other side of the action, or zooming in slightly, or letting tall grass fill the foreground? Would the picture be more interesting if it were framed by horizontal, vertical, or diagonal structures (such as branches, pillars, or a road stretching away)? All of this floats through a veteran photographer's head before the shutter button clicks.

It's easy to think, "Hey, it's a picture, not a painting—I have to shoot what's there." However, the fact is that photography is every bit as creative as painting. You have more control over the composition than you realize.

Note: If the primary thrust of your photographic ambition is to take casual vacation pictures, some of the following suggestions for professional composition may strike you as overkill.

But read them anyway. If you let some of these tips rub off on you, you'll be able to apply them even in everyday snapshot situations. There's no law against casual vacation pictures being *good* casual vacation pictures.

The Rule of Thirds

Most people assume that the center of the frame should contain the most important element of your shot. In fact, 98 percent of all amateur photos feature the subject of the shot in dead center.

Figure 2-1:
Top: When shooting a head and shoulder portrait, frame the shot so that her eyes fall on the upper imaginary line a third of the way down the frame.

Bottom: When shooting a landscape, put the horizon on the bottom-third line if you want to emphasize the sky or tall objects like mountains, trees, and buildings. Put the horizon on the upper third line to emphasize what's on the ground, such as the people in the shot.

For the most visually interesting shots, however, dead center is actually the *least* compelling location for the subject. Artists and psychologists have found, instead, that following the so-called Rule of Thirds ensures better photos.

Imagine that the photo frame is divided into thirds, both horizontally and vertically, as shown in Figure 2-1. The Rule of Thirds contends that the intersections of these lines are the strongest parts of the frame. Putting the most interesting parts of the image at these four points, in other words, makes better composition.

Save the center square of the frame for tight close-ups—and even then, aim for having the subject's eyes on the upper-third line.

Get Closer

Step one to better pictures: Get closer. Step two: Get closer still.

Move your feet toward the subject, and don't stop moving them until the subject fills the frame (Figure 2-2). Of course, the zoom lens on your camera can help with this process quite a bit.

Figure 2-2:
Top: This otter shot seemed like a great photo at the time it was taken. Once it was uploaded to iPhoto, however, it became something of a disappointment. It looks bland, because the otters were too far away and at an uninteresting angle.

Bottom: By getting (or zooming) closer, however, you get far more interesting results. In this case, the photographer had to apply the time-honored skill of patience, waiting for the sea otters to drift within better range. Sometimes getting closer means waiting for the action to come to you.

Try it with your dog. Take the first picture standing where you normally would stand—probably about five feet away and above Rover's head.

Now prepare to take a second picture—but first crouch down so that you see the world at dog level. Come close enough to the dog so that he can almost lick your camera lens. (But don't let him *do* it; dog slobber is very bad for optics.)

Take the second picture. Load both photos into iPhoto and study them. The first shot probably looks pretty boring compared to the second one.

Clearly, you weren't thinking about *composition* the first time. You were thinking about *taking a picture* of your dog.

The point is, *taking a picture* is usually a mindless act that doesn't result in the most memorable photos. Getting closer to create an interesting *composition* makes for compelling photography.

Tip: Filling the frame with your subject also means that you'll have less uninteresting background to crop out before making prints. As a result, you'll get higher resolution (more pixels) in the printout, which enhances the photo's quality.

Eliminate Busy Backgrounds

Busy backgrounds destroy photographs (Figure 2-3, top). Unless the intent of your image is to confuse and irritate the viewer's eye (headbanger music CD album cover, anyone?), do what you can to eliminate distracting elements from your picture. Remember, you want to make it easy for the viewer to find the key elements of your composition, and enjoy them once they're there.

In other words, don't become so enamored with your subject that you don't notice the telephone wires that seem to run through her skull. Train your eye to examine the subject first, and then survey the surrounding scene.

Here are some problems to look out for and avoid in the backgrounds of your shots:

- **All forms of poles.** Telephone poles, fence posts, street signs, and malnourished trees can creep into your photos and ruin them.

- **Linear patterns.** Avoid busy background elements, such as bricks, paneling, fences, and zebra skins.

- **Parts of things.** When people see a "part of a thing" in your picture—for example, the front of a tractor, the leg of a ladder, the rear end of a camel—they can't help but wonder what the rest of it looks like, instead of focusing on your subject.

Tip: Get in the habit of scanning all four corners of your frame before clicking the shutter. That way, you'll catch those telephone poles and street signs that you wouldn't normally see until it's too late.

Look for backgrounds that have subtle tones, soft edges, and nondescript elements. Moving your subject forward, away from the background, can help soften the backdrop even more.

Figure 2-3:
Top: Egads! What's this picture about? The people? The boats? Linear elements in the background usually spell doom for people shots.

Bottom: Avoid the clutter and opt for a more soothing background, such as water, sky, or any other subtle element. Your subjects—and audience—will thank you.

Go Low, Go High

Change your camera angle often. This is where a flip screen comes in handy, as described in Chapter 1.

Put the camera on the ground and study the composition. Raise it over your head and see how the world looks from that angle (Figure 2-4). If possible, walk around the subject and examine it from left to right.

Or adopt this technique: When you first approach an interesting subject, take the picture, just to get a safe one in the camera. Then change your angle and take another shot. If you have time, get closer and take a few more. Work the subject for as long as the opportunity presents itself.

More often than not, the "safe" shot will be your least favorite of the series. You'll probably find the latter frames far more compelling.

Figure 2-4:
Top: To really capture the feel of this break-fast nook, raise the angle of the camera, even if it means standing on a chair to do so.

Bottom: Try going low, too. "Getting to the bottom of things" provides you with dramatic angles and impressive images.

The Right Way to Compose

Finally, one last suggestion: Consider the pointers in this chapter as guidelines only. There is no one right way in photography; when you come down to it, the best photos are the ones you *like*.

Beyond the Simple Snapshot

There you sit, surveying your boxes of old photos. Snapshots of your family. Snapshots on vacation. Snapshots of tourist attractions. But they're all *snapshots.*

Then the professional photos in some magazine or newspaper hit you. There's the brilliant close-up of a ladybug on a leaf, with the bushes in the background gently out of focus. There's the amazing shot of the soccer player butting the ball with his head, frozen in action so completely that you can see individual flecks of sweat flying from his hair. There's the incredible shot of the city lights at night, with car taillights drawing colorful firefly tracks across the frame.

You can't help but wonder: "How do they *do* that? And why can't I do it too?"

Actually, you probably can. Some of these special shots require special gear, but most of them involve nothing more than good technique—and knowing when to invoke which of your camera's special features. With a little practice, you can take pictures just as compelling, colorful, and intimate as the shots you see in the magazines.

This chapter is dedicated to laying bare the secrets of professional photographers. May you never take another dull snapshot.

Action Photography

Everybody's seen those incredible high-speed action photos of athletes frozen in mid-leap. Without these shots (and the swimsuit photos), *Sports Illustrated* would be no thicker than a pamphlet.

Through a combination of careful positioning, focusing, lighting, and shutter-speed adjustments, this kind of photo is within your reach. As a handy bonus, mastering the frozen-action sports picture also means you've mastered frozen-action water splashes, frozen-action bird-in-flight shots, and frozen-action kid moments.

Tip: Don't get frustrated if, despite learning all of the following techniques, many of your pictures don't come out well. Sports photography produces lots of waste. Pros shoot dozens, sometimes hundreds, of frames just to get one good picture.

In short, a very low good-to-bad ratio is par for the course in this kind of shooting. But what the heck? It isn't costing you anything, and one great shot can make the entire effort worthwhile.

Getting Close to the Action

If your digital camera has a zoom lens, it's probably a 3X zoom, meaning that it can magnify the scene three times. Unfortunately, if you're in the stands at the football game, hoping for action shots of an individual player, 3X is not powerful enough. What you really need is one of those enormous, bazooka-like telephoto lenses that protrude three feet in front of the camera (see Figure 3-1).

Figure 3-1:
If action photography is going to be a regular part of your shooting, consider a digital camera with an 8X zoom or greater. Better yet, look into digital SLR (single-lens reflex) cameras, which can accommodate a telephoto lens. This shot, for example, was captured with a 200mm lens on a digital SLR.

But that doesn't mean you can't still capture good shots. Find a position on the sidelines that puts you as close to the action as possible. Zoom in with your camera and then use the trick shown in Figure 3-2.

If it's a bright, sunny day, the standard "automatic everything" setting of the camera might work just fine. Take a few sample shots, trying to get the action as it's coming at you.

Fast Shutter Speeds

If the results are blurry because the motion is too fast, you'll have to instruct the camera to use a faster shutter speed.

Unfortunately, the cheapest, point-and-shoot-only cameras don't offer any such setting—you get what you pay for. But even cameras a slight cut above those basic ones offer a solution to this problem.

Figure 3-2:
You might not be able to afford a digital SLR with a $10,000 super-telephoto lens attachment. But if you have a 4-megapixel camera or an even better one, here's a way to "zoom in" on the action.

Shoot at your camera's highest resolution–zoomed in as much as you can (top). Once the picture is in iPhoto, you can "zoom in" even further by cropping the portion of the picture you want to keep. Thanks to the high resolution of the original photo, you'll still have enough pixels to make a nice print or slideshow, and the photo is much more effective this way (bottom).

A related tip: If your camera's zoom isn't powerful enough by itself, consider turning on the camera's digital zoom. As noted in Chapter 1, you should avoid using the digital zoom most of the time, because it compromises image quality.

Still, at low levels (2X or 3X, for example), the deterioration in image quality might be tolerable. Experimenting with this feature might be worthwhile when covering a spectator sport, for instance.

Shutter-priority mode

As noted in Chapter 1, certain cameras offer manual controls that pay off in just such special occasions as this.

In this case, what you want is the feature called *shutter priority*. In this mode—a time-honored feature of traditional film cameras—you tell the camera that the *speed* of the shot is what matters. You want the "film" exposed for only 1/500th of a second, for example.

Understanding what this mode does is slightly technical, but extremely important.

Whenever you take a picture, the amount of light that enters the camera is determined by two things: the *speed* of the shutter opening and closing, and the *size* of the opening of the diaphragm in the lens (the *aperture*).

If you want to freeze the action, you'll want the shutter to open and close very quickly. As a result, you're admitting less light into the camera. To prevent the picture from being too dark, the camera will have to compensate by opening its "eye" wider for that fraction of a second—that is, you want it to use a larger aperture.

In shutter-priority mode, that's exactly what happens. You say, "I don't care about the aperture—you worry about that, little camera buddy. I just want this picture *fast*." The camera nods in its little digital way and agrees to open up its aperture wide enough to compensate for your fast shutter speed.

Exactly how you turn on shutter-priority mode differs radically by camera. On some cameras, you have to fiddle around with the menu system; on others, you simply turn the little control knob on the top to a position marked *S* or *Tv* (old-time photography lingo for *time value*), as shown in Figure 3-3.

Figure 3-3:
To freeze the action, use a fast shutter speed, like 1/1000th of a second. Find your camera's Shutter Priority mode, which is usually designated by an S on the mode dial. But some cameras, like Canons, use the more traditional abbreviation Tv, which stands for timed value. Either way, you can set the shutter speed; the camera adjusts the aperture automatically to admit the right amount of light.

In any case, once you're in this mode, you must use some kind of dial or slider to indicate how *fast* you want the shutter to snap. You might start with 1/500th or 1/1000th of a second and take another series of shots. (The screen may show only "500" or "1000," but you'll know what it means.) If the result is too dark, slow down the shutter speed to the next notch; the camera is opening the aperture as wide as it can.

Focusing and Shutter Lag

Whenever you try to photograph something fast, you may run headfirst into a chronic problem of digital cameras called *shutter lag*. That's the time the camera takes to calculate the focus and exposure from the instant you squeeze the shutter button to the instant the shutter actually snaps. It's usually at least one second long. Unfortunately, a delay that long means death to perfect sports photography. You'll miss the critical instant every time.

The circuitry in cameras, like the $700 digital SLR models from Canon and Nikon, is fast enough to make shutter lag a non-issue. In other cameras, you should adopt one of these solutions:

- **Prefocus.** Suppose you're trying to get a shot of the goalie in a soccer game. Take advantage of the time when he's just standing there doing nothing. Frame the shot on your camera screen.

  Then, as the opposing team comes barreling down the field toward him, press the shutter button just halfway. Half-pressing the shutter makes the camera calculate the exposure and focus *in advance*. (Making those calculations is what constitutes most of the camera's shutter lag.) Keep the button half-pressed until the moment of truth, when the goalie dives for the ball. *Now* squeeze the shutter the rest of the way. This technique nearly eliminates shutter lag, freezing the action closer to the critical moment.

  This is only one example of how *anticipating* the critical moment pays big dividends in sports photography. With a little practice, you can learn to press the shutter button *right before* the big moment, rewarding you with the perfect shot.

- **Use burst mode.** Most recent digicams offer something called *burst mode,* in which the camera snaps a series of shots in rapid succession, for as long as you hold down the shutter button. It's something like the motor drive on a traditional film camera, so often featured in movies in which the main character is a photographer.

  Most cameras can capture only about two frames per second, but that's still enough to improve the odds that one of your shots will be good. With a little practice, using the burst mode can help you compensate for shutter lag—especially if you anticipate the action.

Light Metering

Ordinarily, a digital camera calculates the amount of light in a scene by averaging all light from all areas of the frame. And ordinarily, that system works perfectly well.

In sports photography, however, the surrounding scene is usually substantially brighter or darker than the athletes, leading to improper exposure of the one thing you really want: the action.

Fortunately, many cameras offer *spot metering.* In this mode, you see little bracket markers (or a square or circle) in the center of your viewing frame (Figure 3-4). You can use these brackets to tell the camera which portion of the scene to pay attention to in calculating the exposure. By turning on this feature for sports shooting, you'll make sure that the athlete is correctly lit, background notwithstanding.

Figure 3-4:
In this picture, the athletes are brighter than the baseball field. If you were to use your camera's normal "averaging" or "evaluative" mode, there's a good chance that the players would be too bright, or overexposed. By using spot metering, you can tell your camera to set the exposure for the smaller area in the center of the frame. Now the subjects of the photo will be correctly exposed.

Portraits

You may have noticed that in most professional photo portraits, the background is softly out of focus. Unless you have the cheapest camera on the planet, you can create a similar great-looking effect yourself.

In photographic terms, a shot with a soft-focus background is said to have a *shallow depth of field*. The term "depth of field" refers to how much of the picture is in focus. When you're photographing your family in front of the Great Wall of China, you'll probably want a *deep* depth of field, so that both the people and the background remain in focus. But in typical headshot-type portraits, you'll want a *shallow* depth of field—and a blurry background. Figure 3-5 should make this point clearer.

So how do you control the depth of field? Here are a few ways.

Trick 1: Zoom In

It might not seem logical that you'd want to use your camera's zoom lens (if it has one) for a portrait. After all, you can get as close as you want to the subject just by walking.

But thanks to a quirk of optics, zooming in helps create a shallow depth of field, which is just what you want for portraits.

Trick 2: Move the Background Back

The farther away your model is from the background, the softer the background will appear. If you choose an ivy-covered wall as your backdrop, for example, position your subject 10, 20, or 30 feet away from the wall—the farther, the better.

Trick 3: Choose a Wide Aperture Setting

You may remember that two factors determine how much light fills a shot: how long the shutter remains open (the shutter speed) and how wide it opens (the aperture).

In sports photography, what you care about most is usually the shutter speed. In portrait photography, what you care about most is the aperture setting—because the size of the aperture controls the depth of field. Low-numbered aperture settings like f-2.8 or f-4 are referred to as *wide aperture settings* by photographers because they let lots of light through the lens. These wide settings also help create soft backgrounds for portraits.

Figure 3-5:
Top: The trick to creating a soft background, whether for a portrait or a landscape, is to use a large aperture setting, like f-2.8 or f-4. (Quirkily enough, low *f-numbers indicate* larger *aperture settings; see the table on page 40.)*

If your camera has an aperture-priority *mode, then you can lock in this setting; the camera sets the correct shutter speed for you. Also, note that the farther away the subject is from the background, the softer the background will appear.*

Bottom: When you want your entire scene in focus, from front to back, then you want a deep *depth of field. You can do this by setting your aperture to f-8, f-11, or f-16.*

The portrait setting (program)

Many cameras offer a *portrait* mode, often designated on the control dial by the silhouette of a human head (Figure 3-6). Setting the camera to this mode automatically creates a short depth of field, blurring the background.

Figure 3-6:
If you don't want to mess with aperture settings, you can use the portrait mode *on your camera, if it has one—indicated on this camera and many others by a silhouette of a human head.*

Aperture-priority mode

More expensive cameras offer more control over depth of field in the form of an *aperture-priority mode*. It lets you tell the camera: "I want to control how much of this shot is in focus; that is, I want to set the aperture. You, the camera, should worry about the other half of the equation—the shutter speed."

Entering aperture-priority mode (if your camera has it) may be as simple as turning a dial to the A or AV position, or as complicated as having to pull up the camera's onscreen menu system.

(See page 36 for detail on how you can turn on shutter-priority mode. Aperture-priority mode is very similar, and is usually located right next to shutter priority.)

In any case, once you've turned on this mode, you adjust the aperture by turning a knob or pressing the up/down buttons. On the screen, you'll see the changing *f-stop* numbers, which represent different size apertures.

This table should offer some indication of what you're in for:

f-stop	diameter of aperture	depth of field	background looks
f-2	very large	very shallow	very soft
f-2.8	large	shallow	soft
f-4	medium	moderate	a little out of focus
f-5.6	medium	moderate	a little out of focus
f-8	small	moderately deep	mostly in focus
f-11	small	deep	sharp
f-16	very small	very deep	very sharp

Making the Shot

Position your model so the backdrop is in the distance. Check for telephone poles or anything else that may appear to pierce the model's head. If you can, shoot on a cloudy day, first thing in the morning or late in the afternoon; these are the best situations for outdoor portraits, when the light is softer and more flattering. Otherwise, try to place the model in open shade, like under a tree.

Adjust the flash settings so the flash is forced to go off, which will provide a nice supplemental burst of light. Don't stand more than ten feet away from your subject or your fill flash won't reach.

Finally, zoom in and start shooting. You'll notice that if you're standing within ten feet (so the flash will reach) and zooming in as much as your lens allows (to help soften the background), your model's upper body will fill the frame. That's what you want. Unwittingly, most snap shooters stand too far away from their subjects.

After a few frames, review your work and adjust as necessary. The soft background effect probably won't be as strong as it would be if you were using a pro camera with a telephoto lens, but you will definitely notice a pleasant difference.

Existing-Light Portraits

Cameras love light, that's for sure. And in general, you need the flash for indoor shots.

But not always. Some of the best interior photos use nothing more than light streaming in from a window. Images that use only ambient light without adding flash are called *existing light* or *natural light* photos.

This technique isn't right for every situation. But when it's appropriate, existing-light photos have these advantages over flash photography:

- **More depth.** The problem with the flash is that it illuminates only about the first ten feet of the scene. Everything beyond that fades to black.

  In existing-light photography, on the other hand, your camera reads the lighting for the entire room. Not only is your primary subject exposed properly, but the surrounding setting is too, giving the picture more depth.

- **Less harsh.** The light in an existing-light photo generally comes from a variety of sources: overhead lights, windows, lamps, and reflections off walls and ceilings. All of this adds up to softer, more balanced light than what you get from the laser beam generated by your built-in flash.

- **More expressive.** Too often, flash pictures produce the "deer in the headlights" look from your subjects—if indeed the close-range flash doesn't whitewash them completely. Existing-light pictures tend to be more natural and expressive, and the people you're shooting are more relaxed when they're not being pelted by bursts of light.

An existing-light indoor portrait has a classic feel, because it's reminiscent of those timeless paintings by great artists like Rembrandt.

Keep It Steady

In a natural-light portrait, keep the flash turned off (that's why it's called *natural* light). The camera's shutter will have to remain open for a relatively long interval to admit enough light for a good picture. As a result, you'll need to keep the camera very steady—which often means you'll need a tripod.

Pocket tripods are great for this type of shooting. They weigh only a few ounces, steady the camera well, and can be used on all kinds of surfaces like tables, countertops, and so on.

Once the tripod is steady, you face another challenge: taking the picture without jiggling the camera when you push the shutter button. Even a little camera shake will blur your entire image, creating an out-of-focus appearance.

If a remote control came with the camera, use it. If not, use the camera's self-timer feature, which counts off, say, ten seconds before snapping the picture automatically.

Tip: If your camera has a burst mode, here's a great chance to use it. Your finger pressing the shutter button is likely to ruin your first shot by introducing camera shake—but because it will thereafter remain down without moving, the second or third shot of the burst will look much steadier.

In either case, do what you can to persuade the subject to keep still; during a long exposure like this, fidgety people mean blurry portraits. (Of course, you can use this effect to your advantage, too, if you want to create a moody interior picture with ghostlike subjects.)

The Camera Setup

If you have adjustable film speed settings (page 21), then you might want to use the 200 or 400 setting to make your camera more light-sensitive. (On the other hand, if you do have enough light for a decent exposure, then don't increase the film speed, because it'll slightly degrade the image quality.)

How can you tell if you don't have enough light and need to increase the film speed? Review your test shot. (Zoom in to the LCD screen, magnifying the photo, to inspect it more closely.) If it's too dark or has motion blur, increase the film speed from 100 to 200. Take another test shot. If things are still looking dark, try one more time at 400 speed. And open the drapes all the way.

Also consider turning on spot metering (page 48). It permits the camera to make exposure decisions based only on the subject, without being affected by the lighting in the surrounding background.

The Model Setup

You'll need a window, tripod, trusty digital camera, and willing model for this project (Figure 3-7). You may want to put the camera on a tripod (page 66) to avoid camera shake.

Tip: Great painters of the past preferred the light coming through a *north* window for their portraits, especially in the early hours of the day. Try this setting for your existing-light portraits.

Now look at the lighting the way the camera would see the scene, not the way you would normally view it (see the box on page 45). If there's a noticeable difference between the brightest area of the model's face and the darkest area, then you may want to add a little of what's called *fill light*.

If you were a serious photographer with actual photographic gear lying around—and maybe you are—you could use a low-power flash as a fill light. Of course, then it would no longer be an *existing*-light portrait.

Figure 3-7:
In this existing-light portrait, notice how the tones trail off quickly from light to dark, which is typical illumination from a window. If you want to brighten the shadow areas, use a reflector to bounce the light back toward the model. You can try a flash for fill light, but be careful not to ruin the mood of the scene. Your best bet is to use the nighttime flash mode, which should preserve some of the scene's ambience.

It's a better idea to find a reflector and position it so that light bounces off it onto the dark side of the model's face. A reflector is a common piece of photographic gear; it's essentially a big white shiny surface on its own pole. If you don't have lighting equipment sitting around the house, but you really want this portrait to look good, just rig a big piece of white cardboard or white foam board to serve as a reflecting surface.

When you think you've balanced the tones, take a picture and review your results. Chances are that the shadow areas look darker to the camera than they do to your eyes. In that case, move the reflector closer to brighten the shadows.

White Balance (Color Balance)

Here's a mind-bending example of the way your eyes and your camera see things completely differently. It turns out that different kinds of lights—regular incandescent lightbulbs, fluorescent office lighting, the sun—cast subtle tinges of color on everything they illuminate. When you shoot non-flash photos indoors or in open shade outside, you'll get a bluish or *cool* cast. If you shoot without a flash under incandescent lighting, then the shots will have a *warm* tint, mostly yellow and red.

So why haven't you ever noticed these different lighting artifacts? Because your brain compensates almost instantly for these different *color temperatures,* as they're called. (Your brain does a lot of compensating for light. Ever noticed how your eyes adjust to a dark room after a couple of minutes?)

But to a camera, tints are tints—and you'll see them onscreen and in your printouts. Unfortunately, they can detract from your photos. For example, portraits with warmer casts are generally more pleasing to the eye. But natural light from the window imparts a bluish cast, which isn't good for skin tones.

Figure 3-8:
Most digital cameras let you adjust color balance. Sometimes the setting is labeled "WB" (white balance, which is essentially the same thing as color balance). Most of the time, you can leave this setting on Auto. But if the tones start looking too cool or too warm, you might want to override auto and make the adjustment yourself. And here's a tip: to warm up the skin tones in existing-light portraits (like the one in Figure 3-7), use the Cloudy white-balance setting.

In the days of traditional film photography, you would have corrected the color temperature by placing a screw-on filter over the lens. On a digital camera, you can change the color temperature by adjusting something called the camera's *white balance* (or *color balance*). Almost every digital camera has this function.

Most cameras have a little knob or menu offering these icons (see Figure 3-8). The sun icon represents normal daylight conditions in direct light; the cloud icon is for overcast days, open shade, and window-illuminated interiors; the lightbulb icon is for incandescent lighting; and the bar icon is for fluorescent lighting.

(If you're used to working with traditional camera filters, the sun is your "Sky 1A" filter, the cloud is your "81B warming" filter, the lightbulb is your "80A cooling" filter, and the tube is the "FLD fluorescent correction" filter.)

Tip: When you're using the flash, change your camera's color balance from Auto to Cloudy. Electronic flashes tend to produce images that have a cool cast. Switching to the Cloudy setting on your digital camera warms them up nicely.

Taking the Picture

With time and practice, you'll be able to "calibrate" your eyes so that they see shadows the same way your camera does. You'll spend less and less time testing before the shoot, and more time creating your classic image.

As you've figured out by now, creating a great natural-light portrait means learning to work with light as though it's a paintbrush. It takes time and practice to become proficient at this, but even your first efforts will probably surprise you with their expressiveness.

Tip: Don't be too quick to delete shots from the camera before viewing them on the computer screen. Existing-light shots sometimes contain subtleties that don't appear on tiny LCD screens. You'll be pleasantly surprised by many of the images that may have looked uninteresting when viewed on your camera's two-inch display.

Self-Portraits

The preceding discussion about blurring the background applies to pictures you take of yourself, too, of course. But there are a few other considerations.

UP TO SPEED

The Tale of Two Perceptions

The reason photographic lighting is such a challenge is that you have two different systems operating at once: your eyes and your camera.

Your pupils are super-advanced apertures that constantly adjust to ambient light. Even in extreme conditions, such as when you go from a completely dark theater to the bright lobby, it only takes seconds for your optical system to adjust.

Furthermore, you can look at a scene that contains both deep shadows and super-bright highlights—and see detail in both areas simultaneously. Your eyes, optical nerves, and brain are constantly adjusting to interpret the ever-changing landscape around you.

Too bad your camera can't do the same.

Whereas your eyes can pick up the entire *tonal range* of a scene (the shades from brightest white to darkest black), a camera can pick up detail in only a slice of it. For example, if you're shooting a bright sky filled with clouds and trees

casting deep shadows on meadow grass, you have a decision to make. Which parts of this scene are most important to you? The bright sky, the trees, or the deep shadows? On a good day, your camera will be able to record detail in two out of the three.

With practice, you can learn to see the world the way your camera does, to the great benefit of your photos. For example, try setting up a natural-light scene, such as a still life with fruit. Put the camera on a tripod. Study the scene with your eyes, and then photograph it. Compare what the lens records with the image in your head.

Are they the same? Probably not. How are the two images different? Make a few notes about your perceptions as compared to what the camera captured, and then repeat the exercise with a different scene.

When the image in your head begins to match the one on the camera's LCD screen, then you've truly begun to see the world with a photographic eye.

If you're on vacation, the natural scenery might be all the backdrop you need. If you're shooting a picture to use on a resumé or to post on your Web page, however, find a well-lit room with some open wall space. The blank wall (preferably light-colored) will serve as your backdrop. Natural light coming in from windows is best for this setup.

Find a stool or a low-back chair without arms, and position it about five feet in front of your backdrop. If possible, it should face the brightest window in the room.

Next, you'll need a way to position your camera. A standard tripod is best, but you can use a pocket tripod on top of a table if necessary. Either way, position the camera about five feet from your stool.

Tip: In a pinch, you can use a standard hotel-room lamp as a tripod. The threads that are designed to secure the lampshade to its support bracket are exactly the right diameter for your camera's tripod socket!

Turn on the flash. The ambient room lighting is often bright enough to provide overall even illumination, but the flash will provide a little burst of front light to smooth out facial blemishes and put a twinkle in your eyes.

The best cameras for self-portraits have a flip screen and a remote control. The flip screen lets you preview how you look in the frame before you shoot the shot, and the remote control lets you actually take the shot while sitting comfortably on your stool.

If you don't have these options, put your camera in self-timer mode. To help you frame the shot while you're not actually on the stool, use a table lamp as a stand-in.

Check your hair and clothing in a mirror, press the shutter button to trigger the self-timer countdown, and then sit on the stool (preferably *after* removing the table lamp).

Once the camera fires, play back the photo on the screen. Did you zoom in close enough? Are you in focus and centered in the frame? How does the lighting look?

If you need to add a little light to one side of your face or the other because it's appearing too shadowy, you can construct a homemade reflector out of white cardboard or similar material. Position your reflector as close to you as possible (although not in the photo itself) and angle it so it bounces light off the brightest light source onto the area requiring illumination. This will help lighten up the dark areas.

Shoot another round. Once you get the basic setup looking good, experiment with different angles and facial expressions. One advantage of taking your own portraits is that you can be more creative. Remember, you can always erase the embarrassing frames—or all of them. Remember, too, that self-portraits don't have to be dull headshots; they can be every bit as interesting as any other photo.

Kid Photography

Children are challenging for all photographers. They're like flash floods: fast, low to the ground, and unpredictable. But with a little patience and perseverance, you can keep up with them and get the shot (Figure 3-9). Here are some tips:

- **Be prepared.** Rule one for capturing great kid pictures is to have your camera handy at all times, charged and with memory-card space to spare. Great kid shots come and go in the blink of an eye. Parents don't have the luxury of keeping their equipment snugly stowed away in a camera bag in the closet.

- **Get down there.** The best kid shots are generally photographed at kid level, and that means getting low. (Flip screens are particularly useful for kid shots, because they let you position the camera down low without actually having to lie on the ground.)

- **Get close.** Your shots will have much more impact if the subject fills the frame, plus you won't have to do as much cropping later in iPhoto.

- **Prefocus.** Shutter lag will make you miss the shot every time. In many cases, you can defeat it by prefocusing—that is, half-pressing the shutter button when the kid's not doing anything special. Keep your finger on the button until the magical smile appears, then press fully to snap the shot.

- **Burst away.** Use your camera's burst mode to fire off several shots in quick succession. Given the fleeting nature of many kids' grins, this trick improves your odds for catching just the right moment.

Figure 3-9:
If you want great-looking kid shots, you've got to play on their turf. That means getting down on your hands and knees, or even your tummy.

• **Force the flash.** Indoors or out, the flash provides even illumination and helps freeze the action. Switch your camera's flash setting so that it's always on.

• **Make it bright.** See page 58 for a discussion of red-eye, but don't bother using the *red-eye reduction* flash mode on your camera. By the time your camera has finished strobing and stuttering, your kid will be in the next zip code.

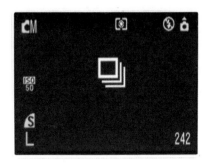

Figure 3-10:
Photographing fast-moving children is easier if you use your camera's burst mode, which lets you hold down the shutter button and fire off a sequence of frames. Chances are, one of them will capture the decisive moment.

On most cameras, you choose burst mode using the onscreen menus. Nicer cameras, in fact, offer a choice of several burst modes: for example, one that captures full-resolution shots but not as quickly, or a more rapid-fire mode that takes lower-res photos.

If red-eye is a problem in your flash photos of kids, make the room as bright as possible, shoot from an angle that isn't dead-on into your kids' eyes, and touch up the red-eye later in iPhoto, if necessary.

• **Fire at will.** Child photography is like shooting a sports event—you'll take lots of bad shots in order to get a few gems. Again, who cares? The duds don't cost you anything. And once you've captured the image of a lifetime, you'll forget about all the outtakes you deleted previously.

Theater Performances

Capturing stage performances is difficult even for professional photographers. What makes theater lighting tricky is that the bright main light on the actors is often right in the same frame with a subdued or even darkened background. If you photograph this composition "as is" in automatic mode, then the camera calibrates the exposure, brightening up the image enough to display the dominant dim background. As a result, the spotlighted actors turn into white-hot, irradiated ghosts.

Your built-in flash is useless under these conditions (unless you climb right up onto the stage beside the actors, which is generally frowned upon by the management). The typical range for the camera's flash is about ten feet, after which it's about as useful as a snow-cone machine in Alaska. *Turn your flash off* at theater performances— because it's annoying to the rest of the audience, because it's worthless, and because it's usually forbidden.

To overcome this challenge, use the other tools built into your camera. If you have a *spot meter mode,* you have a fighting chance. As noted previously, your camera generally gauges the brightness of the scene by averaging the light across the entire frame—a recipe for disaster when you're shooting the stage.

Spot metering, however, lets you designate a particular spot in the scene whose brightness you want the camera to measure. (You indicate what spot that is by positioning a frame marker that appears in the center of the frame.) Point the spot-metering area at the brightly lit actors. The camera then sets the exposure on them instead of on the vast expanse of the dimly lit set.

Not all cameras have a spot-metering mode. But even basic cameras generally offer some kind of *exposure compensation,* an overall brightness control. For theater situations, try lowering the exposure to –1 or –1.5, for example. The objective is to darken the entire scene. The background will be *too* dark, of course, but at least the actors won't be "blown out."

Finally, if you know ahead of time that you want pictures from a particular performance, do what you can to secure a ticket in the first few rows. When it comes to theater shooting, the closer you get, the better.

Tip: Depending on the kind of performance you're trying to photograph, getting the right lighting may be just the tip of the iceberg. Getting *permission* to photograph might be the greater obstacle.

In these cases, consider taking your pictures at the dress rehearsal. (This means you, parents of kids in school plays.) Not only is the management likely to be more permissive, but you'll be able to sit right there in the front row, to the immense benefit of your photos.

Figure 3-11:
You can buy an underwater housing for your digital camera for as little as $100. Olympus and Canon make housings for nearly all of their compact cameras. Other manufacturers offer underwater gear, too.

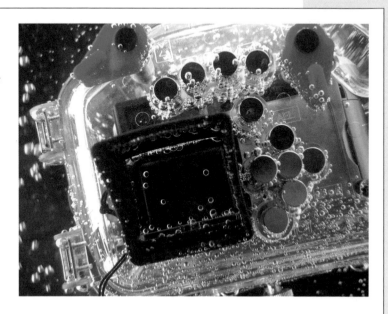

Underwater Photography

Water is the mortal enemy of digital cameras. Still, you can buy waterproof enclosures for many camera models, which opens up a whole new world of photographic possibilities.

Sometimes these enclosures are made by the camera manufacturer; for other models, you can often find enclosures for sale at Web sites like *www.ikelite.com* or *www. uwimaging.com*.

The good news is that these enclosures protect the camera at depths down to 100 feet, for example, and provide access to the camera's controls. The bad news is that the underwater housing can cost as much as the camera!

When shooting underwater, force the flash to turn on; it's dark down there. You might also want to play with the color balance adjustment to help offset the bluish tint of the water. If your camera has a dial that lets you call up different lighting presets, try the Cloudy setting to warm up the tones.

Oh, and don't try to change the batteries while you're down there.

Travel Photography

Digital cameras are perfect vacation companions. Memory cards are easy to pack, there's no film for airport X-rays to wash out, and when the day is done, you can review all of your images on the camera's LCD screen, on your laptop, or on the hotel room TV.

Shooting on the road presents unique photo opportunities that simply aren't available at home—like museums, fjords, and Cinderella's Castle. Here's how to master those moments and add a little spice to your vacation slideshow.

Packing up

Digital cameras may be small and compact, but they're often accompanied by just as much accessory junk as film cameras. Here's a pre-trip checklist:

- **Batteries.** The laws of photography dictate that you'll run out of juice at the precise moment the perfect shot appears. If your camera comes with its own proprietary, rechargeable battery, consider buying a second one. Charge both batteries every night, and take them both with you during the day. (Pack the charger, too.)

  If your camera accepts AA-type batteries instead, you have much more flexibility. Bring your set of NiMH rechargeables, as described as page 15, and their charger. Also pack an emergency set of disposables, like alkaline AAs or Duracell CRV3 lithium disposables, if your camera accepts them.

- **Memory cards.** Nobody ever said, "Oh, I wish I'd bought a smaller memory card." As a rough rule of thumb, figure that you'll wind up keeping 50 shots a day (not including the ones that you delete right off the camera). If you have a 4-megapixel camera, a 128 MB card might be enough for one day of shooting. If you brought a laptop on the trip, you can rush back to the hotel room each night and offload the pictures into iPhoto, freeing up the card for the next day's shooting.

If you don't plan to take the laptop along, buy a much bigger memory card (or several). It's generally cheaper to buy two 256 MB cards than one 512 MB card, but shop around to get the best deal possible (*www.shopper.com,* for example).

And if you plan to use the movie mode to capture video snippets of your adventures, then add one or two 1 GB cards to your kit. Memory-card prices are well below nosebleed territory these days; you can buy 1 GB cards for less than $75.

• **Camera bag.** If your camera didn't come with a case, get one for it. Not only will it protect your camera, but it will keep your batteries, cards, and cables together.

Tip: If you can find a camera bag that doesn't *look* like a camera bag, it's less likely to be ripped off. An insulated beverage bag does nicely, for example.

• **Tripod.** Nobody likes to lug a tripod across Europe—or across town, for that matter. But if you're a serious photographer, or aspire to be one, you'll occasionally need a way to steady your camera.

A miniature tabletop tripod like the UltraPod 2 is an ideal compromise. It weighs only four ounces, costs $22, and provides solid support for your camera in a variety of situations. A quick search at *www.google.com* should help you find a mail-order company that carries it.

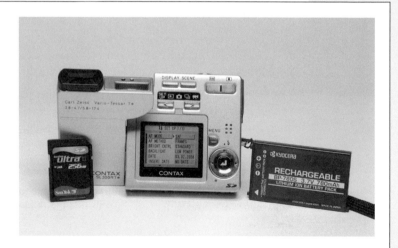

Figure 3-12:
Being prepared for travel mean packing extra memory and batteries. And don't forget the charger!

• **Weatherproofing.** Keep a couple of plastic bags tucked in your carrying case for use in bad weather. Digital cameras hate water, but some of nature's most dramatic shows occur at the beginning and end of storms.

- **Lens cloth.** Microfiber lens cloths are light, inexpensive (about $5), and easy to pack—and they're the best way to keep your optics sparkling clean. They look like a regular soft cloth, but they actually have thousands of microfibers that grab smudges off your lens and whisk them away.

- **Small flashlight.** Don't risk losing a great night shot just because you can't read your camera's controls. Pack a small flashlight to help you work in dim lighting situations.

The Museum Challenge

Many museums permit photography, provided you keep the flash off and don't use a full-size tripod. Digital cameras are particularly well suited to these assignments.

Once you're in, here are some techniques to consider:

- You might want to increase the film speed setting to 200 or 400 to better handle the dimmer interior lighting (see page 21).

- Museums often use halogen lightbulbs to illuminate the artwork, which could lend a red or yellow cast to your photos.

  If your particular camera automatically adjusts its color balance nicely, then no problem. But if your sample shots look too warm (reddish or yellowish), consider switching the camera's white-balance control to the Incandescent setting (usually denoted by a lightbulb icon on the control dial).

  If that doesn't improve the pictures, adjust the camera's white balance as described on page 44 (if your camera offers this feature).

- How do you take a picture of what's in a glass display case without getting nasty reflections?

  The trick is to put the front of your lens barrel right against the glass. You'll probably have to zoom out all the way to frame the shot properly.

- Finally, hold the camera steady when shooting in museums. Because of the low lighting, your camera will probably choose a slow shutter speed, which introduces the possibility that the camera will shake, introducing blur. The steadier you hold your camera, the sharper your shots will be.

Portraits on the Road

In standard headshots, you generally want to frame the subject as tightly as possible. But when you're traveling, you want to include the background so it might suggest your location.

Unfortunately, many travelers include *too much* information about the location. In reality, sometimes you need two shots to convey one message.

Get Creative

Picture taking should be fun while on vacation. You won't be graded on your shots; it's not a term paper to be turned in at the end of the week. So enjoy the process of shooting as much as the trip itself.

Digital cameras encourage playfulness. You can try something silly, look at it on the LCD screen, and—if it's too incriminating—erase it before anyone else discovers just *how* amateur an amateur photographer you really are. The bottom line: taking pictures should be part of your vacation.

Figure 3-13:
When you're taking portraits on location, vary your compositions. Include wide-angle shots, for example, to capture the environment as well as the subjects. Then move in closer for facial expressions.

So here are a few ideas for you to try the next time you're exploring the world:

- **Get in the picture.** Almost every digicam comes with a self-timer. Position the camera so that you have an interesting background, trip the timer, and get in the shot. It's really fun if you're with a group, too.

- **Try the close-up mode.** Almost every digital camera offers a *macro* (super-close-up) mode that lets you get within inches of your subject. The world is a very different place at this magnification. Let your imagination run wild. Everything is a potential shot, from local currency to flower petals.

- **Vary the shots.** The standard shot of your travel companions standing posed in front of the Grand Canyon is fine, but that's only the beginning. The so-called "little shots," such as your son staring out the train window, or your friend buying flowers from a street vendor, are often more compelling than the typical "stand in front of a building and smile" photo. (See Figure 3-13 for an example.)

- **The city lights from your balcony at sunset.** There's a magic moment every day at twilight when the city lights come on right before the sun sets. Grab your camera, park it on a wall or windowsill for stability, and take a few shots.

- **Shoot from the passenger-side window.** Ask your travel companion to take the wheel as you drive along. Sitting on the passenger side of the car, roll down the window and look for interesting pictures. Don't worry about the background blurring and other little glitches, because they're often what make the pictures compelling.

- **Signs and placards instead of notes.** Museums, monuments, and national parks are all loaded with informative signs and placards. Instead of taking notes and lugging brochures, take pictures of these tidbits of information. When you put together your trip slideshow in iPhoto, these will make great introductory shots for each segment.

- **Shooting through shop windows.** Storefront displays say so much about the local culture. But taking pictures through glass can be tricky, thanks to unwanted

Cautions on the Road

Camera-toting tourists are prime targets for thieves—and digital cameras make delicious loot. When you're on the road, keep in mind the following tips, which are designed to help you bring home more than just memories:

- Consider packing your camera gear in a backpack or a fanny pack instead of a traditional camera bag. That way, you're not walking through the streets of India with a bag that screams, "I'm an expensive camera—steal me!"

- Carry your camera bag onto the plane instead of checking it with the luggage.

- Secure the camera strap to your body when touring.

- Be wary when handing your camera to strangers for group shots. They may run away with it. Use the camera's self-timer to take pictures of yourselves—or at least use your best judgment in summing up passersby.

- Keep an eye on your equipment as you go through airport security. The best plan is to have your travel mate go through security first, then send through your collective equipment, then you go through. That way you always have someone close to your stuff.

- Don't leave your camera lying around your hotel room. If you leave it behind, put it in the room's safe.

reflections. As when shooting glass display cases in museums, the trick is to zoom out, and then get the front of the lens barrel as close to the window as possible. The closer you are, the fewer reflections you'll have in your picture.

Now that you're armed with lots of ideas and techniques, you're probably getting the itch to take a vacation. When you go, don't forget your camera, a few memory cards, and plenty of battery power.

Outdoor Portraits

Everybody knows what the camera's built-in flash is for, right? It goes off automatically when there's not enough light.

Unfortunately, everybody also knows how ornery and feeble these flashes are. If you're too close to the subject, the flash blows out the picture, turning your best friend into

Figure 3-14:
Bright backgrounds often fool your exposure meter. The camera might expose the background properly, but throw your subject into darkness. The solution: Force the flash to fire. (This technique is called a fill flash, and it's represented in your camera's mode options by a single lightning bolt.) It's a terrific way to properly expose both the background and the subject—as long as you're within flash range, of course.

a ghost face that looks like it was photographed during a nuclear test. If you're farther than about eight feet away, the flash is too weak to do anything useful at all.

No matter what kind of camera you have, however, you'll take your best pictures when *you* decide to use the flash, not when the camera decides. Believe it or not, the camera's automatic mode is wrong about half the time.

Outdoor portraits represent a perfect example. If you leave the flash setting on automatic when you shoot outdoors, you can guess what will happen: The camera will conclude that there's plenty of light and won't bother to fire the flash.

The camera has correctly concluded that there's enough light *in the entire frame.* But it's not smart enough to recognize that the person you're photographing is, in fact, in shadow (Figure 3-14).

The solution in this situation is to *force* the flash on—a very common trick. Provided you're close enough to the subject, the flash will provide enough *fill light* to balance the subject's exposure with that of the surrounding background. (If you're using your on-camera flash, stand within about eight feet of the subject so you can get enough flash for a proper exposure.)

This kind of fill flash will dramatically improve your outdoor portraits. Not only will it eliminate the silhouette effect when your subject is standing in front of a bright background, but frontal light is very flattering. It softens smile lines and wrinkles, and it puts a nice twinkle in the subject's eyes.

How do you take your flash off auto mode? Most cameras offer a couple different flash settings. Look for the icon that represents a lightning bolt with an arrow tip on the end—the universal icon for electronic flash. Generally, if you push the button next to this icon, it cycles through the flash modes on your camera. These modes usually include *auto flash* (no icon), *red-eye reduction* (eyeball icon), *no flash* (universal "circle with a diagonal line through it" icon) and *flash on*, and *forced flash* (stand-alone lightning bolt icon). For your outdoor portraits, cycle through the icons until you get to the forced-flash mode.

(In full automatic mode, by the way, you may not be allowed to change the flash mode. Try switching into the portrait mode first.)

Tip: If you're that rare digital photographer who owns an external flash attachment, use *it* in situations where you need a fill flash. The more powerful strobe illuminates the subject better and provides a more flexible working distance.

It's also the only way to go if your subject wears glasses. If the flash is on a dedicated cord, you can raise it a couple feet above the camera to minimize the reflection of the flash in the glasses.

Rim Lighting

Once you've experimented with fill flash, try this variation that pros use to create striking portraits: *rim lighting.*

Position the subject with her back to the sun (preferably when it's high in the sky and not shining directly into your camera lens). Now set your camera to fire the flash (the lightning bolt, not the automatic setting). If the sun is shining into the lens, block it using your hand or a lens shade.

The first thing you'll notice is that the sun creates a *rim light* around the subject's hair (Figure 3-15). You'll also notice that her eyes are more relaxed and open. In one swift move, you've made your subject more comfortable and improved your chances for a dramatic portrait.

Figure 3-15:
Remember how you were always told to have the sun at your back when taking a picture? That's not the best advice for portraits. In fact, you want the sun on the model's back to create a rim light *effect. Notice how her hair and her shoulder are highlighted? Remember to turn on your fill flash so the model's face isn't underexposed.*

If you were to shoot the picture right now, without the fill flash, the result would be the classic *backlit photo*. In other words, the background would be nicely exposed—but the subject would be shadowy or even silhouetted. You would join the throngs who, on a daily basis, ruin golden opportunities for great photographs.

Once again, the solution is to force the flash, creating a nice fill light.

Now take a few pictures and review your work onscreen. If your model is too bright, move back a few steps and try again. If she's too dark, move a little closer.

When it works, rim lighting creates portraits that you'll be very proud of. It's not the right technique for every situation, but sometimes it produces jaw-dropping results.

Tip: If your camera accepts filters, try a *softening filter* for your rim-lighting shots. It can reduce facial wrinkles and create a nice glow around the subject's head.

Open Shade

Working in open shade, like the shadow of a tree, produces less dramatic portraits than rim lighting, but very pleasing ones nonetheless.

The open shade eliminates harsh shadows around the face and keeps the subject from squinting. Here again, forcing the flash on your digital camera is a great idea. Look for a subtle background without distracting elements.

The beauty of this technique is that you capture an evenly lit, relaxed subject with a perfectly exposed background. You won't even notice that it was shot in the shade.

Indoor Flash

Over the years, you've probably seen plenty of indoor flash pictures that have a pitch-black background and an overexposed, practically nuked subject.

Many factors conspire to produce these stark, unflattering shots, but one of the major contributors is, once again, your camera thinking on its own. You're letting *it* decide when to turn on the flash and which shutter speed to use.

First of all, you don't always need the flash. Indoor photography offers many opportunities for stunning existing-light portraits and moody interior shots, as described earlier. And when you do have to turn on the flash, you can make certain adjustments to preserve the ambiance of the room so that your background doesn't fall into a black hole.

UP TO SPEED

How to Really Get Rid of Red-Eye

For years now, camera manufacturers have been inflicting *red-eye reduction mode* on their customers. It's a series of bright, strobing flashes that's not only annoying to the people you're photographing, but it doesn't even work.

What causes red-eye? In a dimly lit room, the subject's pupil dilates, revealing more of the retina. On cameras where the flash is close to the camera lens (as it almost always is), the light from the flash shines through the dilated pupil, bounces off the retina, and reflects as a red circle directly back into the lens. (The same thing happens to animals, too, except that the color is sometimes green instead of red.)

The solution is to move the flash away from the camera lens. That way, the reflection from the retina doesn't bounce directly back at the camera. But on a camera that fits in your pocket, it's a little tough to achieve much separation of flash and lens.

Since camera makers couldn't move the flash away, they went to Plan B: firing the flash just *before* the shutter snaps, in theory contracting the subjects' pupils, thereby revealing less retina. Alas, it doesn't work very well, and you may wind up with red-eye anyway.

You have three ways out of red-eye. If you can turn up the lights, do it. If you have that rare camera that accepts an external, detachable flash, use it. And if none of that works, remember that iPhoto has its own red-eye-removal tool (page 154).

IPHOTO 6: THE MISSING MANUAL

Slow-Synchro Interiors

There are two reasons why your flash shots often have a pitch-black background. The first problem is that the light from a typical digital camera's flash reaches only about eight to ten feet. Anything beyond this range, and you've got yourself an inadvertent existing-light photo.

If your camera has a *manual mode* that allows you to dictate both the aperture (f-stop) and shutter speed, you can easily overcome these problems. Once in manual mode, try this combination as a starting point for flash photography indoors:

- Set your film speed to 100 (page 21).

- Set the aperture (f-stop) to f-5.6.

- Set the shutter speed to 1/15th of a second.

- Use the forced-flash mode. (*Don't* use the red-eye reduction feature.)

At these slow shutter speeds, your shots are more vulnerable to camera shake, and therefore to blurriness. Your flash will help freeze everything in its range—but the background, not illuminated by the flash, may blur if the camera isn't steady.

Take a shot. As you review the picture, you'll see that it has more room ambiance and background detail that what you're used to.

If your camera doesn't have a manual mode, all is not lost. Almost every consumer model has a setting called *nighttime* or *slow-synchro* mode. This setting is often indicated by a "stars over a mountain" icon. The intention of this mode is to let you shoot portraits at twilight, as described in the next section. But you can also use Nighttime mode indoors to "open up" the background (Figure 3-16). Granted, you don't have

Figure 3-16:
Tired of having your flash subjects lost in a black hole of darkness? Try using what photographers call slow-synchro flash. *Set your camera's shutter speed and aperture manually to control the exposure of the background. The camera's flash ensures that the subjects are exposed properly.*

as much control with this setting as you do with manual mode, but you might be pleasantly surprised with the results.

Twilight Portraits

Twilight is a magic time for photographers. The setting sun bathes the landscape in a warm glow, providing a beautiful backdrop for portraits. This is an ideal time to shoot any type of shot.

First, you'll need a tripod or some other means to steady the camera. There's far less light during this time of day, and therefore the shutter slows down considerably.

Now inspect your camera's flash options. Look for an option called either Slow-synchro or Nighttime—a setting that synchronizes your flash with the very slow shutter. Look for a "stars and mountain" or "stars and person" icon.

Now position your model in front of the most beautiful part of the landscape and take the picture.

When you push the button, the camera opens the shutter long enough to compensate for the dim twilight lighting, capturing all of the rich, saturated colors. The flash, meanwhile, throttles down, emitting just enough light to illuminate the subject from the front.

The result can be an incredibly striking image that will make your travel pictures the talk of the office. It's a great technique when shooting somebody standing in front of illuminated monuments and buildings at night, sunsets over the ocean, and festive nighttime lighting.

Tip: If your subject is rendered too bright (overexposed by the flash), move back a few feet, zoom in, and try again. Conversely, if your subject is too dark (underexposed by the flash), move in a couple of feet.

Landscape and Nature

Unlike portraiture, where *you* have to arrange the lights and the models, landscape photography demands a different discipline: patience. Nature calls the shots here. Your job is to be prepared and in position.

Shoot with Sweet Light

Photographers generally covet the first and last two hours of the day for shooting (which half explains why they're always getting up at five in the morning). The lower angle of the sun and the slightly denser atmosphere create rich, saturated tones, as well as what photographers call *sweet* light.

It's a far cry from the midday sun, which creates much harsher shadows and much more severe highlights. Landscape shooting is more difficult when the sun is high overhead on a bright, cloudless day.

Layer Your Lights and Darks

Ansel Adams, the most famous American landscape photographer, looked for scenes in sweet light that had alternating light and dark areas. As you view one of these pictures from the bottom of the frame to the top, you might see light falling on the foreground, then a shadow cast by a tree, then a pool of light behind the tree, followed by more shadows from a hill, and finally an illuminated sky at the top of the composition.

A lighting situation like this creates more depth in your pictures (and, yes, lets you "shoot like Ansel").

Highlight a Foreground Object with Flash

Sometimes you can lend nature a helping hand by turning on your flash to illuminate an object in the immediate foreground. Remember, just because your eyes can see detail in the dark area at the bottom of the frame doesn't mean that your camera

POWER USERS' CLINIC

Built-In Flash vs. External Flash

More expensive digital cameras offer serious photographers a wonderful feature: a place to plug in an external flash attachment.

An external flash moves the light source away from the lens, which reduces red-eye, especially if the flash is on its own separate bracket rather than a hot shoe right on the camera. The external flash makes your camera's battery last longer, too, because it has its own batteries. You'll be grateful during long events like weddings.

The most versatile way to attach an external flash is with a standard hot shoe right on top of the camera, as shown here. You can either connect the flash directly, or you can use a *dedicated* flash cord that allows you to move the flash away from the camera, but still retain communication between the two.

Some cameras just aren't big enough to accommodate a hot shoe. To circumvent this problem, some camera makers have engineered a system that uses a tiny socket on

the camera that connects to the flash via a proprietary cord and bracket. This system isn't the height of versatility, but it does allow you the flexibility of an external flash on a very compact camera.

A wedding is one key example of a situation where you'll find this useful. When you're not the primary photographer, you won't get the prime shooting locations during big events (like the cake cutting). Therefore, you'll need all the flash power possible to get the shots even when you're out of position—another advantage of an external flash unit.

Finally, a detached flash attachment gives you more flexibility, because you can use it to bounce light off the wall or ceiling to provide fill lighting for certain shots.

A good external flash with a dedicated cord costs at least $200, and, of course, only the fancier digital cameras can accommodate them. But as you become more serious with your photographic pastime, you'll find that external flashes help you capture shots that on-camera flashes just can't get.

can. Look for an interesting object—a bush, perhaps. Move the camera close to it and zoom out. Then turn on the flash and shoot. The effect can be stunning.

Sunsets

Your camera usually does a good job of exposing the sky during sunset, even in automatic mode. Keep the flash turned off and shoot at will.

Tip: Keep an eye on your shutter speed (if your camera shows it). If it goes below 1/30th of a second, you may need a tripod or some other steady surface to prevent camera shake. Activate the self-timer or remote control to avoid jiggling the camera when you press the shutter.

The biggest mistake people make when shooting sunsets has nothing to do with the sky—it's the *ground* that ruins the shots. Your eyes can make out much more detail in the shadowy ground than your camera will. Therefore, it's not worth trying to split the frame in half, composing it with the sky above and the ground below. The bottom half of your photo will just be a murky black blob in the final image.

Instead, fill your composition with 90 percent sky and 10 percent ground or water. This arrangement may feel funny—at least until you look at your prints and see how much more dynamic they are with this composition.

Tip: Many photographers make the mistake of leaving the scene right after the sun dips below the horizon. Hang around for another 10 minutes or so; sometimes there's a truly amazing after-burst of light.

Weddings

Weddings dominate special event photography, not to mention being the primary income source for a huge percentage of professional photographers.

If you can shoot an entire wedding, then you're prepared for any other event that comes your way. For example, graduations are just weddings without the reception. Birthday parties are just weddings without the ceremony.

If you're a guest, one critical element of successful photography at a wedding is not interfering with the *hired* photographer's posed shots. Introduce yourself to the photographer and ask if it's OK to take a couple of shots right after the pro has finished each setup. You'll generally receive permission—and the opportunity to capture the highlights of the day.

Tip: As a digital photographer, you can bring a new dimension to the celebration that most pros don't even offer: immediacy. If you like, you can hook up your camera to a TV to play the pictures back while the reception is still going on. Or, thanks to iPhoto, you can have shots on the Web before the pro even gets his film to the lab. Put your favorites together and add a little music; suddenly you have a QuickTime movie for downloading.

Shots to Look For

In part, your success at shooting a wedding depends on your ability to anticipate the action. If you've been to any weddings recently, you probably know that you can expect classic photo ops like these:

- **Before the wedding.** Bride making final dress adjustments, alone in dress, with mother, with maid of honor, with bridesmaids, and so on. The groom with his best man, with his ushers, with his family.

- **During the ceremony.** The groom waiting at the altar, his parents being seated, the bride's mother being seated, the processional, the bride coming down the aisle, the vows, the ring ceremony, the kiss, the bride and groom coming back down the aisle. Oh, and of course the obligatory adorable shots of the flower girl and ring-bearer boy walking down the aisle looking dazed.

- **Directly after the ceremony.** The wedding party at the altar, the bride and groom with family, the bride and groom with officiate, close-up of the bride's and groom's hands on the ring pillow.

- **During the reception.** Guests signing the guest book, the bride dancing with groom/father/father-in-law, the groom dancing with mother/mother-in-law, the cake table, the cake cutting, the cake feeding, the toasts, the bouquet tossing, the decorated getaway car.

Tip: One of the advantages you might have over the hired photographer is that you'll *know* people at the wedding. You'll therefore have the opportunity, in theory at least, to take candid, relaxed pictures of the guests—a sure bride-and-groom pleaser.

That's the checklist for a professional photographer, of course. If you're one of the guests, use that list only for inspiration. Wedding days provide dozens of opportunities for memorable pictures. If you get only a fraction of them, you'll still have plenty to share at the end of the day.

Photographing Objects

Most people usually photograph people and places. Every now and then, however, you'll need to photograph *things:* stuff you plan to sell on eBay, illustrations for a report, your personal belongings for insurance purposes, and so on.

The *macro* (close-up) mode of your digital camera makes it easy to shoot objects. All you need to do is set up and light your shot; the camera does the rest.

The Home Studio

The trick to lighting any object professionally, whether it's a painting or a teapot, is to position *two* lights, each at a 45-degree angle to the plane of the subject.

At a hardware store, buy a couple of lamps. Sometimes called *shop lights,* they have clamps and ball joints to lock the lamp at a certain angle.

Note: Buy lamps that accommodate regular lightbulbs, not the high-powered halogen models that melt everything within 50 yards.

Regular 100-watt "soft light" bulbs work fine. While you're at the hardware store, look for some white *butcher paper* or some other paper that will give you a seamless background at least six feet long and four feet wide. (Camera stores also sell paper backdrops for about $30 a roll.)

Figure 3-17:
You don't need to build a home studio to produce great product shots. This picture was created by setting a table next to a north-facing window. A piece of white cardboard was used as a reflector to bounce some light back onto the shadow side of the object.

Now you're ready to set up your temporary photo studio. Slide a table against the wall, then hang your butcher paper about three feet above the table. Tape it to the top surface of the table, making sure that it has a gentle curve as it goes from vertical to horizontal. Place the item that you want to photograph in the center of the table, about a foot in front of the paper curve.

Next, it's time to set up your lights. You can use chair backs to clamp your lights, which should be pointing directly at your subject at a 45-degree angle, about three feet away from the subject, pointing slightly downward.

Note: Some photographers eschew the two-light setup, preferring a bit of shadow on one side of the object. For this effect, use only one light; on the opposite side, create a reflective surface like a white piece of cardboard, aluminum foil, or white foam board. Make sure that the reflector bounces the light toward the object's non-illuminated side.

Now your subject is evenly lit, with a minimum of glare and harsh shadows. Even though this homemade product rig might not look beautiful, the shots you create with it can be very appealing (Figure 3-17).

Some other tips:

- Adjust your camera's white balance for the type of light you're using (page 44). Uncorrected incandescent lights produce an overly warm (reddish) cast; flash tends to produce images a bit on the cool (bluish) side.

- A tripod helps keep the camera in precise position.

- If your camera has a manual-focus mode, use it to lock the focus on the object's area that's most important to you.

- Once your camera is positioned and focused, you may find its remote control or self-timer mode convenient, so you won't have to constantly bend over during the course of a long shoot.

You're ready to shoot.

Natural Lighting for Objects

Of course, you won't always be at home with a bunch of lights and roll paper at your disposal. Many of your object shots will be more spontaneous, impromptu affairs, or you may decide that a home studio isn't your cup of tea. In these cases, let nature provide the lighting.

In taking natural-light shots like this, the trick is to keep your subject out of direct sunlight, which would create harsh contrast and "hot spots" on the object's surface.

Figure 3-18:
Don't wait until complete darkness for this type of shot, or your sky will go pitch black. Twilight is the best time to shoot streaming car lights.

Instead, work in open shade, preferably in the morning or late afternoon hours when the light is the "sweetest." A north-facing window is perfect for this type of shooting.

Once again, pay close attention to the background. You might have to get creative in setting up the shot so that it has a continuous background without any distracting edges.

Finally, set the white balance controls to the Cloudy setting to offset the blue cast created by open shade.

Nighttime Photography

Nighttime pictures can be the most spectacular ones in your portfolio. City lights, river lights, sky lights, and even car lights can stand out like bright colors on a black canvas.

Unfortunately, you won't get far in this kind of photography without a tripod. You can practice the following techniques by bracing the camera against a wall—but you'll find the job infinitely easier with a true tripod.

Trailing Car Lights

You've seen this shot on postcards and in magazines: neon bands of light streaking across the frame, with a nicely lit bridge or building in the background. The trick to these shots is to keep the shutter open long enough for the cars to pass all the way from one side of the frame to the other (Figure 3-18).

When using film cameras, photographers rely on the camera's B setting, in combination with a *cable release* (a shutter button on the end of a cord). The B setting (short for *bulb*) keeps the shutter open for as long as you hold down the release. Many a

---

BUYERS' GUIDE

How to Buy a Tripod

A tripod has two parts: the legs and the *pan head*. The camera attaches to the pan head, and the legs support the head.

You can buy a tripod with any of three pan head types. *Friction heads* are the simplest, least expensive, and most popular with still photographers. *Fluid heads* are desirable if you'll also be using your tripod for a camcorder, as they smooth out panning and tilting. (This means you, iMovie fans.) They're more expensive than friction heads, but are well worth the money if you're after a professional look to your footage. Finally, *geared heads* are big, heavy, expensive, and difficult to use.

The tripod's legs may be made of metal, wood, or composite. Metal is light and inexpensive, but easier to damage by accident (thin metal is easily bent). Wood and composite legs are much more expensive; they're designed for heavier professional broadcast and film equipment. The bottoms of the legs have rubber feet, which is great for use indoors and on hard floors.

Good tripods also have *spreaders* that prevent the legs from spreading apart and causing the entire apparatus to crash to the ground. If your tripod doesn't have spreaders, put the tripod on a piece of carpet, which prevents the legs from slipping apart.

---

photographer has stood out in the cold, thumbs pressing down on icy cable releases, softly counting: "One thousand one, one thousand two, one thousand three…"

Your digital camera probably doesn't have a B setting (although a few do have Bulb modes). But you can capture these dramatic shots if your camera offers a shutter-priority mode (see Figure 3-3). In this mode, you can tell the camera to keep the shutter open for a long time indeed—four seconds or more for car-taillight photos, for example.

Tip: When preparing for nighttime shooting, pack a pocket flashlight so you can see the camera's controls in the dark.

Try to find a vantage point high enough to provide a good overview of the scene. A nicely lit building, bridge, or monument in the background provides a nice contrast to erratic lights created by the cars passing through the scene.

Put your camera on a tripod or some other steady surface, and set it in shutter-priority mode. After you've composed your shot, set the shutter for four seconds. The camera will control the aperture automatically. Use your remote control, if you have one, or your camera's self-timer mode.

When you see cars coming into the scene, trip the shutter. Review the results on the LCD screen. If the streaks aren't long enough, then add a couple seconds to the shutter setting; if the streaks are too long, subtract a second or two.

With a little trial and error, you can capture beautiful, dramatic taillight shots just like those postcards you always see.

Nighttime Portraits

Nighttime portraits can be extremely interesting, especially when your subject is in front of a lit monument or building.

Put your camera on a tripod or steady surface as you compose the background. The key to this shot will be opening the aperture very wide, to admit as much light as possible. You can do this in one of two ways.

Aperture-priority mode

If you can put your camera into *aperture-priority mode* (as described on page 39), set the aperture to f-2.8 or f-4.

Take a shot of just the background and review it onscreen. If it looks good, turn on your flash (forced-flash mode) and position your subject within ten feet of the camera. Ask your subject to stand still until you give the OK to move. When you take the picture, the flash will fire very briefly, but the shutter will stay open for another second or two to soak in enough light to pick up the background.

Review the results on the camera. If your subject is too bright, move the camera farther away. Move closer if the subject is too dark.

Nighttime-flash mode

If your camera doesn't have an aperture-priority mode, it might have a *nighttime-flash* mode. It's pretty much the same idea—it opens the aperture very wide—except that you can't control precisely *how* wide. The camera will attempt to properly expose the background while providing just enough additional flash for your model.

Try it. If your model is too bright or too dark, move closer or farther.

Time-Lapse Photography

Time-lapse photography is an effective way to depict a subject changing from one state of being to another: a butterfly emerging from a cocoon, the unfurling of a rose bud, and so on. Obviously, the result you want is a movie, not a still picture—but that's just fine with you. You've got a Mac, and the Mac has QuickTime.

The idea is that you'll take a picture at regular intervals—once an hour, for example. At the end of eighteen hours, you'll have eighteen images that you can upload to iPhoto for processing. (You'll also be very tired, but that's another story.)

You'll then be able to use iPhoto's Export to QuickTime command, which turns your still frames into a live-action movie at the frame rate you specify. Chapter 11 details this process.

POWER USERS' CLINIC

Star Trails

If you *really* want to impress your friends with your budding photographic skills, try capturing *star trails.* Surely you've seen these dramatic shots: one star, located in the center of the frame, remains a point of light, but all the other stars in the universe seem to carve concentric circle segments around it, as though the galaxy were spinning dizzily.

That one fixed star, in case you were wondering, is the North Star. It remains steady as all the other stars seem to travel in a circular path around it, thanks to the rotation of the earth.

Find some place dark with a clean horizon line. If you want the ground in the shot at all, compose the frame so that the sky fills 90 percent of it, and the ground occupies only the bottom 10 percent.

The setup for this shot is the same as for the taillight trails, except that you have to keep the shutter open much longer—at least fifteen seconds for very short trails as in the example here, or (if your camera can handle it) up to fifteen *minutes* for dramatic star trails. The photo here, showing the Pleiades constellation (sometimes called the Seven Sisters), was captured with a shutter speed of just a few seconds. The stars are already beginning to "trail."

The longer the exposure, the longer the star trails, so push your camera to the limit. If the trails aren't bright enough, then increase your camera's light sensitivity by changing the film speed setting (page 21) to 200 or 400.

When setting up for a time-lapse shoot, keep these things in mind:

- Use a tripod. You want every shot to have precisely the same angle, distance, and composition.

- You don't want a lot of changing background activity in your sequence of shots, since it will distract from the main subject.

- Keep the camera plugged into a wall jack (an AC adapter is an extra purchase with most camera models). Changing the batteries once the time-lapse process has begun is sure to alter the camera's original positioning.

POWER USERS' CLINIC

Infrared Black-and-White Photography

Black-and-white photography no longer dominates the print world as it did during the heyday of *Life* magazine, but it's still popular. Black-and-white shots impart a special artistic feeling that's often lacking in color shots.

Unfortunately, many of the tricks used by expert black-and-white artists aren't readily available to casual photographers employing digital means without a visit to high-end image editors like Photoshop. There is, however, a powerful black-and-white alternative that doesn't require an advanced degree in photo editing: *infrared* photography.

Infrared photography deals with the spectrum of light that you can't see but your digital camera can. It's an option only if your camera accepts filters—and if you're willing to buy an *infrared* filter, which eliminates the visible spectrum and captures only the infrared rays.

The first thing you'll notice in infrared photography is that the blue sky goes dark and that

most trees turn very light. Glare is minimized, as you can see by the road in the before-and-after examples shown here.

The most popular filter for digicam infrared photography is the Hoya R72. If your camera accepts filters, then go to the camera store, attach the R72, and look at a brightly lit scene on the LCD screen. You'll know right away if your camera is suitable for this kind of photography.

Older digital cameras, like the Nikon CoolPix 900, often work better for infrared photography because they don't have the wave-blocking infrared filters of newer models. But even today, certain specialty cameras, like the Canon EOS 20Da, perform well for infrared and astrophotography because they don't have the infrared cutoff filter.

If you're lucky enough to have a camera that can capture infrared images and accept filters, then get your hands on a Hoya R72 and go have some fun. You can create some astonishing pictures that will attract lots of attention.

- Focus manually (if your camera allows it) to ensure sharpness in every frame.

- Avoid the flash. Close-range flash shooting generally blows your subject into blinding white.

- Experiment with exposure intervals. Try one shot every fifteen minutes for one project, and then repeat the project again using 30-minute intervals. With a little trial and error, you'll find the perfect setting for your subject.

Once you've captured your sequence of shots, upload them to iPhoto. Chapter 11 has the full details about creating QuickTime movies of your slide shows. For time-lapse movies, the process is just as described there, with a few additional suggestions. They include:

- Don't crop individual photos. You want them to line up with each other in the finished movie.

- Put all of the pictures into a new album.

- In iPhoto's Export to QuickTime dialog box, choose a duration for each frame along the lines of .25, .50, or 1.0 seconds.

Digital Movies

Movie making probably wasn't what you had in mind when you bought a digital *still* camera. Even so, most cameras offer this feature, and it can come in handy now and then; life is filled with situations when a little movie captures the moment far better than a photo would.

Movie mode lets you capture QuickTime video, often with sound, and save it to your memory card right alongside your still pictures. Some cameras permit only 30 seconds of video per attempt; others let you keep recording until the memory card is full. Most new cameras these days capture video with frame dimensions of 640 x 480—big enough to fill a TV screen on playback. Once you've transferred the movie to your Mac, you can play it, email it to people, post it on a Web page, or burn it to a DVD.

iPhoto 6 gracefully imports the movies along with the still photos. You can find details on importing and playing them on page 89; details on editing them are in Chapter 11. (You can use either iMovie or QuickTime Player Pro.)

Just keep these pointers in mind:

- **Remember your memory.** Digital movies, even these low-quality ones, fill up your memory card in seconds. Remember, you're shooting 15 or 30 little pictures *per second*. This is 512 MB, 1 GB, or 2 GB card territory.

- **Steady the camera.** If you don't have a tripod, put the camera strap around your neck, pull the camera outward so the strap is taut, and only then begin filming. The strap steadies the camera.

- **Don't try it in the dark.** The flash doesn't work for movies, so look for the best lighting possible before composing your shot.

- **Set up the shot beforehand.** Most cameras don't let you zoom or change focus during filming.

Cameraphone Photography

There's an old photographer's saying: the best camera is the one you have with you. The day you're faced with a photo op and your multi-megapixel wonder machine is stashed in your sock drawer at home, you'll be thankful if there's a *cameraphone* in your pocket—a cellphone with a tiny, built-in lens that takes tiny, built-in pictures.

Of course, cameraphones don't have all of the whiz-bang settings that you've come to adore on your digicam, but you can still take perfectly good shots (see Figure 3-19). Here's a look at the most common cameraphone settings and how they can help you take better pictures.

- **Picture size.** This option gives you the choice between two resolution settings: large and small. (They would be more accurately labeled *small* and *smaller*, but that wouldn't fly with the marketing department.) Choose large, which is usually about 640 x 480 pixels or 1.3 megapixels. You can't make a very big print with these images, but they're handy for emailing.

- **Effects.** You may get a menu of oddball settings called *effects* like sepia, black and white, or even negative, which is perfect for that X-ray look you've been yearning

Figure 3-19:
Cameraphones are designed for moderately close portraits. Head-and-shoulders compositions usually turn out well. But avoid super-closeups, especially of friends and family. Those wide-angle lenses built into phones (shown at right on a Treo 600) can distort your subject, potentially resulting in estrangement from loved ones. Compose your portraits as shown at left; you'll get the shot and keep your friends.

When all looks well, hold steady and squeeze the shutter button (often the phone's Enter button, shown here on a Sony Ericsson cameraphone).

for. Don't bother with the options in this menu; shoot your pictures in living color. You can always add an effect later in iPhoto—with much greater control.

- **Self-timer.** Often considered the best way to include the photographer in family group shots, the self-timer is also a great tool for getting sharp pictures in less-than-perfect lighting. Rest the camera on any steady surface, compose the image, activate the self-timer, and press the shutter button. The camera counts for about 10 seconds and then shoots the shot. (As usual, the steadier the camera, the sharper the shot will be.)

Often, you'll want to use these settings in combination, like using night mode and a self-timer to take crisp indoor photos.

Tip: One problem with cameraphones is that there's no tripod socket. How the heck do you compose your self-timer shots without a tripod? Figure 3-20 shows one option.

Figure 3-20:
How do you steady a camera that doesn't have a tripod socket? This beanbag chair for mobile phones is the perfect solution. For a mere $6, Porter's Camera Store (www.porters camerastore.com) will ship you a nifty solution called the Pillow Pod. It's like a beanbag chair for your cameraphone. As simple as it sounds, the Pillow Pod lets you align your phone for just the right composition when using the self-timer.

You're probably not going to win any photo contests taking pictures this way. But in a pinch, at least now you know how to squeeze every drop of quality from the one camera you'll always have with you.

All that's left is figuring out how to get the pictures to your Mac, so you can drag them into iPhoto. Most people manage either by emailing the photos to themselves (right off the phone), transferring them via a wireless Bluetooth connection (to a Mac laptop, for example), or—on cellphones that have tiny memory cards—transferring the card to a card reader hooked up to the computer.

Part Two:
iPhoto Basics

2

Camera Meets Mac

The Ansel Adams part of your job is over. Your digital camera is brimming with photos. You've snapped the perfect graduation portrait, captured that jaw-dropping sunset over the Pacific, or compiled an unforgettable photo essay of your two-year-old attempting to eat a bowl of spaghetti. It's time to use your Mac to gather, organize, and tweak all these photos so you can share them with the rest of the world.

This is the core of this book—compiling, organizing, and adjusting your pictures using iPhoto, and then transforming this random collection of digital photos into a professional-looking slideshow, set of prints, movie, Web page, poster, email, desktop picture set, or bound book.

But before you start organizing and publishing these pictures using iPhoto, they have to find their way from your camera to the Mac. This chapter explains how to get pictures from camera to computer and introduces you to iPhoto.

iPhoto: The Application

iPhoto approaches digital photo management as a four-step process:

- **Import.** Working with iPhoto begins with feeding your digital pictures into the program, either from a camera or from somewhere else on your Mac.

  In general, importing is literally a one-click process. This is the part of iPhoto covered in this chapter.

- **Organize.** This step is about sorting and categorizing your chaotic jumble of pictures so you can easily find them and arrange them into logical groups. You can add searchable keywords like Vacation or Kids to make pictures easier to find. You can change the order of images, and group them into "folders" called albums. As a result, instead of having 94,300 randomly named digital photos scattered about on your three hard drives, you end up with a set of neatly categorized and immediately accessible photo collections. Chapter 5 covers all of iPhoto's organization tools.

- **Edit.** This is where you fine-tune your photos to make them look as good as possible. iPhoto provides everything you need for rotating, retouching, resizing, cropping, color-balancing, straightening, and brightening your pictures. (More significant image adjustments—like editing out an ex-spouse—require another image-editing program.) Editing your photos is the focus of Chapter 6.

- **Share.** iPhoto's best features have to do with sharing your photos, either onscreen or on paper. In fact, iPhoto offers nine different ways of publishing your pictures. In addition to printing pictures on your own printer (in a variety of interesting layouts and book styles), you can display images as an onscreen slideshow, turn the slideshow into a QuickTime movie, order professional-quality prints or a professionally bound book, email them, apply one to your desktop as a desktop backdrop, select a batch to become your Mac OS X screen saver, post them online as a Web page, or "photocast" them (make them available to your fans' copies of iPhoto 6, directly from your copy across the Internet).

Chapters 7 through 12 explain how to undertake these self-publishing tasks.

Note: Although much of this book is focused on using digital cameras, remember this: You don't have to shoot digital photos to use iPhoto. You can just as easily use it to organize and publish pictures you've shot with a traditional film camera and then digitized using a scanner (or had Kodak convert them to a Photo CD). Importing scanned photos is covered later in this chapter.

---

iPhoto Requirements

According to Apple, iPhoto 6 requires a Mac that has a USB (Universal Serial Bus) port, a G3 chip or better, 256 MB of memory or more, and either Mac OS X 10.3.9 or, if you've upgraded to Tiger, 10.4.3 or later. (A faster chip is required for some editing functions and burning slideshows to DVD.)

Tip: The USB port makes it possible to connect a camera or memory card reader for directly importing the photos. But technically, you don't need a USB port, since you can always import photos from the hard drive or a CD, as described later in this chapter.

The truth is, iPhoto may be among the most memory-dependent programs on your Mac. It just *loves* memory. Memory is even more important to iPhoto than your Mac's processor speed. It makes the difference between tolerable speed and sluggishness, or between a 25,000-photo collection and a 250,000-photo collection. So the more memory and horsepower your Mac has, the happier you'll be.

Finally, take a look at how much free hard drive space you have. You need at least 300 MB if you're installing only iPhoto, iMovie, and iTunes. If you want iDVD and

GarageBand too, iLife will eat up 10 GB of disk space—not including the room you'll
need for all your photos.

Getting iPhoto

A free version of iPhoto has been included on every Mac sold since January 2002. If
your Mac falls into that category, you'll find iPhoto in your Applications folder. (You
can tell which version you have by single-clicking its icon and then choosing File→Get
Info. In the resulting info window, you'll see the version number clear as day.)

If you bought your Mac after January 2006, you probably have iPhoto 6 installed.
Otherwise, it's available only as part of Apple's iLife '06 software suite—an $80 DVD
that includes GarageBand, iTunes, iMovie HD, iPhoto, iDVD, and iWeb. You can get the
iLife box from *www.apple.com/store*, mail-order Web sites, or local computer stores.

When you run the iLife installer, you're offered a choice of programs to install. Install
all five programs, if you like, or just iPhoto.

When the installation process is over, you'll find the iPhoto icon in your Applications folder. (In the Finder, choose Go→Applications, or press Shift-⌘-A, to open
this folder.) You'll also find the iPhoto icon—the little camera superimposed on the
palm tree—preinstalled in your Dock, so you'll be able to open it more conveniently
from now on.

UP TO SPEED

The Installer Password

When you run the iLife installer, your efforts are almost
immediately interrupted by a message telling you that you
need an "Administrator password" to install the program.

Not to worry. Like all Mac
OS X software installers,
this one is just checking
to make sure that you, as
the administrator of your
Mac, truly have permission
to load new software on
it. Well-written programs
always ask you to estab-
lish your authority before
installing them.

If you're not sure which user account is the administrator's,
choose ⌘→System Preferences. Click the Accounts icon to
view a list of people with accounts on your Mac. Those who
have been designated as
administrators are clearly
marked.

Bear in mind, you don't
actually have to *log in* as
an administrator to install
the software; you just need
to know an administrator's
name and password. In
other words, if you're not
an administrator, you can

If *you* have an Administrator account on this Mac, just type
your password into the lower box. If not, click the lock icon
in the lower-left corner of the Authorization screen of the
installer. You'll be prompted for the name and password of
an Administrator account for your Mac.

call one over to the machine and ask him to type in his
information so you can proceed with the installation.

Upgrading from earlier versions

If you've used an earlier version of iPhoto, you'd be wise to make a backup of your *iPhoto Library* folder—your database of photos—before running iPhoto 6. That's because iPhoto 6's first bit of business is converting that library into a new, more efficient format that's incompatible with earlier iPhotos (see Figure 4-1, bottom).

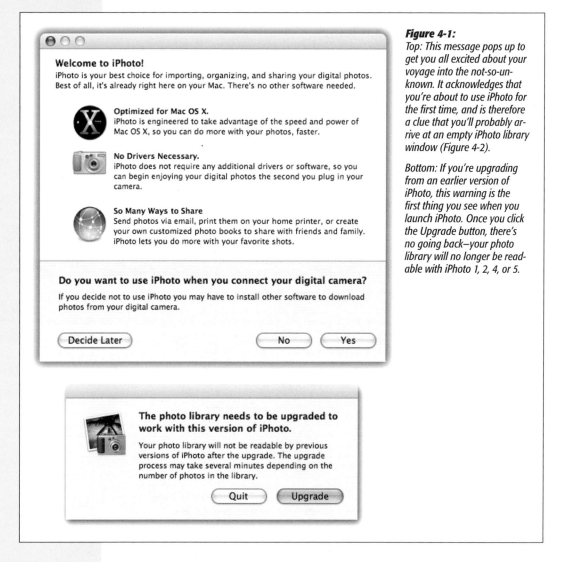

Figure 4-1:
Top: This message pops up to get you all excited about your voyage into the not-so-unknown. It acknowledges that you're about to use iPhoto for the first time, and is therefore a clue that you'll probably arrive at an empty iPhoto library window (Figure 4-2).

Bottom: If you're upgrading from an earlier version of iPhoto, this warning is the first thing you see when you launch iPhoto. Once you click the Upgrade button, there's no going back—your photo library will no longer be readable with iPhoto 1, 2, 4, or 5.

Ordinarily, the upgrade process is seamless: iPhoto smoothly converts and displays your existing photos, comments, titles, and albums. But lightning does strike, fuses do blow, and the technology gods have a cruel sense of humor—so making a backup copy before iPhoto 6 converts your old library is very, very smart.

To perform this safety measure, open your Home→Pictures folder, and then copy or
duplicate the iPhoto Library folder. (This folder may be huge, since it contains copies
of all the photos you've imported into iPhoto. This is a solid argument for copying it
onto a second hard drive, like an iPod, or a burnable DVD.) Now, if anything should
go wrong with the conversion process, you'll still have a clean, uncorrupted copy of
your iPhoto Library files.

Running iPhoto 6 for the First Time

Double-click the iPhoto icon to open the program. After you dismiss the "Welcome to
iPhoto" dialog box (Figure 4-1, top), iPhoto checks to see if you have an older version
and, if so, offers to convert its photo library (Figure 4-1, bottom).

Finally, you arrive at the program's main window, the basic elements of which are
shown in Figure 4-2.

Figure 4-2:
Here's what iPhoto looks like
when you first open it. The large
photo-viewing area is where
thumbnails of your imported photos will appear. The icons at the
bottom of the window represent
all the stuff you can do with your
photos.

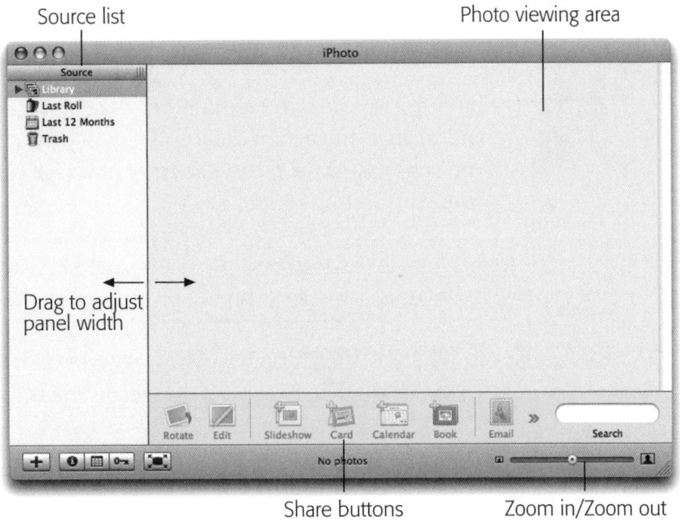

Source list

Photo viewing area

Drag to adjust
panel width

Share buttons

Zoom in/Zoom out

Getting Your Pictures into iPhoto

With iPhoto installed and ready to run, it's time for you to import your own pictures
into the program—a process that's remarkably easy, especially if your photos are going
directly from your camera into iPhoto.

Of course, if you've been taking digital photos for some time, you probably have a
lot of photo files already crammed into folders on your hard drive or on Zip disks or
CDs. If you shoot pictures with a traditional film camera and use a scanner to digitize
them, you've probably got piles of JPEG or TIFF images stashed away on disk already,
waiting to be cataloged using iPhoto.

This section explains how to transfer files into iPhoto from each of these sources.

Connecting with a USB Camera

Every modern digital camera can connect to a Mac using the USB port. If your Mac has more than one USB jack, any of them will do.

Plugging a USB-compatible camera into your Mac is the easiest way to transfer pictures from your camera into iPhoto.

Note: A few cameras require a pre-step right about here: turning the Mode dial on the top to whatever tiny symbol means "computer connection." If yours does, do that.

The whole process practically happens by itself:

1. **Connect the camera to one of your Mac's USB jacks. Turn the camera on.**

   To make this camera-to-Mac USB connection, you need what is usually called an *A-to-B* USB cable; your camera probably came with one. The "A" end—the part you plug into your camera—has a small, flat-bottomed plug whose shape varies by manufacturer. The Mac end of the cable has a larger, flatter, rectangular, standard USB plug. Make sure both ends of the cable are plugged in firmly.

   If iPhoto isn't already running when you make this connection, the program opens and springs into action as soon as you switch on the camera. (It does, that is, unless you've changed the factory settings in Image Capture, a little program that sits in your Applications folder.)

Note: If this is the first time you've ever run iPhoto, it asks if you always want it to run when you plug in the camera. If you value your time, say yes.

   In iPhoto 6, there's no wondering whether iPhoto is ready to do its job; the entire screen changes to show you the "ready" message shown in Figure 4-3.

Tip: If, for some reason, iPhoto doesn't "see" your camera after you connect it, try turning the camera off, then on again.

   In addition, your camera's icon appears in the Source list. That's handy, because it means that you can switch back and forth between the importing mode (click the camera's icon) and the regular working-in-iPhoto mode (click any other icon in the Source list), even while the time-consuming importing is under way.

   (Incidentally, as long as the camera's appearing in the Source list—wouldn't it be cool if you could drag photos *onto* the camera too? Maybe next year.)

2. **If you like, type in a *roll name* and description for the pictures you're about to import.**

   Each time you import a new set of photos into iPhoto—whether from your hard drive, a camera, or a memory card—that batch of imported photos is called a *film roll.*

Of course, there's no real film in digital photography, and your pictures aren't on a "roll" of anything. But if you think about it, the metaphor makes sense. Just as in traditional photography, where each batch of photos you shoot is captured on a separate roll of film, each separate batch of photos you download into iPhoto gets classified as its own film roll.

You'll learn much more about film rolls in Chapter 5. For the moment, typing in a name for each new batch—*Disney, First Weekend* or *Baby Meets Lasagna,* for example—will help you organize and find your pictures later. (Use the Description box for more elaborate textual blurbs, if you like. You could specify the date, who was on the trip, the circumstances of the shoot, and so on.)

3. **Turn on "Delete items from camera after importing," if you like.**

   If you turn on this box, iPhoto will erase your camera's memory card once the pictures and movies are safely on the Mac. The memory card will be all ready for another exciting photo safari.

Figure 4-3:
iPhoto is ready to import, captain! If you have to wait a long time for this screen to appear, it's because you've got a lot of pictures on your camera, and it takes iPhoto a while to count them up and prepare for the task at hand. (The number may be somewhat larger than you expect if you forgot to erase your last batch of photos.)

Now, iPhoto won't delete your pictures until *after* it has successfully copied them all to the Photo Library. However, it's not beyond the realm of possibility that a hard disk could fail during an iPhoto import, or that a file could get corrupted when copied, thereby becoming unopenable. If you want to play it safe, leave the "Delete items from camera after importing" option turned off.

Then, after you've confirmed that all of your photos have been copied safely, you can use the camera's own menus to erase its memory card.

4. Click the Import button.

If you chose the auto-erase feature, you'll see a final "Confirm Move" dialog box, affording you one last chance to back out of that decision. Click Delete Originals if you're sure you want the camera erased after the transfer, or Keep Originals if you want iPhoto to import *copies* of them, leaving the originals on the camera.

A different message appears if you're about to import photos you've *already* imported (see Figure 4-4, top).

In any case, iPhoto swings into action, copying each photo from your camera to your hard drive. You get to see them as they parade by (Figure 4-4, bottom).

Figure 4-4:
Top: If you're not in the habit of using the "Delete items from camera after importing" option, you may occasionally see the "Import duplicates?" message. iPhoto notices the arrival of duplicates and offers you the option of downloading them again, resulting in duplicates on your Mac, or ignoring them and importing only the new photos from your camera. The latter option can save you a lot of time.

Bottom: A nice feature in iPhoto 6: As the pictures get slurped into your Mac, iPhoto shows them to you, nice and big, as a sort of slideshow. You can see right away which ones were your hits, which were the misses, and which you'll want to delete the instant the importing process is complete.

When the process is over, your freshly imported photos appear in the main iPhoto window, awaiting your organizational talents.

5. **"Eject" the camera by clicking the ⏏ button next to its name in the Source list.**

   Or, if the ⏏ button doesn't appear, just drag the camera's icon directly downward onto the Trash icon. You're not actually throwing the camera away, of course, or even the photos on it—you're just saying, "Eject this." Even if the camera's still attached to your Mac, its icon disappears from the Source list.

Tip: Alternatively, you can Control-click or right-click the camera's icon and choose Unmount from the shortcut menu.

---

6. **Turn off the camera, and then unplug it from the USB cable.**

   You're ready to start having fun with your new pictures (page 92).

GEM IN THE ROUGH

The Memory Card's Back Door

When you connect some camera models to the Mac, the memory card shows up as a disk icon at the upper-right corner of your desktop, as shown here.

You get the same effect when you insert a memory card into a card reader attached to your Mac.

Inside the disk window, you'll generally find several folders, each cryptically named by the camera's software. One of them contains your photos; another may contain movies.

Opening this "disk" icon is one way to *selectively* delete or copy photos from the card. (If you do that, though, make sure you eject and reconnect the camera before importing into iPhoto, to avoid thoroughly confusing the software.)

Finding the folder that contains the memory card's photos also offers you the chance to copy photos *from* your hard drive *to* your camera–just drag them to the "disk" icon in the Finder.

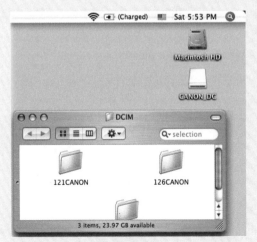

The downside of having your card icon show up is that you must eject it manually after importing your photos into iPhoto. You can drag it to the Trash, Control-click it (or right-click it) and choose Eject, click its ⏏ button in the Sidebar (Mac OS X 10.3 or later), or use any other disk-ejecting tactic you want. You can also use the Unmount command within iPhoto, as described in the Tip that appears above.

If your camera *doesn't* show up as an icon, you can always open the Image Capture program in your Applications folder. It, too, is capable of selectively deleting or importing photos and can also import your digital movies.

Then, after you've confirmed that all of your photos have been copied into the iPhoto Library folder, you can use the camera's own command to erase its memory card.

USB Card Readers

A USB *memory card reader* offers another convenient way to transfer photos into iPhoto. Most of these card readers, which look like tiny disk drives, are under $20, and some can even read more than one kind of memory card.

If you have a reader, then instead of connecting the camera to the Mac, simply remove the camera's memory card and insert it into the reader (which you can leave permanently connected to the Mac). iPhoto recognizes the reader as though it's a camera and offers to import (and erase) the photos, just as described on the previous pages.

This method offers several advantages over the camera-connection method. First, it eliminates the battery drain involved in pumping the photos straight off the camera. Second, it's less hassle to pull a memory card out of your camera and slip it into your card reader (which is always plugged in) than it is to constantly plug and unplug camera cables. Finally, this method lets you use almost *any* digital camera with iPhoto, even those too old to include a USB cable connector.

Tip: iPhoto doesn't recognize most camcorders, even though most models can take still pictures. Many camcorders store their stills on a memory card just as digital cameras do, so a memory card reader is exactly what you need to get those pictures into iPhoto.

Connecting with a USB-compatible memory card reader is almost identical to connecting a camera. Here's how:

1. **Pop a memory card out of your camera and insert it into the reader.**

   Of course, the card reader should already be plugged into the Mac's USB jack.

   As when you connect a camera, iPhoto acknowledges the presence of the memory card reader. A huge camera icon appears in the main window, you see the number of images on the card, and you're offered a chance to type in a roll name and description. As described on page 81, you can also turn on the "Delete items from camera after importing" checkbox if you want iPhoto to automatically clear the memory card after copying the files to your Mac.

2. **Click Import.**

   iPhoto swings into action, copying the photos off the card.

3. **Click the Eject button (⏏) next to the card's name in the Source list, and then remove the card from the reader.**

   Put the card back into the camera, so it's ready for more action.

Importing Photos from Really Old Cameras

If your camera doesn't have a USB connection *and* you don't have a memory card reader, you're still not out of luck.

First, copy the photos from your camera/memory card onto your hard drive (or other disk) using whatever software or hardware came with your camera. Then bring them into iPhoto as you would any other graphics files.

Tip: If your camera or memory card appears on the Mac desktop like any other removable disk, you can also drag its photo icons, folder icons, or even the "disk" icon itself directly into iPhoto.

Importing Existing Graphics Files

iPhoto is also delighted to help you organize digital photos—or any other kinds of graphics files—that are already on your computer, like in a folder somewhere.

In fact, if that's your situation, you've just stumbled onto one of the most profound new features in iPhoto 6.

For years, Mac fans complained about the way iPhoto handled photos that were already on the hard drive: when you imported them into iPhoto, the program duplicated them. You wound up with one set inside iPhoto's proprietary library folder (page 94) in addition to the original folder full of photos. Disk space got eaten up rather quickly as a result. This system also meant that iPhoto couldn't simultaneously track photos that resided on more than one hard drive.

But now, for the first time in history, iPhoto can track, organize, edit, and process photos on your hard drive(s) right in place, *right in the folders that contain them.* The program doesn't have to copy them into the iPhoto Library folder, doesn't have to double their disk-space consumption.

This is a great blessing to people who already have folders filled with photos. You can drag them directly into iPhoto's Source list (or the main viewing area). iPhoto acts like it's importing them, but doesn't really. Yet you can work with them exactly like the ones that iPhoto has actually socked away in its own library.

If you choose to go this route, here are a few tips and notes:

- Very ugly things will happen in iPhoto if you delete a photo "behind its back," in the Finder. When, in iPhoto, you try to open or edit one of the moved photos, an error message will appear, offering you the chance to locate the photo manually. And if you can't find it, the photo opens up as a huge, empty, gray rectangle filled with an exclamation point. (You kind of know what the program means.)

- On the other hand, iPhoto is pretty smart if you rename a photo in the Finder, or even drag it to a different folder. Apple doesn't really want this feature publicized, hopes you won't try it, and won't say how iPhoto manages to track pictures that you move around even when the program isn't running. But it works. Moved or renamed photos still appear in iPhoto, and you can still open, edit, and export them.

- If you delete a photo within iPhoto, you're not actually deleting it from your Mac. It's still sitting there in the Finder, in the folder where it's always been. You've just told iPhoto not to track that photo any more.

• Using this feature, you can use iPhoto to catalog and edit photos that reside on multiple hard drives—even *other computers on the network.* Just make sure those other disks are "mounted" (visible on your screen) before you attempt to work with them in iPhoto.

• On the other hand, iPhoto's new offline smarts do not make it a good choice for managing photos on CDs, DVDs, or other disks that aren't actually connected to, or inserted in, the Mac.

Internal or External?

Now, it's nice that iPhoto can track external photos without having to slurp in its own private copies. But the old way had some advantages, too. When iPhoto copies photos into its own library, they're safer. For example, you can back up your iPhoto Library

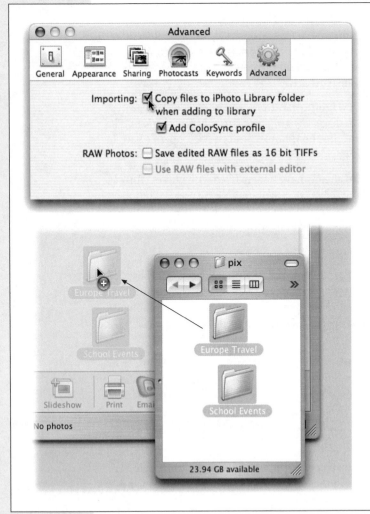

Figure 4-5:
Top: In the Preferences dialog box, click the Advanced button. Here's where you specify whether or not you want iPhoto to duplicate imported photos from your hard drive so that it has its own Library copy. (If you turn off this checkbox, iPhoto will simply track the photos in their current Finder folders.)

Bottom: When you drop a folder into iPhoto, the program automatically scans all the folders inside it, looking for pictures to catalog. It creates a new film roll (Chapter 5) for each folder it finds. iPhoto ignores irrelevant files and stores only the pictures that are in a format it can read.

folder, content in the knowledge that you've really backed up all your photos (instead of leaving some behind because they're not *actually* in the Library folder).

Fortunately, how iPhoto behaves when you import graphics files is entirely up to you. It can *either* copy them into its own Library folder, *or* it can track photos in whatever Finder folders they're already in. You make this choice in the iPhoto→Preferences dialog box (see Figure 4-5, top).

Dragging into iPhoto

No matter what choice you make in the Preferences dialog box, the easiest way to import photos from your hard drive is to drag them into the main iPhoto window. You can choose from two methods:

- Drag the files directly into the main iPhoto window, which automatically starts the import process. You can also drop an entire *folder* of images into iPhoto to import the contents of the whole folder, as shown in Figure 4-5 (bottom).

  You can even drag a bunch of folders at once.

Tip: Take the time to name your folders intelligently before dragging them into iPhoto, because the program retains their names. If you drag a folder directly into the main photo area, you get a new film roll named for the folder; if you drag the folder into the Source list at the left side of the screen, you get a new album named for the folder. And if there are folders inside folders, they, too, become new film rolls and albums. Details on all this reside in Chapter 5.

- Choose File→Import to Library (or press Shift-⌘-I) in iPhoto and select a file or folder in the Open dialog box, shown in Figure 4-6.

These techniques also let you select and import files from other hard drives, CDs, DVDs, Jaz or Zip disks, or other disks on the network.

If your photos are on a Kodak Photo CD, you can insert the CD (with iPhoto already running), and then click the Import button on the Import pane, just as if you were importing photos from a connected camera. iPhoto makes fresh copies of the files you import, storing them in one centralized photo repository (the iPhoto Library folder) on your hard drive. The program also creates thumbnail versions of each image for display in the main iPhoto window.

The File Format Factor

iPhoto can't import digital pictures unless it understands their file format, but that rarely poses a problem. Just about every digital camera on earth saves photos as JPEG files—and iPhoto handles this format beautifully. (JPEG is the world's most popular file format for photos, because even though it's compressed to occupy a lot less disk space, the visual quality is still very high.)

Note: While most digital photos you work with are probably JPEG files, they're not always called JPEG files. You may also see JPEG referred to as JFIF (JPEG File Interchange Format). Bottom line: The terms JPEG, JFIF, JPEG JFIF, and JPEG 2000 all mean the same thing.

But there's more to this story—in iPhoto 6, much more. The program now imports and recognizes some very useful additional formats.

RAW format

Most digital cameras work like this: When you squeeze the shutter button, the camera studies the data picked up by its sensors. The circuitry then makes decisions pertaining to sharpening level, contrast and saturation settings, color "temperature," white balance, and so on—and then saves the resulting processed image as a compressed JPEG file on your memory card.

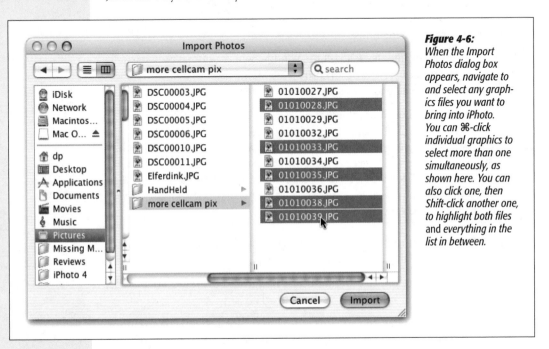

Figure 4-6:
When the Import Photos dialog box appears, navigate to and select any graphics files you want to bring into iPhoto. You can ⌘-click individual graphics to select more than one simultaneously, as shown here. You can also click one, then Shift-click another one, to highlight both files and everything in the list in between.

For millions of people, the resulting picture quality is just fine, even terrific. But all that in-camera processing drives professional shutterbugs nuts. They'd much rather preserve *every last iota* of original picture information, no matter how huge the resulting file on the memory card—and then process the file *by hand* once it's been safely transferred to the Mac, using a program like Photoshop.

That's the idea behind the RAW file format, which is an option in many pricier digital cameras. (RAW stands for nothing in particular, and it's usually written in all capital letters like that just to denote how imposing and important serious photographers think it is.)

A RAW image isn't processed at all; it's a complete record of all the data passed along by the camera's sensors. As a result, each RAW photo takes up much more space on your memory card. For example, on a 6-megapixel camera, a JPEG photo is around

2 MB, but over 8 MB when saved as a RAW file. Most cameras take longer to store RAW photos on the card, too.

But for image-manipulation nerds, the beauty of RAW files is that once you open them up on the Mac, you can perform astounding acts of editing on them. You can actually change the lighting of the scene—retroactively! And you don't lose a single speck of image quality along the way.

Until recently, most people used a program like Photoshop or Photoshop Elements to do this kind of editing. But amazingly enough, humble, cheap little iPhoto 6 can now edit RAW files, too. For details on editing RAW images, see Chapter 6.

Note: Not every camera offers an option to save your files in RAW format. And among those that do, not all are iPhoto compatible. Apple maintains a partial list of compatible cameras at *http://www.apple.com/macosx/upgrade/cameras.html*. (Why are only some cameras compatible? Because RAW is a concept, not a file format. Each camera company stores its photo data in a different way, so in fact, there are dozens of different file formats in the RAW world. Programs like iPhoto must be upgraded periodically to accommodate new camera models' emerging flavors of RAW.)

Movies

In addition to still photos, most consumer digital cameras these days can also capture cute little digital movies. Some are jittery, silent affairs the size of a Wheat Thin; others are full-blown, 30-frames-per-second, fill-your-screen movies (that eat up a memory card plenty fast). Either way, iPhoto can now import and organize them. The program recognizes .mov files, .avi files, and many other movie formats. In fact, it can import any format that QuickTime itself recognizes, which is a very long list indeed.

You don't have to do anything special to import movies, since they get slurped in automatically. To play one of these movies once they're in iPhoto, see Figure 4-7.

Other graphics formats

Of course, iPhoto also lets you load pictures that have been saved in a number of other file formats, too—including a few unusual ones. They include:

• **TIFF.** Most digital cameras capture photos in a graphics-file format called JPEG. Some cameras, though, offer you the chance to leave your photos *uncompressed* on the camera, in what's called TIFF format. These files are huge—in fact, you'll be lucky if you can fit one TIFF file on the memory card that came with the camera. Fortunately, they retain 100 percent of the picture's original quality.

Note, however, that the instant you *edit* a TIFF-format photo (Chapter 6), iPhoto converts it into JPEG.

That's fine if you plan to order prints or a photo book (Chapter 10) from iPhoto, since JPEG files are required for those purposes. But if you took that once-in-a-lifetime, priceless shot as a TIFF file, don't do any editing in iPhoto—don't even rotate it—if you hope to maintain its perfect, pristine quality.

• **GIF** is the most common format used for non-photographic images on Web pages. The borders, backgrounds, and logos you typically encounter on Web sites are usually GIF files—as well as 98 percent of those blinking, flashing banner ads that drive you insane.

• **PNG** and **FlashPix** are also used in Web design, though not nearly as often as JPEG and GIF. They often display more complex graphic elements.

Figure 4-7:
The first frame of each video clip shows up as though it's a photo in your library; only a little camera icon and the total running time let you know that it's a movie and not a photo. iPhoto is no iMovie, though; it can't even play these video clips. If you double-click one, it actually opens up in QuickTime Player, a different program on your Mac that's dedicated to playing digital movies.

See Chapter 11 for details on editing these movies, either in iMovie or in QuickTime Player Pro.

The little camcorder icon says, "This is a movie." Double-click the image...

...to open the movie in QuickTime Player. Tap the Space bar to start or stop playback.

• **BMP** is a popular graphics file format in Windows.

• **PICT** was the original graphics file format of the Macintosh prior to Mac OS X. When you take a screenshot in Mac OS 9, paste a picture from the Clipboard, or copy an image from the Scrapbook, you're using a PICT file.

• **Photoshop** refers to Adobe Photoshop, the world's most popular image-editing and photo-retouching program. iPhoto can even recognize and import *layered* Photoshop files—those in which different image adjustments or graphic elements are stored in sandwiched-together layers.

- **MacPaint** is the ancient file format of Apple's very first graphics program from the mid-1980s. No, you probably won't be working with any MacPaint files in iPhoto, but isn't it nice to know that if one of these old, black-and-white, 8 x 10 pictures, generated on a vintage Mac SE, happens to slip through a wormhole in the fabric of time and land on your desk, you'll be ready?

- **SGI** and **Targa** are specialized graphics formats used on high-end Silicon Graphics workstations and Truevision video-editing systems.

- **PDF** files are Portable Document Format files that open up in Preview or Acrobat Reader. They can be user manuals, brochures, or Read Me files that you downloaded or received on a CD. Apple doesn't publicize the fact that iPhoto can import PDF files, maybe because iPhoto displays only the first page of multipage documents. (Most of the PDFs you come across probably aren't photos; they're usually multipage documents filled with both text and graphics.)

If you try to import a file that iPhoto doesn't understand, you see the message shown in Figure 4-8.

GEM IN THE ROUGH

iPhoto Becomes iSound

OK, so iPhoto now imports and manages still photos, and it imports and manages digital movies. It's only logical, then, that you should also be able to use iPhoto to manage your digital *sound* files. After all, what's a movie but a sound file plus a video file?

Weirdly, though, iPhoto doesn't recognize these sound files if you try to import them.

Apple would probably argue that that's what iTunes is for. Still, there are times when it's far more logical to store them in iPhoto. Consider, for example, the voice annotations that you can record using most digital cameras nowadays. These are sound recordings that you can associate with particular photos as reminder notes.

Fortunately, there's a workaround that lets you store these voice notes right in iPhoto—if, that is, you're willing to putter around in QuickTime Player Pro (Chapter 11).

To pull this off, start in iPhoto. Locate the photo to which the sound annotation was supposed to be attached, and export it to your desktop (see page 326). Choose JPEG format, 640 x 480 resolution.

Drag the exported JPEG graphic onto the icon of QuickTime Player. When the photo appears, choose Edit→Select All, and then Edit→Copy.

Now open the sound file in QuickTime Player, too. (You'll first have to copy it from the camera's memory card, of course, either by dragging in the Finder or by using Image Capture, described on page 360.) It appears as just a scroll bar, with no picture.

Choose Edit→Add Scaled. QuickTime Player responds by creating a video track for the sound file (using the photo as the "video"). Presto! You turned a sound file that iPhoto doesn't recognize into a *video* file that iPhoto *does* recognize!

Choose File→Export to save the resulting "movie" onto the desktop, and then import it into iPhoto as described in this chapter. Now, when you see the photo, you can double-click it to open it in QuickTime Player, where you'll see the photo *and* hear the dulcet tones of your own masterful voice recording as it plays back.

Ingenious workaround or time-wasting kludge? You be the judge.

The Post-Dump Slideshow

Once you've imported a batch of pictures into iPhoto, what's the first thing you want to do? If you're like most people, this is the first opportunity you have to see, at full-screen size, the masterpieces you and your camera created. That's the beauty of iPhoto's slideshow feature, which comes complete with the tools you need to perform an initial screen of the new pictures—like deleting the baddies, rotating the sideways ones, and identifying the best ones with star ratings.

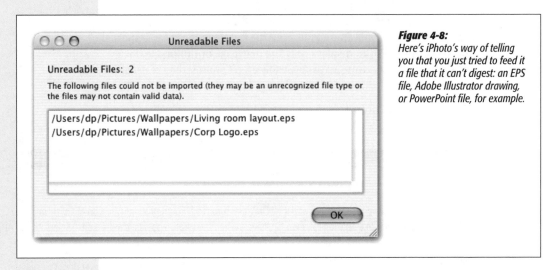

Figure 4-8:
Here's iPhoto's way of telling you that you just tried to feed it a file that it can't digest: an EPS file, Adobe Illustrator drawing, or PowerPoint file, for example.

To begin the slideshow, click the Last Roll icon in the Source list at the left side of the screen to identify which pictures you want to review.

Note: On a freshly installed copy of iPhoto, this icon is labeled Last Roll. If you've fiddled with the iPhoto preference settings, it may say, for example, "Last 2 Rolls" or "Last 3 Rolls," and your slideshow will include more than the most recent batch of photos. If that's not what you want to see, just click the actual photo that you want to begin the slideshow (in the main viewing area).

Now *Option-click* the Play button (▶) at the bottom of the window. (If you don't see it there, it's probably been shoved off to the right by all the other tool icons. Click the >> button to see the word Play, or use the View→Show in Toolbar command to turn off the names of the tool icons you don't use very often.)

iPhoto fades out of view, and a big, brilliant, full-screen slideshow of the new photos begins, accompanied by music.

Tip: If you just click the Play button (instead of adding the Option key), you summon the Slideshow dialog box instead of starting the show. This dialog box has lots of useful options; for instance, you can choose the music for your slideshow. If you merely want a quick look at your new pix, however, Option-clicking is the way to bypass it.

You can read more about slideshows in general in Chapter 7. What's useful here, though, is the slideshow control bar shown in Figure 4-9. You make it appear by wiggling your mouse as the show begins.

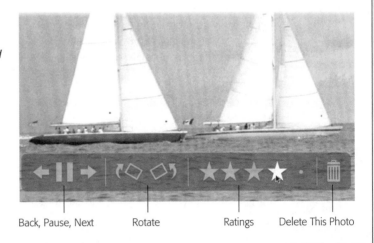

Figure 4-9:
As the slideshow progresses, you can pause the show, go backward, rotate a photo, delete a bad shot, or apply your star rating to a picture, all courtesy of this new control bar.

Back, Pause, Next   Rotate   Ratings   Delete This Photo

This is the perfect opportunity to throw away lousy shots, fix the rotation, and linger on certain photos for more study—all without interrupting the slideshow. You can even apply a rating by clicking the appropriate star in the band of five; later, you can use these ratings to sort your pictures or create *smart albums*. See Chapter 5 for full detail on rating stars and smart albums.

Here's the full list of things you can do when the onscreen control bar is visible:

- Click the Play/Pause button to start and halt the slideshow. The space bar toggles these controls—and the control bar doesn't have to be visible when you press it.

- Click the left and right arrows to browse back and forth through your photos. The left and right arrow keys on your keyboard do the same thing.

- Press the up or down arrow keys on your keyboard to make the slides appear faster or slower.

- Click the rotation icons to flip photos clockwise or counterclockwise, 90 degrees at a time.

- Click one of the five dots to apply a rating in stars, from one at the left to five all the way at the right. Or use the number keys at the top of the keyboard or on the numeric keypad; press 3 to give a picture three stars, for example.

- Click the Trash can icon to delete a photo from the album you're viewing (but not from the Photo Library). Or simply hit Delete (or Del) on your keyboard.

Tip: There are keyboard shortcuts for all of these functions, too, that don't even require the control bar to be on the screen (page 196).

Click the mouse somewhere else on the screen to end the slideshow.

Tip: You might want to use the new full-screen editing mode, rather than the slideshow mode, for your first post-dump look at the pictures (page 110). It doesn't advance the slides automatically, but it does offer far more editing power, plus handy thumbnails that let you see similar shots side-by-side.

Where iPhoto Keeps Your Files

Having entrusted your vast collection of digital photos to iPhoto, you may find yourself wondering, "Where's iPhoto putting all those files, anyway?"

Most people slog through life, eyes to the road, without ever knowing the answer. After all, you can preview, open, edit, rotate, copy, export, and print all your photos right in iPhoto, without actually opening a folder or double-clicking a single JPEG file.

Even so, it's worthwhile to know where iPhoto keeps your pictures on the hard drive. Armed with this information, you can keep those valuable files backed up and avoid the chance of accidentally throwing them away six months from now when you're cleaning up your hard drive.

A Trip to the Library

Whenever you import pictures into iPhoto, the program makes *copies* of your photos, always leaving your original files untouched.

- When you import from a camera, iPhoto leaves the photos right where they are on its memory card (unless you use the "Erase" option).

- When you import from the hard drive into iPhoto, the originals remain in whichever folders they're in. As a result, transferring photos from your hard drive into iPhoto *more than doubles* the amount of disk space they take up. In other words, importing 1 GB of photos requires an additional 1 GB of disk space, because you'll end up with two copies of each file: the original, and iPhoto's copy of the photo. In addition, iPhoto creates a separate thumbnail version of each picture, consuming about another 10 K to 20 K per photo.

iPhoto stores its copies of your pictures in a special folder called iPhoto Library, which you can find in your Home→Pictures folder. If the short name you use to log into Mac OS X is *mozart,* the full path to your iPhoto Library folder from the main hard drive window would be Macintosh HD→Users→mozart→Pictures→iPhoto Library.

Tip: You should back up this iPhoto Library folder regularly—using the Burn command to save it onto a CD or DVD, for example. After all, it contains all the photos you import into iPhoto, which, essentially, is your entire photography collection. Chapter 14 offers much more on this file management topic.

What all those numbers mean

Within the iPhoto Library folder, you'll find a set of mysteriously numbered files and folders. At first glance, this setup may look bizarre, but there's a method to iPhoto's madness. It turns out that iPhoto meticulously arranges your photos within these numbered folders according to the *creation dates* of the originals, as explained in Figure 4-10.

Other folders in the iPhoto Library

In addition to the numbered folders, you'll find several other items nested in the iPhoto Library folder, most of which you can ignore:

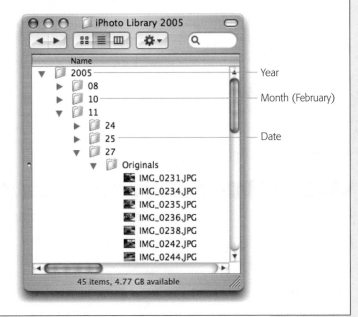

Figure 4-10:
Behold the mysteries of the iPhoto Library. Once you know the secret, this seemingly cryptic folder structure actually makes sense, with all the photos in the library organized by their creation dates.

- **AlbumData.xml.** Here's where iPhoto stores access permissions for the various *photo albums* you've created within iPhoto. (Albums, which are like folders for organizing photos, are described in Chapter 5.) For example, it's where iPhoto keeps information on which albums are available for sharing across the network (or among accounts on a single machine). Details on sharing are in Chapter 9.

- **Dir.data, iPhoto.db, Library.data, Library6.iPhoto.** These are iPhoto's for-internal-use-only documents. They store information about your Photo Library, such as which keywords you've used, along with the image dimensions, file size, rating, and modification date for each photo.

- **Data.** This folder contains index card-sized previews of your pictures—jumbo thumbnails, in effect—organized in the year/month/day structure shown in Figure 4-10.

- **Originals.** This folder, reconceived in iPhoto 6, is the real deal: It's the folder the stores your entire photo collection. Inside, you'll find nested folders organized in the year/month/day structure illustrated in Figure 4-10.

    This folder is also the key to one of iPhoto's most remarkable features: the Revert to Original command.

    Whenever it applies any potentially destructive operations to your photos—like cropping, red-eye removal, brightening, black-and-white conversion—iPhoto *duplicates* the files and stuffs the edited copies in the Modified folder. The pristine, unedited versions remain safely in the Originals folder. If you later decide to scrap your changes to a photo using the Revert to Original command—even months or years later—iPhoto ditches the duplicate. What you see in iPhoto is the Original version, preserved in its originally imported state.

- **Modified.** Here are the latest versions of your pictures, as edited. (Remember, behind the scenes, iPhoto actually duplicates a photo when you edit it.)

Look, don't touch

While it's enlightening to wander through the iPhoto Library folder to see how iPhoto keeps itself organized, don't rename or move any of the folders or files in it. Making such changes will confuse iPhoto to the point where it will either be unable to display some of your photos or it'll just crash.

FREQUENTLY ASKED QUESTION

Moving the iPhoto Library

Do I have to keep my iPhoto Library folder in my Pictures folder? What if I want it stored somewhere else?

No problemo! iPhoto has come a long way since the days when it had to keep its Library folder in your Pictures folder.

Just quit iPhoto. Then move the *whole* iPhoto Library folder (currently in your Home→Pictures folder) to another location—even onto another hard drive.

Then open iPhoto again. It will proclaim that it can't find your iPhoto Library folder. Now click the Find Library button to show the program where you put the folder. Done deal!

The Digital Shoebox

I f you've imported your photos into iPhoto using any of the methods described in the previous chapter, you should now see a neatly arranged grid of thumbnails in iPhoto's main photo-viewing area. You're looking at what iPhoto refers to as your *Library*—your entire photo collection, including every last picture you've ever imported. This is the digital equivalent of that old shoebox you've had stuffed in the closet for the last 10 years, brimming with snapshots waiting to be sorted and sifted, often never to be seen again.

You're not really organized yet, but at least all your photos are in one place. Your journey out of chaos has begun. From here, you can sort your photos, give them titles, group them into smaller sub-collections (called *albums*), and tag them with keywords so you can find them quickly. This chapter helps you tackle each of those organizing tasks as painlessly as possible.

The Source List

Even before you start naming your photos, assigning them keywords, or organizing them into albums, iPhoto imposes an order of its own on your digital shoebox.

The key to understanding it is the *Source list* at the left side of the iPhoto window. This list will grow as you import more pictures and organize them—but right off the bat, you'll find icons like Library, Last 12 Months, and Last Roll.

Library
The first icon in the Source list is called Library. This is a very reassuring little icon, because no matter how confused you may get in working with subsets of photos later

in your iPhoto life, clicking Library returns you to your entire picture collection. It makes *all* of your photos appear in the viewing area.

Library by Year

In early versions of iPhoto, the Library got a bit unwieldy if you had 2,000 pictures in it. But now that iPhoto can handle *250,000 photos,* you need a way to break down this tidal wave of pixels.

Enter the year icons, shown at top in Figure 5-1. When you click the Library flippy triangle, iPhoto's Source list now shows small yellow calendar icons, one for each year going back to 2001 (and a catch-all for earlier images).

Figure 5-1:
Top: You can specify how far back the "Last ___ Months" album goes and how many downloads the "Last ___ Rolls" album includes on the General panel of iPhoto Preferences (bottom).

Don't forget, by the way, that iPhoto isn't limited to grouping your pictures by year. It can also show you the photos that you took on a certain day, in a certain week, or during a certain month. See page 125 for details.

Bottom: While you're in Preferences, don't miss the "Show item counts" option. It places a number in parentheses after each album name in the Source panel, representing how many pictures are inside.

When you import your entire digital photo collection (or upgrade from an earlier version of iPhoto), the program files each photo by the date you took it. You can click Library to see all your photos amassed in one window, or click, say, the 2005 icon to see just the ones you took during that year.

The year icons are also very helpful when you're creating an iPhoto slideshow or trying to pinpoint one certain photo. After all, you usually can remember what year you took a vacation or when someone's birthday was. The year icons help you narrow down your search without requiring that you scroll through your entire Library.

Library by Month

The Last 12 Months icon is the same idea as the calendar-year icons, except that it puts the most recent photos at your fingertips. The idea, of course, is that most of the time, the freshest photos are the most interesting to you.

Actually, it doesn't even have to say "Last 12 Months." You can specify how many months' worth of photos appear in this heap—anywhere from one month to a year and a half—by choosing iPhoto→Preferences and going to the General panel (see Figure 5-1). Like the iPhoto calendar (page 125), this feature is very useful when you want to find the pictures from this past Christmas, photos from your kid's most recent birthday, or wedding pictures from your most recent marriage.

Last Roll

Each batch of imported photos is called one *film roll*.

Most of the time, you'll probably work with the photos that you just downloaded from your camera. Conveniently, iPhoto always keeps track of your most recently added film roll, so you can view its contents without much scrolling.

That's the purpose of the roll-of-film icon called Last Roll in the Source list. With one click, iPhoto displays only your most recent photos, hiding all the others. This feature can save you a lot of time, especially as your Library grows.

In fact, iPhoto lets you specify how *many* film rolls you want listed here; choose iPhoto→Preferences and click the General icon (again, see Figure 5-1). Simply change the number where it says "Show last __ roll album." (In the unlikely event that you don't find this icon useful, you can also hide it entirely by turning off the corresponding checkbox.)

For example, if you've just returned from a three-day Disney World trip, you probably want to see your last *three* imports all at once. In that case, you'd change the last roll setting to *3*.

Tip: If you delete all the photos from the Last Roll category, iPhoto promptly displays the *previous* roll's contents—whatever was the Last Roll before this latest one. It's a handy way to rewind into the past, even if it was many weeks or months ago, in your quest for a lost picture.

Other Icons in the Source List

Library, year icons, and Last Roll icons aren't the only items you'll find in the Source list. Later in this chapter, you'll find out how to create your own arbitrary subsets of pictures called albums, and even how to stick a bunch of related albums into an enclosing entity called a *folder*.

Later in this book, you'll find out how to swipe photos from other people's collections via iPhoto sharing or photocasting. And later in life, you may discover the geeky joy of dumping photos onto CDs or DVDs—and then loading them back into iPhoto whenever you darned well feel like it.

Shared photo collections, CD icons, and DVD icons can all show up in the Source list, too.

Saved slideshows and book layouts get their own icons in the Source list, too (and can be filed, alongside albums, in folders).

As you go, though, remember this key point: Photos in your Library, Last Roll, and Last Months icons are the *real* photos. Delete a picture from one of these three collections, and it's gone forever. (That's *not* true of albums, which store only aliases—phantom duplicates—of the real photos.)

More on Film Rolls

iPhoto starts out sorting your Library by film roll, meaning that the most recently imported batch of photos appears at the bottom of the window. Your main iPhoto window may look like a broad, featureless expanse of pictures, but they're actually in a logical order.

Tip: If you'd prefer that the most recent items appear at the top of the iPhoto window instead of the bottom, choose View→Sort Photos→Descending. (The Ascending/Descending submenu is new in iPhoto 6. You no longer have to open the Preferences dialog box to make this change.)

Using the View→Sort Photos submenu, you can make iPhoto sort all the thumbnails in the main window in a number of useful ways:

- **by Film Roll.** Your photos appear in the order you imported them. (Often that's the same as the date order, but not always.)

    In iPhoto 6, this option means that you can still *sort* the pictures in your Library by film roll even if you opt not to display the film-roll *divider lines* shown in Figure 5-2. You won't be able to see where one film roll ends and the next begins, but the photos will be in the right order.

- **by Date.** This sort order reflects the *creation* date of the photos (rather than the date they were imported).

- **by Keyword.** New in iPhoto 6, this option sorts your photos alphabetically by the *keywords* you've assigned to them (page 127).

FREQUENTLY ASKED QUESTION

Your Own Personal Sorting Order

I want to put my photos in my own order. I tried using View→Sort Photos→Manually, but the command is dimmed out! Did Apple accidentally forget to turn this on?

No, the command works—but only in an album, not in the main Photo Library. If you create a new photo album (as explained later in this chapter) and fill it with photos, you can then drag them into any order you want.

- **by Title.** This arrangement is alphabetical by the photos' *names*. (To name your photos, see page 121.)

- **by Rating.** If you'd like your masterpieces at the top of the window, with the losers way down below, choose this option. (To rate your photos, see page 135.)

- **Manually.** If you choose this option, you can drag the thumbnails around freely within the window, placing them in any order that suits your fancy. To conserve your Advil supply, however, make no attempt to choose this item when you're viewing one of the *film rolls'* contents—do so only in an *album.* See the box on the facing page for details.

Displaying Film Rolls

If you choose View→Film Roll so that the checkmark appears, iPhoto sorts your photos by film roll and adds a labeled, dated divider line above each one (Figure 5-2). (As you now know, iPhoto 6 can also sort the pictures by film roll—using the Sort Photos→by Film Roll option—*without* adding the divider lines.)

Tip: Better yet, use the keyboard shortcut Shift-⌘-F to hide or show the divider lines.

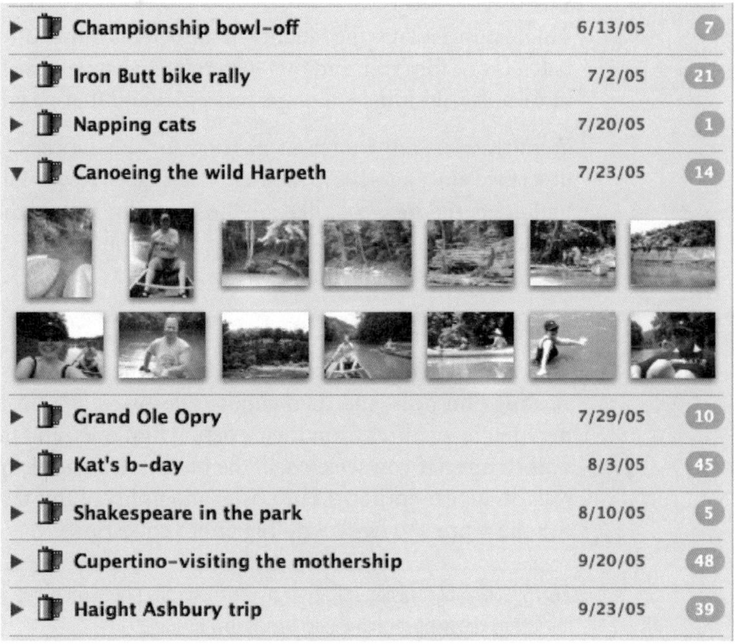

Figure 5-2:
This tidy arrangement is the fastest way to use iPhoto. Display the photos grouped by film roll, and then hide the photo batches you're not working with. Click the triangle beside each header to expand or collapse the film roll, just like a folder in the Finder's list view.

Note that the header for each roll lists the date that you imported this batch (and the number of photos in each). If you dragged a folder of files into iPhoto—or if you named the roll as the pictures were imported—the film-roll header also lists the name of the enclosing folder.

You'll probably find this arrangement so convenient that you'll leave it on permanently. As your Library grows, these groupings become excellent visual and mnemonic aids to help you locate a certain photo—sometimes even months or years after the fact.

Furthermore, as your Library becomes increasingly massive, you may need to rely on these film-roll groupings just for your sanity. By collapsing the flippy triangles next to the groups you're *not* looking at right now (Figure 5-2), you speed up iPhoto considerably. Otherwise, iPhoto may grind almost to a halt as it tries to scroll through ever more photos. (About 250,000 pictures is its realistic limit for a single library on everyday Macs. Of course, you can always start new libraries, as described in Chapter 14.)

Collapsing Film Rolls En Masse

On a related note, here's one of the best tips in this entire chapter: *Option-click* a film roll's flippy triangle to hide or show all of the film rolls' contents. When all your photos are visible, scrolling is slowish, but at least you can see everything. By contrast, when all your film rolls are collapsed, you see nothing but their names, and scrolling is almost instantaneous.

Tip: Click anywhere on the film-roll divider line—on the film roll's name, for example—to simultaneously select all the photos in that roll.

Creating Film Rolls Manually

Film rolls are such a convenient way of organizing your pictures that Apple even lets you create film rolls manually, out of any pictures you choose.

This feature violates the sanctity of the original film-roll concept: that each importing batch is one film roll, and that *albums* are what you use for arbitrary groupings. Still, in this case, usefulness trumps concept—and that's a good thing.

You just select any bunch of pictures in your Library (using any of the techniques described on page 106), then choose File→Create Film Roll. iPhoto creates and highlights the new roll, like any normal film roll. It then gives the newborn roll a generic name like "Roll 54" or whatever number it's up to. You can always rename it, as described on the facing page.

Merging Film Rolls

You can *merge* film rolls using this technique, too. Just select photos in two or more existing film rolls, and then choose File→Create Film Roll. iPhoto responds by removing the pictures from their existing film rolls, and then placing them into a new, unified one. (If you selected *all* the photos in a couple of film rolls, the original film rolls disappear entirely.) The power and utility of this tactic will become more attractive the more you work with big photo collections.

Tip: Speaking of cool film-roll tips: You can move any photo (or group of selected photos) into another film roll just by dragging it onto the film roll's row heading!

Renaming and Dating Film Rolls

As you know from Chapter 4, iPhoto gives you the opportunity to name each film roll as it's created—that is, at the joyous moment when a new set of photos becomes one with your iPhoto library.

If you don't type anything into the Roll Name box that appears at that time, though, iPhoto just labels each film roll with a roll number. In any case, you can easily change any film roll's name at any time.

To edit the name of a roll, see Figure 5-3.

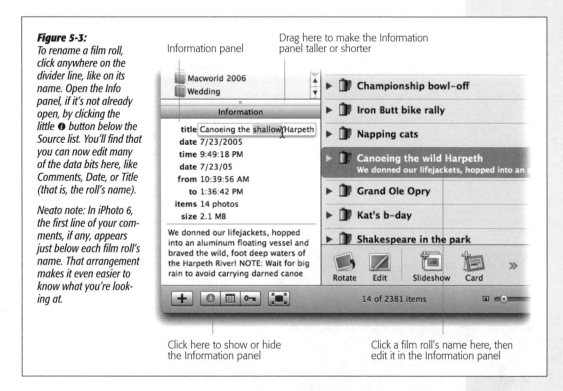

Figure 5-3:
To rename a film roll, click anywhere on the divider line, like on its name. Open the Info panel, if it's not already open, by clicking the little ❶ button below the Source list. You'll find that you can now edit many of the data bits here, like Comments, Date, or Title (that is, the roll's name).

Neato note: In iPhoto 6, the first line of your comments, if any, appears just below each film roll's name. That arrangement makes it even easier to know what you're looking at.

Information panel

Drag here to make the Information panel taller or shorter

Click here to show or hide the Information panel

Click a film roll's name here, then edit it in the Information panel

Using the same technique, you can also change the *date* that appears in the film-roll header. This date usually identifies when you imported the photos, but for most purposes, that date is relatively unimportant. What you probably care more about is the day or month that the photos were actually *taken.*

Once again, start by clicking the roll-of-film icon in the film-roll divider. This time, type a new date in the Information pane's Date text box. You can type the date in a variety of formats—*4 September 2006, September 4, 2006,* and *9/4/06* all work—but you must use a complete date, including day, month, and year. If you don't, iPhoto will take a guess, filling in the missing information for you—and sometimes getting it wrong.

Tip: Another effective way to redate a bunch of pictures at once is to use iPhoto's batch-processing feature, described on page 124.

Scrolling Through Your Photos

All right: You've gotten the hang of the Source list, the Library, and film rolls. Enough learning about iPhoto already—now it's time to start *using* it.

Browsing, selecting, and opening photos is straightforward. Here's everything you need to know:

- Use the vertical scroll bar to navigate through your thumbnails. As you drag the scroll bar's handle, you get to enjoy a new iPhoto 6 feature: a huge, floating "heads-up display" that shows where you are in the collection. Figure 5-4 should make this idea clearer.

  Pressing your Page Up and Page Down keys work, too. (They scroll one screenful at a time.) If your mouse has a scroll wheel on top (or a scroll pea, like Apple's Mighty Mouse), you can also use that to scroll. These shortcuts deprive you of the handy navigational display shown in Figure 5-4, however.

Figure 5-4:
As you drag the vertical scroll bar, this good-looking heads-up display shows where you are in the mass of pictures.

Exactly what you see here depends on what sorting method you've selected in the View menu. For example, if you're sorting your pictures by name, you see letters of the alphabet as you scroll, like handy tabs in a filing folder.

If you've sorted your collection by rating, you see stars appear in this panel—zero through five of them—showing you where you are in your scroll through the ratings.

And so on.

- Scrolling can take awhile if you have a full library, especially if you haven't collapsed the film rolls you're not using. But you can use this standard Mac OS X trick for faster navigation: Instead of dragging the scroll box or clicking the scroll bar arrows,

Option-click the spot on the scroll bar that corresponds to the location you want in your Library. If you want to jump to the bottom of the Library, Option-click near the bottom of the scroll bar. To find photos in the middle of your collection, Option-click the middle portion of the scroll bar, and so on.

Note: By turning on "Jump to here" in the Appearance pane of your System Preferences, you can make this the standard behavior for all Mac OS X scroll bars—that is, you won't need the Option key.

- Press Home to jump to the very top of the photo collection, or End to leap to the bottom.

- You can no longer hide the Source list at the left side of the window; Apple figured that the new Full Screen mode does an even better job of maximizing screen space.

  You can still adjust the width of the Source list, though. To do so, drag the thin, black divider bar (between the Source list and the main photo-viewing area) sideways, or drag the little ribbed handle at the top of the list (where it says Source). When your cursor's in the right place for dragging, it turns into a double-headed arrow.

Tip: You can slightly speed up iPhoto's scrolling by turning off the Drop Shadow option in the Appearance pane of iPhoto's Preferences window.

Size Control

You can make the thumbnails in iPhoto grow or shrink using the Size Control slider (on the right side of the iPhoto window, just under the photo-viewing area). Drag the slider all the way to the left, and you get micro-thumbnails so small that you can fit 200 or more of them in the iPhoto window. If you drag it all the way to the right, you end up with such large thumbnails that you can see only one picture at a time.

Tip: You don't have to drag the Size Control slider; just click anywhere along the slider to make it jump to a new setting. You can also scale all of the thumbnails to their minimum or maximum size by clicking the tiny icons at either end of the slider.

By the way, you might notice that this Size Control slider performs different functions, depending on which mode iPhoto is in. When you're editing a photo, it zooms in and out of an individual image; when you're designing a photo-book layout (Chapter 10), it magnifies or shrinks a single page.

Tip: You may want to adopt a conservative dragging approach when using the Size Control slider, since iPhoto may respond slowly in enlarging or shrinking the photos. Just drag in small movements so the program can keep pace with you.

Selecting Photos

To highlight a single picture in preparation for printing, opening, duplicating, or deleting, click the icon once with the mouse.

That much may seem obvious. But many first-time Mac users have no idea how to manipulate *more* than one icon at a time—an essential survival skill.

To highlight multiple photos in preparation for deleting, moving, duplicating, printing, and so on, use one of these techniques:

Figure 5-5:
You can highlight several photos simultaneously by dragging a box around them. To do so, start from somewhere outside of the target photos and drag diagonally across them, creating a whitish enclosure rectangle as you go. Any photos touched by this rectangle are selected when you release the mouse.

FREQUENTLY ASKED QUESTION

The Mini-Photo Effect

Hey, what's the deal? When I double-click a photo to open it for editing, it appears momentarily as a little, three-inch version. It takes three seconds to fill the window so I can get to work. Do I need to send my copy of iPhoto in for servicing?

No, not exactly.

Today's digital photos are pretty big, especially if you've got one of those cameras that takes giant-sized photos (5 to 13 megapixels, for example).

Now, as it turns out, that's a lot more pixels than even the biggest computer screen has. So the Mac must not only "read" all the photo information off your hard drive, it must then compute a scaled-down version that's exactly the size

of your iPhoto window. Naturally, all of this computation takes time.

In previous versions of iPhoto, Apple tried to disguise this moment of computation by first displaying a full-sized but blurry, low-resolution photo, and then filling in the sharpened details a moment later. It drove people absolutely crazy.

The new approach—in which you first see a small but clear rendition of the photo with the words "Loading Photo"—still doesn't let you begin editing until the full-window computation is complete. What it does do is show you, clearly, which photo you've opened. And if you've opened the wrong one, you don't have to wait any longer; you can click over to a different photo, having wasted no more time than necessary.

- **To select all photos.** Select all the pictures in the set you're viewing by pressing ⌘-A (the equivalent of the Edit→Select All command).

- **To select several photos by dragging.** You can drag diagonally to highlight a group of nearby photos, as shown in Figure 5-5. You don't even have to enclose the thumbnails completely; your cursor can touch any part of any icon to highlight it. In fact, if you keep dragging past the edge of the window, iPhoto scrolls the window automatically.

Tip: If you include a particular thumbnail in your dragged group by mistake, ⌘-click it to remove it from the selected cluster.

- **To select consecutive photos.** Click the first thumbnail you want to highlight, and then Shift-click the last one. All the files in between are automatically selected, along with the two photos you clicked (Figure 5-6, top). This trick mirrors the way Shift-clicking works in a word processor, the Finder, and many other kinds of programs.

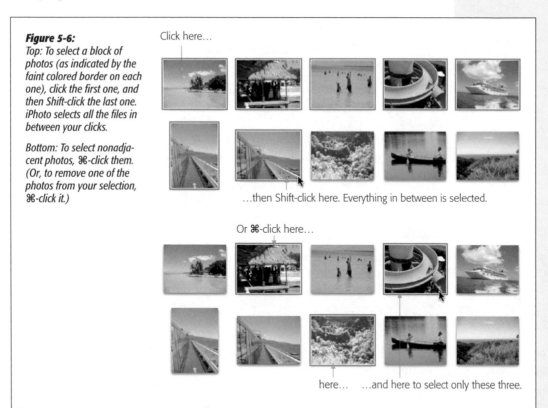

Figure 5-6:
Top: To select a block of photos (as indicated by the faint colored border on each one), click the first one, and then Shift-click the last one. iPhoto selects all the files in between your clicks.

Bottom: To select nonadjacent photos, ⌘-click them. (Or, to remove one of the photos from your selection, ⌘-click it.)

Click here…

…then Shift-click here. Everything in between is selected.

Or ⌘-click here…

here…   …and here to select only these three.

- **To select random photos.** If you only want to highlight, for example, the first, third, and seventh photos in a window, start by clicking photo icon No. 1. Then

⌘-click each of the others. Each thumbnail sprouts a colored border to indicate that you've selected it (Figure 5-6, bottom).

If you're highlighting a long string of photos and then click one by mistake, you don't have to start over. Instead, just ⌘-click it again, and the dark highlighting disappears. (If you do want to start over from the beginning, however, just deselect all selected photos by clicking any empty part of the window.)

The ⌘ key trick is especially handy if you want to select *almost* all the photos in a window. Press ⌘-A to select everything in the folder, then ⌘-click any unwanted photos to deselect them. You'll save a lot of time and clicking.

Tip: You can also combine the ⌘-clicking business with the Shift-clicking trick. For instance, you could click the first photo, then Shift-click the tenth, to highlight the first ten. Next, you could ⌘-click photos 2, 5, and 9 to remove them from the selection.

Once you've highlighted multiple photos, you can manipulate them all at once. For example, you can drag them en masse out of the window and onto your desktop—a quick way to export them. (Actually, you may want to drag them onto a *folder* in the Finder to avoid spraying their icons all over your desktop.) Or you can drag them into an album at the left side of the iPhoto window. Just drag any *one* of the highlighted photos; all other highlighted thumbnails go along for the ride.

In addition, when multiple photos are selected, the commands in the File, Edit, Photos, and Share menus—including Duplicate, Print, Revert to Original, and Email—apply to all of them simultaneously.

Three Ways to Open Photos in iPhoto

iPhoto wouldn't be a terribly useful program if it let you view only postage stamp versions of your photos (unless, of course, you like to take pictures of postage stamps). Fortunately, iPhoto offers three ways to view your pictures at something much closer to actual size.

You'll use these methods frequently when you start editing your photos, as described in Chapter 6. For the moment, though, it's useful to know about these techniques simply for the more common act of viewing the pictures at larger sizes.

Method 1: Right in the Window

The easiest way to open a photo is simply to double-click a thumbnail. Unless you've changed iPhoto's settings, the photo opens in the main iPhoto window, scaled to fit into the viewing area.

This is the way most people open pictures, at least at first. It's comforting to see landmarks like the Source list and toolbar buttons. The downside is that those other screen elements limit the size of the enlarged photo; that's why you might want to consider one of the other photo-opening methods described below.

Tip: In iPhoto 6, you can open up *more than one* photo simultaneously in the Edit window. Just highlight two or more photos, and then double-click any one of them (or click the Edit button). The upper limit ranges from six to twelve photos, depending on the size of your screen. (If you choose more than iPhoto is prepared to handle, it opens up only *one* of the selected photos.)

Either way, this new feature is a great way to compare similar shots for choosing the best one.

Whenever you've opened a photo within iPhoto's window, by the way, you'll see a parade of other photo thumbnails at the top of the window. Feel free to switch to any other photo by clicking its little postage-stamp icon up there (or by clicking the big Previous/Next arrows at the bottom of the window).

Or, if you'd rather hide the thumbnail browser to reclaim the space it's using, choose View→Hide Thumbnails (Option-⌘-T).

To return to your thumbnail-filled, photo-organizing world, click the Done button (at the bottom-right corner of the screen). Or double-click the photo you're editing; the picture itself is a much bigger target than the little Done button.

Method 2: Individual Windows

iPhoto's second method of opening photos is to send each picture into its own window. The advantage here is that you can scale the image up or down by making

Figure 5-7:
When you open photos in their own windows, you can look at several at the same time at reasonably good magnification—a critical feature when comparing similar shots. Plus, you can keep your other thumbnails in view, allowing you to easily open additional photos without closing the open ones.

the window larger or smaller (drag its lower-right corner). You can close an open photo from the keyboard by pressing ⌘-W. You still see all your thumbnails in the background window (Figure 5-7). And you can open multiple pictures, side by side, without confining them to the width of the iPhoto window.

You can set up this separate-window system either permanently or on a case-by-case basis:

- Go to iPhoto→Preferences and change the photo-opening setting. On the General panel, from the "Edit photo" pop-up menu, choose "In separate window." Then close the Preferences window. From now on, double-clicking selected photos will always open them into separate windows.

Tip: Pressing Option reverses whichever choice you make here. That is, if you've chosen "In main window" in the Preferences dialog box, then Option-double-clicking a thumbnail opens the photo into a separate window instead. Conversely, if you've chosen "In separate window," Option-double-clicking a thumbnail overrides your choice and opens it into the main iPhoto viewing area.

(Option-double-clicking has no effect if you've selected one of the other two Preferences options, "Using full screen" or "In application.")

- To open a photo this way only once, Control-click or right-click it. From the shortcut menu, choose "Edit in separate window." (Use this method, for example, when your preferences are set to open photos a different way—because that's how you *usually* like things—but you want the separate-windows effect right now, just this once.)

Method 3: Full-Screen Mode

iPhoto 6 introduces yet another way to get a gander at a photo. Sure, all of these options make the program more complicated, but you'll really like this new feature; it's often the most effective of all. In full-screen mode, a selected photo fills your *entire* monitor, edge to edge. No menu bar, no toolbar, no Source list—just your big, glorious photo, blown up as big as it can go.

This mode is much more interesting when you're *editing* photos, which is why it's described and illustrated at greater length in Chapter 6.

Tip: You can also open several photos in full-screen mode simultaneously. If you highlight several thumbnails before entering full-screen mode, iPhoto displays them side-by-side.

Once again, you can either tell iPhoto that you always want your photos to open this way, or you can invoke full-screen mode manually:

- Go to iPhoto→Preferences. On the General pane, from the "Edit photo" pop-up menu, choose "Using full screen." (Then close Preferences.) Now double-clicking a photo opens it into full-screen mode.

- To open a photo this way only once, Control-click or right-click it. From the shortcut menu, choose "Edit using full screen."

Or, if you're in a real hurry, just click the little Full Screen icon (■)on the bottom edge of the iPhoto window.

To exit full-screen mode, double-click anywhere on the photo, or click the Close Full Screen icon (■).

Albums

No matter how nicely you title, sort, and arrange photos in your digital shoebox, it's still a *shoebox* at this point, with all your photos piled together in one vast collection. To really become organized and present your photos to others, you need to arrange your photos into *albums*.

In iPhoto terminology, an album is a subset of pictures from your Library. It's a collection of photos that you group together for easy access and viewing. Represented by a little album-book icon in the Source list at the left side of the screen, an album can consist of any photos that you select, or it can be a *smart album* that iPhoto assembles by matching certain criteria that you set up—all pictures that you took in 2004, for example, or all photos that you've rated four stars or higher.

While your iPhoto Library as a whole might contain thousands of photos from a hodgepodge of unrelated family events, trips, and time periods, a photo album has a focus: Steve & Sarah's Wedding, Herb's Knee Surgery, and so on.

As you probably know, mounting snapshots in a *real* photo album is a pain—that's why so many of us still have stacks of Kodak prints stuffed in envelopes and shoeboxes. But with iPhoto, you don't need mounting corners, double-sided tape, or scissors to create an album. In the digital world, there's no excuse for leaving your photos in hopeless disarray.

Of course, you're not required to group your digital photos in albums with iPhoto, but consider the following advantages of doing so:

- You can find specific photos faster. By opening only the relevant album, you can avoid scrolling through thousands of thumbnails in the Library to find a picture you want—a factor that takes on added importance as your collection expands.

- Only in a photo album can you drag your photos into a different order. To change the order of photos displayed in a slideshow or iPhoto hardbound book, for example, you need to start with a photo album (see Chapters 7 and 10).

Creating an Album by Clicking

Here are a few ways to create a new, empty photo album:

- Choose File→New Album.

- Press ⌘-N.

- Control-click (or right-click) in a blank area of the Source list and choose New Album from the shortcut menu.

• Click the + button in the iPhoto window, below the Source list.

In each case, a dialog box appears, prompting you to name the new album. Type in a descriptive name (*Summer in Aruba, Yellowstone 2006, Edna in Paris,* or whatever), click OK, and watch as a new photo album icon appears in the Source list. (Several are on display in Figure 5-8.)

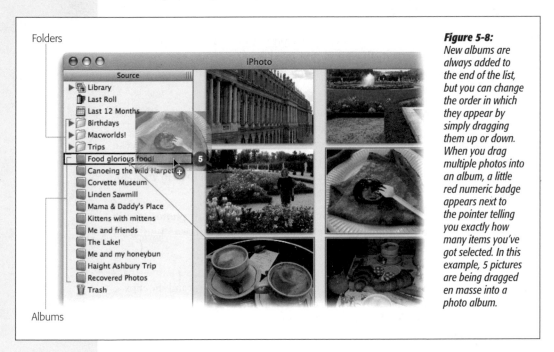

Folders

Albums

Figure 5-8:
New albums are always added to the end of the list, but you can change the order in which they appear by simply dragging them up or down. When you drag multiple photos into an album, a little red numeric badge appears next to the pointer telling you exactly how many items you've got selected. In this example, 5 pictures are being dragged en masse into a photo album.

Now you can add photos to your newly spawned album by dragging in thumbnails from your Library, also as shown in Figure 5-8. There's no limit to the number of albums you can add, so make as many as you need to satisfactorily organize all the photos in your Library.

Creating an Album by Dragging

Creating a new, empty album, however, isn't always the best way to start. It's often easier to create an album and fill it with pictures all in one fell swoop.

For example, you can drag a thumbnail (or a batch of them) from the photo-viewing area directly into an empty portion of the Source list. In a flash—well, in about three seconds—iPhoto creates a new album for you, named Album-1 (or whatever number it's up to). The photos you dragged are automatically dumped inside.

Similarly, you can drag a bunch of graphics files from the *Finder* (the desktop behind iPhoto) directly into the Source list. In one step, iPhoto imports the photos, creates a new photo album, names it after the folder you dragged in, and puts the newly imported photos into that album.

Tip: In the same way, you can drag photos directly from the Finder onto an existing album icon in the Source list, forcing iPhoto to file them there in the process of importing.

Creating an Album by Selecting

Here's a handy, quick, album-creation command: File→New Album From Selection. Scroll through your Library and select any pictures you like, using the methods described on page 106. (They don't have to be from the same film roll, or even the same year.) When you're done, choose New Album From Selection, type a name for the new album, and click OK.

Tip: To rename an existing photo album, double-click its name or icon in the Source list. A renaming rectangle appears around the album's name, with text highlighted and ready to be edited.

Adding More Photos

To add photos to an existing album, just drag them onto its icon. Figure 5-8 illustrates how you can select multiple photos and drop them into an album in one batch.

The single most important point about adding photos to an album is this: Putting photos in an album doesn't really *move* or *copy* them. It makes no difference where the thumbnails start out—whether it's the Library or another album. You're just creating *references*, or pointers, back to the photos in your master photo Library. This feature works a lot like Macintosh aliases; in fact, behind the scenes, iPhoto actually does create aliases of the photos you're dragging. (It stashes them in the appropriate album folders within the iPhoto Library folder.)

What this means is that you don't have to commit a picture to just one album when organizing. One photo can appear in as many different albums as you want. So, if you've got a killer shot of Grandma surfing in Hawaii and you can't decide whether to drop the photo into the Hawaiian Vacation album or the Grandma & Grandpa album, the answer is easy: Put it in both. iPhoto just creates two references to the same original photo in your Library.

Viewing an Album

To view the contents of an album, click its name or icon in the Source list. All the photos included in the selected album appear in the photo-viewing area, while the ones in your Library are hidden.

You can even browse more than one album at a time by highlighting their icons simultaneously:

- To view the contents of several adjacent albums in the list, click the first one, then Shift-click the last.

- To view the contents of albums that aren't consecutive in the list, ⌘-click them.

Tip: Viewing multiple albums at once can be extremely useful when it's time to share your photos. For example, you can make prints or burn an iPhoto CD archive (as explained in Chapters 8 and 14) containing the contents of multiple albums at the same time.

Remember, adding photos to albums doesn't remove them from the Library itself, your master collection. So if you lose track of which album contains a particular photo, just click the Library icon at the top of the Source list to return to the overview of your *entire* photo collection.

Tip: You can put your albums in any order. Just drag them up or down in the Source list.

Moving Photos Between Albums

There are two ways to transfer photos from one photo album to another:

- To *move* a photo between albums, select it and then choose Edit→Cut (or press ⌘-X), removing the photo from the album. Click the destination photo album's name or icon, and then choose Edit→Paste (or press ⌘-V). The photo is now a part of the second album.

- To *copy* a photo into another album, drag it onto the icon of the destination album in the Source list. That photo is now a part of both albums.

Removing Photos from an Album

If you change your mind about the way you've organized your photos and want to remove a photo from an album, open the album and select the photo. (Caution: Be sure that you're viewing the contents of a blue photo *album* and not the main Library, the Last 12 Months collection, or the Last Roll collection. Deleting a photo from those sources really does delete it for good.)

Then do one of the following:

- Choose Edit→Cut (or press ⌘-X).

- Drag the photo's thumbnail onto the little Trash icon.

- Press the Delete key.

- Press the Del (forward delete) key.

- Control-click (or right-click) the photo, and then, from the shortcut menu, choose Cut.

The thumbnail disappears from the album, but of course it's not really gone from iPhoto. Remember, it's still in your Library.

Duplicating a Photo

You can't drag the same photo into an album twice. When you try, the thumbnail simply leaps stubbornly back into its original location, as though to say, "Nyah, nyah, you can't drag the same photo into an album twice."

It's often useful to have two copies of a picture, though. As you'll discover in Chapter 8, a photo whose dimensions are appropriate for a slideshow or photo book (that is, a 4:3 proportion) is inappropriate for ordering prints (4 x 6, 8 x 10, or whatever). To use the same photo for both purposes, you really need to crop two copies independently.

In this case, the old adding-to-album trick isn't going to help you. This time, you truly must duplicate the file, consuming more hard drive space behind the scenes. To do this, highlight the photo and choose Photos→Duplicate (⌘-D). iPhoto switches briefly into Import mode, copies the file, and then returns to your previous mode. The copy appears next to the original, bearing the same name plus the word "copy."

Note: If you duplicate a photo in an album, you'll see the duplicate both there and in the Library, but not in any other albums. If you duplicate it only in the Library, that's the only place you'll see the duplicate.

Putting Photos in Order

If you plan to turn your photo album into an onscreen slideshow, a series of Web pages, or a printed book, you'll have to tinker with the order of the pictures, arranging them in the most logical and compelling sequence. Sure, photos in the main Library or in a smart album (page 116) are locked into a strict sort order—either by creation date, rating, or film roll—but once they're dragged into a photo album, you can shuffle them manually into a new sequence.

To custom-sort photos in an album, just drag and drop, as shown in Figure 5-9.

Figure 5-9:
Arrange photos any way you like by dragging them to a new location within a photo album. In this example, two selected photos from the top-left corner are being dragged to a new location in the next row. The 2 indicates the number of photos being moved; the black vertical bar indicates where iPhoto will insert them when you release the mouse.

Duplicating an Album

It stands to reason that if you have several favorite photos, you might want to use them in more than one iPhoto presentation (in a slideshow and a book, for example). That's why it's often convenient to *duplicate* an album: so that you can create two different sequences for the photos inside.

Just highlight an album and then choose Photos→Duplicate. iPhoto does the duplicating in a flash—after all, it's just duplicating a bunch of tiny aliases. Now you're free to rearrange the order of the photos inside, to add or delete photos, and so on, completely independently of the original album.

Tip: For quick duplicating, you can also Control-click (or right-click) an album in the list and choose Duplicate from the shortcut menu. Duplicating an album creates an identical album, which you can then edit as described on the preceding pages.

Merging Albums

Suppose you have three photo albums that contain photos from different trips to the beach, called Spring Break at Beach, Summer Beach Party, and October Coast Trip. You'd like to merge them into a single album called Beach Trips 2004. No problem.

Select all three albums in the Source list (⌘-click each, for example); the photos from each now appear in the photo-viewing area. Now create a new, fourth album, using any of the usual methods. Finally, select all of the visible thumbnails and drag them into the new album.

You now have one big album containing the photos from all three of the original albums. You can delete the three source albums, if you like, or keep all four around. Remember, albums contain only references to your photos—not the photos themselves—so you're not wasting space by keeping the extra albums around. The only penalty you pay is that you have a longer list of albums to scroll through.

Deleting an Album

To delete an album, select its icon in the Source list, and then press the Delete (or Del) key. You can also Control-click (right-click) an album and choose Delete Album from the shortcut menu. iPhoto asks you to confirm your intention.

Deleting an album doesn't delete any photos—just the references to those photos. Again, even if you delete *all* your photo albums, your Library remains intact.

Tip: If you're a person of steely nerve and unshakable confidence, there is a way to make iPhoto delete an album forever—including all the photos inside it. See page 331…if you dare.

Smart Albums

Albums, as you now know, are the primary organizational tool in iPhoto. Since the dawn of iPhoto, you've had to create them yourself, one at a time—by clicking the + button beneath the Source list, for example, and then filling up the album by dragging photo thumbnails.

iPhoto, though, can fill up albums *for* you, thanks to *smart albums*. These are self-updating folders that always display pictures according to certain criteria that you set up—all pictures with "Aunt Edna" in the comments, for example, or all photos that you've rated four stars or higher. (If you've ever used smart playlists in iTunes, you'll recognize the idea immediately.)

To create a smart album, choose File→New Smart Album (Option-⌘-N), or Option-click the + button below the Source list. Either way, the Smart Album sheet slides down from the top of the window (Figure 5-10).

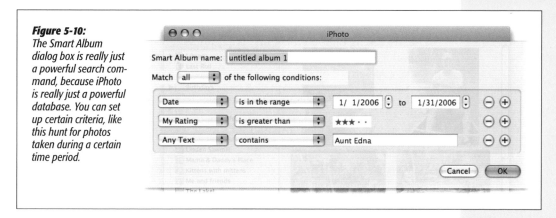

Figure 5-10:
The Smart Album dialog box is really just a powerful search command, because iPhoto is really just a powerful database. You can set up certain criteria, like this hunt for photos taken during a certain time period.

The controls here are designed to set up a search of your photo Library. Figure 5-10 illustrates how to find pictures that you took in the first month of 2006—but only those that have four- or five-star ratings and mention your Aunt Edna in the title or comments.

Click the + button to add a new criterion row to be even more specific about which photos you want iPhoto to include in the smart album. Use the first pop-up menu to choose a type of photo feature (keyword or date, for example) and the second pop-up menu to tell iPhoto whether you want to match it ("is"), eliminate it ("is not"), and so on. The third part of the criterion row is another pop-up menu or a search field where you finally tell iPhoto what to look for.

- You can limit the smart album's reach by limiting it to a certain **Album**. Or, by choosing "is not" from the second pop-up menu, you can *eliminate* an album from consideration. All your albums are listed in the third pop-up menu.

- **Any Text** searches your Library for words or letters that appear in the title, comments, or keywords that you've assigned to your photos.

Tip: If you can't remember how you spelled a word or whether you put it in the Comments or Title field, choose "Any Text," choose "contains" from the second pop-up menu, and in the search field type just the first few letters of the word ("am" for Amsterdam, for example). You're bound to find some windmills now!

- **Comments, Filename, Keyword, and Title** work the same way, except they search *only* that part of the photo's information. Search for "Keyword" "is" "Family" (choose "Family" from the third pop-up menu) to find only those pictures that you specifically assigned the keyword "Family," for example, and not just any old photos where you've typed the word "family" somewhere in the comments.

- **Date** was once one of iPhoto's most powerful search criteria. By choosing "is in the range" from the second pop-up menu, you can use it to create an album containing, for example, only the pictures you took on December 24 and 25 of last year, or for that five-day stretch two summers ago when your best friends were in town. In iPhoto 6, the calendar serves this function much more conveniently.

- The **My Rating** option on the first pop-up menu really puts the fun into smart albums. Let's suppose you've been dutifully giving your pictures star ratings from 1 to 5, as described on page 135.

  Here's the payoff: You can use this smart album feature to collect, say, only those with five stars to create a quick slideshow of just the highlights. Another option is to choose "is greater than" two stars for a more inclusive slideshow that leaves out only the real duds.

- **Roll** lets you make iPhoto look only in, for example, the last five film rolls that you took (choose "is in the last" from the second pop-up menu and type 5 in the box). Or, if you're creating an album of old shots, you can eliminate the last few rolls from consideration by choosing "is not in the last."

- **Aperture, Camera Model, Flash, Focal Length, ISO,** and **Shutter Speed** are new smart album options in iPhoto 6. These are behind-the-scenes data bits that your camera automatically records with each shot, even embedding the information inside the resulting photo file. Thanks to these options, you can use a smart album to round up all of your flash photos, all photos taken with an ISO (light sensitivity) setting of 800 or higher, all pictures with a certain shutter speed, all the ones you shot with your Canon Elph, and so on.

- Click the – button next to a criterion to take it out of the running. For example, if you decide that date shouldn't be a factor, delete any criterion row that tells iPhoto to look for certain dates.

When you click OK, your smart album is ready to show off. When you click its name in the Source list (it has a little gear icon), the main window displays the thumbnails of the photos that match your criteria. The best part is that iPhoto will keep this album updated whenever your collection changes—as you change your ratings, as you take new photos, and so on.

Tip: To change or review the parameters for a smart album, click its icon in the list and then choose Photos→Get Info (⌘-I). The Smart Album sheet reappears.

Folders

Obviously, Apple hit a home run when it invented the album concept. Let's face it: If there were a Billboard Top Software-Features Hits chart, the iPhoto albums feature would have been number one for months on end.

Albums may have become *too* popular, however. It wasn't long before iPhoto fans discovered that their long list of albums had outgrown the height of the Source list. As a result, people grew desperate for some way to organize albums *within* albums, to create subfolders somehow.

Apple's response consisted of one word: "folders."

If you choose File→New Folder, iPhoto promptly creates a new, folder-shaped icon in the Source list called "untitled folder." (Type a name for it and then press Return or Enter.) Its sole purpose in life is to contain *other* Source-list icons—albums, smart albums, saved slideshows, book layouts, and so on. Figure 5-11 shows the details.

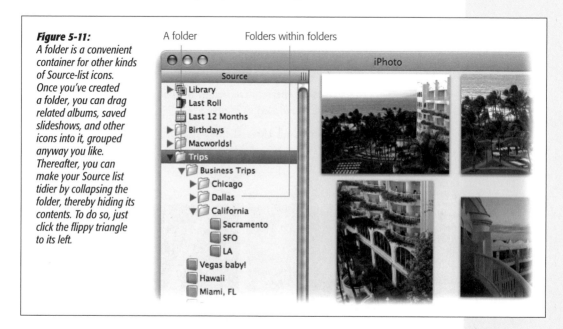

Figure 5-11:
A folder is a convenient container for other kinds of Source-list icons. Once you've created a folder, you can drag related albums, saved slideshows, and other icons into it, grouped anyway you like. Thereafter, you can make your Source list tidier by collapsing the folder, thereby hiding its contents. To do so, just click the flippy triangle to its left.

What's really nice about folders is that they can also contain *other* folders. That is, iPhoto is capable of more than a two-level hierarchy; you can actually create folders within folders within folders within folders, also as shown in Figure 5-11.

Otherwise, folders work exactly like albums. You rename them the same way, drag them up and down the Source list the same way, delete them the same way, and duplicate them the same way.

Clearly, the people have spoken.

Tip: If you've nested a folder within a folder by accident, no problem. You can easily drag it back out again. Just drag the folder upward until it's just below the Last Rolls icons in the Source list—watch the black horizontal line that shows where you are—and then release the mouse.

Three Useful Panels

Just below the Source list, iPhoto can display any of three useful panels:

- **Information.** On this panel, you can view and edit general data about a photo, album, roll, or whatever else you've selected.

- **Calendar.** This feature, new in iPhoto 6, is fantastically useful. It helps you pluck a photo out of your thousands according to the timeline of your life.

- **Keywords.** You can use this list of keywords for tagging your pictures with text labels, from "Robin" to "sunny day" to "prize winner."

To open one of these panels, click the corresponding button beneath the Source list: the blue ❶ for the Information panel, the tiny grid for the Calendar panel, and the little key for the Keywords panel. (You close the panel by clicking the same button again.)

Note, too, that you can adjust the relative height of the panel by dragging the gray divider bar just above it, as illustrated in Figure 5-12.

The following pages describe all three displays, beginning with the information panel.

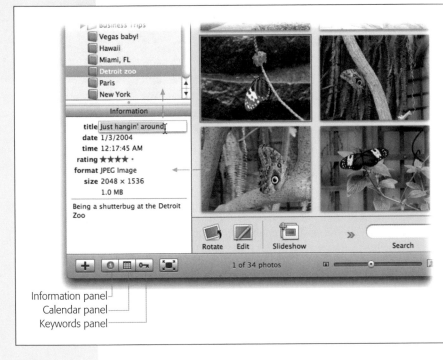

Figure 5-12:
As shown here by the arrows, you can adjust the size of the information panel either horizontally or vertically, just by dragging the gray "metallic" divider bars.

Information panel
Calendar panel
Keywords panel

Information Panel: Titles, Dates, and Comments

When the Information panel is visible, as described in the previous section, you may see any number of different displays (Figure 5-12):

- When a single photo is selected, iPhoto displays that picture's name, rating, creation time and date, dimensions (in pixels), file size, and any comments you've typed.

- When multiple photos are selected, you see the *range* of their creation dates, plus how many photos are selected, and how much disk space they occupy.

- When no photos are selected, the Info area displays information about whatever container is selected in the Source list—the current album or film roll, for example. You get to see the name of the container, the range of dates of its photos, the number of photos, and their total file size on the hard drive.

Tip: When you click the Library at the very top of the Source list, the date-range statistic is pretty cool. It amounts to a stopwatch measuring the span of your interest in digital photography (in the iPhoto era, anyway).

Similarly, the file size info can be extremely useful when creating backups, copying photos to another disk, or burning CDs. One glance at the Info panel—with no photos selected—tells you exactly how much disk space you'll need to fit the current album, film roll, or library.

- When a book, calendar, or card icon is selected (Chapter 10), you get to see its name, theme, dimensions, number of photos, and number of pages, plus any comments you added.

Titles (Renaming Photos)

Just about everything in iPhoto has its own title: every photo, album, folder, film roll, photo book, slideshow, and so on. You can rename them easily enough. Just edit the "title" box in the Information panel, as shown in Figure 5-12.

Most people find this feature especially valuable when it comes to individual photographs. When you import them from your digital camera, the pictures bear useless gibberish names like CRS000321.jpg, CRS000322.jpg, and so on. To change a photo's name to something more meaningful, just select its thumbnail, click once in the Title field, and type in a new title.

While you can make a photo's title as long as you want, it's smart to keep it short (about 10 characters or so). This way, you can see all or most of the title in the Title field (or under the thumbnails).

Tip: A great keystroke makes life a lot easier when naming a whole bunch of photos in a row (like a batch you've just imported). Edit the title box for the first photo, and then press ⌘-] (right bracket) to select the next one. Each time you press ⌘-], iPhoto not only highlights the next picture, but also pre-highlights all of the text in its "title" box so you don't need to click anything before typing a new name for it. (Pressing ⌘-[takes you back one photo, of course.)

This simple keystroke is your ticket to quickly naming a multitude of unique photos, without ever taking your hands off the keyboard.

Changing titles, dates, or comments en masse

The trouble with naming your photos is that hardly anybody takes the time. Yes, the keystroke described in the Tip above certainly makes it easier to assign every photo its own name with reasonable speed—but are you really going to sit there and make up individual names for 25,000 photos?

Mercifully, iPhoto lets you change the names of your photos all at once, thanks to a new "batch processing" command. No, each photo won't have a unique, descriptive name, but at least they can have titles like *Spring Vacation 2* and *Spring Vacation 3* instead of *IMG_1345* and *IMG_1346*.

To use it, choose Photos→Batch Change, or press Shift-⌘-B, or Control-click some selected photos and choose Batch Change from the shortcut menu. The Batch Change sheet drops down from the top of the window (see Figure 5-13). Make sure that the first pop-up menu says Title.

Tip: Don't be fooled by the command name Batch Change. iPhoto still can't edit a batch of photos. You can't, for example, scale them all down to 640 x 480 pixels, or apply the Enhance filter to all of them at once.

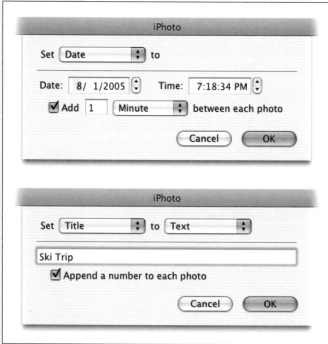

Figure 5-13:
iPhoto's batch-processing feature lets you specify Titles, Dates, and Comments for any number of photos you select.

Top: When you assign a date and time to a batch of pictures, turn on "Add ___ minute between each photo" to give each a unique time stamp, which could come in handy later when you're sorting them. Besides, you didn't take them all at the exact same moment, did you?

Bottom: When you title a batch of pictures, turn on "Append a number to each photo" to number them in sequence as well.

Your options, in the second Batch Change pop-up menu, are as follows:

- **Empty.** Set the titles to "empty" if you want to un-name the selected photos, so they're all blank. You might appreciate this option when, for example, you're working on a photo book (Chapter 10) and you've opted for titles to appear with each photo, but you really want only a few pictures to appear with names under them.

- **Text.** This option produces an empty text box into which you can type, for example, *Ski Trip.* When you click OK, iPhoto names all of the selected pictures to match.

  If you turn on "Append a number to each photo," iPhoto adds digits after whatever base name you choose—for example, *Ski Trip 1, Ski Trip 2,* and so on.

- **Roll Info.** Choose this command to name all the selected photos after the roll's name—"Grand Canyon 2006," for example. iPhoto automatically adds the photo number after this base name.

- **Filename.** If you've been fooling around with naming your photos, and now decide that you want their original, camera-blessed file names to return (IMG_1345 and so on), use this command.

- **Date/Time.** Here's another approach: Name each photo for the exact time it was taken. The dialog box gives you a wide variety of formatting options: long date, short date, time of day, and so on.

Tip: Once you've gone to the trouble of naming your photos, remember that you can make these names appear right beneath the thumbnails for convenient reference. Choose View→Titles to make it so.

Photo Dates

When you select a single photo, you can actually *change* its creation date by editing the Info pane's Date field. For example, you can switch the date from the day the digital file was created to the day the photo was actually taken.

In fact, you can also use the Batch Change command to rewrite history, resetting the dates of a group of photos all at once, as shown in Figure 5-13.

(We trust you won't use this feature for nefarious ends, such as "proving" to the jury that you were actually in Disney World on the day of the office robbery.)

Comments

Sometimes you need more than a one- or two-word title to describe the contents of a photo, album, folder, book, slideshow, or film roll. If you want to add a lengthier description, you can type it in the Comments field in the Photo Info pane, as shown in Figure 5-14.

Even if you don't write full-blown captions for your pictures, you can use the Comments field to store little details such as the names, places, dates, and events associated with your photos.

The best thing about adding comments is that they're searchable. After you've entered all this free-form data, you can use it to quickly locate a photo using iPhoto's search command.

Tip: If you speak a non-English language, iPhoto makes your life easier. As you're typing comments, you can choose Edit→Special Characters. Mac OS X's Character Palette opens, where you can add international letters like É, ø, and ß. Of course, it's also ideal for classic phrases like "I ♠ my cat."

Keep the following in mind as you squirrel away all those bits and scraps of photo information:

- You don't have to manually *type* to enter data into the Comments field. You can paste information in using the standard Paste command, or even drag selected text from another program (like Microsoft Word) right into the Comments box.

- If you feel the need to be verbose, go for it; the Comments box holds thousands of words. Careful, though: The field has no scroll bars, so there's a limit as to how much of what you paste or type will actually be visible. (You can, however, scroll the text by pressing the Page Up and Page Down keys, or by pressing the up or down arrow keys, or by dragging the cursor until the insertion point bumps the top or bottom edge of the box. If you've got a lot to say, your best bet is to make the box taller and the Source list wider, as shown in Figure 5-14.)

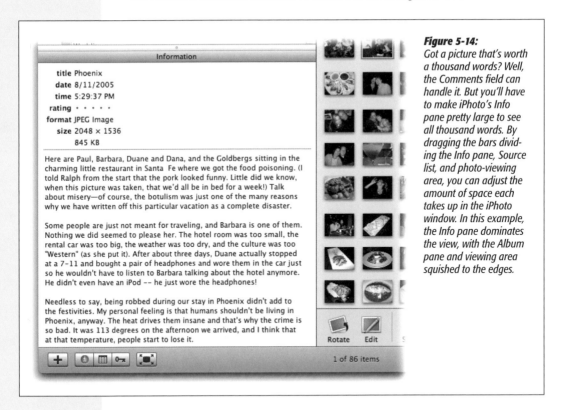

Figure 5-14:
Got a picture that's worth a thousand words? Well, the Comments field can handle it. But you'll have to make iPhoto's Info pane pretty large to see all thousand words. By dragging the bars dividing the Info pane, Source list, and photo-viewing area, you can adjust the amount of space each takes up in the iPhoto window. In this example, the Info pane dominates the view, with the Album pane and viewing area squished to the edges.

- If no photos, or several photos, are selected, the notes you type into the Comments box get attached to the current *album*, rather than to the pictures.

- You can add the same comment to a group of photos using iPhoto's Batch Change command. For example, ⌘-click all the pictures of your soccer team, choose Photos→Batch Change, choose Comments from the first pop-up menu, and type a list of your teammates' names in the Comments field. Years later, you'll have a quick reminder of everyone's name.

You can just as easily add comments for an album, folder, slideshow icon, book, or film roll whose name you've highlighted.

Comments as captions

While the Comments field is useful for storing little scraps of background information about your photos, you can also use it to store the *captions* that you want to appear with your photos. In fact, some of the book layouts included with iPhoto's book-creation tools (Chapter 10) automatically use the text in the Comments field to generate a caption for each photo.

(On the other hand, you don't *have* to use the Comments box text as your captions. You can always add different captions when you're editing the book.)

The Calendar

iPhoto has always offered a long list of ways to find certain photos: visually, by film roll, by album, by searching for text in their names or comments, and so on. But as the years went by, rival programs like Photoshop Album added what, in retrospect, seemed like an obvious and very natural method of finding specific pictures: by consulting a calendar.

After all, you might not know the file names of the pictures you took during your August 2004 trip to Canada. You might not have filed them away into an album. But one thing's for sure: You know you took that trip in August of 2004, and the new iPhoto calendar will help you find those pictures fast.

To use the calendar, start by indicating what container you want the calendar to search: an album or folder, for example, or one of the Library or Last __ Roll icons.

Now make the calendar appear by clicking the tiny blue calendar-grid button at the bottom of the Source list (see Figure 5-15).

At first, you get a year-at-a-glance view. This display may look clear and crisp and simple, but it contains a lot of power—and, if you look closely, a lot of different places to click the mouse. Here's how you can use the calendar to pinpoint photos taken in a certain time period.

- **Photos in a certain month.** See the names of the months in the year view? The names in **bold type** are the months where you took some photos. Click the name of a boldfaced month to see the thumbnails of those photos; they'll appear in the main viewing area. (To scroll to a different year, click the tiny up and down triangle buttons on either side of the word Calendar at the top of the display, as shown in Figure 5-15.)

• **Photos on a certain date.** In Year view, start by double-clicking the appropriate month name. The calendar now changes to show you the individual dates within that month, shown in Figure 5-15 at right. Once again, bold type lets you know that photos are awaiting. Click a date square to see the photos you took that day. (Here again, the up and down triangle arrows above the calendar let you scroll to different months. You can return to the year view by clicking the left-pointing arrow next to the uppermost month's name.)

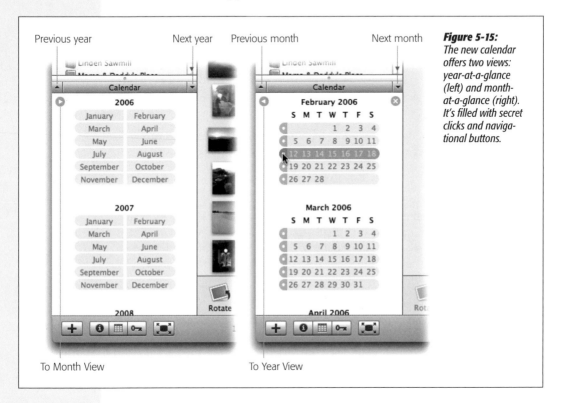

Previous year   Next year   Previous month   Next month

Figure 5-15:
The new calendar offers two views: year-at-a-glance (left) and month-at-a-glance (right). It's filled with secret clicks and navigational buttons.

To Month View   To Year View

• **Photos in a certain week.** Once you've drilled down into the Month view, as described above, you can also round up the photos taken during an entire week: Just click the little dot to the left of the week in question. (It's indicated by the cursor in Figure 5-15.) The horizontal week bar of the calendar is now highlighted in color, and the photos taken during any of those seven days appear in the main viewing area.

It's possible to develop some fancy footwork when you work with this calendar, since, as it turns out, you can select more than one week, month, or day at a time. In fact, you do that using exactly the same keyboard shortcuts that you would use to select individual photo thumbnails. For example:

• You can select multiple adjacent time units by clicking the first and then shift-clicking the last. For example, in Year view, you can select all the photos from June through August by first clicking June, and then Shift-clicking August. (You can use the same trick to select a series of days or weeks in the month view.)

***

Tip: Alternatively, you can just drag the mouse across the dates on the Month view, the days of the week, or the months on the Year view to select consecutive time periods.

***

- You can select multiple time units that *aren't* adjacent by ⌘-clicking them. For example, in Month view, you can select November 1, 5, 12, 20, and 30 by ⌘-clicking those days. In the photo-viewing area, you'll see all the photos taken on all of those days combined.

- Here's an offbeat shortcut that might actually be useful someday: You can round up all the photos taken during a specific month, week, or day *from every year in your collection* by holding down the Option key as you select.

  For example, you can round up six years' worth of Christmas shots by Option-clicking the December button in the Year view. Or you can find the pictures taken every year on your birthday (from all years combined) by Option-clicking that date in the month view.

Apple really went the extra mile on behalf of shortcut freaks when it designed the calendar. Here are a few more techniques that you probably wouldn't stumble upon by accident:

- In Year view, select all the days in a month by double-clicking the month's name. In Month view, you can do the same by triple-clicking any date number.

- Return to Year view by quadruple-clicking any date, or by clicking the month's name.

- Skip ahead to the next month or year (or the previous month or year) by turning the scroll wheel on your mouse, if you have one.

- Deselect anything that's selected in the calendar by clicking the small gray circular X button at the top-right corner of the calendar.

Keywords

Keywords are descriptive words—like *family*, *vacation*, or *kids*—that you can use to label and categorize your photos, regardless of which album they're in.

The beauty of keywords in iPhoto is that they're searchable. Want to comb through all the photos in your library to find every closeup taken of your children during summer vacation? Instead of browsing through multiple photo albums, just perform an iPhoto search for photos containing the keywords *kids, vacation, closeup,* and *summer.* You'll have the results in seconds.

Keywords are also an integral part of iPhoto's smart albums feature, as described on the previous pages.

Editing Keywords

Apple offers you a few sample entries in the Keywords list to get you rolling: Favorite, Family, Kids, Vacation, Birthday, Movie, and Raw. But these are intended only as a starting point. You can add as many new keywords as you want—or delete any of Apple's—to create a meaningful, customized list:

- To add, delete, or rename keywords, choose iPhoto→Preferences. Click the Keywords button to reveal the panel shown in Figure 5-16. Now click the + button to produce a new entry called "untitled" in the Keywords list, ready to be edited.

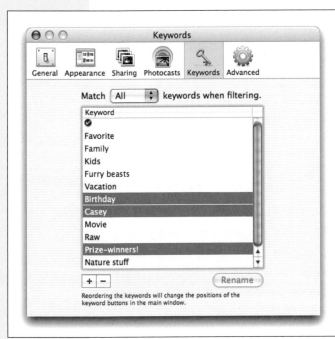

Figure 5-16:
Apple completely rejiggered the whole Keyword process back in iPhoto 5 so that it's a lot easier to figure out—unless, of course you're used to the old, iPhoto 2/4 way. Now, you create and destroy keywords in iPhoto's Preferences dialog box.

Finally, just type in your new keyword name and then press Return or Enter.

- To delete a keyword, select it in the list and then click the – button. As usual in iPhoto, you can select multiple keywords for deletion by Shift-clicking or (for noncontiguous selections) ⌘-clicking them in the list before clicking Remove. (When you remove a keyword from the list, iPhoto also removes that keyword from any pictures to which it had been applied.)

- To rename a keyword, select it in the list, click the Rename button below the list, and then edit the name.

Note: Be careful about renaming keywords after you've started using them; the results can be messy. If you've already applied the keyword Fishing to a batch of photos, but later decide to replace it with Romantic in your keyword list, all the Fishing photos automatically inherit the keyword Romantic. Depending on you and your interests, this may not be what you intended.

It may take some time to develop a really good master set of keywords. The idea is to assign labels that are general enough to apply across your entire photo collection, but specific enough to be meaningful when conducting searches.

Here's a general rule of thumb: Use *albums* to group pictures of specific events—a wedding, family vacation, or beach party, for example. (You can use *film rolls* for the same purpose, if you prefer; see page 100.) Use *keywords* to focus on general characteristics that are likely to appear through your entire photo collection—words like Mom, Dad, Casey, Robin, Family, Friends, Travel, and Vacation.

Suppose your photo collection includes a bunch of photos that you shot during a once-in-a-lifetime trip to Rome last summer. You might be tempted to assign *Rome* as a keyword. Don't…because you probably won't use *Rome* on anything other than that one set of photos. It would be smarter to create a photo album or film roll called *Trip to Rome* to hold all those Rome pictures. Use your keywords to tag the same pictures with descriptors like Travel or Family. It also might be useful to apply keywords that describe attributes of the photos themselves, such as Closeup, Landscape, Portrait, and Scenic—or even the names of the people *in* the photos, like Harold, Chris, and Uncle Bert.

Assigning and Unassigning Keywords

iPhoto offers two different methods of applying keywords to your pictures. No matter which method you prefer, keep one fortunate fact in mind: You can apply as many keywords to an individual photo as you like. A picture of your cousin Rachel at a hot dog eating contest in London might bear all these keywords: Relatives, Travel, Food, Humor, and Medical Crises. Later, you'll be able to find that photo no matter which of these categories you're hunting for.

Method 1: Drag the picture

One way to apply keywords to photos is, well, to apply the *photos* to the *keywords*.

If it's not already visible, expose the Keywords panel by clicking the little key button below the Source list (Figure 5-17).

Figure 5-17:
Left: You apply a keyword by dragging a photo onto the corresponding button.

Right: This dialog box is faster if you intend to apply a lot of keywords to a single photo or batch of photos.

Once your keyword buttons are visible, you can drag relevant photos directly onto them, as shown in Figure 5-17. You can drag them one at a time, or you can select the whole batch first, using any of the selection techniques described on page 106.

This method is best when you want to apply a whole bunch of pictures to one or two keywords. It's pretty tedious, however, when you want to apply a lot of different keywords to a single photo. That's why Apple has given you a second method, described next.

Note: If you press the Option key as you drag a thumbnail onto a keyword button, you *remove* that keyword assignment from the picture.

Method 2: Get Info
Highlight a pictures thumbnail and then choose Photos→Get Info. The Photo Info dialog box appears (Figure 5-17, right).

Now click the Keywords tab. Here, you find a simple checklist of all your keywords. Turn on all the checkboxes that correspond to the currently selected photo.

The beauty of this system is that you can keep the little Keywords window open on the screen as you move through your photo collection. Each time you click a photo—or, in fact, select a group of them—the checkboxes update themselves to reflect the keywords of whatever is now selected. Select some pictures, turn on Travel, select some others, turn on Family, and so on, without ever having to close the palette.

(It should be pretty obvious how you can use this method to *remove* keyword assignments from a certain picture or group of pictures, too—just turn off the checkboxes.)

Viewing Keyword Assignments
Once you've tagged a few pictures with keywords, you can see those keywords in either of two ways:

• Look at the Keywords window described above. When you select a photo, its assigned keyword checkboxes light up in the Keywords list.

• Set up iPhoto to show the actual text of the keywords right in the main photo-viewing area. To do this, choose View→Keywords, or press Shift-⌘-K. Figure 5-18 shows the resulting effect.

The Checkmark "Keyword"
You may have noticed that one entry in the keyword panel is not a word, but a symbol—a small checkmark. You can't edit this particular entry; it's always just a checkmark.

The checkmark works just like the other keyword entries, with one exception. Instead of assigning a particular keyword to photos, it flags them with a small checkmark symbol, as shown in Figure 5-19.

So what does the checkmark mean? Anything you want it to mean; it's open to a multitude of personal interpretations. The bottom line, though, is that you'll find this marker extremely useful for temporary organizational tasks.

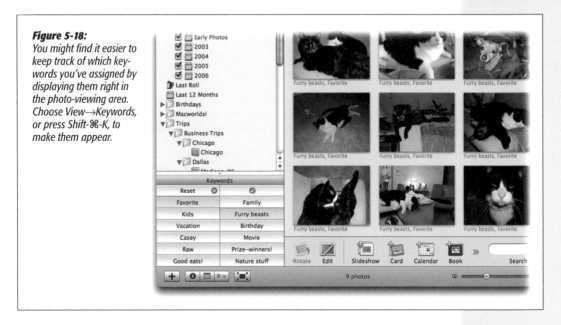

Figure 5-18:
You might find it easier to keep track of which keywords you've assigned by displaying them right in the photo-viewing area. Choose View→Keywords, or press Shift-⌘-K, to make them appear.

Figure 5-19:
The idea behind the checkmark button is to provide an easy, uncomplicated way of earmarking a series of photos while sifting through your collection.

For example, you might want to cull only the most appropriate images from a photo album for use in a printed book or slideshow. As you browse through the images, use the checkmark button to flag each shot you want. Later, you can use the Search function (described next) to round up all of the images you checkmarked, so that you can drag them all into a new album en masse.

You remove checkmarks from photos just as you remove any other keywords, as described in the previous sections.

Tip: Just after moving your checkmarked photos to an album, remember to remove the checkmark from all of them while they're still selected. This way, you won't get confused the next time you want to use the checkmark button for flagging a batch of photos.

Using Keywords

Whether you tag photos with the checkmark symbol or a series of keywords, the big payoff for your diligence arrives when you need to get your hands on a specific set of photos, because iPhoto lets you *isolate* them with one quick click.

Start by opening the Keywords panel below the Source list. (Click an album, folder, or roll in the Source list at this point, if you like, to confine your search.)

Here's where the fun begins: When you click one of the keyword buttons, iPhoto immediately rounds up all photos labeled with that keyword, displays them in the photo-viewing area, and hides all others.

Here are the important points to remember when using iPhoto's keyword searches:

- To find photos that match multiple keywords, click additional keyword buttons. For example, if you click Travel and then click Holidays, iPhoto reveals all the pictures that have *both* of those keywords.

Tip: New feature alert! In iPhoto 6, you can, if you prefer, perform an "or" keyword roundup instead—that is, to find pictures with *either* Travel *or* Holidays keywords. The trick is to choose iPhoto→Preferences, click the Keywords button, and make the pop-up menu say "Match *Any* keywords when filtering."

Every button stays "clicked" until you click it a second time; you can see several of the keyword buttons "lit up" in Figure 5-18.

- Suppose you've rounded up all your family pictures by clicking the Family keyword. The trouble is, your ex-spouse is in half of them, and you'd really rather keep your collection pure.

No problem: *Option*-click the Ex-Spouse keyword button. iPhoto obliges by removing all photos with that keyword from whatever is currently displayed. In other words, Option-clicking a keyword button means, "find photos that don't contain this keyword."

- You can confine your search to a single album by selecting it before searching. Similarly, clicking the Library (or Last Roll, or Last 12 Months) in the list before searching means that you want to search that photo collection. You can even select multiple albums and search only in those.

- Click Reset to restore the view to the whole album or whole Library you had visible before you performed the search.

Searching for Photos by Text

The keyword mechanism described above is an adequate way to tag photos with textual descriptions. But as you know by now, there are other ways. The name you give a picture might be significant; its original file name on the hard drive might be important; and maybe you've typed some important clues into its Comments box or given its film roll an important name.

Anyway, that's the purpose of the Search box in the lower-right corner of the window (Figure 5-20).

Tip: iPhoto 6 is capable of searching your photos' *metadata,* too—the photographic details like camera manufacturer, F-stop, flash status, exposure settings, and so on. But you don't use the Search box for that; you must create a Smart Album, as described on page 116.

Figure 5-20:
As you type into the Search box, iPhoto hides all pictures except the ones that have your typed phrase somewhere in their names, keywords, comments, file names, or film-roll titles. (To cancel your search and reveal all the pictures again, click the round gray X at the right end of the Search box.)

IMG_1351.JPG

Backseat driver

Seal Madonna & Child

Hilton Of the Seas

The Photo Info Window

The small Information pane below the Source list displays only the most basic information about your photos: title, date, time, rating, format, and size. For more detailed information, you need the Get Info command. It opens the Photo Info window, where iPhoto displays a surprisingly broad dossier of details about your photo: the make and model of the digital camera used to take it, for example, and even exposure details like the f-stop, shutter speed, and flash settings.

To open the Photo Info window (Figure 5-21), select a thumbnail and then choose Photos→Get Info (or press ⌘-I). (If more than one photo is selected, you'll get only a bunch of dashes in the info window.)

In addition to the Keywords tab described above, the Photo Info window contains Photo and Exposure tabs. The Photo panel contains information about the image file itself—when it was originally created, when it was first imported, and when it was last modified. If the image was shot with a digital camera (as opposed to being scanned or imported from disk), the make and model of the camera appear at the bottom of the window (see Figure 5-21).

Tip: Comparing the details on the Exposure panel with the advice in Chapters 2 and 3 can be eye-opening. For example, if you put your camera into its automatic mode and snap a few pictures, you can find out—and learn from—the shutter and lighting settings the camera used.

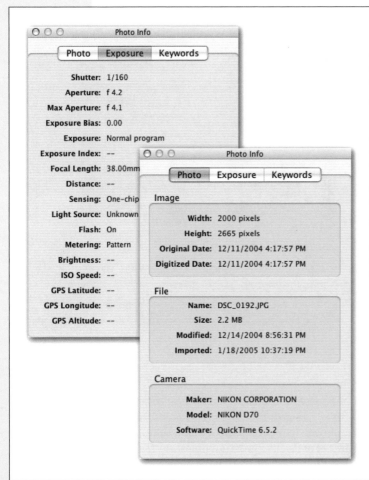

Figure 5-21:
The Photo Info window reports details about your photos by reading the EXIF tags that your camera secretly embeds in your files.

Left: On the Exposure panel, you can tell at a glance that this photo was shot with a flash, at a shutter speed of 1/160, and with an f-stop setting of 4.2. Tracking this information can be useful in determining which settings on your camera produce the best-quality digital photos in a certain set of conditions.

Right: iPhoto uses the Original Date (or lacking that, Modified date) information to sort your photos in the Photo Library and place them in their respective year albums.

How on earth does iPhoto know so much about how your photos were taken? Most digital cameras embed a wealth of image, camera, lens, and exposure information in the photo files they create, using a standard data format called *EXIF* (Exchangeable Image Format). With that in mind, iPhoto automatically scans photos for EXIF data as it imports them.

Note: Some cameras do a better job than others at embedding EXIF data in photo files. iPhoto can extract this information only if it's been properly stored by the camera when the digital photo is created. Of course, most (if not all) of this information is missing altogether if your photos didn't come from a digital camera (if they were scanned in, for example).

Rate Your Photos

iPhoto offers a great way to categorize your pictures: by how great they are! You can assign each picture a rating of 0 to 5 stars, then use the ratings to sort your photo Library, or gather only the cream of the crop into a slideshow, smart album, or photo book.

Here are the ways you can rate your digital masterpieces:

- Select a photo (or several) and choose Photos→My Rating; from the submenu, choose from 1 through 5 stars. You can even do this while you're editing a single photo.

Tip: If the top of the screen is just too far away, you can also Control-click (or right-click) any one of the selected thumbnails (or, in Edit mode, anywhere on the photo) and choose the My Rating command from the shortcut menu. Its submenu is exactly the same as what you'd find in the Photos→My Rating command.

- If you're not a mousy sort of person, you can perform the same stunt entirely from the keyboard. Press ⌘-1 for one star, ⌘-2 for two stars, and so on. Press ⌘-0 to strip away any existing ratings.

- During a slideshow, twitch the mouse to bring up the onscreen control bar. In the bar, click the row of dots to turn them into rating stars (click the third dot to give the current photo 3 stars, for example). Or just press the number keys on the keyboard to bestow that number of stars as the slides go by.

- To remove a rating, select the photo and choose Photos→My Ratings→None. You're saying, in effect, "This photo has not yet been rated." Keyboard shortcut: ⌘-0.

Tip: Once you've applied your star ratings, you can view the actual little stars right under the corresponding thumbnails by choosing View→My Ratings (or pressing Shift-⌘-R).

Deleting Photos

As every photographer knows—well, every *good* photographer—not every photo is a keeper. So at some point, you'll probably want to delete some of your photos.

The iPhoto Trash

iPhoto has a private Trash can that works just like the Finder's Trash. It's sitting there at the bottom of the Source list. When you want to purge a photo from your Library, simply drag it to the Trash. Instead of deleting the photo immediately, iPhoto lets it sit there in the Trash "album," awaiting permanent disposal via the Empty Trash command. This feature gives you one more layer of protection against accidentally deleting a precious picture.

In the main thumbnails view, you can relegate items to the Trash by selecting one or more thumbnails in the Library (not in an album) and then performing one of the following:

• Drag the thumbnails into the Trash.

• Control-click (or right-click) a photo and choose Move to Trash from the shortcut menu.

• Press ⌘-Delete or choose Photos→Move to Trash.

Tip: To delete a photo from a smart album or from Edit mode, press Option-⌘-Delete.

To view the photos that you have sentenced to the great shredder in the sky, click the Trash icon, as shown in Figure 5-22. However, if you suddenly decide you don't really want to get rid of any of these trashed photos, it's easy to resurrect them: Just drag the thumbnails out of the Trash and onto the Library icon in the Source list. (Alternatively, you can Control-click the photo or photos and, from the shortcut menu, choose Restore to Photo Library.)

FREQUENTLY ASKED QUESTION

Undeletable Photos?

iPhoto won't delete photos of my sister. I thought I got rid of a bunch of unflattering pictures of her the other day, and then I found them again when browsing through my Library. Why aren't they staying deleted?

Possibility 1: You deleted the pictures from an album instead of the Library itself (the first icon in the list). When you remove a photo from an album, it removes only a reference to that picture from the album, leaving the photo itself untouched in the Library.

If the pictures of your sister are really horrendous, click the Library icon in the Source list, move the offending photos to the Trash, and then empty the Trash. That'll get rid of them once and for all.

Possibility 2: You're trying to delete the photo from inside a smart album (page 116). Remember, you have to delete such photos from the Library itself, or from the Last __ Months or Last __ Rolls collections.

You've just rescued them from photo-reject limbo and put them back into your main photo collection.

Tip: You can also move photos from the Trash back into your Library by selecting them—yes, in the Trash "album"—and then pressing ⌘-Delete. Think of it as the un-Trash command.)

Figure 5-22:
When you dump a photo into iPhoto's Trash, it's not really gone—it's just relocated to the Trash folder. Clicking the Trash icon in the Source list displays all the photos in the Trash and makes the Info panel show the total number of trashed photos, their date range, and their sizes.

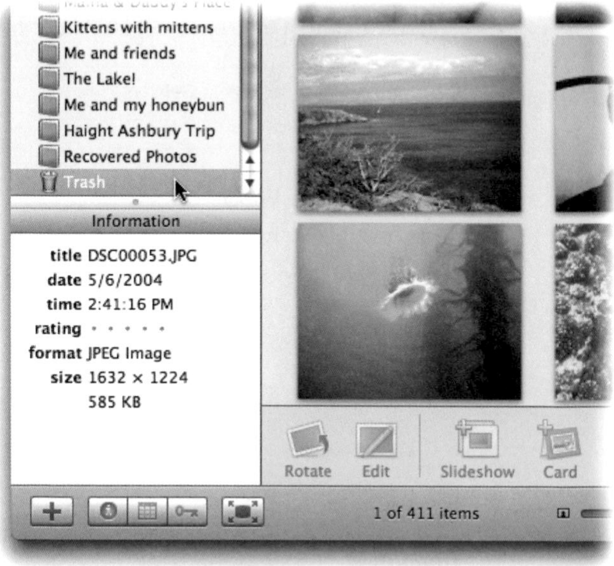

To *permanently* delete the photos in the Trash, choose iPhoto→Empty Trash, or Control-click the Trash icon to access the Empty Trash command via a shortcut menu. iPhoto then displays an alert message, warning you that emptying the Trash removes these photos permanently and irreversibly.

(Of course, if you imported the photos from files on disk or haven't deleted them from your camera, you can still recover the original files and reimport them.)

Note: As you might expect, dragging photos into the Trash doesn't reduce the total size of your iPhoto Library by a single byte, because iPhoto is still storing a copy of each photo in its Trash folder. Only when you empty the Trash does the iPhoto Library folder actually shrink in size.

Whatever pictures you throw out by emptying the Trash also disappear from any albums you've created. (Deleting a photo from an *album* is different.)

Note: If you use iPhoto to track photos that are not actually in iPhoto (they remain "out there" in folders on your hard drive), deleting them in iPhoto doesn't do much. They no longer show up in iPhoto, but they're still out there on the hard drive, right where they always were. See page 85 for more on this external photo-tracking feature.

Customizing the Shoebox

iPhoto starts out looking just the way you probably see it now, with each picture displayed as a small thumbnail against a plain white background. This view makes it easy to browse through photos and work with iPhoto's various tools.

But hey, this is *your* digital shoebox. With a little tweaking and fine-tuning, you can completely customize the way iPhoto displays your photos.

Start with a visit to iPhoto→Preferences and click the Appearance button.

Tip: You can open the iPhoto Preferences window at any time by pressing ⌘-comma. This keystroke is blissfully consistent across all the iLife programs.

Changing the View

The controls in the Appearance panel of the Preferences window let you make some pretty significant changes to the overall look of your Library. See Figure 5-23 for an example.

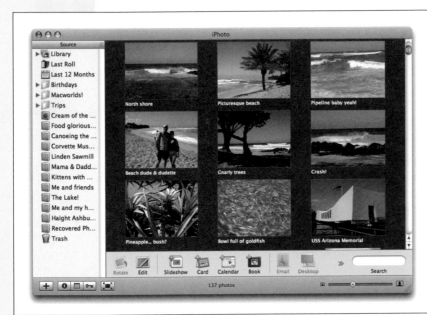

Figure 5-23:
Here's a typical Library with a very different look. Instead of the usual white background with drop-shadowed thumbnails, this view presents large thumbnails, with borders, against a dark gray background. The font for the Source list is enlarged, and the titles for each photo are displayed.

Here are your options:

- **Add or remove a border or shadow.** The factory setting, Drop Shadow, puts a soft black shadow behind each thumbnail in the photo-viewing pane, a subtle touch that gives your Library an elegant 3-D look.

  As pretty as this effect is, however, there's also a decent reason to turn it *off*: It slows iPhoto down slightly, as the program has to continually redraw or resize those fancy shadows behind each thumbnail whenever you scroll or zoom. Switch to either the Border or No Border setting and you'll be rewarded with faster scrolling and smoother zooming whenever you change the size of thumbnails (as described in the next section). The Border setting puts a thin white frame around each picture. You won't see this border unless you change the background color, as explained in the next paragraph.

- **Change the background color.** Right under the No Border radio button, a slider lets you adjust the background color of the photo-viewing pane. Actually, the term "color" is a bit of an overstatement, since your choices only include white, black, or any shade of gray in between. Not exactly a rainbow of colors.

- **Adjust the Alignment.** Turn on the "Align photos to grid" checkbox if you want the thumbnails in your Library to snap into evenly spaced rows and columns, even if your collection includes thumbnails of varying sizes and orientations, as shown in Figure 5-24.

Figure 5-24:
The "Align to grid" op-
tion does nothing if all
photos have the same
orientation. But with
mixed horizontal and
vertical images, photos
stay in strict rows and
columns (right) despite
their shape differences.
At left: an "unaligned"
version of the same
thumbnails.

- **Change the date order.** Turning on "Place most recent photos at the top" puts them at the top of the main iPhoto window. It's sort of like seeing your most recent email messages at the top of your inbox. If you turn this checkbox off, you'll have to scroll all the way down to see your most recent pictures.

- **Choose text size.** The pop-up menu at the bottom of the Appearance panel lets you choose Small or Large for the album names in the Source list, depending on your eyesight. As for keywords and the other text in the iPhoto window, you're stuck with one size—tiny.

Showing/Hiding Keywords, Titles, and Film Roll Info

If you want your thumbnails to appear with their titles and/or keywords, choose View→Titles (Shift-⌘-T) or View→Keywords (Shift-⌘-K). Titles and keywords appear under each thumbnail.

As with most of iPhoto, your formatting options are limited. You can't control the font, style, color, or size of this text. Your only choice is to either display the title and keywords or to keep them hidden.

Editing Your Shots

Straight from the camera, digital snapshots often need a little bit of help. A photo may be too dark or too light. The colors may be too bluish or too yellowish. The focus may be a little blurry, the camera may have been tilted slightly, or the composition may be somewhat off.

Fortunately, one of the amazing things about digital photography is that you can fine-tune images in ways that, in the world of traditional photography, would require a fully equipped darkroom, several bottles of smelly chemicals, and an X-Acto knife.

OK, iPhoto isn't a full-blown photo-editing program like Adobe Photoshop, but it does include a handful of useful tools. This chapter shows you how to use each of the tools in iPhoto's digital darkroom to spruce up your photos—and how to edit your photos in other programs if more radical image enhancement is needed.

Editing in iPhoto

You can't paint in additional elements, mask out unwanted backgrounds, or apply 50 different special effects filters in iPhoto, as you can with editing programs like Photoshop and GraphicConverter. Nonetheless, iPhoto is designed to handle basic photo fix-up tasks in three categories: one-click fixes, one-click effects, and advanced fine-tuning. Here's a quick summary; details appear later in the chapter.

One-Click Fixes
iPhoto presents these tools front and center, right at the bottom of the editing window. They're nearly idiot-proof:

- **Enhance.** With one click, this tool endeavors to make photos look more vibrant by tweaking the brightness and contrast settings and adjusting the saturation to compensate for washed-out or oversaturated colors.

- **Cropping.** The cropping tool lets you cut away the outer portions of a photo to improve its composition or to make it the right size for a printout or Web page.

- **Retouch.** This little brush lets you paint out minor imperfections like blemishes, freckles, and scratches.

- **Red-Eye.** This little filter gets rid of a very common photo glitch—those shining red dots that sometimes appear in a person's eyes as the result of flash photography. Who wants to look like a werewolf if it's not necessary?

One-Click Effects

It's not entirely clear how often you'll use these eight special effects, new in iPhoto 6, but they'll be here when you need them. Among them, you'll find an inexplicable abundance of effects designed to make your photos look old and bleached out (Black & White, Sepia, Fade Color, Antique), and three options for fading out the photo at its corners or edges (Matte, Vignette, Edge Blur).

Advanced Controls

This floating panel is aimed at power users who used to go galloping off to Photoshop every time they needed greater control over photo editing. It includes sliders for these parameters:

- **Brightness/Contrast.** These sliders can tone down bright, overexposed images or lighten up those that look too dark and shadowy. While the Enhance button takes an all-or-nothing approach to fixing a photo, the Brightness and Contrast controls let you make tiny adjustments to the settings.

- **Saturation, Temperature, Tint.** These sliders affect the overall color of a picture: its vividness, warmth, and color cast.

- **Sharpness.** There's no rescuing a completely out-of-focus shot. But this slider can take a photo a few percentage points closer to sharp, or—in situations where a traditional photographer might smear a little Vaseline on the lens—blur the picture softly to hide your subject's wrinkles and flaws.

- **Straighten.** Here's a really fun new control. In one quick twitch of the mouse, you can rotate a crooked shot slightly so that it appears square with the horizon.

- **Exposure.** Like magic, this slider lets you fix most over- and underexposed shots, allowing you to crank up the flash or bring details out of shadow.

- **Levels.** Using these sophisticated controls, you can compress or expand the lights and darks across a photo's spectrum—a function that will make a lot more sense when you try it.

For anything beyond these touch-up tasks, you need to manipulate your photos in a more powerful editing program.

Using the Editing Tools

All iPhoto editing is performed in a special editing mode, where editing tool icons appear along the bottom (Figure 6-1). You enter Edit mode either by double-clicking a photo's thumbnail (the quick way) or by highlighting the thumbnail and then clicking the Edit icon at the bottom of the screen (the long way).

Figure 6-1:
iPhoto's editing tools appear in the toolbar when you open a photo for editing. A >> symbol at the right end of the toolbar (as shown here) means that the window is too narrow to display all the tools. Just drag the window wider to show all tools, or click the double-arrow to access the tools via a pop-up menu.

As you may recall, however, iPhoto offers you several different layouts of this Edit world. First, there's the one where the photo appears right in the iPhoto window. Second, there's the one where the photo opens up in a separate window of its own. Third, there's the new full-screen mode, where the photo fills your entire screen, and elements like the menu bar, Source list, and thumbnails display are temporarily hidden.

A reminder: You specify which arrangement you prefer in the iPhoto→Preferences dialog box. Then again, you can decide on an individual basis, too. To do so, Control-click (or right-click) a thumbnail or a photo in its own window; from the shortcut menu, choose "Edit," "Edit in separate window," or "Edit using full screen," depending on your preference.

Review pages 108-110 for details on these different editing modes. But considering how much better the full-screen mode is than any other method, it's worth taking a few moments to learn about its ins and outs.

Full-Screen Mode

Mac screens come in all sizes and resolutions these days, but one thing is for sure: Even the biggest ones usually can't show you an entire digital photo at full size. A five-megapixel photo (2784 x 1856), for example, is still too big to fit entirely on Apple's 30-inch Cinema Display (2560 x 1600 pixels) without shrinking it.

The bottom line: For most of your iPhoto career, you'll be working with scaled-down versions of your photos. That's a particular shame when it comes to editing those photos, when you need as much clarity and detail as possible.

That's why the invention of full-screen mode, new in iPhoto 6 (and borrowed from Aperture, Apple's professional photo program), is such a big deal. In this mode, the selected photo is magnified to fill your entire screen. You don't sacrifice a single pixel to menu bars, tool bars, window edges, or other screen-eating elements. It's *awesome*.

Here's what you need to know about full-screen mode:

- There are three ways to enter it, as described on page 110. The quickest: Click the full-screen mode icon (▣) at the bottom of the iPhoto window.

- You have at your disposal a *thumbnail browser* at the top of the screen (so you can choose a different photo to work on) and an *editing toolbar* at the bottom (so you can fix up what you're seeing). But both of these strips are self-hiding. They don't appear unless you push your cursor to the top or bottom of the screen for a moment. Figure 6-2 illustrates.

Figure 6-2:
The thumbnail browser and editing toolbar, as seen in full-screen mode.

When the arrow cursor moves toward the middle of the screen, the thumbnails and editing tools disappear, making more room for you to enjoy your photograph.

Tip: If you prefer, you can force the row of thumbnails, the toolbar, or both to remain on the screen all the time, rather than hiding themselves when they're feeling unwanted. Just slide your mouse to the top of the screen so that the menu bar appears. Now choose View→Show Thumbnails or View→Show Toolbar. You'll notice that the thumbnail browser or toolbar sticks around, even when your cursor is in the middle of the screen.

To restore the self-hiding behavior, choose View→Hide Thumbnails or View→Hide Toolbar.

- The Compare button (at the left end of the self-hiding toolbar) displays the currently selected photo and the one to its right, side-by-side, for handy comparison. To compare the original photo with a different shot, mouse up to the top of the screen so that the thumbnail browser appears, and then ⌘-click the comparison shot you want.

  To restore the single-photo view, click the Compare button again.

Note: Suppose you're looking at Photo A. When you click the Compare button, iPhoto shrinks Photo A so that you can see Photo B beside it.

At this point, however, Photo B is highlighted, meaning that iPhoto now thinks *that's* the picture you want to work on. So if you click Compare again to turn the effect off, you'll be left with Photo B filling the screen.

- You're not limited to comparing *two* photos side-by-side. You can compare three, four, or however many your screen can fit.

  If you're the kind of person who thinks ahead, you can select a batch of pictures (using the techniques described on page 106) and then click the full-screen mode button. You'll enter full-screen mode with all of those photos displayed.

  But if you're *already* in full-screen mode, just ⌘-click or Shift-click to select additional photos in the thumbnail browser, exactly as described on page 106. iPhoto makes room for yet another photo to appear with its comrades. (To remove a photo from the comparison, ⌘-click its thumbnail again.)

- If you click the little ❶ button at the left side of the toolbar (when it's visible), you summon a floating-palette version of the regularly scheduled Info panel (page 120). Here, without leaving the comfort of full-screen mode, you can rename a photo, edit its comments, and so on.

- Deleting a photo from full-screen view is really easy; just press the Delete key. The visible photo (or, if you were comparing some, the highlighted photo) immediately disappears. (It's in the iPhoto Trash.) The next photo in the album or library appears in its place.

- To exit full-screen mode, either double-click a photo, tap the Esc key, or click the Exit Full-Screen button at the right end of the editing toolbar.

- Remember that if you find yourself using full-screen mode a lot, you may as well save yourself some effort by making it your new standard editing view. To do that, choose iPhoto Preferences, click General, and from the "Edit photo" pop-up menu, choose "Using full screen." Thereafter, you can open full-screen mode just by double-clicking a photo thumbnail.

Notes on Zooming and Scrolling

Before you get deeply immersed in the editing process, it's well worth knowing how to zoom and scroll around, since chances are you'll be doing quite a bit of it.

Zooming in Any Editing View

You can press the number keys on your keyboard—0, 1, and 2—to zoom into any of iPhoto's editing modes. Hit 1 to zoom in so far that you're viewing every single pixel (colored dot) in the photo; that is, one pixel of the photo occupies one pixel of your screen. The photo is usually bigger than your screen at this point, so you're now viewing only a portion of the whole—but it's great for detail work.

Hit 2 to double that magnification level. Now each pixel of the original picture consumes *four* pixels of your screen, a handy superzoom level when you're trying to edit individual skin cells.

Finally, when you've had quite enough of super-zooming, tap your zero (0) key to zoom out again so the whole photo fits in the window. (Zooming into "edit in separate window" mode, by the way, disables iPhoto's zoom-by-changing-the-window-size feature. Tapping the 0 key lets you once again zoom in or out by dragging the window's corner.)

Zooming in "Separate Window" View

If you've opened a photo into its own window, one way to zoom is to change the size of the window itself. Enlarge the window to zoom in; shrink it to zoom out.

But you can make a window only so big before you run out of screen. Therefore, you need a way to magnify the photo independently of its window size.

That's why Apple has given you the Size pop-up menu on iPhoto's Editing toolbar. If it's hidden at the moment, make sure you've opened a photo in its own window, and then click the >> button in the lower-right corner of the window (Figure 6-1). You'll find the Size submenu, complete with larger-than-life settings like 150% and 200%.

Zooming in Full-Screen View

Even though you're getting the biggest view of your photo ever available in iPhoto, that's not the end of the magnification possibilities. You can use the size slider at the bottom of the window (or the 0, 1, or 2 keystroke) to blow it up even more. In fact, once the photo is enlarged so that it no longer fits on the screen, a handy little navigation panel appears (Figure 6-3). You can change your position on the super-enlarged photo by dragging the tiny "you are here" rectangle within the navigator.

Scrolling Tricks (Any Editing View)

Once you've zoomed in, you can scroll the photo in any direction by pressing the Space bar as you drag the mouse. That's more direct than fussing with two independent scroll bars.

Better yet: If you've equipped your Mac with a mouse that has a scroll wheel on the top, you can scroll images up and down while zoomed in on them by turning that wheel. To scroll the zoomed area *horizontally*, press Shift while turning.

Figure 6-3:
While zooming in full-screen mode, you get a handy little navigation panel allowing you to change your position on the super-huge photo by dragging a tiny "you are here" rectangle, as shown here.

The "Before and After" Keystroke

After making any kind of edit, it's incredibly useful to compare the "before" and "after" versions of your photo. So useful, in fact, that Apple has dedicated one whole key to that function: the Control key at the lower corner of your keyboard.

Hold it down to see your unenhanced before photo; release it to see the after image.

By pressing and releasing the Control key, you can toggle between the two versions of the photo to assess the results of the enhancement.

Backing Out

As long as you remain in Edit mode, you can back out of your changes no matter how many of them you've made. For example, if you've adjusted the Brightness and Contrast sliders, you can remove those changes using the Edit→Undo Brightness/Contrast command (⌘-Z).

The only catch is that you must back out of the changes one at a time. In other words, if you rotate a photo, crop it, then change its contrast, you must use the Undo command three times—first to undo the contrast change, then to un-crop, and finally, to un-rotate.

But once you leave Edit mode—either by closing the photo's window or by clicking the Done button—you lose the ability to undo your edits. At this point, the only way to restore your photo is to choose Photos→Revert to Original, which removes all the edits you've made to the photo since importing it.

Tip: If you prefer to edit your photos in the main iPhoto window (rather than in a separate window), you'll be tempted by the presence of a big fat Done button that you can click when you're finished editing. But if you plan to edit another photo, you can save yourself a click by not clicking on the Done button, and clicking instead on another thumbnail (at the top of the editing window). iPhoto saves the changes to your existing image, then opens the next one for you.

One-Click Fixups: The Rotate Button

Unless your digital camera has a built-in orientation sensor, iPhoto imports all photos in landscape orientation (wider than they are tall). The program has no way of knowing if you turned the camera 90 degrees when you took your pictures. Once you've imported the photos, just select the sideways ones and rotate them into position (if you didn't do so during your first slideshow, as described in Chapter 4).

Remember, you don't have to be in Edit mode to rotate photos. You can select thumbnail images when you're in Organize mode and then use one of the following methods to turn them right-side up:

- Choose Photos→Rotate→Counter Clockwise (or Clockwise).

- Click the Rotate button at the bottom of the main iPhoto window. (Option-click this button to reverse the direction of the rotation.)

- Press ⌘-R to rotate selected photos counter-clockwise, or Option-⌘-R to rotate them clockwise.

- Control-click (or right-click) a photo and choose Rotate→Clockwise (or Counter Clockwise) from the shortcut menu.

Tip: After importing a batch of photos, you can save a lot of time and mousing if you select all the thumbnails that need rotating first (by ⌘-clicking each, for example). Then use one of the rotation commands above to fix all the selected photos in one fell swoop.

Incidentally, clicking Rotate (or pressing ⌘-R) generally rotates photos counter-clockwise, while Option-clicking that button (Option-⌘-R) generally rotates them clockwise. If you want, you can swap these directions by choosing iPhoto→Preferences and changing the Rotate setting on the General pane of the dialog box.

Note: When you rotate an image saved in GIF format in iPhoto, the resulting rotated picture is saved as a JPEG file. The original GIF is stored unchanged in an Originals folder in the iPhoto Library folder (see Chapter 4).

Cropping

Think of iPhoto's cropping tool as a digital paper cutter. It neatly shaves off unnecessary portions of a photo, leaving behind only the part of the picture you really want.

You'd be surprised at how many photographs can benefit from selective cropping. For example:

- **Eliminate parts of a photo you just don't want.** This is a great way to chop your brother's ex-girlfriend out of an otherwise perfect family portrait, for example (provided she was standing at the end of the lineup).

- **Improve a photo's composition.** Trimming a photo allows you to adjust where your subject matter appears within the frame of the picture. If you inspect the professionally shot photos in magazines or books, for example, you'll discover that many pros get more impact from a picture by cropping tightly around the subject, especially in portraits.

- **Get rid of wasted space.** Huge expanses of background sky that add nothing to a photo can be eliminated, keeping the focus on your subject.

- **Fit a photo to specific proportions.** If you're going to place your photos in a book layout (Chapter 10) or turn them into standard size prints (Chapter 8), you may need to adjust their proportions. That's because there's a substantial discrepancy between the *aspect ratio* (length-to-width proportions) of your digital camera's photos and those of film cameras—a difference that will come back to haunt you if you order prints. The following discussion covers all the details.

UP TO SPEED

When Cropping Problems Crop Up

Remember that cropping always shrinks your photos. Remove too many pixels, and your photo may end up too small (that is, with a resolution too low to print or display properly).

Here's an example: You start with a 1600 x 1200 pixel photo. Ordinarily, that's large enough to be printed as a high-quality, standard 8 x 10 portrait.

Then you go in and crop the shot. Now the composition is perfect, but your photo measures only 800 x 640 pixels. You've tossed out nearly a million and a half pixels.

The photo no longer has a resolution (pixels per inch) high enough to produce a top-quality 8 x 10. The printer is forced to blow up the photo to fill the specified paper size, producing visible, jaggy-edged pixels in the printout. The 800 x 640 pixel version of your photo would make a great 4 x 5 print (if that were even a standard size print), but pushing the print's size up further noticeably degrades the quality.

Therein lies a significant advantage of using a high-resolution digital camera (5 or 6 megapixels, for example). Because each shot starts out with such a high resolution, you can afford to shave away a few hundred thousand pixels and still have enough left over for good-sized, high-resolution prints.

Moral of the story: Know your photo's size and intended use—and don't crop out more photo than you can spare.

How to Crop a Photo

Here are the steps for cropping a photo:

1. **Open the photo for editing.**

   You can use any of the methods mentioned earlier in this chapter.

2. **Make a selection from the Constrain pop-up menu, if you like (Figure 6-4).**

   The Constrain pop-up menu controls the behavior of the cropping tool. When the menu is set to None, you can draw a cropping rectangle of any size and proportions, in essence going freehand.

Figure 6-4:
When you crop a picture, you drag out (draw) a rectangle in any direction using the crosshair pointer to define the part of the photo you want to keep. (To deselect this area—when you want to start over, for example—click anywhere in the foggy area.)

Top: The three different cursor shapes you may see, depending on where you move the pointer: the + crosshair for the initial drag, the black double arrow when you're near a boundary (for reshaping), or the pointing-hand for sliding the entire rectangle around the photo.

Bottom: Once you've drawn the rectangle and clicked Crop, the excess margin falls to the digital cutting-room floor, thus enlarging your subject.

When you choose one of the other options in the pop-up menu, however, iPhoto constrains the rectangle you draw to preset proportions. It prevents you from coloring outside the lines, so to speak.

The Constrain feature is especially important if you plan to order prints of your photos (Chapter 8). When doing so, you'll notice that you can order prints only in standard photo sizes: 4 x 6, 5 x 7, 8 x 10, and so on. You may recall, however, that most digital cameras produce photos whose proportions are 4 to 3 (width to height). This size is ideal for DVDs and iPhoto books (Chapter 10), because your television and iPhoto book layouts use 4 to 3 dimensions, too—but it doesn't divide evenly into standard print photograph sizes.

That's why the Constrain pop-up menu offers you canned choices like 4 x 6, 5 x 7, and so on. Limiting your cropping to one of these preset sizes guarantees that your cropped photos will fit perfectly into Kodak prints. (If you don't constrain your cropping this way, Kodak—not you—will decide how to crop them to fit.)

___

Note: Even though the Constrain menu ensures the right proportions, it doesn't in any way guarantee that the total size of the final photos is adequate. See the box "When Cropping Problems Crop Up" on page 149 for more about properly sizing your photos.

___

Other crop-to-fit options in the Constrain menu let you crop photos for use as a desktop picture ("1024 x 768 [Display]," or whatever your actual monitor's dimensions are), as a 4 x 6-inch print, to fit into one of the Book layouts available in iPhoto's Book mode (Chapter 10), and so on.

___

Tip: Here's a bonus feature: the item in the Constrain pop-up menu called Custom. Inside the two text boxes that appear, you can type any proportions you want: 4 x 7, 15 x 32, or whatever your eccentric design needs call for.

___

As soon as you make a selection from this pop-up menu, iPhoto draws a preliminary cropping rectangle—of the proper dimensions—on the screen, turning everything outside it dim and foggy.

In general, this rectangle always appears in either landscape (horizontal) or portrait (vertical) orientation, according to the shape of the photo itself. If you've selected "4 x 3" (Book), you can reverse the orientation of the starter rectangle by opening the pop-up menu a second time and choosing Constrain as Portrait (or Constrain as Landscape).

___

Tip: Actually, there's a quicker way to rotate the selection from horizontal to vertical (or vice versa): Option-drag across the photo to draw a new selection rectangle, as described in the next step. The selection rectangle crisply turns 90 degrees.

___

Now, the cropping area that iPhoto suggests with its foggy-margin rectangle may, as far as you're concerned, be just right. In that case, skip to step 5.

More often, though, you'll probably want to give the cropping job the benefit of your years of training and artistic sensibility by *redrawing* the cropping area. Here's how:

3. **Click anywhere in the foggy area to get rid of the rectangle. Then position the mouse pointer (which appears as a crosshair) at one corner of your photo. Drag diagonally across the portion of the picture that you want to *keep*.**

   As you drag a rectangle across your photo, the portions *outside* of the selection—the part of the photo that iPhoto will eventually trim away—are dimmed out once again (Figure 6-4).

Tip: Even if you've turned on one of the Constrain options in step 2, you can override the constraining by pressing ⌘ after you begin dragging.

Don't worry about getting your selection perfect, since iPhoto doesn't actually trim the photo until you click the Crop button.

4. **Adjust the cropping, if necessary.**

   If the shape and size of your selection area are OK, but you want to adjust which part of the image is selected, you can move the selection area without redrawing it. Position your mouse over the selection so that the pointer turns into a hand icon. Then drag the existing rectangle where you want it.

   You can even change the *shape* of the selection rectangle after you've released the mouse button, thanks to an invisible quarter-inch "handle" that surrounds the cropping area. Move your cursor close to any edge or corner so that it changes to a + shape (near the corner) or a double-headed arrow (near the edge). Now you can drag the edge or corner to reshape the rectangle (see Figure 6-4).

   If you get cold feet, you can cancel the operation by clicking once anywhere outside the cropping rectangle (to remain in Edit mode), or by double-clicking anywhere on the photo (to return to thumbnails mode). Or, if the photo is open in its own window, just close the window.

Note: Despite its elaborate control over the relative dimensions of your cropping rectangle, iPhoto won't tell you its actual size, in pixels. Therefore, if you want to crop a photo to precise pixel dimensions, you must do the job in another program, like GraphicConverter or Photoshop Elements. (See page 171 for instructions on flipping into a different editing program.)

---

5. **When the cropping rectangle is just the way you want, click the Crop button.**

   Alternatively, Control-click (or right-click) the photo and choose Crop from the shortcut menu, or just press Return.

   If throwing away all those cropped-out pixels makes you nervous, relax. Remember that when you click Crop, iPhoto, behind the scenes, makes a safety copy of the original photo—a handy backup for the day you decide to revert back to the uncropped version, months or years later.

If you realize immediately that you've made a cropping mistake, you can choose Edit→Undo Crop Photo to restore your original.

If you have regrets *weeks* later, on the other hand, you can always select the photo and choose Photos→Revert to Original. After asking if you're sure, iPhoto promptly reinstates the original photo from its backup, discarding every change you've ever made.

Note: When you crop a photo, you're changing it in all albums in which it appears (Chapter 5). If you want a photo to appear cropped in one album but not in another, you must first duplicate it (highlight it and then choose Photos→Duplicate), then edit each version separately.

The Enhance Button

The Enhance button provides a simple way to improve the appearance of less-than-perfect digital photos. You click one button to make colors brighter, skin tones warmer, and details sharper (Figure 6-5). It's a lot like the Auto Levels command in Photoshop.

Figure 6-5:
The Enhance command works particularly well on photos that are slightly dark and that lack good contrast, like the original photo on the left. Using iPhoto's Brightness and Contrast sliders alone might have helped a little, but the Enhance button produces a faster and overall better result, as shown at right.

But if you want to know *exactly* what the Enhance button does, well, good luck. Apple guards that information like a top-secret meatloaf recipe.

What's clear is that the Enhance button analyzes the relative brightness of all the pixels in your photo and attempts to "balance" the image by dialing the brightness or contrast up or down and intensifying dull or grayish-looking color. In addition to this overall adjustment of brightness, contrast, and color, the program makes a particular effort to identify and bring out the subject of the photo. Usually, this approach at least makes pictures look somewhat richer and more vivid.

To enhance a photo, just click the Enhance button. (You'll find it on the bottom toolbar in any of iPhoto's three editing views.) That's it…there's nothing to select first, and no controls to adjust.

Tip: You can also Control-click (or right-click) a photo to choose Enhance from the shortcut menu.

Remember that iPhoto's image-correcting algorithms are just guesses at what your photo is supposed to look like. It has no way of knowing whether you've shot an overexposed, washed-out picture of a vividly colored sailboat, or a perfectly exposed picture of a pale-colored sailboat on an overcast day.

Consequently, you may find that Enhance has no real effect on some photos, and only minimally improves others. Remember, too, that you can't enhance just one part of a photo—only the entire picture at once. If you want to selectively adjust specific portions of a picture, you need a true photo-editing program like GraphicConverter or Photoshop Elements.

Tip: If using the Enhance command does improve your photo, but just not enough, you can click it repeatedly to amplify its effect—as many times as you want, really. However, applying Enhance more than three times or so risks turning your photo into digital mush.

If you go too far, remember that you can press ⌘-Z (or choose Edit→Undo) to backtrack. In fact, you can take back as many steps as you like, all the way back to the original photo.

In some cases, you'll need to do more than just click the Enhance button to coax the best possible results from your digital photos. You may have to tweak away with the Brightness and Contrast sliders, as explained later in this chapter.

Red-Eye

Let's say you snap a near-perfect family portrait: The focus is sharp, the composition is balanced, everyone's smiling. And then you notice it: Uncle Mitch, standing dead center in the picture, looks like a vampire bat. His eyes are glowing red, as though illuminated by the evil within.

You've been victimized by *red-eye,* a common problem in flash photography. This creepy possessed-by-aliens look has ruined many an otherwise-great photo.

Red-eye is actually light reflected back from your subject's eyes. The bright light of your camera's flash passes through the pupil of each eye, illuminating the blood-red retinal tissue at the back of the eye. This illuminated tissue, in turn, is reflected back into the camera lens. Red-eye problems worsen when you shoot pictures in a dim room, because your subject's pupils are dilated wider, allowing even more light from the flash to illuminate the retina.

Page 58 offers advice on avoiding red-eye to begin with. But if it's too late for that, and people's eyes are already glowing demonically, there's always iPhoto's Red-Eye tool. It lets you alleviate red-eye problems by digitally removing the offending red pixels.

Start by opening your photo for editing. Change the zoom setting, if necessary, so that you have a close-up view of the eye with the red-eye problem (Figure 6-6).

Now click the Red-Eye button. Use the crosshair pointer to click inside each red-tinted eye; with each click, iPhoto neutralizes the red pixels, painting the pupils solid black. Of course, this means that everybody winds up looking like they have black eyes instead of red ones—but at least they look a little less like the walking undead.

Figure 6-6:
Top: When you click the Red-Eye tool, a pop-up message informs you of the next step: Click carefully inside each affected eye. (If you don't see the Red-Eye tool, you may have to use the >> menu at the right end of the toolbar to find the Red-Eye command.)

Bottom: Truth be told, the Red-Eye tool doesn't know an eyeball from a pinkie toe. It just turns any red pixels black, regardless of what body part they're associated with. Friends and family members look more attractive–and less like Star Trek characters–after you touch up their phosphorescent red eyes with iPhoto.

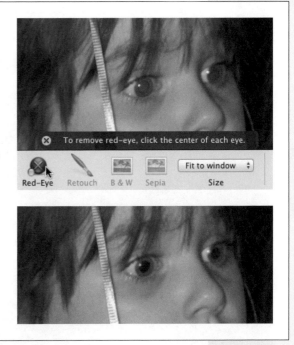

Retouching Freckles, Scratches, and Hairs

Sometimes an otherwise perfect portrait is spoiled by the tiniest of imperfections—a stray hair or an unsightly blemish, for example. Professional photographers, whether working digitally or in a traditional darkroom, routinely remove such minor imperfections from their final prints—a process known as *retouching,* for clients known as *self-conscious.*

iPhoto's Retouch brush lets you do the same thing with your own digital photos. You can paint away scratches, spots, hairs, or any other small flaws in your photos with a few quick strokes.

The operative word here is *small.* The Retouch brush can't wipe out a big blob of spaghetti sauce on your son's white shirt or completely erase somebody's mustache. It's intended for tiny fixups that don't involve repainting whole sections of a photo. (For that kind of photo overhaul, you need a dedicated photo-editing program.)

The Retouch brush works its magic by blending together the colors in the tiny area that you're fixing. It doesn't cover the imperfections you're trying to remove, but *blurs* them out by softly blending them into a small radius of surrounding pixels. You can see the effect in Figure 6-7.

Tip: The Retouch brush is particularly useful if your Photo Library contains traditional photographs that you've scanned in. You can use it to wipe away the dust specks and scratches that often appear on film negatives and prints, or those that are introduced when you scan the photos.

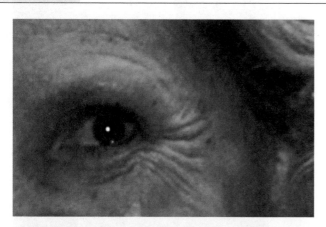

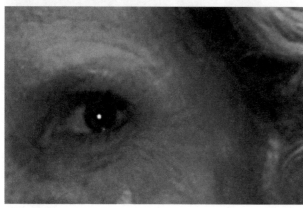

Figure 6-7:
The key to using the Retouch brush is to target small areas and use restraint so that you don't overblur the area you're working on. Notice how the Retouch brush was used on the original photo (top) to soften wrinkles around the eye and remove imperfections in the upper-left corner (bottom), like an application of digital Botox.

Using the Retouch Brush

The Retouch brush appears at the bottom of the window as soon as you open a photo for editing. You can also switch to it whenever you're in Editing mode, by Control-clicking (or right-clicking) a photo and choosing Retouch from the shortcut menu.

Once you've selected the Retouch brush, your pointer turns into a small crosshair with a hole in the middle. Using the center of the crosshair, target the imperfection and "paint" over it, using a series of short strokes to blend it with the surrounding portion of the picture (Figure 6-7). Don't overdo it: If you apply too much retouching, the area you're working on starts to look noticeably blurry and unnatural, as if someone smeared Vaseline on it.

Fortunately, you can use the Edit→Undo command (⌘-Z) to take back as many of your brush strokes as necessary.

Note: On high-resolution photos, it can take a moment or two for iPhoto to process each individual stroke of the Retouch brush. If you don't see any results, wait a second for iPhoto to catch up with you.

The Effects Palette

It's hard to imagine that Apple added this new iPhoto 6 feature because the masses were screaming for it, but never mind. It's here if you want it: a set of five photo effects (like black-and-white and Antique), plus three effects that soften a photo's borders.

Figure 6-8:
By clicking the Effects button while in editing mode, you can summon up a free-floating palette filled with nine different clickable effects, good for a solid 10 minutes of photo-editing fun.

Shown here is the Sepia effect.

To open this new palette, click the Effects icon shown in Figure 6-8. No matter which editing mode you're in (in-window, separate window, full-screen), the floating, tick-tack-toe–looking Effects palette appears (also shown in Figure 6-8).

There's nothing to it. Click a button to apply the appropriate effect to the photo in front of you:

- **B & W (Black and White), Sepia.** These tools drain the color from your photos. B & W converts them into moody grayscale images (a great technique if you're going for that Ansel Adams look); Sepia repaints them entirely in shades of antique brown (as though they were 1865 daguerreotypes).

Tip: If you don't have the strength to deal with the Effects palette just now, there's another way: Control-click (or right-click) the photo and choose the corresponding command from the shortcut menu.

- **Antique.** A heck of a lot like Sepia, but not quite as severe. Still gets light brownish, but preserves some of the original color—like, say, a photo from the 1940s.

- **Fade Color.** The colors get quite a bit faded, like a photo from the 1960s.

- **Current.** Click this center button to undo all the playing you've done so far, taking the photo back to the way it was when you first opened the Effects palette.

- **Boost Color.** Increases the color saturation, making colors look more vivid.

- **Matte.** This effect whites out the outer portion of the photo, creating an oval-shaped frame around the center portion.

- **Vignette.** Same idea as Matte, except that the image darkens toward the outer edges instead of lightening.

- **Edge Blur.** Same idea again, except instead of creating an oval of white or black around the photo, creates an out-of-focus oval. The main, central portion of the photo is left in focus.

Tip: You can click any of these effect buttons repeatedly to intensify the effect.

The Adjust Panel

For thousands of people, the handful of basic image-fixer tools described on the previous pages offer plenty of power. But power users don't like having to trot off to a program like Photoshop to make more advanced changes to their pictures, like fiddling with saturation (the intensity of colors) or sharpness.

That's where the Adjust panel comes in (Figure 6-9). It appears whenever you click the Adjust button in any of the editing views.

Note: Except for the Brightness and Contrast controls, the Adjust palette doesn't work unless your Mac has at least a G4 processor or something faster. And if you want to apply these effects to photos in the RAW format, you need Mac OS X 10.3.6 or later.

Now, before you let the following pages turn you into a tweak geek, here are some preliminary words of advice concerning the Adjust panel:

• **When to use it.** Plenty of photos need no help at all. They look fantastic right out of the camera. And plenty of others are ready for prime time after only a single click on the Enhance button described earlier.

The beauty of the Adjust panel, though, is that it permits infinite *gradations* of the changes that the Enhance button makes. For example, if a photo looks too dark and murky, you can bring details out of the shadows without blowing out the highlights. If the snow in a skiing shot looks too bluish, you can de-blue it. If the colors don't pop quite enough in the prize-winning soccer goal shot, you can boost their saturation levels.

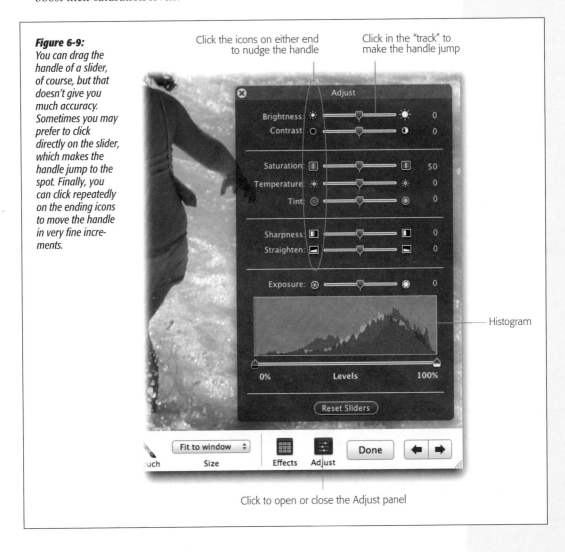

Figure 6-9:
You can drag the handle of a slider, of course, but that doesn't give you much accuracy. Sometimes you may prefer to click directly on the slider, which makes the handle jump to the spot. Finally, you can click repeatedly on the ending icons to move the handle in very fine increments.

Click the icons on either end to nudge the handle

Click in the "track" to make the handle jump

Histogram

Click to open or close the Adjust panel

In short, there are fixes the Adjust panel can make that no one-click magic button can touch.

- **How to play.** You can fiddle with an Adjust panel slider in any of three ways, as illustrated in Figure 6-9.

- **Backing out.** You can always apply the Undo and Revert to Original commands to work you perform with the Adjust panel. But the panel also has its own Reset Sliders button, which essentially means, "undo all the Adjust-panel changes I've made during this session."

Tip: The Reset Sliders button is also useful when you just want to play around with an image. You can make some adjustments, see how they look, then hit Reset Sliders before closing the window or clicking the Done button. In this case, iPhoto leaves the photo just as it was.

- **Moving on.** The Adjust panel is a see-through, floating entity that lives in a plane of its own. You can drag it anywhere on the screen, and—here's the part that might not occur to you—you can move on to a different photo without having to close the panel first. (Click another photo among the thumbnails at the top of the screen, for example, or click the big Previous and Next arrows at the bottom.)

Introduction to the Histogram

Learning to use the Adjust panel effectively involves learning about its *histogram,* the colorful little graph at the bottom of the panel.

The histogram is the heart of the Adjust palette. It's a self-updating visual representation of the dark and light tones that make up your photograph. If you've never encountered a histogram before, this all may sound a little complicated. But the Adjust palette's histogram is a terrific tool, and it'll make more sense the more you work with it.

Within each of the superimposed graphs (red, blue, green), the scheme is the same: The amount of the photo's darker shades appears toward the left side of the graph; the lighter tones are graphed on the right side.

Therefore, in a very dark photograph—a coal mine at midnight, say—you'll see big mountain peaks at the left side of the graph, trailing off to nothing toward the right. A shot of a brilliantly sunny snowscape, on the other hand, will show lots of information on the right, and probably very little on the left.

The best-balanced pictures have some data spread across the entire histogram, with a few mountain-shaped peaks here and there. Those peaks and valleys represent the really dark spots (like the background of a flash photo) and bright spots (a closeup face in that flash picture). Those mountains are fine, as long as you have some visual information in other parts of the histogram, too.

The histogram for a *bad* photo, on the other hand—a severely under- or overexposed one—has mountains all bunched at one end or the other. Rescuing those pictures involves spreading the mountains across the entire spectrum, which is what the Adjust palette is all about.

Three Channels

As noted on the previous page, the histogram actually displays three superimposed graphs at once. These layers—red, green, and blue—represent the three "channels" of a color photo.

When you make adjustments to a photo's brightness values—for example, when you drag the Exposure slider just above the histogram—you'll see the graphs in all three channels move in unison. Despite changing shape, they essentially stick together. Later, when you make color adjustments using, say, the Temperature slider, you'll see those individual channels move in different directions.

Exposure

Most of the sliders in the Adjust palette affect the histogram in some way. But where do you begin?

Here's a general suggestion: Make exposure adjustments first. In the simplest terms, the Exposure slider makes your picture lighter when you move it to the right and darker when you move it to the left.

Its effects differ slightly depending on which file format a photo has:

• When you're editing **JPEG** graphics (that is, most photos from most cameras), the Exposure slider primarily affects the middle tones of a photo (as opposed to the brightest highlights and darkest shadows). If you're used to advanced programs like Photoshop, you may recognize this effect as a relative of Photoshop's gamma controls. (Gamma refers to the middle tones in a picture.)

• When you're working with **RAW** files, however (page 87), Exposure is even more interesting. It actually changes the way iPhoto interprets the dark and light information that your camera recorded when it took the picture. A photographer might say that it's like changing the ISO setting before snapping the picture—except that now you can make this kind of change long *after* you snapped the shutter.

The Exposure slider demonstrates one of the advantages of the RAW format. In a RAW file, iPhoto has a lot more image information to work with than in a JPEG file. As a result, you can make exposure adjustments without sacrificing the overall quality of the photograph.

Watch the data on the histogram as you move the Exposure slider. Make sure you don't wind up shoving any of the "mountain peaks" beyond the edges of the Histogram box. If that happens, you're discarding precious image data; when you print, you'll see a loss of detail in the darks and lights.

The first step in fine-tuning a photo, then, is to drag the Exposure slider until the middle tones of the picture look acceptable to you (Figure 6-10). You can't add details that simply aren't there, but brightening a dark shadowy image, or deepening the contrast on a washed-out image, can coax out elements that were barely visible in the original photo.

If the dark and light areas aren't yet perfect, don't worry; you'll improve those areas next with the Levels control.

Adjusting the Levels

After you've spent some time working with the middle tones of your picture, you can turn your attention to the endpoints on the histogram, which represent the darkest and lightest areas of the photo.

If the mountains of your graph seem to cover all the territory from left to right, you already have a roughly even distribution of dark and light tones in your picture…so you're probably in good shape. But if the graph comes up short on either the left (darks) or the right (lights) side of the histogram, you might want to make an adjustment.

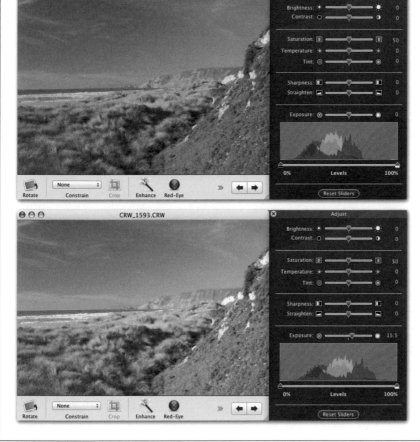

Figure 6-10:
Top: Here's a promising landscape shot that will serve as the basis for all the Adjust-panel manipulations described in this chapter. The camera was in Program mode, with Auto White Balance turned on. Unfortunately, you can see by looking at the histogram that much of the tonal information is bunched in the middle of the graph. As a result, the photo looks a little "flat," without much contrast.

Bottom: Step one in the repair job, then, is to move the Exposure slider a little to the right to improve the midtones. Because the graph in the histogram is elongated as a result, you've also improved the contrast.

To do so, drag the right or left pointer on the Levels slider *inward,* toward the base of the "mountain" (Figure 6-11). If you're moving the *right* indicator inward, for example, you'll notice that the whites become brighter, but the dark areas stay pretty much the same; if you drag the *left* indicator inward, the dark tones change, but the highlights remain steady.

Tip: Instead of dragging these handles inward, you may prefer to simply click the slider track itself at the outer base of the mountain. That's faster and gives you better control of the handle's landing point.

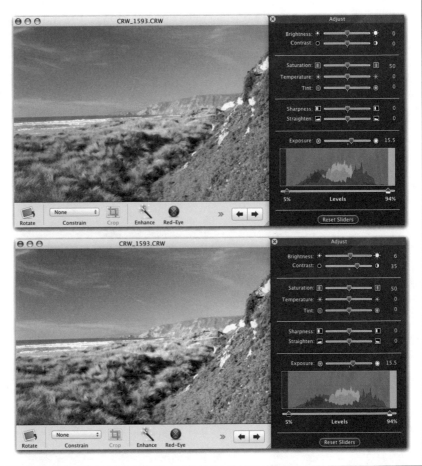

Figure 6-11:
Here's that same photo, now showing the results of the second Adjust-panel tweak: You've moved the endpoints of the Levels slider inward, boosting the shadow and highlight tones. In this case, moving them all the way to the point where they're touching the sides of the "mountains" would overdo it, creating too much contrast for this particular image. The base of the mountains is usually your target, but the visual results should always be your primary guide. Besides, you can always perform additional tweaks using the Brightness and Contrast sliders.

In general, you should avoid moving these endpoint handles inward *beyond* the outer edges of the mountains. Doing so adds contrast, but also throws away whatever data is outside the handles, which generally makes for a lower quality printout.

Brightness and Contrast Sliders

Once you've massaged the Exposure and Levels controls, the overall exposure for a picture usually looks pretty good. In effect, you've managed to create a full range of tones from dark to light.

So why, then, does Apple include Brightness and Contrast sliders, which govern similar aspects of your photo's appearance?

Reason #1: They've always been part of iPhoto, and millions of people are used to them.

Reason #2: They're not quite the same as Exposure and Levels.

Brightness

When you move the Brightness slider, you're making the *entire* image lighter or darker. You're literally sliding the entire histogram to the left or right without changing its

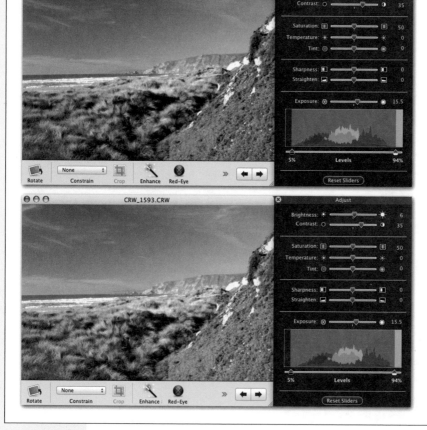

Figure 6-12:
Top: Moving the Contrast slider to the right added more punch. Instead of moving the Levels endpoints inward, the mountains moved outward toward the endpoints. Remember, the farther outward you stretch the graph, the more difference you create between the darkest and lightest tones.

Bottom: Once the contrast looks right, you can use the Brightness slider. This control moves the entire graph to the left or right of the histogram. Here, moving it a little to the right brightened the image—a good preparation for the color corrections that will follow in the next steps, because they usually darken the picture slightly.

shape (Figure 6-12). (Remember that the Exposure and Levels controls affect the midtones, highlights, and shadows independently.)

In other words, if the picture's contrast is already exactly as you want it, but the whole picture could use darkening or lightening, Brightness should be your tool of choice.

Contrast

The Contrast slider, on the other hand, does change the shape of the histogram. Contrast is the difference between the darkest and lightest tones in your picture. If you increase the contrast, you "stretch out" the shape of the histogram, creating darker blacks and brighter whites. When you decrease the contrast, you're scrunching the shape of the histogram inward, shortening the distance between the dark and light endpoints. Since the image data now resides in the middle area of the graph, the overall tones in the picture are duller. Photographers might call this look "flat" or "muddy."

Color Balance

If all you ever shoot is black-and-white photos, then Exposure/Levels or Brightness/Contrast may be all you ever need. If you're like most people, though, you're also concerned about a little thing called color.

Truth is, digital cameras (and scanners, too) don't capture color very accurately. Digital photos sometimes have a slightly bluish or greenish tinge, producing dull colors, lower contrast, and sickly-looking skin tones. In fact, the whole thing might have a faint green or magenta cast. Or maybe you just want to take color adjustment into your own hands, not only to get the colors right, but to also create a specific mood for an image. Maybe you want a snowy landscape to look icy blue so friends back home realize just how darned cold it was!

The Adjust panel offers three sliders that wield power over this sort of thing: Tint, Temperature, and Saturation. And it offers two ways to apply such changes: the manual way and the automatic way.

FREQUENTLY ASKED QUESTION

Battle of the Sliders

All right, first you said that I can create a well-balanced histogram with the Exposure and Levels sliders. Then you said that the Brightness and Contrast sliders do pretty much the same thing. So which should I use?

Photography forums everywhere are overflowing with passionate comments advocating one approach over the other.

The bottom line is, for most normal JPEG photos, you can use whichever you prefer, as long as you wind up creating a histogram whose peaks generally span the entire graph.

If you have no preference, you may as well get into the habit of using the Exposure and Levels sliders. One day, when you begin editing super-high-quality RAW files (page 87), you'll appreciate the clever way these controls interpret the data from the camera's sensors with virtually no loss of quality.

Manual Color Adjustment

These three sliders in the middle of the Adjust Palette provide plenty of color adjustment power. In particular, the Tint and Temperature sliders govern the *white balance* of your photo. (Different kinds of light—fluorescent lighting, overcast skies, and so on—lend different color casts to photographs. White balance is a setting that eliminates or adjusts the color cast according to the lighting.)

For best results, start at the bottom slider and work your way upward.

- **Tint.** Like the tint control on a color TV, this slider adjusts the photo's overall tint along the red-green spectrum. Nudge the slider to the right for a greenish tint, left for red. As you go, watch the histogram to see how iPhoto is applying the color.

Figure 6-13:
Moving the Tint slider just a little to the right removed a little red. Nudging the Temperature slider to the right warmed up the colors, making the grass more appealing. To make the colors more vibrant, move the Saturation slider to the right—not too far, unless you're after a Mars-like, otherworldly effect.

POWER USERS' CLINIC

Coping with Fluorescent Lighting

You can correct most pictures using the automatic gray-balance feature or the Tint, Temperature, and Saturation sliders described in this chapter. Some images, however, will frustrate you—no amount of tweaking will seem to make their colors look realistic. Pictures taken under fluorescent lighting can be particularly troublesome.

The problem with fluorescent bulbs is that they don't produce light across the entire color spectrum; there are, in effect, spectrum gaps in its radiance. Your best color-correction tool, the Temperature slider, only works on images where a full spectrum of light was captured, so it doesn't work well on fluorescently lit shots.

You'll have some luck moving the Tint slider to the left to remove the green cast of fluorescent lighting. But the overall color balance still won't be as pleasing as with pictures shot under full spectrum lighting, such as outside on a sunny day.

The best time to fix fluorescent-light color-balance problems, therefore, is at the moment you take the picture. Use the camera's flash, ensuring that it's the dominant light source, where possible. Its light helps to fill in the gaps in the fluorescent spectrum, making color correction much easier in iPhoto later.

Adjusting this slider is particularly helpful for correcting skin tones and compensating for difficult lighting situations, like pictures you took under fluorescent lighting (see Figure 6-13).

• **Temperature.** This slider, on the other hand, adjusts the photo along the blue-orange spectrum. Move the slider to the left to make the image "cooler," or slightly bluish. Move the slider to the right to warm up the tones, making them more orangeish—a particular handy technique for breathing life back into subjects that have been bleached white with a flash. A few notches to the right on the Temperature slider, and their skin tones look healthy once again!

Professional photographers *love* having color-temperature control; in fact, many photographers could handle the bulk of their image correction with nothing but the Exposure and Temperature controls.

• **Saturation.** Once you're happy with the color tones, you can increase or decrease their intensity with the Saturation slider. Move it to the right to increase the intensity and to the left for less saturation.

When you increase the saturation of a photo's colors, you make them more vivid; essentially, you make them "pop" more. You can also improve photos that have harsh, garish colors by dialing *down* the saturation, so that the colors end up looking a little less intense than they appeared in the original snapshot. That's a useful trick in photos whose *composition* is so strong that the colors are almost distracting.

(iPhoto's Enhance button automatically adjusts saturation when "enhancing" your photos, but provides no way to control the *degree* of its adjustment.)

Automatic Color Correction

Dragging the Tint, Temperature, and Saturation sliders by hand is one way to address color imbalances in a picture. But there's an easier way: iPhoto also contains a fairly secret feature that adjusts all three sliders *automatically.*

Technically, this tool is a *gray balance* adjuster. It relies on your ability to find, somewhere in your photo, an area of what *should* appear as medium gray. If you can adjust the color balance so that this spot does in fact appear the correct shade of gray, iPhoto can take it from there—it can adjust all of the other colors in the photo accordingly, shifting color temperature, tint, and saturation, all with a single click. This trick works amazingly well on some photos.

Before you use this feature, though, make sure you've already adjusted the overall *exposure* of the photo, using the steps described on the previous pages.

Next, scan your photo for an area that should appear as a neutral gray. Slightly dark grays are better for this purpose than bright, overexposed grays (Figure 6-14).

Once you've found such a spot, ⌘-click it.

Instantly, iPhoto automatically adjusts the color-balance sliders to balance the overall color of the photo. If you don't like iPhoto's correction, choose Edit→Undo and try again on a different gray area.

Thankfully, there's a good way to check how well iPhoto corrected the image. Find a spot in the picture that should be plain white. If it's clean (no green or magenta tint), you're probably in good shape; if not, undo the gray balance adjustment and try again on another area of gray.

Tip: If you're a portrait photographer, here's a trick for magically correcting skin tones. The key is to plan ahead by stashing a photographer's gray card somewhere in the composition that can be cropped out of the final print. Make sure the card receives about the same amount of lighting as the subject.

Later, in iPhoto, you can ⌘-click the gray card in the composition, and presto: perfect skin tones. Now crop out the gray card and make your print, grateful for the time you've just saved.

Figure 6-14:
Indoor settings often present tricky lighting situations. Here, this existing light shot has a greenish cast to it.

Bottom: By ⌘-clicking a gray midtone spot—in this case, the case of the inkjet printer on the desk (see the cursor?), you tell iPhoto, "This is supposed to be gray. Use this information to correct all the other colors appropriately."

If you don't like iPhoto's correction, choose Edit→Undo and try again on a different gray area.

Straightening

Many a photographer has remarked that it's harder to keep the horizon straight when composing images on a digital camera's LCD screen than when looking through an optical (eyepiece) viewfinder. Whether that's true or not, off-axis, tilted photos are a fact of photography, and especially of scanning—and a new iPhoto 6 feature makes fixing them incredibly easy. Figure 6-15 shows the secrets of the Straighten slider.

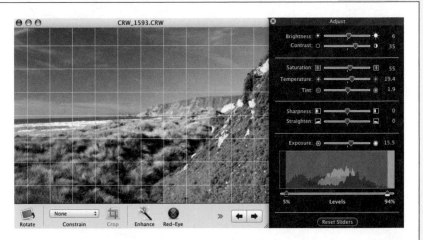

Figure 6-15:
The minute you click the Straighten slider, iPhoto superimposes a yellow grid on your picture. By moving the slider in either direction, you rotate the image. Use the yellow grid to help you align the horizontal or vertical lines in the photo.

Now, if you think about it, you can't rotate a rectangular photo without introducing skinny empty triangles at the corners of its "frame." Fortunately, iPhoto sneakily eliminates that problem by very slightly magnifying the photo as you straighten it. Now you're *losing* skinny triangles at the corners, but at least you don't see empty triangular gaps when the straightening is over.

In other words, the straightening tool isn't a free lunch. Straightening an image decreases the picture quality slightly (by blowing up the picture, thus lowering the resolution) and clips off tiny scraps at the corners. You have to view the before and after pictures side by side at high magnification to see the difference, but it's there.

So, as cool as the Straighten slider is, it's not a substitute for careful composition with your camera. However, it can help you salvage an otherwise wonderful image that's skewed. (And besides—if you lose a tiny bit of clarity in the straightening process, you can always apply a little sharpening afterward. Read on.)

Sharpening

The Sharpen command (see Figure 6-16) seems awfully tempting. Could technology really solve the problem of blurry, out-of-focus photos?

Um, no.

Instead, the Sharpen tool that now appears in iPhoto works by subtly increasing the contrast among pixels in your photo, which seems to enhance the crispness of the image. In pro circles, applying a soupçon of sharpening to a photo is a regular part of the routine.

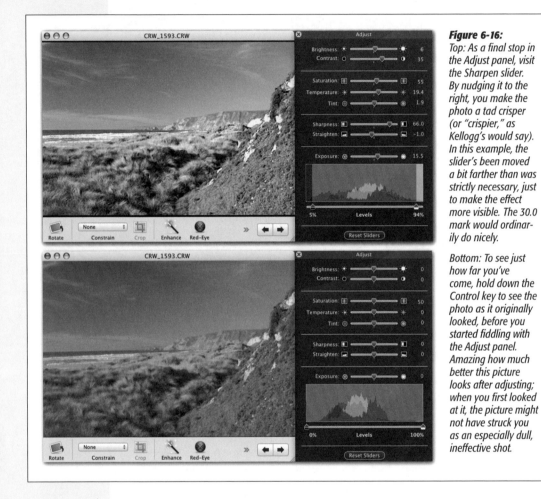

Figure 6-16:
Top: As a final stop in the Adjust panel, visit the Sharpen slider. By nudging it to the right, you make the photo a tad crisper (or "crispier," as Kellogg's would say). In this example, the slider's been moved a bit farther than was strictly necessary, just to make the effect more visible. The 30.0 mark would ordinarily do nicely.

Bottom: To see just how far you've come, hold down the Control key to see the photo as it originally looked, before you started fiddling with the Adjust panel. Amazing how much better this picture looks after adjusting; when you first looked at it, the picture might not have struck you as an especially dull, ineffective shot.

In iPhoto, move the Sharpen slider to the right to increase the sharpness, or to the left to soften the look.

Now, lest you think otherwise, too much sharpening can also ruin a photo, since, eventually, the pixels become grainy and weird-looking. Fortunately, Apple has mostly protected you from this sort of disaster by keeping both the effects and the side effects of the Sharpen control to a minimum. You can help matters by moving the slider in small increments.

Generally speaking, sharpening should be the last Adjust-panel adjustment you make to the picture. If you apply other corrections after sharpening, you may discover that you have to return and sharpen again.

Also, keep in mind that *softening* (or unsharpening) can be effective for portraits that are "too sharp," or for landscapes where you want to create a more dreamy effect. Sometimes applying just a little softening will smooth out skin tones and take the edge off the overall appearance of the portrait.

Beyond iPhoto

Thanks to the Adjust panel, iPhoto's editing tools have come a long, long way. There's a lot less reason now to invest in a dedicated editing program like Photoshop.

But that doesn't mean that there are *no* reasons left. The Auto Levels command (in Photoshop and Photoshop Elements) is still a better color-fixer than iPhoto's Enhance button. Photoshop-type programs are also necessary if you want to scale a photo up or down to specific pixel dimensions, superimpose text on a photo, combine several photos into one (a collage or montage), apply special-effect filters like Stained Glass or Watercolor, or adjust the colors in just a *portion* of the photo.

Photoshop is by far the most popular tool for the job, but at about $600, it's also one of the most expensive. Fortunately, you can save yourself some money by buying Photoshop Elements instead. It's a trimmed-down version of Photoshop with all the basic image-editing stuff and just enough of the high-end features. It costs less than $100, and a free trial version is available online.

Opening Photos in Other Programs

You can open a photo in a "real" editing program in any of several ways. First, you can install that program's icon on your Dock. (For example, drag the Photoshop icon onto the Dock from your Applications folder.)

Then, any time you want to edit a photo in Photoshop, drag its thumbnail image directly onto Photoshop's Dock icon. In fact, you can even drag several thumbnails at once to open all of them simultaneously.

Don't use Photoshop's File→Open command to open an iPhoto photo directly. You'll have to navigate through the oddly numbered folders of the labyrinthine iPhoto Library folder just to locate the picture you want.

Tip: When you edit a photo in another program, you're essentially going behind iPhoto's back; the program doesn't have a chance to make a safety copy of the original. Therefore, you're sacrificing your ability to use the Revert to Original command to restore your photo to its original state in case of disaster (page 172).

The sneaky workaround: Just make one tiny change to the photo *in iPhoto* before you drag its thumbnail onto another program's icon. Any small change, even rotating it all the way around, forces iPhoto to create a backup. Thereafter—whether you edit the photo in another program or not—you can restore the photo to its original condition at any time.

Setting up a default editing program

The drag-and-drop approach is fine if you *occasionally* want to open a photo in another program. But if you find yourself routinely editing your photos in another program, there's a much easier method: Just set up iPhoto to open your photos in that program automatically when you double-click. You set up this arrangement as follows:

1. **Choose iPhoto→Preferences. In the dialog box, click General. From the "Edit photo" pop-up menu, select "In application."**

   A standard Open dialog box appears so you can navigate to your favorite photo-editing program.

2. **Choose the program you want to use for editing, then click Open.**

   When you're done, close the Preferences window.

Now, whenever you double-click a thumbnail (or click the Edit button at the bottom of the screen), iPhoto fires up the designated editing program and uses *it* to open your photo.

One big advantage of this method is that it lets iPhoto track your editing activity—yes, even in other programs. iPhoto subsequently updates its thumbnail versions of your photos to reflect the changes. It also preserves the original versions of the photos you edit externally, so that you can later use the Revert to Original command if disaster should ever strike, as explained later in this chapter.

Freedom of choice

Sure, it's nice to be able to edit photos in external programs, but it's a lot of trouble to switch that feature on and off, since a trip to iPhoto→Preferences is involved every time. If you're like many photo fans, what you want is to use iPhoto's convenient editing features *most* of the time, ducking out to other programs only when you need more industrial-strength features.

Fortunately, iPhoto offers a trick that lets you switch to an external editor only on demand: If you Control-click (or right-click) a thumbnail, the shortcut menu offers you four choices: "Edit" (in the main iPhoto window), "Edit in separate window," "Edit using full screen," or "Edit in external editor." (The last option is available only if you've selected an editing program as described above.) No matter what your settings in Preferences may be, this route always gives you the choice of all four editing modes.

Reverting to the Original

iPhoto includes built-in protection against overzealous editing—a feature that can save you much grief. If you end up cropping a photo too much, cranking up the brightness of a picture until it seems washed out, or accidentally turning someone's lips black with the Red-Eye tool, you can undo all your edits at once with the Revert to Original command. Revert to Original strips away *every change you've ever made* since the picture arrived from the camera. It leaves you with your original, unedited photo.

The secret of the Revert to Original command: Whenever you use any editing tools, iPhoto—without prompting and without informing you—instantly makes a duplicate of your original file. With an original version safely tucked away, iPhoto lets you go wild on the copy. Consequently, you can remain secure in the knowledge that in a pinch, iPhoto can always restore an image to the state it was in when you first imported it.

Note: The unedited originals are stored in an Originals folder inside your Home→Pictures→iPhoto Library folder. The edited versions appear in a folder called Modified. (The Modified folder doesn't exist until you edit at least one photo.)

To restore an original photo, undoing all cropping, rotation, brightness adjustments, and so on, select a thumbnail of an edited photo or open the photo in Edit mode. Then choose Photos→Revert to Original, or Control-click (or right-click) a photo and choose the command from the shortcut menu. Now iPhoto swaps in the original version of the photo—and you're back where you started.

As noted earlier, iPhoto does its automatic backup trick whenever you edit your pictures (a) within iPhoto or (b) using a program that you've set up to open when you

In iPhoto, Less is More

I just finished editing a batch of photos, cropping each picture to a much smaller size. But now my iPhoto Library folder is taking up more space on my hard drive! How can making the photos smaller *increase the size of my photo collection? Shouldn't throwing away all those pixels have the opposite effect–shrinking things down?*

Your cropped photos do, in fact, take up much less space than they previously did. Remember, though, that iPhoto doesn't let you monkey with your photos without first stashing away a copy of each original photo, in case you ever want to use the Revert to Original command to restore a photo to its original condition.

So each time you crop a picture (or do any other editing) for the first time, you're actually creating a new, full-size file on your hard drive, as iPhoto stores both the original and the edited versions of the photo. Therefore, the more photos you edit in iPhoto, the more hard drive space your photo collection will occupy.

Incidentally, it's worth noting that iPhoto may be a bit over-zealous when it comes to making backups of your originals. The simple act of rotating a photo, for example, creates a backup (which, considering how easy it is to re-rotate it, you might not consider strictly necessary). If you've set up iPhoto to open a double-clicked photo in another program like Photoshop, iPhoto creates a backup copy even if you don't end up changing it in that external program.

If this library-that-ate-Cleveland effect bothers you, you might investigate the free program iPhoto Diet (available from the "Missing CD" page of *www.missingmanuals.com,* for example). One of its options offers to delete the backups of photos that have simply been rotated. Another option deletes perfect duplicates that iPhoto created when you opened those photos in another program without editing them.

There's even an option to delete *all* backups–a drastic measure for people who believe that their photos will never be better than they are right now.

double-click a picture. It does *not* make a backup when you drag a thumbnail onto the icon of another program. In that event, the Revert to Original command will be dimmed when you select the edited photo.

Bottom line: If you want the warmth and security of Revert to Original at your disposal, don't edit your pictures behind iPhoto's back. Follow the guidelines in the previous two paragraphs so that iPhoto is always aware of when and how you're editing your pictures.

Editing RAW Files

As noted in Chapter 4, iPhoto can handle the advanced photographic file format called RAW—a special, unprocessed file format that takes up a lot of space on your memory card but offers astonishing amounts of control when editing later on the Mac. (Also as noted in Chapter 4, the RAW format is available only on certain high-end cameras.)

Actually, iPhoto can do more than handle RAW files. It can even edit them...sort of.

iPhoto is, at its heart, a program designed to work with JPEG files. Therefore, when it grabs a RAW file from your camera, it instantly creates a JPEG version of it, which is what you actually see onscreen. The RAW file is there on your hard drive (deep within the labyrinth known as the iPhoto Library folder). But what you see onscreen is a JPEG interpretation of that RAW file. (This conversion to JPEG is one reason iPhoto takes longer to import RAW files from a camera than other kinds of files.)

This trick of using JPEG lookalikes as stand-ins for your actual RAW files has two important benefits. First, it lets you work with your photos at normal iPhoto speed, without the lumbering minutes of calculations you'd endure if you were working with the original RAW files. Second, remember that your iPhoto photos are also accessible from within iDVD, iMovie, iWeb, Pages, and so on—and these programs don't recognize RAW files.

So the question naturally comes up: What happens if you try to edit one of these RAW-file stunt doubles?

No problem. iPhoto accepts any changes you make to the JPEG version of the photo. Then, behind the scenes, it reinterprets the original RAW file, applying your edits; finally, it generates a new JPEG for you to view.

Outside RAW Image Editors

It's nice that iPhoto comes with more powerful editing tools, and it's nice that you can use them with your original RAW files. Nevertheless, iPhoto still isn't Photoshop, and it still doesn't offer every conceivable editing tool. So what happens if you want to edit one of your RAW files in another program, while still using iPhoto to organize them?

Here, life can get a little complicated—and a little different from the way iPhoto 5 handled things.

First, return to Preferences and click the Advanced tab (Figure 6-17). Turn on "Use RAW files with external editor." You've just told iPhoto that you want to work with RAW files in a different program, which is probably Adobe Camera Raw (the RAW-file editor that comes with Photoshop).

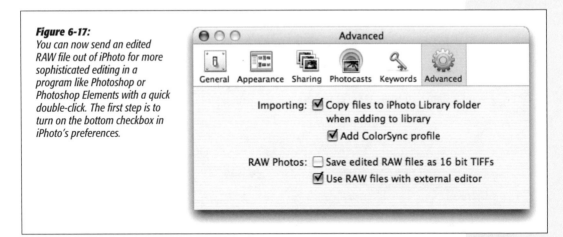

Figure 6-17:
You can now send an edited RAW file out of iPhoto for more sophisticated editing in a program like Photoshop or Photoshop Elements with a quick double-click. The first step is to turn on the bottom checkbox in iPhoto's preferences.

Now, if the RAW file is fresh off the camera and unedited, you *can* drag its thumbnail right out of iPhoto and onto the Dock icon of the external editing program (like Photoshop), just as in iPhoto 5. Photoshop responds by opening up the photo in its Adobe Camera Raw helper program. At this point, you now have Photoshop's advanced controls for super-fine-tuning that prize-winning shot.

But iPhoto 6 offers an easier twist: You can just double-click the thumbnail. Thanks to your setting in Preferences, it opens promptly in Adobe Camera Raw—no drag-and-drop necessary.

Just make sure you haven't *previously* edited the picture in iPhoto. If you have, iPhoto sends the edited JPEG file to Photoshop instead of the RAW file. You can correct this case of mistaken identity by using the Revert to Original command in iPhoto to strip away your previous edits, and *then* double-click the picture to open it in your external RAW editor.

But beware! You can't just click the Save button and smile, confident that you'll see the edited version of the photo when you return to iPhoto. (That may be how things work with JPEG graphics, as described earlier in this chapter—but not with RAW-format files.)

Instead, you must use Camera Raw's Save command to save the edited picture as a new file on your hard drive (see Figure 6-18, top). You'll most likely want JPEG because that's the easiest format to work with in all of the iLife applications. (And remember, your original RAW file is still tucked away safely in the iPhoto Library if you want to revisit it. All you have to do is double-click its thumbnail again, and you're right back in

Camera Raw.) When you click Save, a JPEG version of your edited RAW file is waiting for you on the Desktop. Click Done in Adobe Camera Raw to make it go away.

Your last step, believe it or not, is to reimport the edited JPEG file back into iPhoto. First, though, you may want to make sure that the file number (say, IMG_6268.jpg) is the same as the original RAW version in iPhoto (IMG_6268.CR2). Why? Because you're going to wind up with the edited JPEG and the original RAW file side by side in your library (Figure 6-18, bottom).

This roundabout method of editing a RAW file is not, ahem, the height of convenience. However, if you want to use high-level image controls for your RAW files, this is the path you must take, grasshoppa.

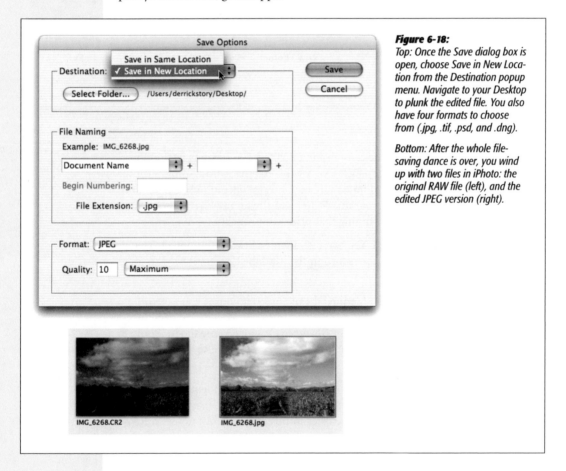

Figure 6-18:
Top: Once the Save dialog box is open, choose Save in New Location from the Destination popup menu. Navigate to your Desktop to plunk the edited file. You also have four formats to choose from (.jpg, .tif, .psd, and .dng).

Bottom: After the whole file-saving dance is over, you wind up with two files in iPhoto: the original RAW file (left), and the edited JPEG version (right).

Part Three:
Meet Your Public

3

The iPhoto Slideshow

i Photo's slideshow feature offers one of the world's best ways to show off your digital photos. Slideshows are easy to set up, they're free, and they make your photos look fantastic. This chapter details not only how to put together an iPhoto slideshow, but how to give presentations that make you and your photos look their absolute best.

About Slideshows

When you run an iPhoto slideshow, your Mac presents the pictures in full-screen mode—no windows, no menus, no borders—with your images filling every inch of the monitor. Professional transitions take you from one picture to the next, producing a smooth, cinematic effect. If you want, you can even add a musical soundtrack to accompany the presentation. The total effect is incredibly polished, yet creating a slideshow requires very little setup.

You always begin by selecting the pictures you want—by clicking an album or a Library icon, for example. At this point, you can kick off a slideshow in three different ways, each one offering a different degree of instant gratification and flexibility:

- **Option-click.** Option-click the Play button (▶) at the bottom of the iPhoto window (see Figure 7-1). A moment later, your Mac's screen fades to black, and then the show begins.

- **Instant.** If you click the Play button *without* the Option key, you get the Slideshow dialog box shown in Figure 7-2. It lets you choose the music for the slideshow, adjust its speed, and make other settings. Only when you dismiss the dialog box by clicking the Play button does the show begin.

• **Saved.** In the early days of iPhoto, each album had its own associated slideshow settings. The album was, in essence, the container for the slideshow.

That was a convenient approach, but not the most flexible. For example, it meant that if you wanted a slideshow that displayed only half the pictures in an album, you had to make a new album just for that purpose. It also meant that you couldn't create different slideshow versions of the same album's worth of photos—a 2-seconds-per-shot version for neighbors, for example, and a 10-seconds-per-shot version for adoring grandparents.

Figure 7-1:
The quickest way to kick off a slideshow in iPhoto is to Option-click the Play button in the main iPhoto window, shown here by the cursor (and the helpful tooltip label). While there's no keyboard shortcut, you can hit any key except the arrow keys and the Space bar to stop a show once it's running.

Now, therefore, iPhoto offers something called a *saved* slideshow, an icon that appears in the Source list and is saved forever, independent of any album. It works a lot like an album in many ways. For example, the photos inside are only "pointers" to the real photos in the Library, and you can drag them into any order you like. On the other hand, unlike an album, a saved slideshow contains special advanced controls for building a really sophisticated slideshow.

This chapter covers each of these three slideshow techniques in order.

Option-Click Slideshows

There's mercifully little to learn about instantaneous slideshows—the ones that begin when you Option-click the Play button beneath the Source list. The slideshow begins automatically and instantaneously. Each photo is displayed full screen for two seconds, and then softly fades out as the next one dissolves into view. The default musical soundtrack—J. S. Bach's *Minuet in G*—plays in the background.

As noted in Chapter 4, this is a terrific feature for reviewing photos you've just dumped into the Mac from the camera. In fact, that delicious moment when you first see the pictures at full-screen size—after having viewed them only on the camera's two-inch screen—is just what Apple's engineers had in mind when they designed the Play button.

Remember to wiggle your mouse during the slideshow when you want to summon iPhoto's onscreen control bar (page 93).

Option-Click
Slideshows

When you've had enough, click the mouse or press almost any key to end the show and return to the iPhoto window. (Otherwise, iPhoto will run the show in a continuous loop forever.)

Finish the show by clicking the mouse.

Note: The Play button generally appears at the lower-right corner of the iPhoto toolbar (at the bottom of the screen). If the toolbar is full of buttons, the Play button may not fit. In that case, you can either click the >> button to see the Play command, or you can get rid of some of the buttons on your toolbar, using the View→Show in Toolbar commands.

Which Photos

Among the virtues of this slideshow type is the freedom you have to choose which pictures you want to see. For example:

- If no photos are selected, iPhoto exhibits all the pictures currently in the photo-viewing area, starting with the first photo in the album, book, or Photo Library.

  Most people, most of the time, want to turn one *album* into a slideshow. That's easy: Just click the album before starting the slideshow. It can be any album you've created, a smart album, the Last Roll album, or one of iPhoto's built-in monthly or yearly albums. As long as no individual pictures are selected, iPhoto will reveal all the pictures in the album currently open.

Tip: You can also create an Option-click or instant slideshow from multiple albums. That is, you can select more than one album simultaneously (by ⌘-clicking them); when you click Play, iPhoto creates a slideshow from all of their merged contents, in order.

- If one photo is *selected*, iPhoto uses that picture as its starting point for the show, ignoring any that come before it. Of course, if you've got the slideshow set to loop continuously, iPhoto will eventually circle back to display the first photo in the window.
- If you've selected more than one picture, iPhoto includes *only* those pictures.

Tip: If a slideshow icon (described momentarily) is highlighted in the Source list, you don't need the Option key to begin a slideshow immediately. Use the Option key only if an album or a batch of photos are selected.

Photo Order

iPhoto displays your pictures in the same order you see them in the photo-viewing area. In other words, to rearrange your slides, drag the thumbnails around within their album. Just remember that you can't drag pictures around in the Photo Library, a smart album, the Last 12 Months collection, or the Last Roll folder—only within a photo album.

Note: If iPhoto appears to be shamelessly disregarding the order of your photos when running a slideshow, it's probably because you've got the "Present slides in random order" option turned on in the Slideshow dialog box, as described in the following section.

Instant Slideshows

An *instant* slideshow, for the purposes of this book, is one that you begin by clicking the triangular Play button beneath the Source list *without* the Option key. It makes the Slideshow dialog box appear, so that you can make a few quick changes to the slideshow settings. (Slide selection and slide sequence, as described in the previous paragraphs, work the same way.)

The Slideshow dialog box has two panels—Settings and Music—as shown in Figure 7-2. In iPhoto 6, you have more ways than ever to customize your slideshow:

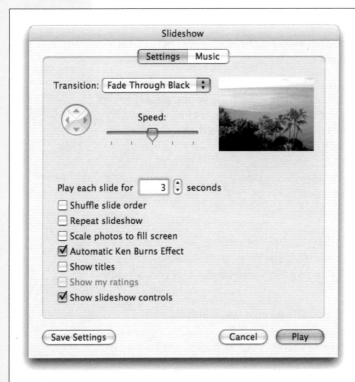

Figure 7-2:
The Slideshow dialog box is where you set slideshow timing for each show. You can set it to go as fast as 1 second per slide, or bump the number up to 60 seconds each for a very leisurely presentation. (You can type a number larger than 60 in the "Play each slide for…" field, but iPhoto will ignore you. It refuses to spend any more than one minute on each shot, no matter how good a photographer you are.)

Using the pop-up menu and Speed slider at the top of this dialog box, you can choose from 13 transition effects and decide how quickly you want them to go by.

Transitions

You can choose from 13 different types of transition effects between slides—for example, the crossfade or *dissolve,* in which one slide gradually fades away as the next "fades in" to take its place. Here's a summary:

- **None.** An abrupt switch, or simple cut, to the following image.

- **Cube.** Imagine that your photos are pasted to the sides of a box that rotates to reveal the next one. If you've ever used the Fast User Switching feature introduced in Mac OS 10.3, you've got the idea.

- **Dissolve.** This classic crossfade should be familiar to users of previous versions of iPhoto or the screen saver feature in Mac OS X.

- **Droplet.** This wild effect resembles animated, concentric ripples expanding from the center of a pond—except that a new image forms as the ripples spread.

- **Fade Through Black.** After each slide has strutted and fretted its time upon the stage, the screen fades momentarily to black before the next one fades into view. The effect is simple and clean, like an old-fashioned living-room slideshow. Along with Dissolve, you should consider this effect one of the most natural and least distracting choices.

- **Flip.** The first photo seems to flip around, revealing the second photo pasted onto its back.

- **Mosaic Flip Large, Mosaic Flip Small.** The screen is divided into several squares, each of which rotates in turn to reveal part of the new image, like puzzle pieces turning over. (The two options refer to two sizes of the puzzle pieces.)

- **Page Flip.** Apple's just showing off here. The first photo's lower-right corner actually peels up like a sheet of paper, revealing the next photo "page" beneath it.

- **Push, Reveal, Wipe.** Three variations of "new image sweeping onto the screen." In Push, Photo A gets shoved off the other side of the screen as Photo B slides on. In Reveal, Photo A slides off, revealing a stationary Photo B. And in Wipe, Photo A gets covered up as Photo B slides on.

- **Twirl.** Photo A literally spins, furiously, shrinking to a tiny dot in the middle of the screen—and then Photo B spins onscreen from that spot. The whole thing feels a little like the spinning-newspaper effect used to signify breaking news in old black-and-white movies.

In most cases, choosing a transition effect makes two additional controls "light up" just below the pop-up menu:

- **Direction.** Determines the direction the new image enters from. Choose Right to Left, Top to Bottom, or vice versa in both cases. (Most people find left to right the most comfortable way to experience a transition, but a slow top-to-bottom wipe is pleasant, too.)

- **Speed.** Move the slider to the right for a speedy transition, or to the left for a leisurely one. Take into account your Timing setting, described below. The less time your photo is onscreen, the better off you are with a fast transition, so that your audience has time to see the picture before the next transition starts. However, moving the Speed slider *all* the way to the right produces a joltingly fast change.

Slide Timing

If left to its own devices, iPhoto advances through your pictures at the rate of one photo every 3 seconds. If that seems too brisk or too slow, you can simply change the rate.

In the Slideshow dialog box, use the "Play each slide for __ seconds" controls to specify a different interval, as shown in Figure 7-2.

Tip: You can also adjust the speed *during* the slideshow, just by pressing the up or down arrow keys. Behind the scenes, iPhoto adjusts the number of seconds in the Slideshow dialog box accordingly.

Shuffle Slide Order

An iPhoto slideshow normally displays your pictures in the order they appear in the photo-viewing area. But if you'd like to add a dash of surprise and spontaneity to the proceedings, turn on the "Shuffle slide order" checkbox. iPhoto will then shuffle the pictures into whatever order it pleases.

Repeat Slideshow

When iPhoto is done running through all your photos in a slideshow, it ordinarily starts playing the whole sequence from the beginning again. If you want your photos to play just once through, turn off the "Repeat slideshow" checkbox.

Scale Photos to Fill Screen

If any photos in your slideshow don't match your screen's proportions, you may want to turn on "Scale photos to fill screen." For example, if your slideshow contains photos in portrait orientation—that is, pictures taken with the camera rotated—iPhoto fills up the unused screen space on each side with vertical black bars.

Turning on "Scale photos" makes iPhoto enlarge the picture so much that it completely fills the screen. This solution, however, comes at a cost: Now the top and bottom of the picture are lost beyond the edges of the monitor.

When the middle of the picture is the most important part, this option works fine. If the black bars bother you, the only other alternative is to crop the odd-sized pictures in the slideshow album so that they match your monitor's shape. (See "Cropping" on page 149.)

Note: This option doesn't mean "Enlarge smaller photos to fill the screen"; iPhoto always does that. This option affects only photos whose *proportions* don't match the screen.

Automatic Ken Burns Effect

Apple first introduced what it calls the "Ken Burns effect" in iMovie, not iPhoto. It's a special effect designed to address the core problem associated with using still photos in a movie—namely, that they're *still!* They just sit there without motion or sound, wasting much of the dynamic potential of video.

For years, professional videographers have addressed the problem using special sliding camera rigs that produce gradual zooming, panning, or both, to bring photographs to life.

Among the most famous practitioners of this art is Ken Burns, the creator of PBS documentaries like *The Civil War* and *Baseball*—which is why Apple, with Burns' permission, named the feature after him.

And now your own humble slideshows can have that graceful, animated, fluid Ken Burns touch. No photo ever just sits there motionless on the screen. Instead, each one flies gracefully inward or outward, sliding and zooming.

It's a great effect, but it can occasionally backfire, too. Every now and then, for example, the actual subject of the photo won't be centered, or the photo won't make it completely onto the screen before the next one begins to zoom on. (One of the virtues of the *saved* slideshow, described below, is that *you* control where the Ken Burns panning and zooming begins and ends.)

Show Titles

Show titles? Sure—*Fiddler on the Roof! West Side Story! Cats!*

Just kidding.

As noted on page 121, every photo in your collection can have a name—a title, in other words. If you turn on this option, iPhoto superimposes each photo's title during the slideshow in a small white-on-black box in the upper-left corner of the screen.

Needless to say, the cryptic file names created by your digital camera (IMG00034.jpg) usually don't add much to your slideshow. But if you've taken the time to give your photos helpful, explanatory names ("My dog age 3 mos"), then by all means turn on the "Show titles" checkbox.

Show My Ratings

As described on page 135, you can differentiate your stunning award-winners from the photographic dogs by adding ratings to each, on a one-to-five-star scale. If you turn on this option, iPhoto superimposes a small ratings bar on the bottom of each slideshow picture. (Unfortunately, you can't change the rating using this mini-bar, since it's for display purposes only. Of course, a quick mouse wiggle summons the full-blown control bar, complete with its own star-rating panel that you *can* change.)

Note: The control bar and the star-rating panel occupy the same space near the bottom of the slideshow "canvas," so they can't both be onscreen at the same time. That's why the "Show my ratings" checkbox is grayed out whenever "Show slideshow controls" is turned on.

Show Slideshow Controls

You can always summon iPhoto's new onscreen control bar by twitching the mouse during a slideshow; then, if a few seconds go by without any mouse activity, the bar politely fades away again.

If you turn on "Show slideshow controls," however, then the control bar appears automatically every time this slideshow begins—no mouse wiggling required—and remains onscreen all the time.

Music: Soundtrack Central

Perhaps more than any other single element, *music* transforms a slideshow, turning your ordinary photos into a cinematic event. When you pair the right music with the right pictures, you do more than just show off your photos; you create a mood that can stir the emotions of your entire audience. So if you really want your friends and family to be transfixed by your photos, add a soundtrack.

That's especially easy if, like many Mac OS X fans, you've assembled a collection of your favorite music in iTunes, the free MP3-playing software that comes with every Mac. (It's also included with the $80 iLife package, or you can download it from *www.apple.com.*)

For the background music of an iPhoto slideshow, you have the choice of an individual song from your iTunes Library or an entire *playlist.* Gone are the days of listening to the same tune repeating over and over again during a lengthy slideshow—a sure way to go quietly insane (unless, of course, you *really* like that song).

The possibilities of this new feature are endless, especially combined with iPhoto's smart albums feature. You can create a smart album that contains, say, only photos of your kids taken in December, and give it a soundtrack composed of holiday tunes, created effortlessly using a smart playlist in iTunes. Instant holiday slideshow!

Your first iPhoto slideshow is born with a ready-to-use soundtrack—J. S. Bach's *Minuet in G.* In fact, Apple sends iPhoto to you equipped with two Bach classics—the *Minuet in G* and *Jesu, Joy of Man's Desiring.* They're listed in the Sample Music category.

Not to knock Bach, but it's fortunate that you're not limited to two of his greatest hits. To switch to a soundtrack of your own choosing, click the Music button at the top of the Slideshow dialog box (Figure 7-2). If you use iTunes, every track in your iTunes Library automatically appears here. You can search and sort through your songs and playlists, just as though you were in iTunes itself.

To get started, click the Music button near the top of the Slideshow dialog box. As shown in Figure 7-3, a folder called Sample Music appears at the top, containing the two Bach pieces mentioned above. A second category, called GarageBand, appears if you've used GarageBand to create musical masterpieces of your own. Finally, if you have songs of your own in iTunes, click the iTunes flippy triangle (and then click Library) to access them.

Your iTunes playlists appear at this point, too. (For iTunes songs, a playlist represents what an album is in iPhoto: a hand-picked subset of the larger collection.) In other words, you can use this list either to select an entire playlist to use as your soundtrack, or to call up a playlist for the purpose of listing the individual songs in it, thereby narrowing your search for the one song you seek.

- To listen to a song before committing to it as a soundtrack, click its name in the list and then click the triangular Play button (▶). (Click the same button, darkened during playback, when you've heard enough.)

Figure 7-3:
The Music tab of the Slideshow dialog box lets you choose a playlist (or your entire iTunes Library). By clicking the column headings, you can sort the list by Song, Artist, or Time. You can also use the Search box, as shown here, to pinpoint an individual song.

If you have a long slideshow, use the list to choose an iTunes playlist rather than an individual song. iTunes will repeat the song (or playlist) for as long as your slideshow lasts.

- To use an entire playlist as a soundtrack for your slideshow, select it from the list. At slideshow time, iPhoto will begin the slideshow with the first tune in the playlist and continue through all the songs in the list before starting over.

- To use an individual song as a soundtrack, click its name in the list. That song will now loop continuously for the duration of the slideshow.

- Rather than scroll through a huge list, you can locate the tracks you want by using the capsule-shaped Search field below the song list. Click in the Search field, and then type a word (or part of a word) to filter your list. iPhoto searches the Artist, Song, and Album fields of the iTunes Library and displays only the matching entries. To clear the search and view your whole list again, click the X in the search field.

- Click one of the three headers—Artist, Song, or Time—to sort the iTunes music list alphabetically by that header.

- You can also change the arrangement of the three columns by grabbing the headers and dragging them into a different order.

Once you've settled on (and clicked) an appropriate musical soundtrack for the currently selected album, click Save Settings (to memorize that choice without starting the slideshow) or Play (to begin the slideshow right now). From now on, that song or playlist will play whenever you run a slideshow from that album. (It also becomes the *proposed* soundtrack for any new slideshows you create.)

Alternatively, if you decide you don't want any music to play, turn off the "Play music during slideshow" checkbox above the list.

Note: You can't select multiple songs from the song list in the Slideshow dialog box. If you have in mind a group of several songs that would make a perfect backdrop for your slideshow, the solution is to create a new playlist in iTunes, taking care to drag into it the desired songs from your Music Library, in the order that you want them to play. Switch back to iPhoto, and choose that playlist from the pop-up menu in the Slideshow dialog box (see Figure 7-3).

Different Shows, Different Albums

You can save different slideshow settings for each icon in your Source list.

To save settings for a specific photo album, for example, first choose the album from the Source list, then click the Slideshow icon in the lower pane of the iPhoto window to open the Slideshow dialog box. Pick the speed, order, repeat, and music settings you want, then click Save Settings. The settings you saved will automatically kick in each time you launch a slideshow from that album.

Tip: Thereafter, you can Option-click the Play button to start the show without interruption by the dialog box; iPhoto recreates the show just the way you had it last.

Saved Slideshows

iPhoto 6 also offers *saved* slideshows, each of which appears as an icon in your Source list. As noted earlier, the beauty of this system is that you can tweak a slideshow to death—you can even set up different transition and speed settings for *each individual slide*—and then save all your work as an independent clickable icon, ready for playback whenever you've got company.

The key to all of this is the Slideshow icon at the bottom of the iPhoto window (Figure 7-4). It tosses you into the new Slideshow editing mode, which has some features of Edit mode and some features of regular old thumbnail-organizing mode.

Here's how you create and fine-tune a saved slideshow:

1. **Select the photos you want to include.**

   You can select either a random batch of slides (using any of the techniques described on page 106) or an icon in the Source list (like an album or book).

Tip: By Shift-clicking or ⌘-clicking, you can actually select several icons in the Source list simultaneously. When you proceed to step 2, iPhoto will intelligently merge their photo contents into one glorious slideshow.

2. **Click the Slideshow button beneath the photo-viewing area.**

   Thunder rumbles, the lights flicker—and you wind up in the slideshow editing mode shown in Figure 7-4. At the same time, a new icon appears in the Source list, with the word "Slideshow" tacked onto the name. (The icon looks like a little pile of actual slides.)

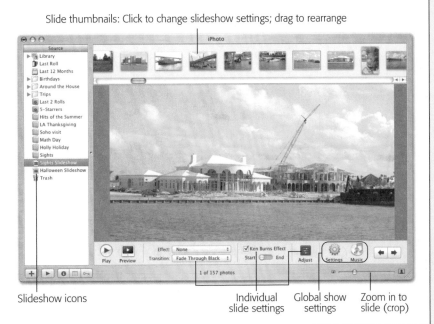

Figure 7-4:
In the new slideshow editor, the window shape is designed to mimic your Mac's monitor shape (or whatever screen proportions you've specified in the Settings box); that's why gray bars may appear. Some of the settings affect the entire slideshow, and some affect only the currently displayed photo, as identified here.

Slide thumbnails: Click to change slideshow settings; drag to rearrange

Slideshow icons

Individual slide settings

Global show settings

Zoom in to slide (crop)

3. **Choose a playback order for your pictures.**

   The trick here is to drag the thumbnails horizontally at the top of the window. Don't forget that you can move these en masse, too. For example, click slide #1, Shift-click slide #3, and then drag the three selected thumbnails as a group to a different spot in the lineup.

4. **By clicking the Settings and Music buttons, set up the global playback options.**

   That is, set up the preferences will affect *all* slides in the show (like timings and transitions), using the controls at the bottom of the window. You can read about what these controls do in the next section.

5. **If you like, walk through the slides one at a time, taking the opportunity to set up their individual characteristics.**

   For example, you can choose one slide to linger longer on the screen, another to dissolve (rather than wipe) into the next picture, and so on. These options, too, are described below.

6. **Preview the show.**

   If you click the Preview button, iPhoto plays a quick, miniature, abbreviated slideshow. It's only two slides long, featuring the currently selected slide (in the thumbnails up top) and whatever follows it. The idea is that you can judge the timing of the currently selected slide, as well as its transition into the next one. (There's no music, and the entire thing plays right in the editing window instead of filling your screen.)

7. **Roll it!**

   When everything looks ready, click the Play button (the big one, next to Preview) to play the actual slideshow.

When it's over, you can do all the usual things with the slideshow icon that now resides in your Source list:

- **Delete it.** Drag it onto the iPhoto Trash icon, as you would an album. When you're asked if you're sure, click Delete or press the Return key.

- **File it away.** Drag it into an iPhoto folder (page 119) to keep it organized with the related albums and books.

- **Rename it.** Double-click its icon and then type away.

- **Edit it.** Click its icon and then change the bottom-of-screen controls.

Global Settings

As indicated by the preceding steps, you can make two kinds of changes to a saved slideshow: global ones (which affect all slides) and individual ones.

Most of the global options are hiding behind the Settings and Music buttons, which summon the two dialog boxes shown in Figure 7-5.

The Music dialog box

The Music dialog box should look familiar; it's identical to the dialog box shown in Figure 7-3. Here's where you choose the music that will accompany your slideshow, as described on page 186.

The Settings dialog box

The Settings button, however, brings up a dialog box that only *seems* familiar (Figure 7-5, top right). It contains many of the same options described on pages 182 through 188 (transition style, slide duration, Ken Burns effect, choice of music track or playlist, options to show your photos' titles and ratings, and so on).

In this incarnation, though, you get a few new options. First, iPhoto wants to know how it should handle slideshows that aren't exactly the same length as the music you've selected for their soundtracks. Your options are "Repeat music during slideshow" (loops the music as necessary to fit the slides) or "Fit slideshow to music" (plays the music only once, but squeezes or stretches the slides' time on the screen to fit the music).

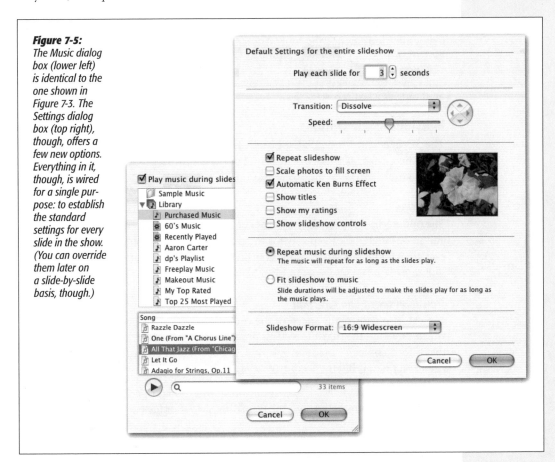

Figure 7-5:
The Music dialog box (lower left) is identical to the one shown in Figure 7-3. The Settings dialog box (top right), though, offers a few new options. Everything in it, though, is wired for a single purpose: to establish the standard settings for every slide in the show. (You can override them later on a slide-by-slide basis, though.)

Second, you get a Slideshow Format pop-up menu. Here, you can tell iPhoto what *shape* the screen will be.

Now, that may strike you at first as a singularly stupid statement; after all, doesn't the Mac know what shape its own screen is? But there's more to this story: Remember that you can build slideshows that aren't intended to be played on your screen. You might want to export a slideshow to play on other people's screens, or even on their TV sets, by burning the slideshow to a DVD. That's why this pop-up menu offers three choices: Current Display; 4:3 iDVD, TV (that is, a standard squarish TV set); and 16:9 Widescreen (for high-definition TV sets and other rectangular ones).

In any case, the changes you make here affect *all* photos in the slideshow. Click OK when you're done, confident in the knowledge that you can always override these settings for individual slides.

The Effect pop-up menu

This pop-up menu lists three choices: None, Black and White, and Sepia (that is, brownish, old-fashioned monochrome). You could argue that Black and White makes a slideshow look artsier and more Ansel Adamsish, and that Sepia makes the pictures look more nostalgic and old-fashioned.

You could also argue that both of these options are pretty gimmicky and should be used only as a last resort.

Individual-Slide Options

The Settings and Music dialog boxes offer plenty of control, but the changes you make there affect *all* slides in the show. For the first time, though, iPhoto 6 also offers control over *individual* slides. For example:

Transition

The options in this pop-up menu are the different crossfade effects (Cube, Dissolve, and so on) that you can specify for the transition from one slide to another. (Whatever you choose here governs the transition *out* of the currently selected slide; every slideshow *begins* with a fade in from black.)

Transition speed and direction

You can also control the speed of the transitions on a slide-by-slide basis, and even which direction the transition effect proceeds across the screen (for transition styles that offer a choice). Because Apple figures this isn't the sort of control most people need every day, it hid these controls away.

To see them, click the black Adjust button shown in Figure 7-6. Dragging the Speed slider left or right gets through the transition slower or faster.

Tip: The idea behind the design of the strangely see-through Adjust panel is that you can leave it open. You can park it anywhere onscreen as you work through the slides in your show. Simply put, as you click a new slide, the Adjust panel changes to reflect whatever settings are in place for that photo. In other words, don't waste your time closing and reopening it.

Slide timing

As you know, the Settings dialog box (Figure 7-5) is where you specify how long you want each slide to remain onscreen—in general. But if you want to override that setting for a few particularly noteworthy shots, the Adjust panel (Figure 7-6) is once again the solution.

With the specially blessed photo on the screen before you, summon the Adjust panel (click the Adjust button, if the panel isn't already open). Use the "Play this slide for __ seconds" control to specify this slide's few seconds of fame.

Tip: If you click the Reset to Defaults button in the Adjust panel, iPhoto wipes out any individual-slide customizations. It then reapplies your global transition and slide-timing settings to the selected photo.

Cropping and zooming

Here's a totally undocumented feature: You can choose to present only *part* of a photo in a slideshow, in effect cropping out portions of it, without actually touching the original.

To enlarge the photo (thus cropping out its outer margins), just drag the Size slider at the lower-right corner of the iPhoto window. Whatever photo size you create here is how it will appear during the slideshow.

What you may not realize, though, is that you can also drag *inside* the picture itself to shift the photo's position onscreen. Between these two techniques—sizing and sliding—you can set up a very specific portion of the photo. (Heck, you could even present the photo *twice* in the same slideshow, revealing half of it the first time, half of it the next.)

Figure 7-6:
The Adjust panel offers some less frequently used individual-slide settings. For example, it lets you change the speed of a transition effect and the amount of time an individual slide remains onscreen. (The Transition pop-up menu here is identical to the one at the bottom of the iPhoto window.)

Click here to open or close the Adjust panel

The Ken Burns Effect checkbox

If you flip back a few pages, you'll be reminded that the Ken Burns effect is a graceful, panning, zooming effect that brings animation to the photos of your slideshow, so that they float and move instead of just lying there.

Figure 7-7:
The idea behind the Ken Burns effect is that you set up the start and end points for the gradual zooming/panning effect. iPhoto, meanwhile, will automatically supply the in-between frames, producing a gradual shift from the first position to the second. In this case, the Ken Burns effect lets you save the "punch line" of this story-telling photo for the end of its time onscreen.

Top: Click Start. Use the Size slider (lower right) to magnify the photo, if you like. Once you've magnified it, you can drag inside the photo to reposition it inside the "frame" of your screen.

Bottom: Click End. Once again, use the Size slider and then drag inside the photo, if you like, to specify the final degree of zoom and movement. In this shot, you can see the tiny "grabbing hand" cursor that appears whenever your mouse wanders into the magnified-photo area.

You'll also be reminded that when you apply the effect to an entire slideshow, you have no control over the pans and zooms. iPhoto might begin or end the pan too soon, so that the primary subject gets chopped off. Or maybe it zooms too fast, so that your viewers never get the chance to soak in the scene—or maybe it pans or zooms in the *wrong direction* for your creative intentions.

Fortunately, the Ken Burns Effect controls located here let you control every aspect of the panning and zooming for one photo at a time. (Note: The settings you're about to make *override* whatever global Ken Burns setting you've made.) As you can see in Figure 7-7, it works like this:

1. **Select the photo. Turn on the Ken Burns Effect checkbox at the bottom of the window.**

   If more than one photo is selected, iPhoto will apply the effect only to the first one.

2. **Click Start. Drag the Size slider (at the lower-right corner of the iPhoto window) until the photo is as big as you want it at the *beginning* of its time onscreen. Drag inside the picture itself to adjust the photo's initial position.**

   In other words, you're setting up the photo the way it appears at the beginning of its time onscreen. Often, you won't want to do anything to it at all. You want it to start on the screen at its original size—and then zoom in from there.

   But if you hope to create a zooming *out* effect, you'd begin here by dragging the Size slider to the right, thus magnifying the photo, and then dragging the picture itself to center it properly.

3. **Click End. Use the Size slider to set up the picture's final degree of magnification. Drag inside the photo to specify the photo's final position.**

   You've set up the starting and ending conditions for the photo.

   Take a moment now to click the Preview button. The animated photo goes through its scheduled motion inside the window, letting you check the overall effect. Repeat steps 2 and 3 as necessary.

Tip: If you accidentally set up the End position when you actually meant to set up the Start position, Option-click the word Start. iPhoto graciously copies your End settings into the Start settings. Now both Start and End are the same, of course, but at least you can now edit just the End—only one set of settings instead of two. (The same trick works in the other direction.)

Now that you've specified the beginning and ending positions of the photo, iPhoto will interpolate, calculating each intermediate frame between the starting and ending points you've specified.

Simply click the Preview button to see the fully animated results of your programming.

Control Over the Show

All types of iPhoto slideshows run themselves, advancing from photo to photo according to the timings you've specified. However, you can still control a slideshow after it starts running in a number of ways. Although some of these functions are represented by icons on the control bar, it's nice to know that you can also trigger them from the keyboard, with or without the control bar. Your options:

- **Pause it.** Press the Space bar at any point to pause a slideshow. The music keeps playing, but the photos stop advancing. If the control bar isn't onscreen, a glowing Pause indicator briefly appears in the lower portion of the picture. When you're ready to move to the next slide and resume the auto-advancing of pictures, press Space again. A small Play indicator appears onscreen momentarily to confirm that iPhoto understands your command.

- **Manual advance.** Press the right or left arrow keys to advance to the next or previous photo, overriding the preset timing. In fact, once you hit either arrow key, the slideshow shifts into manual mode and stops advancing the photos altogether. A small translucent bar with arrows and a Play button appears onscreen to indicate that iPhoto is listening to your key presses.

  At this point, you can continue to use the arrow keys to move through all the photos—or stay on one photo for the rest of your life, for all iPhoto cares. As with the pause command, the music track keeps on playing. (To stop the music, you must end the slideshow.)

  In short, this is a terrific setup for a slideshow that you're narrating in person.

- **Back to auto-advance.** To return a slideshow to autoplay mode after you've used one of the arrow keys, press the Space bar. The photos advance automatically once again. Another option is to just wait a moment. As the onscreen arrows or control bar fade away, auto-advancing will resume.

- **Speed it up or slow it down.** Press the up or down arrow keys to speed up or slow down the slideshow on the fly. You'll discover that iPhoto can't create a stroboscopic, three-frames-per-second effect; one picture per second is about its maximum speed. (Give the poor thing a break—it's got a *lot* of data to scoop off the hard drive and throw onto your screen.)

Note: The changes you make manually are temporary. The next time you run a slideshow, you'll start again with the timing set in the Slideshow dialog box.

- **Rate the photos.** Even if you haven't summoned the control bar, you can rate pictures as they flash by just by tapping the corresponding number keys on your keyboard: 1, 2, 3, 4, or 5 for the corresponding number of stars, or 0 to remove the rating altogether.

- **Rotate the photos.** If a photo appears sideways, press ⌘-R to rotate it counter-clockwise, or Option-⌘-R to rotate it clockwise. (Or vice versa, if you've fooled around with iPhoto's Preferences dialog box.)

- **Delete the duds.** When a forgettable photo appears, press the Delete or Del key on your keyboard to move it to the iPhoto Trash, without even interrupting the show. (Unless you have very understanding family and friends, you may want to do this *before* you show the pictures to others for the first time.)

Slideshow Tips

The following guidelines will help you build impressive slideshows that truly showcase your efforts as a digital photographer:

Picture Size

Choosing photos for your slideshow involves more than just picking the photos you like the best. You also have to make sure you've selected pictures that are the right size.

iPhoto always displays slideshow photos at full-screen dimensions—and on today's monitors, that means at least 1024 x 768 pixels. If your photos are smaller than that, iPhoto stretches them to fill the screen, often with disastrous results (Figure 7-8).

Figure 7-8:
Here's an example of what happens when a 320 x 240–pixel photo ends up in a slideshow. Projected at full-screen dimensions, a photo that looks great at its normal size becomes jaggy-edged and fuzzy–unflattering to both subject and photographer. If you plan to use your photos in a slideshow, make sure your digital camera is set to capture pictures that are at least 1024 x 768 pixels.

Note: Although iPhoto blows up images to fill the screen, it always does so proportionately, maintaining each photo's vertical-to-horizontal aspect ratio. As a result, photos often appear with vertical bars at the left and right edges when viewed on long rectangular screens like the Apple Cinema Display, the 17-inch iMac, and so on. To eliminate this effect, see "Scale Photos to Fill Screen" on page 184.

Determining the size of your photos

If you're not sure whether your photos are big enough to be slideshow material, iPhoto provides two easy ways to check their sizes:

- Click a thumbnail in the photo-viewing area, and then look at the Size field in the Information pane. (If the Information pane isn't open, click the little ➊ button beneath the Source list.) You'll see something like "1600 x 1200." That's the width and height of the image, measured in pixels.

- Select a thumbnail and choose Photos→Show Info, or press ⌘-I to open the Show Info window. The width and height of the photo are the first two items listed in the Image section of the Photo pane.

- As shown in Figure 7-8, very small photos are ugly when blown up to full-screen size. Very large ones look fine, but iPhoto takes longer to display them, and the crossfade transitions might not look smooth. For the best possible results, make your photos the same pixel size as your screen.

- To whatever degree possible, stick with photos in landscape (horizontal) orientation, especially if you have a wide monitor screen. With portrait-oriented (vertical) photos, iPhoto displays big black borders along the sides.

FREQUENTLY ASKED QUESTION

Slideshow Smackdown: iPhoto vs. iMovie

I've read that iMovie makes a great slideshow program, too. Supposedly, I can import my photos, add music, and play it all back, full-screen, with cool cross-dissolves, just like you're saying here. Which program should I use?

The short answer is: iPhoto for convenience, iMovie for control.

In iMovie, you can indeed import photos. Just as in iPhoto, you have individual control over their timing, application of the Ken Burns effect, and crossfades between them.

But the music options are much more expansive in iMovie. Not only can you import music straight from a music CD (without having to use iTunes as an intermediary), but you can actually record a narration into a microphone as the

slideshow plays. And, of course, you have a full range of title and credit-making and special-effects features at your disposal, too.

Still, iPhoto has charms of its own. Creating a slideshow is much less work in iPhoto, for one thing. If you want a slideshow to loop endlessly—playing on a laptop at somebody's wedding, for example, or at a trade show—iPhoto is also a much better bet. (iMovie can't loop.)

Remember, too, that iPhoto is beautifully integrated with your various albums. Whereas building an iMovie project is a serious, sit-down-and-work proposition that results in one polished slideshow, your Photo Library has as many different slideshows as you have albums—all ready to go at any time.

- For similar reasons, try to stick with photos whose proportions roughly match your screen. If you have a traditionally shaped screen, use photos with a 4:3 width to height ratio, just as they came from the camera. However, if you have a wide-screen monitor (Cinema Display, 17-inch iMac, and so on), photos cropped to 6:4 proportions are a closer fit.

Tip: If you don't have time to crop all your odd-sized or vertically oriented photos, consider using the "Scale photos" feature described on page 184. It makes your pictures fill the screen nicely, although you risk cutting off important elements (like heads and feet).

- Preview images at full size before using them. You can't judge how sharp and bright an image is going to look based solely on the thumbnail.

- Keep the timing brief when setting the playing speed—maybe just a few seconds per photo. Better to have your friends wanting to see more of each photo than to have them bored, mentally rearranging their sock drawers as they wait for the show to advance to the next image. Remember, you can always pause a slideshow if someone wants a longer look at one picture.

- Give some thought to the order of your photos. An effective slideshow should tell a story. You might want to start with a photo that establishes a location—an overall shot of a park, for example—and then follow it with closeups that reveal the details.

WORKAROUND WORKSHOP

Small Photos, Big Show

You can't control the size of your pictures as they appear during a slideshow, as they always fill the screen. To ensure that the results look professional, you must make sure all your photos are sized to fill the screen properly, as mentioned earlier in this chapter.

But what if you're stuck with photos that simply aren't big enough? Suppose you're charged with putting together a slideshow for the family reunion, and the only pictures you have of Uncle Rodney happen to be scanned photos that are only 640 x 480 pixels?

You can't cut Rodney out of the slideshow, but at the same time, you know Aunt Lois won't take kindly to having her husband appear onscreen hideously distorted. ("Why does Rod look so jagged?" you can imagine her saying. "What did you do to him?") Here's one simple way to display smaller photos in a slideshow and keep everyone happy:

Using a program like GraphicConverter or Photoshop Elements, create a new document that's exactly the right size for your screen. If your monitor's set to 1024 x 768 pixels, create a document that's 1024 x 768 pixels. Fill the background of the blank document so that it's black, to match the black between slides. (Actually, you can use whatever background you like.)

Now open the small photo that you want to include in your slideshow. Paste a copy of it into the center of your blank document. Save the results and then import the image file into iPhoto.

You now have a new picture, perfectly sized for your slideshow. Your small photo will appear onscreen at the proper size, with a black border around it. No, the photo won't fill the screen, but at least it will appear just as clear and distortion-free as the larger photos.

- If your viewers fall in love with what you've shown them, you have four options: (a) save the slideshow as a QuickTime movie that you can email them or burn onto a CD for their at-home enjoyment (Chapter 11); (b) turn the show into an interactive DVD using Apple's iDVD software (see Chapter 12); (c) create a .Mac slideshow (page 238); or (d) make your admirers buy their own Macs.

Slideshows and iDVD

If you have a Mac equipped with a DVD-burning SuperDrive, you have yet another slideshow option: Instead of running a presentation directly from iPhoto, you can send your slideshow—music and all—from iPhoto to iDVD, Apple's simple DVD-authoring software. Using iDVD, you can transform the pictures from your album into an interactive slideshow that can be presented using any DVD player. (Just picture the family clicking through your photos on the big-screen TV in the den!)

Learn how to perform the iPhoto-to-iDVD conversion in Chapter 12.

Making Prints

There's a lot to love about digital photos that remain digital. You can store hundreds of them on a single CD; you can send them anywhere on earth by email; and they won't wrinkle, curl, or yellow until your monitor does.

Sooner or later, though, most people want to get at least some of their photos on paper. You may want printouts to paste into your existing scrapbooks, to put in picture frames on the mantle, to use on homemade greeting cards, or to share with your Luddite friends who don't have computers.

Using iPhoto, you can create such prints using your own printer. Or, for prints that look, feel, and smell like the kind you get from a photo-finishing store, you can transmit your digital files to Kodak Print Services, an online photo-processing service. In return, you receive an envelope of professionally printed photos on Kodak paper that are indistinguishable from their traditional counterparts.

This chapter explains how to use each of iPhoto's printing options, including the features that let you print greeting cards, contact sheets, and other special items from your digital photo collection. (Ordering greeting cards, postcards, calendars, and books is covered in Chapter 10.)

Making Great Prints

Using iPhoto to print your pictures is pretty easy. But making *great* prints—the kind that rival traditional film-based photos in their color and image quality—involves more than simply hitting the Print command.

One key factor, of course, is the printer itself. You need a good printer that can produce photo-quality color printouts. Fortunately, getting such a printer these days is pretty easy and inexpensive. Even some of the cheapo inkjet printers from Epson, HP, and Canon can produce amazingly good color images—and they cost less than $100. (Of course, what you spend on those expensive ink cartridges can easily double or triple the cost of the printer in a year.)

Tip: If you're really serious about producing photographically realistic printouts, consider buying a model that's specifically designed for photo printing, such as one of the printers in the Epson Stylus Photo series or the slightly more expensive Canon printers. What you're looking for is a printer that uses six, seven, or eight different colors of ink instead of the usual "inkjet four." The extra colors do wonders for the printer's ability to reproduce a wide range of colors on paper.

Even with the best printer, however, you can end up with disappointing results if you fail to consider at least three other important factors when trying to coax the best possible printouts from your digital photos. These factors include the resolution of your images, the settings on your printer, and your choice of paper.

Resolution and Shape

Resolution is the number of individual pixels squeezed into each inch of your digital photo. The basic rule is simple: The higher your photo's resolution, or *dpi* (dots per inch), the sharper, clearer, and more detailed the printout will be. If the resolution is too low, you end up with a printout that looks blurry or speckled.

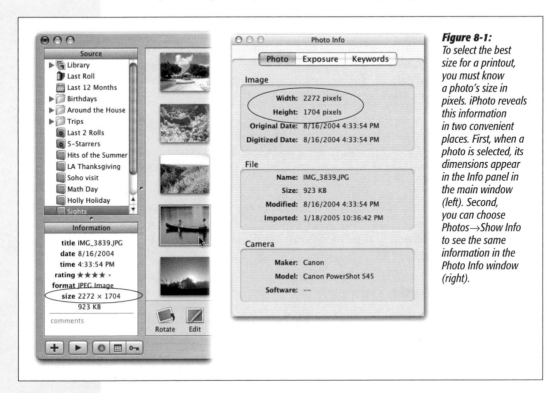

Figure 8-1:
To select the best size for a printout, you must know a photo's size in pixels. iPhoto reveals this information in two convenient places. First, when a photo is selected, its dimensions appear in the Info panel in the main window (left). Second, you can choose Photos→Show Info to see the same information in the Photo Info window (right).

Low-resolution photos are responsible for more wasted printer ink and crumpled photo paper than any other printing snafu, so it pays to understand how to calculate a photo's dpi when you want to print it.

Calculating resolution

To calculate a photo's resolution, divide the horizontal or vertical size of the photo (measured in pixels) by the horizontal or vertical size of the print you want to make (usually measured in inches).

Suppose a photo measures 1524 x 1016 pixels. (How do you know? See Figure 8-1.) If you want a 4 x 6 print, you'll be printing at a resolution of 254 dpi (1524 pixels divided by 6 inches = 254 dpi), which will look fantastic on paper. Photos printed on an inkjet printer look their best when printed at a resolution of 220 dpi or higher.

But if you try to print that same photo at 8 x 10, you'll get into trouble. By stretching those pixels across a larger print area, you're now printing at just 152 dpi—and you'll see a noticeable drop in image quality.

While it's important to print photos at a resolution of 250 to 300 dpi on an inkjet printer, there's really no benefit to printing at higher resolutions—600 dpi, 800 dpi, or more. It doesn't hurt anything to print at a higher resolution, but you probably won't notice any difference in the final printed photos, at least not on inkjet printers. Some inkjets can spray ink at finer resolutions—720 dpi, 1440 dpi, and so on—and using these highest settings produces very smooth, very fine printouts. But bumping the resolution of your *photos* higher than 300 dpi doesn't have any perceptible effect on their quality.

Aspect ratio

You also have to think about your pictures' *aspect ratio*—their proportions. Most digital cameras produce photos with 4-to-3 proportions, which don't fit neatly onto standard print paper (4 x 6 and so on). You can read more about this problem on page 151. (Just to make sure you're completely confused, some sizes of photo paper are measured *height by width,* whereas digital photos are measured *width by height.*)

If you're printing photos on letter-size paper, the printed images won't have standard Kodak dimensions. (They'll be, for example, 4 x 5.3.) You may not particularly care. But if you're printing onto, say, precut 4 x 6 photo paper (which you choose in the File→Page Setup dialog box), you can avoid ugly white bands at the sides by first cropping your photos to standard print sizes.

Tweaking the Printer Settings

Just about every inkjet printer on earth comes with software that adjusts various print quality settings. Usually, you can find the controls for these settings right in the Print dialog box that appears when you choose File→Print. To reveal these printer-specific controls in iPhoto, click the Advanced Options button in the Print dialog box, and then choose an additional command from the pop-up menu (Figure 8-2).

Before you print, verify that you've got these settings right. On most printers, for example, you can choose from several different quality levels when printing, like Draft, Normal, Best, or Photo. There might also be a menu that lets you select the kind of paper you're going to use—plain paper, inkjet paper, glossy photo paper, and so on.

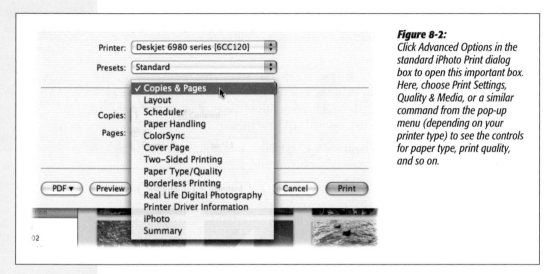

Figure 8-2:
Click Advanced Options in the standard iPhoto Print dialog box to open this important box. Here, choose Print Settings, Quality & Media, or a similar command from the pop-up menu (depending on your printer type) to see the controls for paper type, print quality, and so on.

Choose the wrong settings, and you'll be wasting a lot of paper. Even a top-of-the-line Epson photo printer churns out awful photo prints if you feed it plain paper when it's expecting high-quality glossy stock. You'll end up with a smudgy, soggy mess. So each time you print, make sure your printer is configured for the quality, resolution, and paper settings that you intend.

Paper Matters

When it comes to inkjet printing, paper is critical. Regular typing paper—the stuff you'd feed through a laser printer or copier—is too thin and absorbent to handle the amount of ink that gets sprayed on when you print a photo. You may end up with flat colors, slightly fuzzy images, and paper that's rippled and buckling from all the ink. For really good prints, you need paper designed expressly for inkjets.

Most printers accommodate at least five different grades of paper. Among them:

- Plain paper (the kind used in most photocopiers).

- High Resolution paper (a slightly heavier inkjet paper—not glossy, but with a silky-smooth white finish on one side).

- Glossy Photo paper (a stiff, glossy paper resembling the paper that developed photos are printed on).

- Photo Matte paper (a stiff, non-glossy stock).

- Most companies also offer an even more expensive glossy *film*, made of polyethylene rather than paper (which feels even more like traditional photographic paper).

These better photo papers cost much more than plain paper, of course. Glossy photo paper, for example, might run $25 for a box of 50 sheets, which means you'll be spending about 50 cents per 8 x 10 print—not including ink.

Still, by using good photo paper, you'll get much sharper printouts, more vivid colors, and results that look and feel like actual photographic prints. Besides, at sizes over 4 x 6 or so, making your own printouts is still less expensive than getting prints from the drugstore, even when you factor in printer cartridges and photo paper.

Tip: To save money, use plain inkjet paper for test prints. When you're sure you've got the composition, color balance, and resolution of your photo just right, load up your expensive glossy photo paper for the final printouts.

Printing from iPhoto

When you choose File→Print (⌘-P) in iPhoto, you don't see the standard Mac OS X Print dialog box—the one that asks you how many copies you want to print, which pages you want included, and so on. (As shown in Figure 8-2, you must click Advanced Options to see these controls.)

Advanced Printing Options

As mentioned earlier, the "advanced" printing options that appear when you click the Advanced Options button in the Print dialog box aren't really advanced. They're the standard, everyday options that you find in the Print dialog box when printing from any other Mac OS X program, as shown in Figure 8-2.

You can safely ignore many of these options, which vary depending on which printer you're using. For example, unless you're using a fancy printer equipped with multiple paper trays and double-sided printing capabilities, there's no need to concern yourself with the Duplex and Paper Feed options. The Error Handling panel, which appears if you're using a PostScript printer, controls arcane details about how your printer reports PostScript errors; you'll be happier if you don't even think about it. And the Summary panel is just a window showing your current printer settings, with nothing to turn on or off.

Some of these other printing options are more useful:

- **Copies & Pages.** You don't have to use this panel to choose the number of copies you want printed; you do that using the standard iPhoto print options. However, this panel does allow you to set a specific *range* of pages for printing, which can be helpful. You can print just the first page or two of a 26-page contact sheet, for example, to test your print settings.

- **Output Options.** This panel offers another way to save your print job as a PDF file, exactly like the one described on page 215.

- **Printer Features.** This panel is important, since it's where you can make adjustments that are specific to *your* particular printer. Depending on the make and model of your printer, this might be where you set print resolution, quality, and speed settings.

Instead, you're presented with iPhoto's own private version of the Print command, with six photo-specific printing options at your disposal: Standard Prints, Full Page, Greeting Cards, Contact Sheet, N-Up, and Sampler.

Each of these six printing styles is discussed in detail below.

Standard-Sized Prints

Use this method to print out photos that conform to standard photo sizes, like 5 x 7 or 8 x 10. This is especially useful if you intend to mount your printed photos in store-bought picture frames, which are designed to handle photos in these standard dimensions.

1. **Select the thumbnail(s) of the photo(s) you want to print.**

   Alternatively, you can open the photo in Edit mode before you print it; the Print command is accessible in all of iPhoto's modes. You can also select more than one photo—a good idea if you want to get the most out of your expensive inkjet paper (see step 5). Just highlight the ones you want, using the techniques described on page 106.

2. **Choose File→Print, or press ⌘-P.**

   The iPhoto Print dialog box appears.

3. **From the Style pop-up menu, choose Standard Prints.**

   This is the factory setting, but if you've been printing in other formats, you may have to switch it back.

4. **Using the Size pop-up menu, choose the print size you want.**

   You have several standard photo sizes to choose from—4 x 6, 5 x 7, and so on. Remember, though, that choosing a larger size stretches the pixels of your photo across a larger area, reducing the photo's resolution and potentially degrading its print quality. For best results, don't choose 8 x 10 unless the picture you're printing is at least 1200 x 1800 pixels. (A yellow triangle warns you if the resolution is too low; see Figure 8-3.)

   The Preview panel displays how your photo will be positioned on the paper, as shown in Figure 8-3.

5. **Select the number of photos you want printed on each page.**

   When the "One photo per page" checkbox is turned off, iPhoto fits as many photos as it can on each page, based on the paper size (which you select using the File→Page Setup command) and the photo size that you've chosen. Conversely, when the checkbox is turned on, you get one photo at the center of each page.

   On letter-size paper, iPhoto can fit nine 2 x 3, four 3 x 5, two 4 x 6, or two 5 x 7 pictures on each page. (If you're printing one photo per sheet—on 4 x 6 paper, for example—use the Full Page option described later, not "One photo per page.")

6. **Choose the number of copies you want to make.**

   You can either type the number into the Copies field or click the arrows to increase or decrease the number.

7. **Click the Print button (or press Enter).**

   Your printer scurries into action, printing your photos as you've requested.

Tip: Printing photos using these standard sizes works best if your digital photos are trimmed so that they fit perfectly into one of the three preset dimensions—4 x 6, 5 x 7, or 8 x 10. Use iPhoto's Constrained Cropping tool, explained on page 149, to trim your photos to precisely these sizes.

Figure 8-3:
See that warning icon on the top right corner of the preview? That's iPhoto's warning that the selected print size is too large, given the resolution of your photo. If you ignore the warning, your printout will likely have jagged edges or fuzzy detail.

Greeting Cards

When you choose Greeting Card from the Style pop-up menu of the Print dialog box, iPhoto automatically rotates and positions your photo (Figure 8-4). You could conceivably print out cards on standard letter-size paper and then fold them into halves or quarters, but this option is actually designed for printing on special blank inkjet greeting cards. This kind of glossy or matte paper stock, made by Epson and others, comes prescored and perforated for tidy edge-to-edge printing and crisp folding.

Here's how you print out a greeting card:

1. **Select or open the photo(s) you want to print.**

   Only one photo goes on each card. If you've selected more than one picture, you'll see only the first one illustrated in the preview.

2. **Choose File→Print, press ⌘-P, or click the Print button at the bottom of the iPhoto window.**

The Print dialog box appears.

3. **From the Style menu, choose Greeting Card. Pick a greeting card style using the radio buttons.**

   You have two choices: Single-fold, which prints your photo onto a half sheet of paper; or Double-fold, which fits your photo into a quarter-page printing area. The Preview panel on the left side of the Print dialog box illustrates how each of these options will appear in the final printout.

4. **In the Copies field, enter the number of copies you want to make.**

   If you selected multiple photos in step 1, iPhoto prints multiple greeting cards, one per photo. The number you enter here is different, in that it tells iPhoto how many *duplicates* of each one to print.

5. **Click the Print button (or press Enter).**

   Your cards emerge from your printer, ready to fold, sign, and mail.

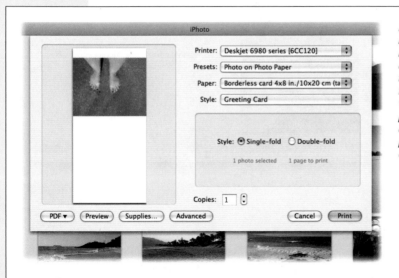

Figure 8-4:
iPhoto's Greeting Card printing doesn't create any actual greeting card content—no titles, holiday-themed icons, fancy borders, or pithy verses here. All you get is a printout of your photo on an otherwise blank sheet of paper, ready for you to fold over like a greeting card.

FREQUENTLY ASKED QUESTION

Changing Page Sizes

iPhoto's Print command lets me choose the size of the photos I want to print, but not the size of the paper I'm printing them on. Can't I pick a different paper size?

Yes, but remember that you change this kind of setting in the Page Setup dialog box, not the Print dialog box. Choose File→Page Setup, and then select the paper size you want using the Paper Size pop-up menu.

Printing Full Page Photos

iPhoto's Full Page printing option reduces or enlarges each photo so that it completely fills a single page.

To make Full Page prints, select the photo(s) you want to print, press ⌘-P, and then choose Full Page from the Style pop-up menu in the Print dialog box (Figure 8-5).

With Full Page printing, it takes 10 pages to print 10 photos, of course. But when you make Standard, N-Up, Sampler, or Contact Sheet prints, iPhoto can fit more than one photo on each page.

Tip: iPhoto's print dialog box tells you how many photos you've selected and how many pages it will take to print them all. However, this information is easy to miss because it appears in dim, grayed-out text near the center of the dialog box, under the Margins slider (Figure 8-5).

Figure 8-5:
Use the Margins slider to change the width of the margins around your photo. You can add margins of up to one inch. You can also specify zero margins, although that doesn't mean you'll get edge-to-edge printing. You will, however, get the smallest margins your particular printer can muster.

Contact Sheets

The Contact Sheet option prints out a *grid* of photos, tiling as many as 120 pictures onto a single letter-size page (8 columns of 14 rows, for example).

Photographers use contact sheets as a quick reference tool when organizing photos—a poor man's iPhoto, if you think about it. But this printing option is also handy in some other practical ways:

• By printing several pictures side by side on the same page, you can easily make quality comparisons among them without using several sheets of paper.

• Use contact sheet printing to make test prints, saving ink and paper. Sometimes a 2 x 3 print is all you need to determine if a picture is too dark or if its colors are wildly off when rendered by an inkjet printer. Don't make expensive full-page prints until you're sure you've adjusted your photo so that it will print out correctly.

- You can easily print multiple copies of a *single* picture if you want to produce lots of wallet-sized (or smaller) copies. (You can also make wallet sizes using the N-Up option.)

Contact Sheet printing options

To make Contact Sheet prints, choose Contact Sheet from the Style pop-up menu in the Print dialog box. Your printing options vary:

- If you've selected no specific photos, the Contact Sheet option prints *all* the photos in the Photo Library (or the current album, if you've selected one). Use the Across slider (Figure 8-6) to change the size of the grid and, therefore, the number of photos that appear on each printed page. iPhoto will print as many pages as needed to include all the photos in your current view.

Figure 8-6:
To fit even more pictures on a contact sheet, turn on the Save Paper checkbox, which appears only when you're printing more than one photo. It not only squishes the pictures closer together on the page, but also automatically rotates vertical photos so that they fit into an evenly spaced grid, again reducing white space. With more photos squeezed onto each page (bottom), you end up using less paper than you would otherwise (top).

- If you select several photos, iPhoto prints a contact sheet containing only those.

- When you select only *one* photo, iPhoto clones that one photo across the whole grid, printing one sheet of duplicate images at whatever size you specify using the slider control.

N-Up

With the N-Up option, you can tell iPhoto exactly how many photos you want printed on each page. The five preset grid configurations let you tile 2, 4, 6, 9, or 16 pictures on each sheet of paper. iPhoto automatically rotates photos as needed to make them fit perfectly into the grid size you choose.

N-Up printing may sound an awful lot like the Contact Sheet option just described, but it's slightly different. When printing Contact Sheets, you specify how many *columns* you want in your photo grid and, based on your choice, iPhoto crams as many photos on the page as it can—even if they end up the size of postage stamps. With N-Up Printing, you control the total number of pictures printed on each page, with a maximum of 16 photos in a 4 x 4 grid.

Tip: If you need your photos to be printed at a specific size—to fit in a 5 x 7 picture frame, for example—use the Standard Prints option instead of N-Up. With Standard Prints, you can specify the exact *size* of the photos; with N-Up, you can't.

Figure 8-7:
Need a sheet of wallet-sized photos to send to relatives? One way to make them is via the N-Up printing option. Just turn on the "One photo per page" checkbox so that you have two, three, or four rows of duplicate pictures. You can print up to 16 copies of a photo on each sheet.

N-Up printing options

As with printing contact sheets, your N-Up printing options depend on what you've got selected in the iPhoto window when you choose the Print command and choose N-Up from the Style menu.

- If you've selected no specific photos, the N-Up option prints *all* the photos in the Photo Library (or the current album, if you've selected one). Use the "Photos per page" pop-up menu (Figure 8-7) to change the size of the grid and, therefore, the number of photos that appear on each printed page. iPhoto will print as many pages as needed to include all the photos in your current view.

- If you select several photos, iPhoto prints a grid containing only those.

- When you select only *one* photo, iPhoto prints one sheet of duplicate images at whatever grid size you specify.

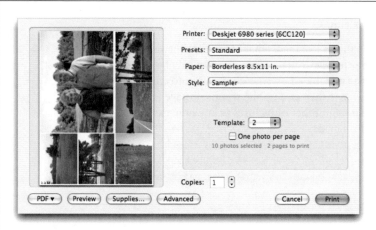

Figure 8-8:
You can print a neatly arranged combination of large and small photos on each page using one of the Sampler templates.

GEM IN THE ROUGH

Portraits & Prints

iPhoto's Sampler option prints *combination* templates like the portrait galleries delivered by professional photographers, but it doesn't offer much flexibility. You can't specify exactly which photos you want where, for example.

Fortunately, a $20 companion program called Portraits & Prints nicely compensates for iPhoto's printing weaknesses. (You can download it from, for example, the "Missing CD" page at *www. missingmanuals.com.*)

Once again, the idea is that you drag selected photos directly out of the iPhoto window and, in this case, into the Portraits

& Prints window. There, you can boost or reduce color intensity, sharpen, crop, rotate, add brightness, and remove red-eye. (If you designate Portraits & Prints as your preferred external photo editing program, any changes you make while in Portraits & Prints will be reflected in iPhoto's thumbnails.)

But all that is just an appetizer for the main dish: a delicious variety of printing templates, like the one shown here. The program comes with six "portrait sets" that let you arrange different pictures at different sizes on the same sheet. You can even save your layouts as *catalogs*, so you can reuse them or reprint them at a later date.

Sampler Pages

While the Contact Sheet and N-Up options produce a straight grid of evenly-sized photos on each printed page, the Sampler option lets you print a grouping of photos at *different sizes* on a single page—just like the portrait galleries you might get from a professional photographer. For example, you can print a sheet that contains a combination of one large photo and five smaller photos, as shown in Figure 8-8.

Once you choose Sampler from the Style menu in the Print dialog box, you can choose from two different Sampler templates from the Template pop-up menu. Sampler 1 puts three pictures on each page—one large photo on the top, with two smaller ones beneath it. Sampler 2 produces the six-photo layout shown in Figure 8-8.

Tip: For even more flexibility when printing a combination of photo sizes on a single page, see the box on the facing page.

The Sampler option offers the same "One photo per page" checkbox available with N-Up printing (explained in Figure 8-7). Turn it on to fill each page with multiple copies of a single photo, just like the school photos brought home by fourth-graders worldwide each year.

Figure 8-9:
The thing to keep in mind when setting up Sampler pages is that the first photo in your current selection is always the one that iPhoto picks as the "large" photo in the layout. If you want a specific photo to end up in the jumbo photo slot, make sure it's either the first one in the album or first among those you select. If you decide to rearrange the photos on the soon-to-be-printed page, close the Print dialog box, drag the thumbnails into a different order in the main iPhoto window, and then choose Print again.

Positioning photos in Sampler templates

You can pick exactly which of the photos from your collection are included in Sampler printouts by selecting them in the iPhoto window *before* choosing the Print command. If you have no photos selected, iPhoto will build Sampler pages using *all* the photos currently visible in the iPhoto window. If you have just one photo selected, iPhoto will fill the Sampler page with duplicates of the single photo. The order of the photos in your Photo Library determines how they're positioned in the printout, as explained in Figure 8-9.

The Preview Button

A mini-preview of your printout-to-be is always visible on the left side of the Print dialog box. But this postage stamp preview is far too small to show much detail. Worse, it shows you only the *first page* of a multipage job.

For a better preview, click Preview. iPhoto processes the print job, just as if you had hit Print—a "Print" progress bar appears at this point, indicating that the job is "on its way" to the printer. Instead of transmitting the job to your printer hardware, however, iPhoto creates a temporary PDF (Acrobat) file. It opens in Preview, the free graphics-viewing program that comes with Mac OS X.

Tip: Depending on the size of your print job, building a preview can take awhile. iPhoto must process all the image data involved, just as if it were really printing.

You end up with a full-size, full-resolution electronic version of your printout. Using the commands in Preview's Display menu, you can zoom in or out to view details, scroll across pages, and move from page to page (to preview every page of a contact sheet, for example). You're seeing exactly how iPhoto is going to render your printout when it actually hits the printer, using the print options you selected.

Figure 8-10:
The documents generated by the Preview command are temporary. If you close one, it disappears without even asking if you want to save it.

To save a preview document permanently, choose File→Save As or File→Export. The difference between the two commands: Save As lets you save only as a PDF document; Export lets you choose other formats, like JPEG or TIFF. Save As can create a multipage PDF from a bunch of selected pictures; Export saves only the first *page in a selection.*

If you like what you see in the PDF preview, you have the following two choices:

• Close the Preview window, return to iPhoto, and choose File→Print again (the Print dialog box will have closed itself automatically). Now, confident that you're going to get the results you expect, click the Print button and send the printout to your printer.

- If you want to *keep* the preview—in order to distribute an electronic version of a contact sheet, for example—you can save it, using one of the options shown in Figure 8-10. You can save it, for example, as a PDF file, which anyone with a Mac, Windows PC, or Unix machine can open using the free Acrobat Reader program that comes on every computer.

Save As PDF

The PDF button, a standard part of all Mac OS X Print dialog boxes, lets you save a printout-in-waiting as a PDF file instead of printing it on paper. It lets you convert any type of iPhoto printout—greeting card, contact sheet, sampler, and so on—to PDF. After opening the Print dialog box, set up your print options the way you want. Then, in Mac OS X 10.4, choose Save as PDF from the PDF pop-up button; in Mac OS X 10.3, click the Save As PDF button.

Now name the PDF in the Save to File dialog box, and click Save. (Saving the file can take awhile if you're converting several pages of photos into the PDF.)

Tip: You can also save a printout as a PDF file *after* you've previewed the results; see Figure 8-10.

Ordering Prints Online

Even if you don't have a high-quality color printer, traditional prints of your digital photos are only a few clicks away—if you have an Internet connection and you're willing to spend a little money, that is.

Thanks to a deal between Apple and Kodak, you can order prints directly from within iPhoto. After you select the size and quantity of the pictures you want printed, one click is all it takes to have iPhoto transmit your photos to Kodak Print Services and bill your credit card for the order. The rates range from 19 cents for a single 4 x 6 print to about $23 for a jumbo 20 x 30 poster. Within a couple of days, Kodak sends you finished photos printed on high-quality glossy photographic paper.

Tip: If you plan to order prints, first crop your photos to the proper proportions (4 x 6, for example), using the Crop tool as described in Chapter 6. Most digital cameras produce photos whose shape doesn't quite match standard photo-paper dimensions. If you send photos to Kodak uncropped, you're leaving it up to Kodak to decide which parts of your pictures to lop off to make them fit. (More than one Mac fan has opened the envelope to find loved ones missing the tops of their skulls.)

By cropping the pictures to photo-paper shape before you place the order, *you* decide which parts get eliminated. (You can always restore the photos to their original uncropped versions using iPhoto's Revert to Original command.)

Here's how the print buying process works:

1. **Select the photos you want to print.**

Click an album in the album list to order prints of everything in it, or select only the specific photos you want. Only the photos you select will appear in the Order Prints window.

2. **Choose Share→Order Prints (or click the Order Prints toolbar button, if you see it).**

Now the Mac goes online to check in with the Kodak processing center. (If the Mac can't make an Internet connection at all, the Order Prints window, shown in Figure 8-11, doesn't open.)

3. **Click Set Up Account, if necessary.**

The Set Up Account button appears at the lower-right corner of the dialog box if you've never before ordered anything from Apple. Clicking it initiates a series of dialog boxes where you surrender your identity and credit card info. You'll also see the option to turn on the "1-Click Ordering system," which is mandatory if you want to order prints. (All of this is a one-time task designed to save you time when you place subsequent orders.)

For details on the process, see page 278. When the Summary screen finally appears, click Done to return to the Order Prints window.

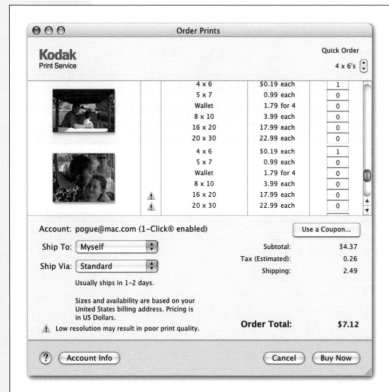

Figure 8-11:
The Order Prints window lets you order six different types of prints from your photos–from a set of four wallet-sized prints to mammoth 20 x 30 posters. Use the scroll bar on the right to scroll through all the photos you've selected to specify how many copies of each photo you want to order. If you need to change your shipping, contact, or credit card information, click the Account Info button to modify your Apple ID profile.

4. **Select the sizes and quantities you want.**

If you want 4 x 6 or 5 x 7 prints of every photo, just use the Quick Order pop-up menu at the top of the dialog box.

For more control over sizes and quantities of individual photos, ignore that pop-up menu. Instead, fill in the numbers individually for each photo, scrolling down through the dialog box as necessary. The total cost of your order is updated as you make selections.

Tip: If you want *mostly* prints of one size—5 x 7, for example—type the quantity into the "5 x 7 prints, quantity" box at the top of the window, so that iPhoto fills in that number for every photo. Now you're free to *change* the quantity for the few photos that you *don't* want to order at 5 x 7.

As you order, pay heed to the alert icons (little yellow triangles) that may appear on certain lines of the order form (visible in Figure 8-11). These are iPhoto's standard warning symbols, declaring that certain photos don't have a high enough resolution to be printed at the specified sizes. A photo that looks great at 5 x 7 may look terrible as a 16 x 20 enlargement. Unless you're the kind of person who thrives on disappointment, *never* order prints in a size that's been flagged with a low-resolution alert.

Tip: You'll see the same warning icon when you print your own photos and order photo books, cards, or calendars (Chapter 10). As always, you have few attractive choices: order a smaller print, don't order a print at all, or order the print and accept the lower quality that results.

---

5. **Click the Buy Now button.**

Your photos are transferred, your credit card is billed, and you go sit by the mailbox.

UP TO SPEED

How Low Is Too Low?

When you order photos online, the Order Prints form automatically warns you when a selected photo has a resolution that's too low to result in a good-quality print. But just what does Kodak consider too low? Here's the list of Kodak's official minimum resolution recommendations.

To order this size picture:	Your photo should be at least:
Wallet-sized	640 x 480 pixels
4 x 5	768 x 512 pixels
5 x 7	1152 x 768 pixels
8 x 10	1536 x 1024 pixels

These are *minimum* requirements, not suggested settings. Your photos will look better in print, in fact, if you *exceed* these resolution settings.

For example, a 1536 x 1024 pixel photo printed at 8 x 10 inches meets Kodak's minimum recommendation, but has an effective resolution of 153 x 128 dpi—a relatively low resolution for high-quality printing. A photo measuring 2200 x 1760 pixels, printed at the same size, would have a resolution of 220 dpi—and look much better on paper, with sharper detail and subtler variations in color.

A dialog box appears, showing the reference number for your order and a message saying you'll be receiving a confirmation via email.

A batch of 24 standard 4 x 6 snapshots costs about $4.50, plus shipping, which is about what you'd pay for processing a roll of film at the local drugstore.

Better yet, you get to print only the prints that you actually want, rather than developing a roll of 36 prints only to find that only two of them are any good. It's far more convenient than the drugstore method, and it's a handy way to send top-notch photo prints directly to friends and relatives who don't have computers. Furthermore, it's ideal for creating high-quality enlargements that would be impossible to print on the typical inkjet printer.

iWeb, Photocasting, & Network Sharing

Holding a beautifully rendered glossy color print created from your own digital image is a glorious feeling. But unless you have an uncle in the inkjet cartridge business, you could go broke printing your own photos. Ordering high-quality prints with iPhoto is terrific fun, too, but it's slow and expensive.

For the discerning digital photographer who craves both instant gratification and economy, the solution is to put your photos *online*—by emailing them to others, posting them on the Web, or *photocasting* them (a new photo-transmission feature in iPhoto 6).

All of this is particularly easy and satisfying in iPhoto 6.

Emailing Photos

Emailing from iPhoto is perfect for quickly sending off a single photo—or even a handful of photos—to friends, family, and co-workers. (If you have a whole *batch* of photos to share, on the other hand, consider using the Web-publishing or photocasting features described later in this chapter.)

The most important thing to know about emailing photos is this: *full-size photos are usually too big to email.*

Suppose, for example, that you want to send three photos along to some friends—terrific shots you captured with your 5-megapixel camera.

First, a little math: A typical 5-megapixel shot might consume two or three megabytes of disk space. So sending along just three shots would make at least a 6-megabyte package.

Why is that bad? Let us count the ways:

- It will take you 24 minutes to send (using a dial-up modem).

- It will take your recipients 24 minutes to download. During that time, the recipients must sit there, not even knowing what they're downloading. And when you're done hogging their time and account fees, they might not consider what you sent worth the wait.

- Even if they do open the pictures you sent, the average high-resolution shot is much too big for the screen. It does you no good to email somebody a 5-megapixel photo (3008 x 2000 pixels) when his monitor's maximum resolution is only 1024 x 768. If you're lucky, his graphics software will intelligently shrink the image to fit his screen; otherwise, he'll see only a gigantic nose filling his screen. But you'll still have to contend with his irritation at having waited 24 minutes for so much superfluous resolution.

- The typical Internet account has a limited mailbox size. If the mail collection exceeds 5 MB or so, that mailbox is automatically shut down until it's emptied. Your massive 6-megabyte photo package will push your hapless recipient's mailbox over its limit. She'll miss out on important messages that get bounced as a result.

For years, this business of emailing photos has baffled beginners and enraged experts.

It's all different when you use iPhoto. Instead of unquestioningly attaching a multi-megabyte graphic to an email message and sending off the whole bloated thing, its first instinct is to offer you the opportunity to send a scaled-down, reasonably sized version of your photo instead (see Figure 9-1). If you take advantage of this feature, your modem-using friends will savor the thrill of seeing your digital shots without enduring the agony of a half-hour email download.

Figure 9-1:
The Mail Photo dialog box not only lets you choose the size of photo attachments, it also keeps track of how many photos you've selected and estimates how large your attachments are going to be, based on your selection.

The Mail Photo Command

iPhoto doesn't have any emailing features of its own. All it can do is get your pictures ready and hand them off to your existing email program. iPhoto works with four of the most popular Mac email programs—Microsoft Entourage, America Online,

Qualcomm's Eudora, and Apple's own Mail (the free email program that came with your copy of Mac OS X).

If you currently use Apple's Mail program to handle your email, you're ready to start mailing photos immediately. But if you want iPhoto to hand off to AOL, Entourage, or Eudora, you have to tell it so. Choose iPhoto→Preferences (or press ⌘-comma), click General, and then choose the email program you want from the Mail pop-up menu.

Once iPhoto knows which program you want to use, here's how the process works:

1. **Select the thumbnails of the photo(s) you want to email.**

   You can use any of the picture-selecting techniques described on page 106. (If you fail to select a thumbnail, you'll get an error message asking you to select a photo and try again.)

2. **Click the Email icon at the bottom of the iPhoto window.**

   The dialog box shown in Figure 9-1 appears.

3. **Choose a size for your photo(s).**

   This is the critical moment. As noted above, iPhoto offers to send a scaled-down version of the photo. The Size pop-up menu in the Mail Photo dialog box, shown in Figure 9-1, offers four choices.

   Choose **Small (Faster Downloading)** to keep your email attachments super small (320 x 240 pixels)—and if you don't expect the recipient of your email to print the photo. (A photo this size can't produce a quality print any larger than a postage stamp.) On the other hand, your photos will consume less than 100 K apiece, making downloads quick and easy for those with dial-up connections.

   Choosing **Medium** yields a file that will fill a nice chunk of your recipient's screen, with plenty of detail. It's even enough data to produce a slightly larger print—about 2 x 3 inches (640 x 480 pixels). Even so, the file size (and download time) remains reasonable; this setting can trim a 2 MB, 4-megapixel image down to an attachment of less than 150 K.

   The Large (Higher Quality) setting downsizes even your large photos to about 450 K, preserving enough pixels (1280 x 960) to make good 4 x 6 prints and completely fill the typical recipient's screen. In general, send these sparingly. Even if your recipients have a cable modem or DSL, these big files may still overflow their email boxes.

   Despite all the cautions above, there may be times when a photo is worth sending at **Actual Size (Full Quality),** like when you're submitting a photo for printing or publication. This works best when both you and the recipient have high-speed Internet connections and unlimited-capacity mail systems.

   In any case, this option attaches a copy of your original photo at its original dimensions.

Note: iPhoto retains each picture's proportions when it resizes them. But if a picture doesn't have 4:3 proportions (maybe you cropped it, or maybe it came from a camera that wasn't set to create 4:3 photos), it may wind up *smaller* than the indicated dimensions. In other words, think of the choices in the Size pop-up menu as meaning, "this size or smaller."

4. **Include Titles and Comments, if desired.**

   Turn on these checkboxes if you want iPhoto to copy the title of the photo and any text stored in the Comments field into the body of the email. When Titles is turned on, iPhoto also inserts the photo's title into the Subject line of the email message.

Note: If multiple photos are selected when you generate an email message, the Titles option produces a generic subject line: "5 great iPhotos" (or whatever the number is). You can edit this proposed text, of course, before sending your email.

5. **Click Compose.**

   At this point, iPhoto processes your photos—converting them to JPEG format and, if you requested it, resizing them. It then launches your email program, creates a new message, and attaches your photos to it. (Behind the scenes, iPhoto uses AppleScript to accomplish these tasks.)

6. **Type your recipient's email address into the "To:" box, and then click Send.**

   Your photos are on their merry way.

Tip: iPhoto always converts photos into JPEG format when emailing them. If you to want preserve the files' original format when emailing Photoshop files or PDFs, *don't* use the Mail Photo feature. Instead, create a new email message manually, and then drag the thumbnails from iPhoto directly into the message window to attach them. (If you want to resize the photos, export them first using the Share→Export command, which offers you a choice of scaling options.)

FREQUENTLY ASKED QUESTION

Using iPhoto with PowerMail, QuickMail Pro, MailSmith...

Hey, I don't use Entourage, Eudora, AOL, or Apple Mail! How can I get iPhoto to send my photos via QuickMail? It's not listed as an option in the iPhoto's Mail Preferences.

You're right. Even if you have a different email program selected in the Internet panel of System Preferences, iPhoto won't fire up anything but Entourage, AOL, Eudora, or Mail when you click the Compose button.

There's a great workaround, though, thanks to the programming efforts of Simon Jacquier. Using his free utility, iPhoto Mailer Patcher, you can make iPhoto work obediently with MailSmith, PowerMail, QuickMail Pro, or even the aging Claris Emailer. It replaces the Mail button on iPhoto's bottom-edge panel with the icon of your preferred email program. You can download iPhoto Mailer Patcher from *http://homepage.mac.com/jacksim/software.*

Publishing Photos on the Web

Putting your photos on the Web is the ultimate way to share them with the world. If the idea of enabling the vast throngs of the Internet-using public to browse, view, download, save, and print *your* photos sounds appealing, read on. It's amazingly easy to get your photos from iPhoto to the Internet.

Three Roads to Webdom

iPhoto actually provides three different Web-publishing routes.

- **The easiest, most hands-off approach:** Use iWeb, one of the other iLife '06 programs. iPhoto can hand off any batch of photos to iWeb with only a couple of mouse clicks; from there, you can post them online with a single command.

  What's especially nice about the resulting Web page is that it presents a tidy collection of thumbnail images—a gallery that downloads relatively quickly into your audience's browsers. Then, when visitors click one of the thumbnails, a new window opens up to display the picture at full size (see Figure 9-2).

Note: This two-click business is available only if you have a .Mac account. That's Apple's suite of Internet services: email accounts, secure file backup, Web-site hosting, and a few other extras. If you don't already have a .Mac account, see the "Getting a .Mac Account" box on page 225. Follow the directions, and you'll have one in less than five minutes. (A .Mac membership costs $100 per year; a two-month trial account is free.)

You can still use iWeb to create photo-gallery Web sites if you don't have a .Mac account; see page 227. It just takes a few additional steps.

- **More effort, more design and layout options:** Copy photos from iPhoto to the Pictures folder of your iDisk (an Internet-based "virtual hard drive" that comes with a .Mac account). Then use the HomePage features at Apple's Web site (instead of the layout tools in iPhoto) to set up your pages.

- **For the experienced Web page designer:** If you already have a Web site, you can use either of two approaches to generate Web pages (HTML documents): either the Export command or the new Send to iWeb command. You can upload these files, with the accompanying graphics, to your Web site, whether that's a .Mac account or any other Web-hosting service. (Most Internet accounts, including those provided by AOL and Earthlink, come with free space for Web pages uploaded in this way.)

  This is the most labor-intensive route, but it offers much more flexibility if you know how to work with HTML to create more sophisticated pages. It's also the route you should take if you hope to incorporate the resulting photo gallery into an existing Web site (that is, one in which the photos aren't the only attraction).

All of these methods are detailed in the following pages.

Method 1: Use iWeb

Web publishing doesn't get any easier than it is with iWeb. Your photos end up on a handsome-looking Web page in just a few quick steps—and you don't have to know the first thing about HTML.

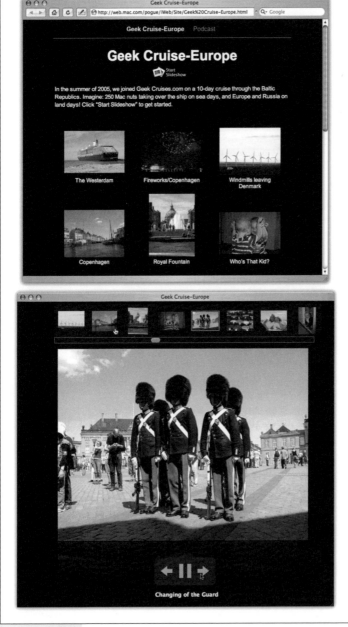

Figure 9-2:
You'd be nuts to stuff your full-size pictures onto the Web. The 70 percent of the population who uses dial-up modems would come after you with a lynch mob.

Top: Fortunately, iWeb adopts a respectful approach: It uploads only a gallery of smallish thumbnails. When visitors click one of them, a larger version of it opens in a separate window.

Bottom: Best of all, though, is the Start Slideshow button. It offers a big-screen version of the photo. A set of navigation buttons fades in when your mouse moves near the bottom of the window; navigation thumbnails fade into view when your mouse approaches the top of the window. Cool.

All of this takes a lot of time to load, though, even with a high-speed Internet connection. If it winds up causing too many headaches for your audience, consider adopting one of the other Web-publishing approaches described in this chapter.

1. In iPhoto, select the photos you want to put on the Web, or click the album that contains them.

   The selection can be one you've dragged pictures into, a smart album, the Last Roll(s) album, a year album, and so on. Or use the selection techniques described on page 106 to isolate a bunch of photos within an album.

Note: The iWeb photo-gallery template can't handle more than 99 photos per Web page. If you want to "publish" more than that, you'll have to create a series of separate pages.

---

2. Choose Photos→Send to iWeb→Photo Page (or, if the iWeb button appears on the toolbar at the bottom of the screen, choose Photo Page from its pop-up menu).

   If you choose Photos→Send to iWeb→Blog instead, you'll create a different sort of Web page—not so much an art gallery as a daily journal page, with spaces where you can type up comments about your pictures. The steps are exactly the same as described here, except that you should begin by selecting, at most, three photos.

UP TO SPEED

Getting a .Mac Account

.Mac, Apple's subscription online service, provides everything you need to put a collection of your photos online–and on your network. Unfortunately, the service isn't free (as it was when it was called iTools and didn't include as many features). A .Mac membership will set you back $100 per year.

The good news is that Mac OS X makes it incredibly easy to sign up for an account, and a two-month trial account is free. (There are a few limitations on the trial account; it grants you 20 MB of iDisk space instead of 125 MB, for example.) If you don't already have an account, here's how you get one:

Choose →System Preferences. When you click the Internet icon, the .Mac tab is staring you in the face. Click Sign Up.

Now you go online, where your Web browser opens up to the .Mac sign-up screen. Fill in your name and address, make up an account name and password, and, if you like, turn off the checkbox that invites you to receive junk mail.

You're also asked to make up a question and answer (such as, "First grade teacher's name?" and "Flanders"). If you ever forget your password, the .Mac software will help you–provided you can answer this question correctly. Click Continue.

An account summary screen now appears; print it or save it. On the next screen, the system offers to send an email message to your friends letting them know about your new email address (which is *whatever-name-you-chose@mac.com*).

The final step is to return to the Internet pane of System Preferences. On the .Mac tab, fill in the account name and password you just composed. You're now ready to use your .Mac account.

After a moment, iWeb appears.

3. **Choose a background design, either black or white.**

The window immediately displays a mock-up of your finished Web page (Figure 9-3), displaying the thumbnails in whatever order they appeared in iPhoto.

Figure 9-3:
In iWeb, iPhoto shows you what your yet-to-be-published Web page is going to look like.

To adjust the layout, click the Inspector button (❶) at the bottom of the window. In the Inspector palette (shown at left), click the third icon from the right to view the Layout options. (If they don't appear, make sure you've clicked the thumbnail area so it's highlighted.)

4. **Edit the page title, subtitle, and individual photo titles.**

Don't be concerned by the presence of all the Latin ("Lorem ipsum dolor amet…"); that's intended to be placeholder text. Drag your cursor through it and type new stuff to replace it.

If you don't bother changing the photo names, iPhoto will simply use whatever titles the photos have in the program itself.

5. **Edit the design of the photo grid, if you like.**

Click the Inspector button at the bottom of the window. As shown in Figure 9-3, clicking its fifth tab opens up a palette of photo-grid options. You can control whether it's a two- or three-column grid, how tall the caption boxes are, whether you want an outline around the grid, and so on.

6. **Click the Publish button (shown at lower left in Figure 9-3).**

This is the big moment: iPhoto connects to the .Mac Web site, scales down your photos to a reasonable size, and then transfers them to the server. This magic requires, of course, that you already have a .Mac account, and that you've entered your account name and password as described on page 225. It can also take a *very* long time.

When the uploading process is complete, as indicated by the alert dialog box (Figure 9-4, bottom), you can go to the page and see your results.

Note: You don't have to have a .Mac account to use iWeb. If you maintain your own Web site, for example, choose File→"Publish to a Folder" in this step. You wind up with a folder of correctly linked HTML documents and images folders on your hard drive. All you have to do is upload them manually to your Web site, as described on page 235.

Figure 9-4:
You can see your finished page on the Web by clicking Visit Site Now, but pay heed to the URL listed above the buttons; that's the Web address you need to give out if you want others to visit the page. (You can drag across it to copy it.)

If you include larger photos in your Web page, iPhoto automatically scales them down to reasonably sized JPEG files, so that they can be more easily loaded and displayed in a Web browser. If you want your Web pages to include *exact* copies of your original photos—regardless of size or file format—you must copy them to your iDisk yourself and then use the online HomePage tools to create your Web pages, as described later in this chapter. Or use the "Export Web Pages" option described on page 232.

What you get when you're done

When you see what you've created with iWeb, you'll be impressed: It's a professional-looking, stylishly titled Web page with thumbnails neatly arranged in a grid. Clicking a thumbnail opens an enlarged version of the picture in its own window; clicking the Start Slideshow button creates a full-window, beautiful slideshow complete with Previous and Next buttons and, when the cursor moves to the top of the window, even a little thumbnail browser (Figure 9-2). You can return to your main index page at any time by closing the slideshow window.

Tip: In the URLs for your .Mac-hosted Web sites (such as *http://web.mac.com/casey/iWeb/Site/Summertime .html*), capitalization counts—a point not to be forgotten when you share the site's address with friends. If you type one of these addresses into a Web browser with incorrect capitalization, you'll get only a "missing page" message.

Then again, maybe it's better to send your friends a much shorter, easier to remember address. You can convert long URLs into shorter ones using a free URL redirection service. At *www.tinyurl.com,* for example, you can sign up to turn *http://web.mac.com/gladys/iWeb/Site/pickles.html* into *http://tinyurl.com/bus4.* (Or do your own shopping for similar services by searching Google for "free URL redirection.")

Editing or deleting the Web page

Within iWeb, make your changes (delete photos or add them using the Media Browser, rearrange them, rename them, and so on) and then click the Publish button again at the bottom of the screen. iWeb sets about updating the gallery online.

To delete a photo-gallery page, click its name in iWeb's left-side panel (the Site Organizer) and press the Delete key. Then click Publish at the bottom of the window (meaning, "OK, make the online version of my site match what I now have in iWeb").

Deleting a photo page like this also deletes all of the online photo files, which frees up space on your iDisk.

Method 2: Use .Mac's HomePage Feature

Although using iWeb is incredibly simple, it entails a lot of sitting and waiting for the program to compute and upload things. You don't have much freedom of design, either: it's black or white, and that's it. HTML aficionados complain, too, that iWeb's behind-the-scenes HTML code is bloated and a tad unorthodox.

Fortunately, there's another way to go about creating, editing, and managing your photo galleries online: visit your .Mac Web site (Figure 9-5). The advantage here is that you can make changes to your photo gallery even when you're far from home,

---

FREQUENTLY ASKED QUESTION

Where Did All the Photos Go?

When iWeb transfers my photos to the .Mac Web site, where are they going?

Everything gets stored on your iDisk, the virtual disk that comes with your .Mac account. (Your iDisk looks and behaves like a miniature hard drive, but it's really just a privately reserved chunk of space on one of Apple's secure servers.)

The HTML pages generated by iWeb automatically go in the Web→Sites→iWeb folder on your iDisk. (In fact, if you know how to use a Web page creation program like Dreamweaver, you can make changes to your Web pages by editing these documents.)

The photos themselves get dumped into folders called Images within that iWeb folder on the iDisk.

---

using any Web-connected computer. As a bonus, Apple offers templates that lets you use your photos in Web pages that aren't photo-gallery designs—there's a nice baby announcement page, for example.

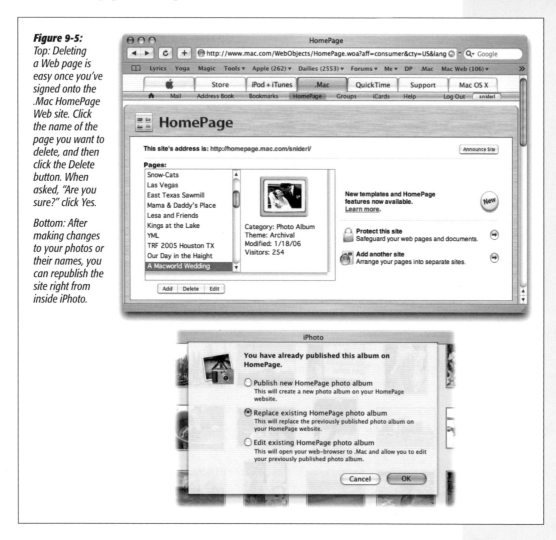

Figure 9-5:
Top: Deleting a Web page is easy once you've signed onto the .Mac HomePage Web site. Click the name of the page you want to delete, and then click the Delete button. When asked, "Are you sure?" click Yes.

Bottom: After making changes to your photos or their names, you can republish the site right from inside iPhoto.

To get started with HomePage, you first must copy the photos you want to publish from iPhoto to the Pictures folder of your iDisk—in fact, into a *new folder* in the Pictures folder, one folder per Web page. (If your iDisk isn't already onscreen, just choose Go→iDisk→My iDisk in the Finder, so that its icon appears on your desktop.) You can drag thumbnails directly out of iPhoto and into the Pictures folder on the iDisk.

Once your photos are in the iDisk's Pictures folder, you're ready to create your Web pages. Go to *www.mac.com*, sign in, click the HomePage button, then click one of the "Create a page" tabs on the HomePage screen to view the styles of pages you can create. Some of the formatting options available are shown in Figure 9-6.

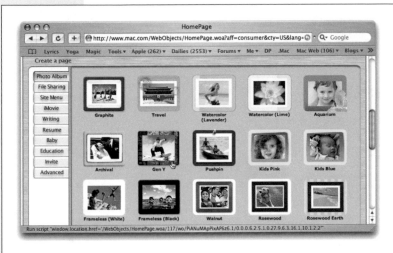

Figure 9-6:
Your Web-publishing options multiply considerably once you hit HomePage. In addition to the photo album themes shown here, you can also create résumés, personal newsletters, baby announcements, and party invitations. You can find these other options by clicking the "Create a page" tabs along the left side of the screen in the main HomePage screen.

The first tab, Photo Album, offers photo-gallery layouts in a far wider range of styles than iWeb offers. But you're free to use your photos in the other Web page designs here, too, like the baby announcements, writing samples, invitations, and so on.

If you choose Photo Album, click the miniature image of the design you want. HomePage next asks which photos folder in your Pictures folder you want to place

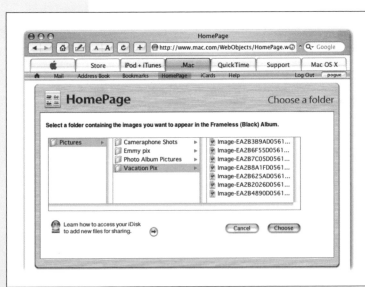

Figure 9-7:
Tell HomePage which photos to use. Two things to remember here: First, the pictures you choose must be in the Pictures folder of your iDisk, or HomePage won't see them; second, you can only choose a folder, not individual files. To include specific photos on a page, put them into a folder of their own in your Pictures folder before you start building the page.

on your new Web page, as shown in Figure 9-7. Select a folder of pictures, and then click Choose. After a few moments, your new photo album page appears with photos already inserted in the appropriate spots.

(If you choose any other Web page design, like Baby, the routine is pretty much the same, except that you have to click Edit at the top of the page in order to choose the photos you want.)

To finish the project, click Edit at the top of the page to change the chunks of dummy text on the page. (Make an effort to avoid misspellings and typos, unless you want an audience of 400 million to think you slept through fourth-grade English.)

Finally, click Preview to see how the Web page will look. When everything is just the way you want it, click Publish. The page goes live, as indicated by the confirmation dialog box shown at the bottom of Figure 9-4.

Tip: You can create as many Web pages as your iDisk will hold, by the way. When you return to the main HomePage screen, a list of your existing Web pages appears, complete with New Page, Edit Page, and Delete Page buttons.

Password Protection

When you publish your photos using HomePage, the pages you create become accessible to the whole Web-browsing world. Specifically, anyone with a Web browser and an Internet connection can view, and even download, your pictures.

If you don't feel comfortable sharing your photos quite so freely, you can add a password to your HomePage-generated sites, thereby controlling access to your photos. All right, you may not particularly care who sees your dog photos—indeed, you may be trolling for a dog-photo agent. But if you'd rather eliminate the possibility that your boss might see your bachelor party shots, or that your husband might see shots of your old boyfriend, password-protect the page,

and then distribute the password only to those who need to know.

To password-protect your site, access the screen shown in Figure 9-5. Select the name of your site from the Site list at the left side of the page, and then click the Edit button beneath it. On the "Edit your site" screen, turn on the Password On checkbox, insert the password of your choice, and then click Apply Changes.

After you've turned on password protection, anyone who comes to one of your .Mac-hosted Web pages will be prompted to enter the password (as shown here) before gaining access to your photos.

Corporations and professional Web designers may sniff at the simplicity of the result, but it takes *them* a lot longer than two minutes to do their thing.

Method 3: Export Web Pages

If you already have your own Web site, you don't need .Mac or iWeb to create an on-line photo album. Instead, you can use iPhoto's Export command to generate HTML pages that you can upload to any Web server. You're still saving a lot of time and effort—and you still get a handy, thumbnail gallery page like that shown back in Figure 9-2.

The Web pages you export directly from iPhoto don't include any fancy designs or themed graphics. In fact, they're kind of stark; just take a look at Figure 9-11.

But they offer more flexibility than the pages made with HomePage. For example, you can specify the dimensions of thumbnails and images, and choose exactly how many thumbnails you want included on each page.

This is the best method if you plan to post the pages you create to a Web site of your own—especially if you plan on tinkering with the resulting HTML pages yourself.

Preparing the export

Here are the basic Web exporting steps:

1. **In iPhoto, select the photos you want to include on the Web pages.**

   The Export command puts no limit on the number of photos you can export to Web pages in one burst. Select as many photos as you want; iPhoto will generate as many pages as needed to accommodate all the pictures into your specified grid.

Tip: If you don't select any photos, iPhoto assumes you want to export all the photos in the current album, including the Photo Library or Last Roll(s) album.

---

2. **Choose File→Export, or press Shift-⌘-E.**

   The Export Photos dialog box now appears.

3. **Click the Web Page tab.**

   You see the dialog box shown in Figure 9-8.

4. **Set the Page attributes, including the title, grid size, and background.**

   The title you set here will appear in the title bar of each exported Web page, and as a header in the page itself.

Tip: For maximum compatibility with the world's computers and operating systems, use all lowercase letters and no spaces.

Use the Columns and Rows boxes to specify how many thumbnails you want to appear across and down your "index" page. (The little "1 page" indicator tells you how many pages this particular index gallery requires.)

Figure 9-8:
As you change the size of the thumbnail grid or the size of the thumbnails, the number of pages generated to handle the images changes. The page count, based on your current settings, appears just to the right of the Rows field. The total count of the photos you're about to export appears in the lower-left corner of the window.

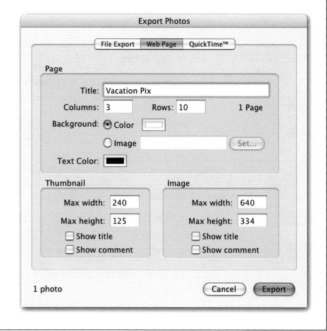

Figure 9-9:
Left: Drag the right-side slider all the way up to see the spectrum of colors available to you. Drag downwards to view darker colors.

Right: Alternatively, click one of the other color-picking buttons at the top of the dialog box. The crayon picker delights with both ease of use and creative color names, like Banana.

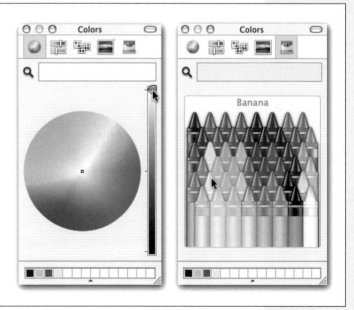

If you'd like a background page color other than white, click the rectangular swatch next to the word Color, and follow the instructions in Figure 9-9. You can also pick a color for the text that appears on each page by clicking the Text Color swatch.

You can even choose a background *picture* instead of a solid background color. To make it so, click the Image button, and then the Set button to select the graphics file on your hard drive. Be considerate of your audience, however. A background graphic makes your pages take longer to load, and a busy background pattern can be very distracting.

5. **Specify how big you want the thumbnail images to be, and also specify a size for the expanded images that appear when you click them.**

   The sizes iPhoto proposes are fine *if* all of your photos are horizontal (that is, in landscape orientation). If some are wide and some are tall, however, you're better off specifying *square* dimensions for both the thumbnails and the enlarged photos—240 x 240 for the thumbnails and 640 x 640 for the biggies, for example.

6. **Turn on "Show title" and "Show comment," if desired.**

   This option draws upon the titles you've assigned in iPhoto, centering each picture's name underneath its thumbnail. The larger version of each picture will also bear this name when it opens into its own window.

   Turning on the "Show comment" option displays any text you've typed into the Comments field for each picture in iPhoto. Depending on which checkboxes you turn on, you can have the comments appear under each thumbnail, under each larger size image, or both.

7. **Click Export.**

   The Save dialog box appears.

8. **Choose a folder to hold the export files (or, by clicking New Folder, create one) and then click OK.**

   The export process gets under way.

Examining the results

When iPhoto is done with the export, you end up with a series of HTML documents and JPEG images—the building blocks of your Web-site-to-be. A number of these icons automatically inherit the name of the *folder* into which you've saved them. If you export the files into a folder named Tahiti, for example, you'll see something like Figure 9-10:

- **Tahiti.html.** This is the main HTML page, containing the first thumbnails in the series that you exported. It's the home page, the index page, and the starting point for the exported pages.

- **Page1.html, Page2.html...** You see these only if you exported enough photos to require more than one page of thumbnails—that is, if iPhoto required *multiple* "home" pages.

- **Tahiti-Thumbnails.** This folder holds the actual thumbnail graphics that appear on each of the index pages.

- **Tahiti-Pages.** This folder contains the HTML documents (named Image1.html, Image2.html, Image3.html, and so on) that open when you click the thumbnails on the index pages.

- **Tahiti-Images.** This folder houses the larger JPEG versions of your photos. Yes, these are the *graphics* that appear on the Image HTML pages.

Tip: Some Web servers require that the default home page of your site be called *index.html.* To force your exported Web site to use this name for the main HTML page, save your exported pages into a folder called "index." Now the home page will have the correct name (*index.html*) and all the other image and page files will be properly linked to it. (After exporting, feel free to rename the folder. Naming it "index" was necessary only during the exporting process.)

Figure 9-10:
This is what a Web site looks like before it's on the Internet. All the pieces are here, filed exactly where the home page (called, in this example, Tahiti.html) can find them.

Once you've created these pages, it's up to you to figure out how to post them on the Internet where the world can see them. To do that, you'll have to upload all the exported files to a Web server, using an FTP program like the free RBrowser (available from the "Missing CD" page of *www.missingmanuals.com*).

Only then do they look like real Web pages, as shown in Figure 9-11.

Enhancing iPhoto's HTML

If you know how to work with HTML code, you don't have to accept the unremarkable Web pages exported by iPhoto. You're free to tear into them with a full-blown Web authoring program like Adobe GoLive, Macromedia Dreamweaver, or the free

Netscape Composer (*www.netscape.com*) to add your own formatting, headers, footers, and other graphics. (Heck, even Microsoft Word lets you open and edit HTML Web pages—plenty of power for changing iPhoto's layout, reformatting the text, or adding your own page elements.)

If you're a hard-core HTML coder, you can also open the files in a text editor like BBEdit or even TextEdit to tweak the code directly. With a few quick changes, you can make your iPhoto-generated Web pages look more sophisticated and less generic. Some of the changes you might want to consider making include:

- Change font faces and sizes.

- Change the alignment of titles.

- Add a footer with your contact information and email address.

- Add *metadata* tags (keywords) in the *page header,* so that search engines can locate and categorize your pages.

- Insert links to your other Web sites or relevant sites on the Web.

Figure 9-11:
Here's what a Web page exported straight from iPhoto looks like. The no-frills design is functional, but not particularly elegant. You have no control over fonts or sizes. On the other hand, the HTML code behind this page is 100 percent editable.

If you're *not* an HTML coder—or even if you are—you can perform many of these adjustments extremely easily with the BetterHTMLExport plug-in for iPhoto, described next.

Better HTML

iPhoto's Export command produces simple, serviceable Web page versions of your photo albums. Most people assume that if they want anything fancier, they need either HTML programming chops or a dedicated Web design program.

Actually, though, you can add a number of elegant features to your photo site using an excellent piece of add-on software that requires absolutely no hand coding or special editing software.

Figure 9-12:
Top: BetterHTMLExport works by adding a new panel called Better Web Page to the standard Export Photos dialog box. It in turn offers panels of features for customizing the Web pages you export from iPhoto. For instance, you can have your pages display your titles and comments beneath all thumbnail images. Other gems include the "Links On Bottom" and "Links On Top" checkboxes, shown below.

Bottom: Thanks to these numbered links, your viewers won't have to keep ducking back to the index page to jump to a different photo; they'll have a row of underlined number buttons (1 2 3 4 5) to click at the top or bottom of each page. BetterHTML Export can also add the "index" link that returns you to the main thumbnail page and the Original Photo link that loads the original photo file—at full, multimegapixel size.

It's the fittingly named BetterHTMLExport, an inexpensive iPhoto plug-in that extends the features of iPhoto's own HTML Exporter. (See page 329 for more on iPhoto plug-ins.)

You can download a copy of BetterHTMLExport from the "Missing CD" page of *www.missingmanuals.com,* among other places. The version for iPhoto 6 is a $20 shareware program.

Here are some of the great things you can do with BetterHTMLExport:

- Add comments (not just titles) on index and image pages.
- Insert "Previous" and "Next" links on each individual image page, so that you can jump from picture to picture without returning to the index (thumbnail) page.
- Control the JPEG quality/compression setting used to create copies of your photos.
- Create links to your *original* images instead of just JPEG versions of them.
- Choose where on the page you want to include navigation hyperlinks.

See Figure 9-12 for a quick tour of this valuable add-on.

The .Mac Slideshow

Here is perhaps the weirdest and wildest way to share your photos online and on your network—publish them as a *.Mac slideshow.*

When you send your photos out into the world as .Mac slides, other Mac OS X fans can *subscribe* to your show, displaying your pictures as their screen saver without manually downloading any files. (They do, of course, need an Internet connection.) In a minute or so, your latest photos can appear as full-screen slides on the Macintosh of a friend, family member, co-worker, or anyone else who knows your .Mac membership name.

Note: If your fans have iPhoto 6 or later, both you and they might much prefer the newer *photocasting* feature described on page 243.

Creating a .Mac Slideshow

Before any other Mac users can connect to your slideshow pictures, you have to make them available via your .Mac account. (If you don't have a .Mac account, you'll be prompted to sign up for one when you attempt to use the .Mac feature. See the box on page 225.) Here are the steps for publishing your slideshow:

1. **In iPhoto, select the photos you want to make available as screen saver slides.**

   You can use one album, several albums, or even the whole Photo Library.

2. **Choose Share→.Mac Slides.**

A dialog box opens, asking if you're sure you really want to publish your personal photos to the Internet. It's a question that deserves some consideration. Once you create .Mac slides, your pictures will be freely available to hundreds of thousands of Internet-connected Mac OS X fans around the world. All they need to know (or guess) is your .Mac membership name. If you have any reservations about making these glimpses of your life available to the world at large, now's the time to click Cancel.

Otherwise, read on:

3. **Click Publish to begin uploading your photos.**

One by one, iPhoto grabs your photos and copies them to your iDisk, dropping them into a special location in the Pictures→Slideshows→Public folder.

When all the photos are safely online, a confirmation dialog box appears, letting you know that your slideshow is now available. (If you look at the uploaded files on your iDisk, you'll notice that iPhoto has renamed your pictures according to its own private naming scheme. It's only the uploaded copies that have been renamed, however, not the photos on your Mac.)

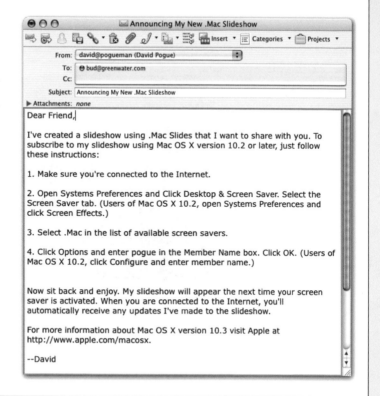

Figure 9-13:
Once you've made your photos available to the whole world for use as a screen saver, iPhoto can help you tell everyone about it, too. Click the Announce Slideshow button in the confirmation dialog box to launch your email program and generate an announcement email. As you can see here, the announcement contains complete instructions for accessing the slideshow using the Screen Effects or Screen Saver panel of System Preferences.

Note: You can publish any number of Web sites on your .Mac account, but only *one* set of .Mac slides. Each time you upload photos for a .Mac slideshow, you *replace* any earlier slideshow photos you've uploaded.

4. **Click Announce Slideshow, if you like (see Figure 9-13).**

If you'd rather not email your friends to let them know about your slides, click Quit instead. Then use your Mac's screen saver feature, as outlined in the next section, to see the fruits of your labor.

Subscribing to a .Mac Slideshow

After you've uploaded your photos as .Mac slides, you, or anyone else with Mac OS X 10.2 or later and an Internet connection, can subscribe to the show and make it into a screen saver. Here's how:

1. **Choose →System Preferences. Open the proper preferences pane by clicking the Screen Effects (Mac OS X 10.2) or Desktop & Screen Saver icon (Mac OS X 10.3 or later).**

Switch to the Screen Effects (Mac OS X 10.2) or Screen Saver (Mac OS X 10.3 or later) tab of the window, if it's not already displayed. This is where you choose the particular effect that your Mac will use as a screen saver.

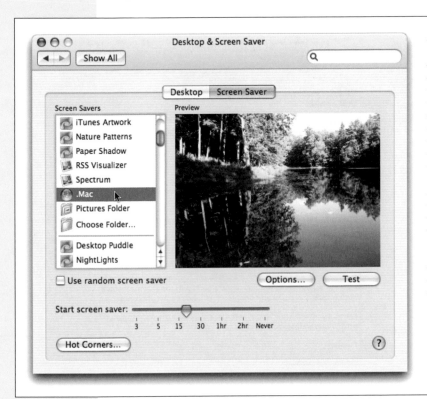

Figure 9-14:
You can connect to screen savers created by other Mac users around the world by using the .Mac Screen Effects option. Don't forget to visit the other two tabs in the Screen Effects panel—Activation and Hot Corners. On the Activation tab, you can tell your Mac how long it must sit idle before your custom screen saver kicks in. The options in the Hot Corners tab let you flip screen effects on or off by moving your mouse into a designated corner of the screen.

2. **Click *.Mac* in the Screen Effects list.**

   On the little Preview screen, shown in Figure 9-14, you can click the Configure (Mac OS X 10.2) or Options (Mac OS X 10.3 and later) button to select a slideshow and set up the playback options.

3. **Click the Configure (or Options) button.**

   The Subscriptions window appears. The controls here determine which slideshows you can see on your Mac and how they're displayed.

4. **In the .Mac Membership Name box, enter the name of the .Mac member whose slideshow you want to see.**

   There's no way to *get* this name. Unless you find the creator's name at the *http://dotmac.info* Web page (see the box on the next page), you just have to know it.

Tip: You can subscribe to as many different .Mac slideshows as you want. As you do, their names accumulate in the Subscriptions window.

---

5. **Choose your Display Options.**

   Adjust the checkboxes in the lower portion of the window to change the way the slides are to be presented on your screen. You can control zooming, crossfades, and other options, as shown in Figure 9-15.

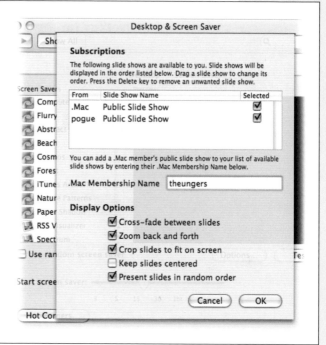

Figure 9-15:
Your Mac remembers each show you've sub-scribed to. You can have it use or ignore any combination of shows by turning the Selected checkbox next to each title on or off. You can also change the order in which the shows are presented by dragging them into a different order in this list.

6. **Click OK to return to the main Screen Effects window.**

   This is the big moment: The Mac hooks up to the .Mac site(s) you've specified and finds the shared slideshow. Seconds later, you see the results of your tinkering. The slides you've subscribed to appear on the little Preview screen in a miniature version of the slideshow, complete with zooming effects and crossfades.

Note: If the slideshow you've subscribed to is very large, the Preview screen may remain black for a minute or two as the images get downloaded to your Mac.

---

7. **Click the Test button to preview the slideshow at full size.**

   Your screen goes black, and then the first of the slides to which you've subscribed fills the screen. Depending on the options you've selected, the slideshow progresses with photos slowly zooming and crossfading into each other. To end the test, just click your mouse.

You've now got a remote slideshow that will play back on your screen according to the rules you've set up in the Activation and Hot Corners tabs of the Screen Effects panel. Of course, at any time, you can go back into Screen Effects and reconfigure the .Mac slide settings: add additional slideshows to your subscriptions, rearrange their playback order, or (when the kid in your cousin's new-baby slideshow turns 21, perhaps) delete .Mac slideshows from the list.

FREQUENTLY ASKED QUESTION

Trolling for .Mac Slides

The idea of sharing .Mac slides with friends sounds great, and I would do it in a heartbeat—if I had more friends. As it turns out, I don't know another soul running Mac OS X. Am I destined to watch my same boring photos crossfade into each other, day after day, in utter solitude?

Fortunately, no. Thousands of .Mac members have already made their slideshows available to the world, and they're just waiting for you to subscribe to them.

The trick is to visit *http://dotmac.info*, where you'll find a listing of movies, photo albums, calendars, Web sites, and .Mac slideshows, all contributed by other .Mac members. You can search for specific items or just browse the listings, then subscribe to any number of slideshows. Thanks to the miracle of modern technology, you can now fill your screen with the photos of total strangers.

Want to give the world access to *your* slideshow, too? Click the Add a Page button on the *dotmac.info* home page. Add a description of your slides along with your membership name, so that anyone who wants to can subscribe to your slides from their Mac.

Photocasting

One of the perks of being Apple is that you make the whole widget: computer, operating system, and programs. And when you make the whole widget, you can create clever interconnections between them; after all, you already know all your own trade secrets, and you don't have to ask yourself permission.

Photocasting, new in iPhoto 6, is a case in point. It's a direct pipe from your copy of iPhoto into somebody else's. You "publish" an album (baby pictures, for example); they "subscribe" to it (grandparents, let's say). From now on, whenever you make changes to that album—you add more photos, for example—the grandparents see the changes in their own copies of iPhoto.

To make matters even juicier, your subscriber fans aren't just *seeing* your pictures. They can also drag them into their *own* copies of iPhoto—the full-resolution originals.

The idea of photocasting is so strong, and its appeal to families and loved ones so great, that the fine print may crush your spirit: to make photocasting work, you need not only iPhoto 6, but also a .Mac account and Mac OS X 10.4 or later.

Subscribing to a photocast doesn't require anything more than an RSS reader—for Mac or even Windows (more on this shortly). But the good stuff—like copying the photos into your own stash, or watching the album update itself—requires that subscribers, too, have at least Mac OS X 10.4 and iPhoto 6.

Publishing

Here's how you go about making your prized pictures available to the up-to-date Mac masses.

1. **Click the album you want to publish.**

   You can't pick only some photos in an album; it's the whole album or nothing.

2. **Choose Share→ Photocast.**

   The dialog box shown at top in Figure 9-16 appears.

3. **From the pop-up menu, choose the photo size you want.**

   The larger the pictures, the longer they'll take to "publish," and the slower they'll be to appear at the other end. (On the other hand, time may not be an issue, since all of this happens in the background.)

Note: If you choose Actual Size, the photos will remain at their current size. That's a good choice if you want to give your fans the opportunity to print the pictures at full resolution. However, note that iPhoto always photocasts your photos in JPEG format, even if they began life in iPhoto in RAW or some other format. (That is, "Actual Size" does not necessarily mean "original files.")

---

4. **Click the checkboxes worth clicking.**

"Automatically update when album changes" means that your subscribers will see any changes you make on your end (adding photos, deleting photos, editing photos). Of course, this works only if they have iPhoto 6 and Mac OS X 10.4. "Require name and password" ensures that if the photocast's address falls into the wrong hands, the spies won't be able to see your pictures. Make up a name and password here, and distribute this information only to authorized friends and relatives. (They'll have to enter this information when they try to subscribe.)

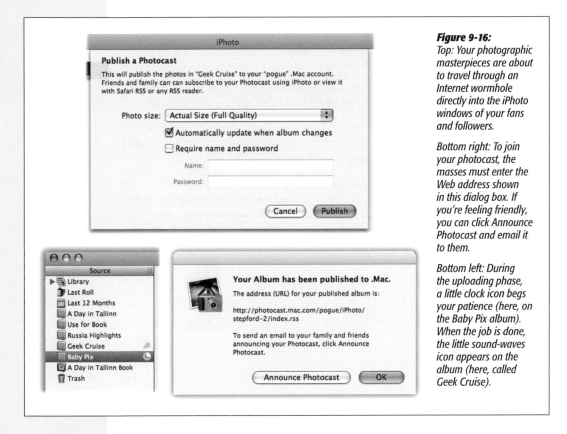

Figure 9-16:
Top: Your photographic masterpieces are about to travel through an Internet wormhole directly into the iPhoto windows of your fans and followers.

Bottom right: To join your photocast, the masses must enter the Web address shown in this dialog box. If you're feeling friendly, you can click Announce Photocast and email it to them.

Bottom left: During the uploading phase, a little clock icon begs your patience (here, on the Baby Pix album). When the job is done, the little sound-waves icon appears on the album (here, called Geek Cruise).

5. **Click Publish.**

   iPhoto begins transmitting your album to your .Mac account. It can take a very long time; Apple tries to entertain you with a little ticking-clock animation (the tiny icon next to the album's name).

   When the uploading is complete, sometime the following week, you see the message shown in Figure 9-16 at bottom right.

6. **Tell your followers that the photocast is available.**

   The easiest way is to click Announce Photocast. Your email program opens automatically, and an outgoing message appears, ready to address and send. It provides the lucky recipient with instructions on how to subscribe to your photographic masterpieces.

(A synopsis: "To subscribe, just click the following link. If you have iPhoto 6, this Photocast will appear in your iPhoto Source list. Whenever you are connected to the Internet, iPhoto will automatically update this Photocast so you see the latest photos I've added.

"If you don't have iPhoto 6, you can view the photos in this Photocast with Safari RSS or any compatible RSS reader on Mac, Windows or other computers by using the link above. Note: If this Photocast is password protected, please contact me for the username and password.")

That's all there is to it. A special photocast icon appears next to the album's name (see Figure 9-16, lower left) to remind you that you've made it public.

(If email isn't possible or convenient, you can just write down the photocast's Web address, as it appears in the dialog box, and hand it to someone, or read it over the phone instead. And if you ever need to look up the photocast address again, just open the album's Info panel as described on page 120.)

Ending the Photocast

Photocast as many albums as you like. There's no real downside; it doesn't slow down your Mac, it doesn't eat up memory, and it doesn't occupy any disk space on your Mac. In fact, iPhoto doesn't even have to be running. (Your .Mac account is doing all the grunt work.)

But if you're running out of space on your iDisk or just getting bored with the whole idea, you can turn off the photocast. Click the album, choose Share→ Photocast, and, in the dialog box that appears, click Stop Publishing.

Subscribing to a Photocast

Now pretend that the shoe's on the other foot. Suppose that you've received an invitation to subscribe to someone else's photocast.

Tip: Want to play both roles—publisher and subscriber—just to get a feel for both ends of the process? Then publish a photocast. On the very same Mac, switch to a different account (that you've created ahead of time in the Accounts panel of System Preferences). Open iPhoto there, and use the following steps to subscribe to the photocast that you just sent yourself.

- **If you have iPhoto 6.** Click the link that was sent to you by email. iPhoto opens automatically. A message appears that says, "Are you sure you want to subscribe to this photocast?" (Unless, of course, you previously turned on the checkbox that says "Do not ask about subscribing to photocasts again.")

  When you click Subscribe (and enter the name and password, if required), a new album appears near the top of your Source list. The tiny sound-waves icon reminds you that it's a subscribed photocast (and not one of your own photo collections).

After a long time—once again, the little clock icon asks your patience—the photocasted photos appear in the main iPhoto window. You can use them like any other pictures: print them, email them, make a slideshow of them, order books, cards, or calendars.

Remember, though, that these photos technically belong to somebody else, so you can't delete them or edit them (although for some reason, you can rotate or crop them). But if you drag the photos into one of your own albums, they're yours now. You can edit them to your heart's content, and even photocast them to somebody else.

- **If you don't have iPhoto 6.** Not everyone has iPhoto 6—and that's putting it mildly. Think about the 95 percent of the world where Microsoft Windows rules supreme, or the millions who use older versions of the Mac (or of iPhoto), or the legions of Linux fans. What are they, chopped liver?

Fortunately, they, too, can enjoy your photos. All they need is a program called an RSS reader. (RSS is a terrible name for a great technology; it can stand for either Rich Site Summary or Really Simple Syndication. It's a system of signing up for free "subscriptions" to Web sites so you don't have to check them for updates.)

Mac fans should note that the Safari Web browser itself is an RSS reader (at least in Mac OS X 10.4 and later), but there are plenty of RSS shareware programs, like NetNewsWire. For Windows, some popular readers are Newz Crawler, Feed-Demon, and Bloglines. Anyone on any platform can get RSS feeds using Web sites like Google Reader (http://reader.google.com).

Each RSS feeder has a URL (address) box where you can type the address of an RSS feed that you want to receive. Paste in the iPhoto link you've been emailed, wait a moment or two for the photos to arrive, and you're in business.

Photo Sharing on the Network

One of the coolest features of iTunes is the way you can "publish" certain playlists on your home or office network, so that other people in the same building can listen to your tunes. Why shouldn't iPhoto be able to do the same thing with pictures?

In fact, it can. Here's how it works.

For this example, suppose that you're the master shutterbug who has all the cool shots. On your Mac, choose iPhoto→Preferences and click Sharing. Turn on "Share my photos" (Figure 9-17).

You might be tempted to turn on "Share entire library," so that no crumb of your artistry will go unappreciated—but don't. Even the fastest Macs on the fastest networks will grind to a halt if you try to share even a medium-sized photo library. You are, after all, attempting to cram gigabytes of data through your network to the other Macs.

It's far more practical to turn on the checkboxes for the individual albums you want to share, as shown in Figure 9-17.

Unless you also turn on "Require password" (and make up a password), everyone on the network with iPhoto 4 or higher can see your shared pictures.

Finally, close the Sharing window.

Figure 9-17:
If you turn on "Share entire library," you make all of your pictures available to others on the network—and doom your fans to a lifetime of waiting while gray empty boxes fill their iPhoto screens.

Alternatively, click "Share selected albums" and turn on the individual albums that you want to make public.

Either way, turning on Sharing makes only photos available on the network—not movie clips.

Figure 9-18:
You can't delete or edit the photos you've summoned from some other Mac. But you can drag them into your own albums (or your own Photo Library) to copy them. (The topmost category shown here, Shared Photos, appears only if iPhoto detects more than one shared iPhoto collection on the network.)

When you've had enough, click the Eject button. The flippy triangle, the list of albums, and the Eject button itself disappear. The names of shared collections (like "Casey's Photos" and "Robin's Photos" in this example) remains on the screen, in case you want to bring them back for another look later.

All shared photo libraries   Individual shared photo libraries   "Eject" button

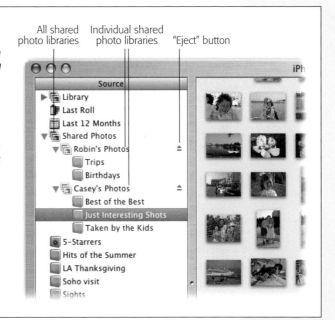

At this point, other people on your network will see *your* albums show up in *their* Source lists, above the list of their own albums; see Figure 9-18. (Or at least they will if they have "Look for shared photos" turned on in their iPhoto Preferences.)

As you may know, when you share iTunes music over a network, other people can only *listen* to your songs—they can't actually *have* them. (The large, well-built lawyers of the American record companies have made sure of that.)

But iPhoto is another story. Nobody's going to issue you a summons for freely distributing your own photos. So once you've jacked into somebody else's iPhoto pictures via the network, feel free to drag them into your own iPhoto albums, thereby copying them onto your own Mac. Now you can edit them, print them, and otherwise treat them like your own photos.

Photo Sharing Across Accounts

Mac OS X is designed from the ground up to be a *multiple-user* operating system. You can set up Mac OS X with individual *user accounts* so that everyone must log in. When the Mac starts up, in other words, you have to click your account name and type a password before you can start using it.

Upon doing so, you discover the Macintosh universe just as you left it, including *your* icons on the desktop, Dock configuration, desktop picture, screen saver, Web browser bookmarks, email account, fonts, startup programs, and so on. This accounts feature adds both convenience and security. As you can imagine, this feature is a big deal in schools, businesses, and families.

This feature also means that each account holder has a separate iPhoto Library folder. (Remember, it lives inside your own Home folder.) The photos *you* import into iPhoto are accessible only to you, not to anyone else who might log in. If you and your spouse each log into Mac OS X with a different account, you each get your own Photo Library—and neither of you has access to the other's pictures in iPhoto.

But what if the two of you *want* to share the same photos? Ordinarily, you'd be stuck, since iPhoto can't make its library available to more than a single user. You could transfer the photos by CD or by photocasting, of course, but here are two easier solutions to this common conundrum.

Easy Way: Share Your Library

iPhoto's sharing feature isn't just useful for sharing photos across the network. It's equally good at sharing photos between *accounts* on the same Mac.

To make this work, iPhoto has to be running in the account that will be sharing the pictures. And you have to turn on Fast User Switching. (To find this checkbox, open the Accounts panel of System Preferences. Click the Login Options button.)

Now you're ready. Log in as, say, Dad. Share some albums.

Now Mom chooses her name from the little Fast User Switching menu at the upper-right corner of the screen, thereby switching to her own account (and shoving Dad's to the background). She'll find that Dad's albums show up in her copy of iPhoto, exactly as shown in Figure 9-17. She can copy whichever pictures she likes into her own albums.

Geeky Way: Move the Library

The problem with the Share Your Library method is that you wind up with *copies* of the pictures. In some situations, you may want to work on exactly the same set of pictures. You want, in other words, to share the *same iPhoto Library.*

What will trip up any normal person's attempt to share an iPhoto Library is a little thing called *permissions.* That term refers to the insanely complex web of invisible Unix codes that keep your files and folders out of the hands of other account holders, and vice versa.

Figure 9-19:
Top: To share your Photo Library with other user-account holders on your Mac, start by moving its folder into your Mac's Shared folder. For clarity, the iPhoto library has been named "iPhoto Library (Shared)" here.

Bottom: Now add the shared library to the list of iPhoto libraries in the freeware program iPhoto Library Manager. (That involves clicking Add Library at the top of the window and navigating to that Shared folder.)

Set the iPhoto Library (Shared) folder's three pop-up menus to "Read & write," as shown here. Finally, turn on the shared library's checkmark and then click Launch iPhoto.

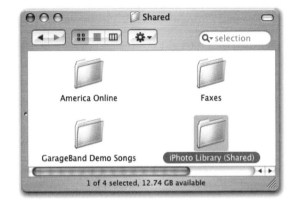

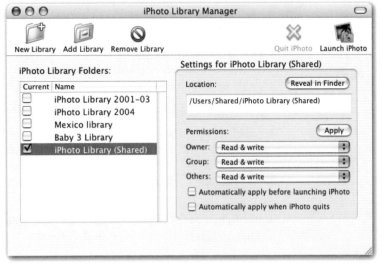

The trick here, then, is to perform a two-step maneuver (one of which requires the assistance of a piece of free software). First, put your photo library somewhere where every account holder has access to it. Second, change its permissions from "mine" to "everyone's." Here's the drill. (Quit iPhoto first.):

1. **In the Finder, drag your iPhoto Library folder into the Shared folder.**

   Your iPhoto Library folder contains all of your pictures (and all of the information associated with them, like albums, comments, and so on). It's probably sitting, at this moment, in your Home→Pictures folder. To move it, you'll probably have to open two Finder windows side-by-side, so you can see your starting and ending points at the same time.

   Your destination is the Shared folder, which is in your Macintosh HD→Users folder. Drag the iPhoto Library folder into the Shared folder.

   You've done most of the setup. Now comes a step that each individual account holder must take individually. Suppose, for example, that you're now your mom.

2. **Log in to your account. Don't open iPhoto yet. Open iPhoto Library Manager instead.**

   The gloriously useful (and gloriously free) iPhoto Library Manager program is described at length in Chapter 14. (You can download it from, for example, the "Missing CD" page at *www.missingmanuals.com.*)

3. **Click the Add Library button. Navigate to the Macintosh HD→Users→Shared folder, click the iPhoto Library folder, and click Open.**

   Now the shared photo library appears in iPhoto Library Manager's list of libraries, as shown in Figure 9-19. Make sure it's highlighted.

4. **Set all three pop-up menus to "Read & write," as shown in Figure 9-19. Also turn on "Automatically apply before launching iPhoto."**

   Your mom has just made your iPhoto Library folder her own. And every time she opens iPhoto (from within iPhoto Library Manager, that is), those pesky permission bits will be set automatically to give her ownership for this editing session.

5. **Turn on the iPhoto Library folder's checkbox, and then click Launch iPhoto.**

   Incredibly, iPhoto opens up that iPhoto library in your account—even if it wasn't yours to begin with. You're free to edit the photos. And you won't have to repeat any of these steps, either; from now on, just opening iPhoto (from within iPhoto Library Manager) will take you straight to the pictures.

   Better yet, each family member (account holder) can set things up the same way for themselves, by repeating steps 2 through 5. (Only one person can actually have the library open for editing at a time, though.)

Books, Calendars, & Cards

At first, gift-giving is fun. During those first 20, 30, or 40 birthdays, anniversaries, graduations, Valentine's Days, Christmases, and so on, you might actually *enjoy* picking out a present, buying it, wrapping it, and delivering it.

After a certain point, however, gift-giving becomes exhausting. What the heck do you get your dad after you've already given him birthday and holiday presents for 15 or 35 years?

If you have iPhoto, you've got an ironclad, perennial answer. The program's Book feature lets you design and order (via the Internet) a gorgeous, professionally bound photo book, printed at a real bindery and shipped to the recipient in a slipcover. Your photos are printed on glossy, acid-free, single-sided pages, complete with captions, if you like. It's a handsome, emotionally powerful gift *guaranteed* never to wind up in an attic, at a garage sale, or on eBay.

These books ($20 and up) are amazing keepsakes to leave out on your coffee table—the same idea as most families' photo albums, but infinitely classier and longer lasting (and not much more expensive).

In iPhoto 6, in fact, the self-publishing business has expanded. Not only is the quality better (300 dpi instead of 150), but you can now create equally great-looking calendars (covering any year, or an arbitrary bunch of months), postcards, and greeting cards.

Fortunately for you, the designing-and-ordering tools are the same for all of these photo-publishing categories. This chapter begins with a tour of the book-making process, and follows up with calendars, greeting cards, and postcards.

Phase 1: Pick the Pix

The hardest part of the whole book-creation process is winnowing down your photos to the ones you want to include. Many a shutterbug eagerly sits down to create his very first published photo book—and winds up with one that's 99 pages long (that is, $109).

In general, each page of your photo book can hold a maximum of six or seven pictures. (iPhoto also offers canned book designs called Catalog and Yearbook, which hold up to 32 tiny pictures per page in a grid. At this size, however, your pictures don't exactly sing. Instead, the whole thing more closely resembles, well, a catalog or yearbook.)

Even the six-per-page limit doesn't necessarily mean you'll get 120 photos into a 20-page book, however. The more pictures you add to a page, the smaller they have to be, and therefore the less impact they have. The best-looking books generally have varying numbers of pictures per page—one, four, three, two, whatever. In general, the number of pictures you'll fit in a 20-page book may be much lower—50, for example.

Either way, winnowing down your brilliant pictures to the most important few can be an excruciating experience, especially if you and a collaborator are trying to work together. ("You can't get rid of that one! It's adorable!" "But honey, we've already got 139 pictures in here!" "I don't care. I *love* that one.")

You can choose the photos for inclusion in the book using any selection method you like. You can select a random batch of them (page 106), or you can file them into an album as a starting point. You can even select a group of albums that you want included, all together, in one book.

If you opt to start from an album, take this opportunity to set up a preliminary photo *sequence*. Drag them around in the album to determine a rough order. You'll have plenty of opportunity to rearrange the pictures on each page later in the process, but the big slide–viewer-like screen of an album makes the process easier. Take special care to place the two most sensational or important photos first and last (for the cover and the last page of the book).

Phase 2: Publishing Options

Once you've selected an album or a batch of photos, click the Book button below the main picture area (Figure 10-1), or choose File→New Book.

Now you see something like Figure 10-1: a dialog box in which you can specify what you want your book to look like. The dialog box looks pretty simple, but it's crawling with important design options.

Book Type

This pop-up menu, shown open in Figure 10-1, lets you specify whether you want to publish your book as a hardbound volume (classier and more durable, but more expensive) or as a paperback. If you choose the softcover option, you can also choose one of three book sizes. The options are 11 x 8½ inches, which feels the slickest and most formal; 8 x 6, which is more portable; and 3½ x 2⅝.

This last option gives you a tiny, wallet-size flip book, with one photo filling each page, edge to edge. You must order these in sets of three (for $12), which suggests that Apple imagines them to serve as simultaneous giveaways to relatives, wedding guests, business clients and so on. In any case, they're absolutely adorable (the booklets, not the business clients).

Figure 10-1:
You can change these settings later, even after you've started laying out your book pages. But if you have the confidence to make these decisions now, you'll save time, effort, and (if you want captions for your photos) possibly a lot of typing.

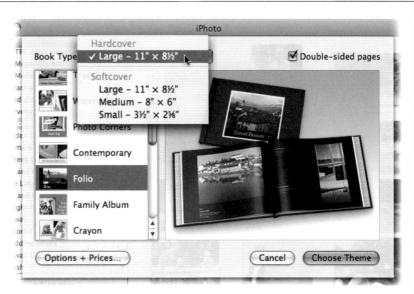

Double-Sided Pages

The pages of *all* softcover book styles are printed with photos on both sides.

If you choose a hardback book, though, you can choose either double-sided printing or single-sided, meaning that each left-hand page is blank. The single-sided printing style tends to give each photo page more weight and drama because it's isolated, but of course your book winds up costing more because it's longer.

Theme Choices

And now, the main event: choosing a *theme*—a canned design, typography, and color scheme—for the cover and pages of your book. The scrolling list of named icons at the left side of the dialog box contains 19 professionally designed page templates, each dedicated to presenting your photos in a unique way.

As you click each one's name in the list, the right side of the dialog box reveals a photograph of a representative book that's been published in that style.

Several of them are new in iPhoto 6. Some are designed to cover even the background of the page with textures, shadows, passport stamps, ripped-out clippings, and other photorealistic simulations.

Here's a brief description of each:

- **Picture Book.** This design's motto could be "maximum photos, minimum margins." There's nowhere for text and captions, and the photos stretch gloriously from one edge of the page to the other—a *full bleed*, as publishers say.

  This dramatic design can be emotionally compelling in the extreme. The absence of text and minimization of white space seems to make the photos speak—if not shout—for themselves.

  (Plenty of people start out believing that captions will be necessary. But once they start typing "Billy doing a belly flop" or "Dad in repose," they realize they're just restating the obvious.)

Tip: Keeping in mind that the book is published horizontally, in landscape mode, will help you maximize page coverage. For example, on pages with only one photo, a horizontal shot looks best, since it'll fill the page, edge to edge. On pages with two photos, two side-by-side vertical (portrait-mode) shots look best. They'll appear side by side, filling the page top to bottom.

- **Modern Lines.** Each page can have up to four photos on it, with plenty of white margin, plus fine gray "modern lines" that separate the pictures. You can add a one-line caption to the bottom of each page, or you can leave the pages text-free.

- **Formal.** Think "wedding" or "graduation." When you order this book, the photos are printed to look like they've been mounted on fancy album pages. You can choose, for each page, either a textured or untextured gray background textures; up to six photos can occupy a page. (The texturing is a hoax, of course. The paper is the same acid-free, shiny stuff of every iPhoto book; it's just *printed* to look like it's textured.)

  You'll have the chance to add a short caption to the bottom of each page.

- **Travel.** If you choose this option, iPhoto will publish a book with beige- and gold-colored page backgrounds (Figure 10-2). The photos are also given a graphic treatment that make them appear to have been taped into a scrapbook, usually at a slight angle to the page. Some of the photos will look like they've actually been folded and then unfolded; others will seem to have been built from 25 smaller ones, all assembled into one larger mosaic image. Adding captions to the pages is optional; if you want them, they'll appear on strips that look like they've been ripped, jagged edge and all, from a piece of stationery.

  Overall, the effect is casual and friendly—not what you'd submit to *National Geographic* as your photographic portfolio, of course, but great as a cheerful memento of some trip or vacation.

- **Watercolor.** "Watercolor," in this case, refers to the page backgrounds, which appear in gentle, two-toned pastel colors. This time, you can choose to have your photos "mounted" on the pages either slightly askew, for an informal look, or neatly parallel to the page edges. Note, though, that this design doesn't offer an option for photo captions, so you'll have to let the pictures tell the story.

- **Photo Corners.** Cute—real cute. Your pictures (up to six per page) look like they've been printed as a cluster, on a single sheet of white photo paper that's affixed to the page using scrapbook-makers' "photo corners." Figure 10-2 shows the effect.

Figure 10-2:
As you click the names of the themes (in the dialog box that's starring in Figure 10-1), you see a little photographic preview of what the book will look like.

Pay special attention to the selection of fonts, the availability of captions, and the photo sizes.

Travel

Family Album

Contemporary

Folio

Baby Boy

Yearbook

Each page can be text-free or labeled with a whole-page caption.

- **Contemporary.** The page backgrounds are white, the photos are all clean and square to the page, and captions, if you want them, appear in light gray, modern type (Figure 10-2). The maximum number of photos on a page is three, ensuring that they remain large enough to make a bold statement. Clearly, though, Apple's hoping that you'll choose only one maximum-impact photo per page; it offers you four different "white-space" treatments for one-photo pages.

- **Folio.** This design is among the most powerful of the bunch, primarily because of the glossy jet-black page backgrounds. (You can also choose plain white.) It looks really cool (Figure 10-2).

This template must have been some designer's pet project, because it's the only one that offers special layout designs for a title page, About page, and explanatory-text page, all done up in great-looking fonts in white, gray, and black. Caption space is also provided.

- **Family Album.** OK, now Apple's officially gone nuts with this "printing pages to look like they're physical scrapbook pages." In this design, photos look like they've been affixed to the page using every conceivable method: attached using "photo corners," taped into photo montages made up of 25 smaller images, licked like giant postage stamps with perforated edges, fastened by inserting their corners into little slits in the page, or even inserted into one of those school-photo binders with an oval opening so your charming face peers out. Up to six pix can occupy a page, and a page caption is optional (Figure 10-2).

- **Crayon.** Here's another design where the pages are photographically printed to look like they're textured paper. For each page, you can choose either a photos-mounted-askew layout or—get this—a straight layout in which each photo has a frame "drawn" around it with a crayon. And to keep with that Crayola-ish theme, you can choose from any of 10 background colors for each page.

You can place up to six photos on a page. Oddly enough, though, you're offered the opportunity to include captions only on the two-photo page design.

- **Baby.** You can choose either Boy (light blue accents on the page backgrounds) or Girl (pink); see Figure 10-2. For each page, you can choose a page-background pattern in stripes, calico, gingham, or canvas. You can also opt to have your photos askew or aligned, but you can't include captions.

Not that you'd really need them. These book designs are obviously included as baby-announcement books—there's even an Information page template with blanks to fill in like Gender, Weight, Time, and Place.

If you've opted for a hardcover book, and you scroll down far enough into the list of design templates, you'll find a second set of them called Old Themes. These were the design choices in iPhoto 4. True, they may be old in computer time (2004—ooh! Ancient!), but they're still perfectly usable (at least for hardback books; they're not available in softcover). In fact, because iPhoto 6 offers double-sided printing, these older designs have been given new life. They include:

- **Picture Book.** This theme is identical to the new, improved Picture Book theme described above. The only differences are that the new one lets you place up to 16 photos per page (instead of six), has more modern-looking type on the cover and Introduction page, and lets you choose how you want the photos arranged on a six-photo page.

- **Catalog.** This design looks exactly like a mail-order catalog: a picture on the left, and a name and description on the right. There are eight pictures per page (or one, or four). It's neatly aligned and somewhat conservative.

  This design would also be an ideal "face book" (with mini-biographies) for, say, a dating agency or personnel director. It's also a candidate for a regular photo album, in the event you're the kind of person who wants it to look square and gridlike, like a "real" photo album from Office Max.

- **Classic.** It's easy to deduce the philosophy behind this conservative, clean design: maximum photos, minimum text. Photos are as large as possible on the page (up to six per page), and each offers only enough room for a title and a very short caption.

- **Collage, Storybook.** These designs are wacky, energetic layouts in which *no* photos are square with the page. Everything falls as though tossed onto a coffee table. Photos may even overlap.

  Collage and Story Book are very similar, except that Collage lacks captions. (Collage does offer a page design called "One with Text" that harbors one photo with a tall, skinny text block next to it.)

- **Portfolio.** Modeled after a photographer's portfolio, this design has elements of both Catalog and Picture Book. Like Catalog, it provides text boxes that accommodate a title and description for each photo. But as with Picture Book, the photos are otherwise displayed at maximum size, with very little white space between them.

  The whole effect is a tad industrial-looking, so you probably wouldn't want to use it as a "memory book" for some trip or event. It's useful in situations where Catalog would be right, except that it's more interesting to look at, thanks to the varied photo sizes.

- **Year Book.** This theme lets you fit up to 32 photos on each page—just as in a high school yearbook (Figure 10-2). Of course, if you choose greater quantities, the photos themselves get smaller—but iPhoto always leaves you enough room for a title ("Chris Jones") and a little description ("Swim team '06; voted Most Likely to Enter the Priesthood").

The Options+Prices button in the corner of the dialog box takes you online to a special Web page that fills you in on the details of the options you've selected, including the maximum number of pages, dimensions, and, oh yeah…the price.

Once you've settled on a design theme for your book, your initial spate of decision-making is mercifully complete. Click Choose Theme.

Tip: You can always revisit your choice of theme—or even book type (size, hardcover, and so on)—by clicking the Themes button at the bottom of the iPhoto window, pictured in Figure 10-4.

Phase 3: Design the Pages

iPhoto is nearly ready to lead you into Book Layout Land, where you'll see, for the first time, *your* pictures inserted into Apple's page designs.

First, though, an important message appears shown in Figure 10-3. It's letting you know that, at least for the moment, your book is completely blank; gray rectangles appear where pictures ought to be. It's your job to put the photos on the pages. And there's two ways to go about it:

- **Use the Autoflow button.** You can use this button if you're in a hurry or you're not especially confident in your own design skills. iPhoto will arrange the photos, in the sequence you've specified, on successive pages of the book.

  No doubt, it's a fast and easy way to lay out the pages of your book, but of course you may not agree with iPhoto's choices. It may clump that prizewinning shot of the dog nosing the basketball through the hoop on the same page as three less impressive pictures.

  On the other hand, you can always touch up the layout afterward, accepting *most* of iPhoto's design but punching it up where necessary, as described on the following pages.

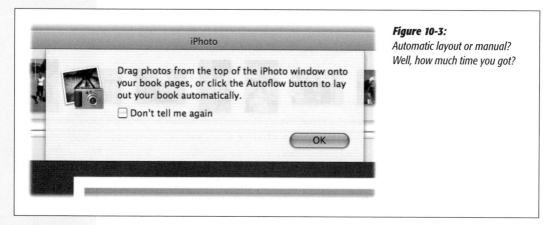

Figure 10-3:
Automatic layout or manual?
Well, how much time you got?

- **Manually.** At the top of the screen, you'll see thumbnails of the pictures you selected; you can drag them onto the gray rectangles, thus assembling your book by hand.

Think about it, and then click OK.

Two things have now happened. First, a new icon appears in your Source list, representing the book layout you're about to create. You can work with it as you would other kinds of Source-list icons. For example, you can delete it by dragging it to the iPhoto Trash, rename it by double-clicking, file it in a folder by dragging it there, and so on.

___

Note: If you're used to previous iPhoto versions, this is a happy bit of news. It means that a book is no longer tied to an album. Therefore, rearranging or reassigning photos in the original album no longer wreaks havoc with the book design that's associated with it.

___

Figure 10-4:
Book mode is a miniature page-layout program right in iPhoto. Use the picture-size slider to zoom in or out from the page you're working on, which can be handy when you're editing captions at small type sizes. Also note the single-page/ two-page switch at the lower-left corner. For books with two-sided printing, it lets you specify whether you want to edit single pages or two-page spreads.

Page thumbnails
Unplaced photos

Page/photo browser

Single-page view/Double-page view

Zoom in/ Zoom out

Previous page/ Next page

Second, you now see something like Figure 10-4. The page you're working on always appears at nearly full size in the main part of the window. Up above, you see a set of thumbnails, either of your photos or of your book pages (more on this in a moment); that's the *photo browser*. iPhoto has just turned into a page-layout program.

Once you've selected an album and a theme, the most time-consuming phase begins: designing the individual pages.

Open a Page

That photo browser at the top of the window has two functions, as represented by the two tiny icons at its left edge.

When you click the top one (the blue page button), you see miniatures of the pages in your book. This is your navigation tool, your master scroll bar. When you click one of the page thumbnails, the full-sized (well, fuller-sized) image of that page appears in the main editing area.

The lower icon presents a desktop, a pasteboard, a temporary scrapbook, for *unplaced photos*—pictures that you've said you want in your book, but haven't yet inserted. (You can see this view of the photo browser in Figure 10-9.) The unplaced-photos area is also convenient for dragging the photos into a satisfying sequence before you transfer them onto the book's pages.

In any case, the first step in building your book is to click a page to work on. Most people start with the Cover page—the first thumbnail in the row. When it's selected, the cover photo appears in the main picture area. This is the picture that will appear, centered, on the linen or glossy cover of the actual book. You can't do much with the cover except to change the title or subtitle; see "Editing Text" on page 271. You'll choose the cover color in a later step.

Tip: The picture you see here is the first picture in the album or selected group. If it's not the photo you want on the cover, you can drag a different photo into its place, as described in the following pages.

Choose a Page Type

After you're finished working with the cover, open the next page you want to work on. If you did some preliminary photo-arranging work (in an album, for example), your photos should already be in roughly the right *order* for the book pages—but not necessarily the right *groupings*.

Whether you opted to have your photos placed into the book manually or automatically, you can see that iPhoto cheerfully suggests varying the number of photos per page. Two-per-page on the first page, a big bold one on the next, a set of four on the next, and so on.

If you approve of the photos-per-page proposal, great. You can go to work choosing which photos to put on each page, as described in the following pages.

Sooner or later, though, there will come a time when you want three related photos to appear on a page that currently holds only two. That's the purpose of the Page Type pop-up menu shown in Figure 10-5. It's a list of the different page designs that Apple has drawn up to fit the overall design theme you've selected.

You control how many pictures appear on a page by choosing from the Page Type pop-up menu. Your choices are:

- **Cover.** The first thumbnail in your book *must* have the Cover design.

(You can choose Cover from the pop-up menu for subsequent pages, too, but that's just a bug; it doesn't actually affect the design of the chosen page.)

- **Introduction.** In most themes, this special page design has no photos at all. It's just a big set of text boxes that you can type (or paste) into. Here's where you can let the audience know about the trip, the company, or the family; tell the story behind the book; praise the book's lucky recipient; scare off intellectual-property thieves with impressive-sounding copyright notices; and so on.

Tip: An Introduction page (one of the choices in the Page Type pop-up menu) doesn't have to be the first page of the book after the cover. Truth is, you can turn *any* page into an Introduction page. Such pages make terrific section dividers.

They're especially useful in designs that use the Picture Book theme, where no text accompanies the photos. In this case, an Introduction page can set the scene and explain the following (uncaptioned) pages of pictures.

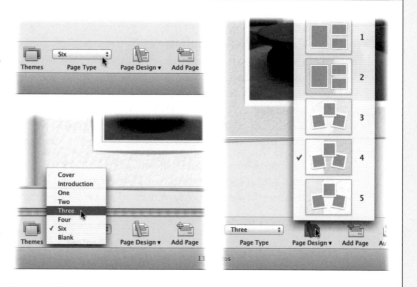

Figure 10-5:
The Page Type pop-up menu (top left, lower left) lets you specify how many photos you want on this page, and lists bonus page types like Cover and Introduction.

Right: Once you've chosen a Page Type, you can use the Page Design pop-up menu. It shows tiny previews of the different layouts available for the Page Type you've selected.

- **One, Two, Three, Four...** These commands let you specify how many photos appear on the selected page. iPhoto automatically arranges them according to its own internal sense of symmetry. (Most themes offer up to six or seven photos per page.)

Use these options to create a pleasing overall layout for the book and give it variety. Follow a page with one big photo with a page of four smaller ones, for example.

You can also use these commands to fit the number of photos you have to the length of your book. If you have lots of pictures and don't want to go over the 10-page minimum, then choose higher picture counts for most pages. Conversely, if iPhoto warns you that you have blank pages at the end of your book, spread your photos out by choosing just one or two photos for some pages.

- **One with Text, Title Page, Text Page, About Page, Contact Page.** Some themes, especially the Folio theme, offer their own private page designs. In general, they're designed to hold specialized blobs of text that are unique to that book design.

- **Blank.** Here's another way to separate sections of your book: Use an empty page. Well, empty of *pictures*, anyway; most of the new iPhoto 6 themes still offer a choice of "look" for a blank page, such as a choice of color or simulated page texture.

- **End.** The Story Book theme offers a bonus page design called End. Use it for the last page of the book.

The End page is designed to hold three pictures, and you'd be well advised to fiddle with your album until the last page does, in fact, have three photos on it. Otherwise, you'll wind up with a strange, half-filled look on the End page. For example, if there's only one photo on it, that picture will sit halfway off the left margin, as though sailing off to the left ("Later, dude!"), and the rest of the page will be blank.

Pick a Layout Variation

Once you've chosen how *many* photos you want on a page, the Page Design pop-up menu becomes available to you. As shown at right in Figure 10-5, it contains tiny thumbnail representations of the various photo layouts available. If you chose Three as the number of photos, for example, the Page Design pop-up menu may offer you a choice of page background (for a three-photo layout) or a couple of different arrangements of those three photos—big one on top, two down the side, or whatever.

In some themes, especially the older ones, you're not offered any choices at all. There's only one arrangement for a two-photo layout, one for a three-photo layout, and so on. In some themes, a page type may offer over a dozen variations. Try before you buy.

Lay Out the Book

The key to understanding iPhoto 6's book-layout mode is realizing that all photos are *draggable*. Dragging is the key to all kinds of book-design issues.

In fact, between dragging photos and using a handful of menu commands, you can perform every conceivable kind of photo- and page-manipulation trick there is.

FREQUENTLY ASKED QUESTION

Doubling the Cover Photo

I want to use my cover photo as one of the pages in the book, just like they do in real coffee-table photo books. How do I do it?

Find the photo in its album, or in your Library; click the photo

and then choose Photos→Duplicate (⌘-D).

Now you have two copies of the photo. Use one as the cover, and then drag the other onto the desired interior page layout.

Ways to manipulate photos

Here are all the different ways to move photos around in your book (see Figure 10-6 for a summary):

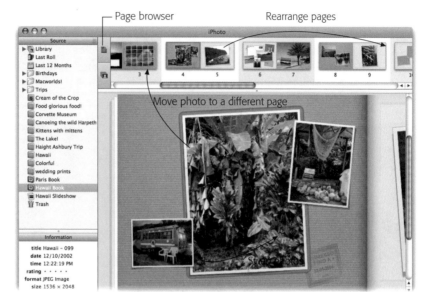

Figure 10-6:
iPhoto's book-layout mode is absolutely crawling with tricks that let you move photos around, add them to pages, remove them, and so on. The fun begins when you finally understand the difference between the page browser (top) and the unplaced-photos browser (bottom).

For example, you can add new photos to your book only via the unplaced-photos browser. Use the page browser more as a navigational tool.

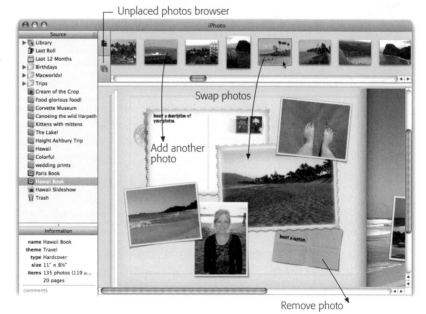

• **Swap two photos on the same page (or two-page spread)** by dragging one directly on top of the other. When the existing picture sprouts a colored border, let go of the mouse button; the two pictures swap places.

• **Move a photo to a different page of the book** by dragging it onto a different page in the photo browser.

• **Remove a photo from a page** by clicking its icon and then pressing your Delete key. Its icon moves up into the unplaced-photos area (Figure 10-6). (You can also drag the photo directly into the unplaced-photos browser, if it's visible.) There it will remain until you move it back onto a book page or delete it.

Figure 10-7:
In some book themes, photos have been "tossed" onto the page so that they overlap slightly. In the rare event that an important part of a photo is covered up by another, you can rearrange their front-to-back order using the shortcut menu shown at left. Here, the lower photo (left) is being slipped underneath the upper photo (right).

• **Remove a photo from the book altogether** by (a) moving it to the unplaced-photos area as described above (or just dragging it off the page), then (b) clicking it *again* (in its current photo-browser location) and, finally, (c) pressing Delete *again*.

Note that removing a photo also changes the resulting page type from a four-photo page layout (for example) to a three-page layout. In other words, the three remaining pictures snap into a different arrangement to fill up the new space. (And if you delete the last remaining photo on a page, you wind up with a big gray placeholder.)

• **Shove one overlapping photo "under" another** by Control-clicking it and, from the shortcut menu, choosing Send to Back. Figure 10-7 reveals all.

• **Add an unplaced photo to a page** by dragging it out of the unplaced-photos browser (Figure 10-4) onto a *blank* spot of the page. iPhoto automatically increases the number of photos on that page, even changing the Page Type pop-up menu to match.

Note: This won't work if the page already has the maximum number of photos on it, according to the theme you've chosen. For example, the Folio theme permits a maximum of two pictures per page.

- **Swap in an unplaced photo** by dragging it out of the unplaced-photos browser *onto* a photo that's already on a page of your book. iPhoto swaps the two, putting the outgoing photo back into the unplaced-photos browser.

- **Add new photos to the unplaced-photos area** by dragging them onto the book's Source-list icon. For example, you can click any album, smart album, slideshow, or Library icon to see what photos are inside—and then drag the good ones onto your book icon.

  Once these photos have arrived in the unplaced-photos area, you can drag them onto individual pages as described above.

- **Fill in an empty gray placeholder frame** by dragging a photo onto it from the unplaced-photos area.

- **Fill in *all* the gray placeholders with photos** by clicking the Autoflow button at the bottom of the window. (Those gray placeholders appear when you choose the Manual layout option described on page 258, or whenever your book has more pages than photos you've put on them.)

  Either way, clicking Autoflow "pours" all of the unplaced photos into the gray placeholders of your book, front to back. When they arrive, they'll be in the same order as they appeared in the thumbnails browser.

  If the results aren't quite what you expected, you can always use the Edit→Undo command to backtrack.

- **Enlarge or crop a picture,** right there on the page, by double-clicking it. A tiny zoom slider appears above the photo, which you can use to magnify the picture or shift it inside its boundary "frame" (see Figure 10-8). For now, it's worth remembering that this trick is helpful when you want to call attention to one part of the photo, or to crop a photo for book-layout purposes without actually editing the original.

- **Edit a photo** by Control-clicking it and, from the shortcut menu, choosing Edit Photo. In a flash, book-layout mode disappears, and you find yourself in the edit-

---

FREQUENTLY ASKED QUESTION

The Save Command

Yo…where's the Save command?

There isn't one. iPhoto automatically saves your work as you go.

If you want to make a safety copy along the way—that is, a fallback version—Control-click the book's icon in the Source

list and then, from the shortcut menu, choose Duplicate. This process takes virtually no extra memory or disk space, but it's good insurance. If you change the layout or theme of a book, iPhoto vaporizes all the text you've entered (and often a lot of the layout work). If that ever happens, you'll be glad you had a backup.

---

ing mode described in Chapter 6. (Either the picture appears in its own window, or the Edit tools fill the bottom toolbar, depending on your iPhoto preference settings.)

When you're finished editing, click Done (or, if you're editing in a separate window, close it). You return to the layout mode, with the changes intact.

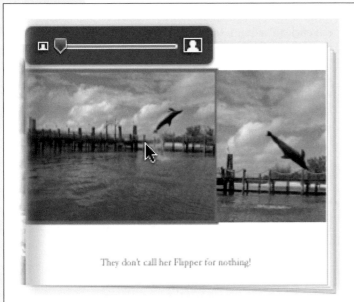

Figure 10-8:

Top: Double-click a photo to make its zoom slider appear. Drag the slider to the right to enlarge the photo.

Bottom: At this point, you can drag inside the photo to adjust its position within its "frame."

None of this affects the actual photo (as using the iPhoto cropping tool would). You're basically just changing the relationship between the photo and its boundary rectangle on the page template. Of course, you'll have to be careful not to enlarge the photo so much that it triggers the dreaded yellow-triangle low-resolution warning.

Ways to manipulate pages

Photos aren't the only ones having all the fun. You can drag and manipulate the pages themselves, too:

- **Move pages around within the book** by dragging their thumbnails horizontally in the photo browser.

- **Remove a page from the book** by clicking its photo-browser icon and then either pressing Delete or choosing Edit→Remove Page. (If you use the Delete-key method, iPhoto asks if you're sure you know what you're doing.)

   Note that removing a page never removes any *pictures* from the book. They just fall into the unplaced-photos area, ready to use later if you like. But removing a page *does* vaporize any captions you've carefully typed in.

- **Insert a new page into the book** by clicking the Add Page button at the bottom of the window, or by choosing Edit→Add Page.

   Before you go nuts with it, though, note that iPhoto inserts the new page *after* the page you're currently viewing. It's helpful, therefore, to begin by first clicking the desired page thumbnail (in the page browser at the top of the window).

   If you have some leftover pictures in the unplaced-photos area, iPhoto uses them to fill the new page; if not, you just get empty gray placeholders. (iPhoto takes it upon itself to decide how many photos appear on the new page.) In any case, now you know how to change the number of photos on that page, or at least how to replace the pictures that iPhoto put there.

Tip: As a shortcut, you can also Control-click (or right-click) a blank spot on any page and, from the shortcut menu, choose Add Page or Remove Page.

Layout strategies

Sometimes chronological order is the natural sequence for your photos, especially for memento books of trips, parties, weddings, and so on. Of course, there's nothing to stop you from cheating a bit—rearranging certain scenes—for greater impact and variety.

As you drag your pictures into order, consider these effects:

- Intersperse group shots with solo portraits, scenery with people shots, vertical photos with horizontal ones.

- On multiple-photo pages, exploit the direction your subjects face (Figure 10-8). On a three-picture page, for example, you could arrange the people in the photos so that they're all looking roughly toward the center of the page, for a feeling of inclusion. You might put a father looking upward to a shot of his son diving on a photo higher on the page, or a brother and sister back-to-back facing outward, signifying competition.

- Group similar shots together on a page.

Making Your Photos Shape Up

iPhoto's design templates operate on the simple premise that all of your photos have a 4:3 aspect ratio. That is, the long and short sides of the photo are in four-to-three proportion (four inches to three inches, for example).

In most cases, that's what you already have, since those are the standard proportions of standard digital photos. If all your pictures are in 4:3 (or 3:4) proportion, they'll fit neatly and beautifully into the page-layout slots iPhoto provides for them.

Figure 10-9:
Variety is good—but thematic unity is effective. Here, two photos taken at the same event, moments apart, feel comfortable together. They tell a little story and add action to your book. (This illustration also shows the unplaced-photos area at the top of the window. Its thumbnails represent all the currently homeless pictures, the ones that you haven't yet placed on a page—or that were on a page, but you removed them. It's a handy temporary storage shelf.)

But not all photos have a 4:3 ratio. You may have cropped a photo into some other shape. Or you may have a camera that can take pictures in the more traditional 3:2 film dimension (1800 x 1200 pixels, for example), which work better as 4 x 6 prints.

When these photos land in one of iPhoto's page designs, the program tries to save you the humiliation of misaligned photos, which was a chronic problem in iPhoto 4. Rather than leave unsightly strips of white along certain edges (therefore producing photos that aren't aligned with each other), iPhoto 6 automatically blows up a mis-cropped photo so that it perfectly fills the 4:3 space allotted to it. Figure 10-9 shows the effect.

Unfortunately, this solution isn't always ideal. Sometimes, in the process of enlarging a nonstandard photo to fill its 4:3 space, iPhoto winds up lopping off an important part of the picture—somebody's forehead, say.

Here, you have two alternatives. First, you can use the Fit Photo to Frame Size command described in Figure 10-10.

Second, you can crop your non-4:3 photos using the Constrain pop-up menu (page 149) set to "4 x 3 (Book)." This way, *you* get to decide which parts of the photo get lopped off. (Or just use the adjustment technique shown in Figure 10-8.)

Figure 10-10:
Top: When you first start working on a book, the photos all look nice together. They nestle nicely side by side. Every now and then, however, you may be disheartened to find that iPhoto is lopping off a dear one's head.

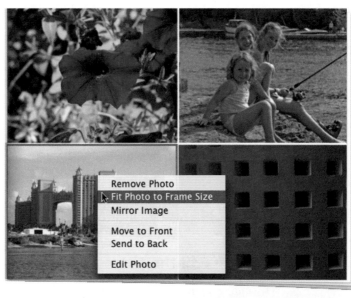

Bottom: If you Control-click a photo and choose Fit Photo to Frame, you'll discover that the problem is a photo that doesn't have 4:3 proportions (on this page, that's three of them). iPhoto thought it was doing you a favor by blowing it up enough to fill the 4:3 box. Now you get ugly white gaps, but, hey, at least you're seeing the entire photo.

Page Limits

The book can have anywhere from 10 to 100 pages (or 20 to 100 for double-sided pages). If you try to create more than that, iPhoto scolds you and dumps the excess photos onto your unplaced-photos shelf.

Of course, if you really have more than 100 pages' worth of pictures, there's nothing to stop you from creating multiple books. ("Our Trip to New Jersey, Vol. XI," anyone?)

Hiding Page Numbers

Don't be alarmed if iPhoto puts page numbers on the corners of your book pages—that's strictly a function of the theme you've chosen. (Some have numbering, some don't.) In any case, you never have to worry about a page number winding up superimposed on one of your pictures. A picture *always* takes priority, covering up the page number.

Even so, if it turns out that your theme *does* put numbers on your pages, and you feel that they're intruding on the mood your book creates, you can eliminate them. Click the Settings button at the bottom of the window. In the resulting dialog box, you'll see a "Show page numbers" checkbox that you can turn off.

Tip: As a shortcut, you can also Control-click a blank spot on any page and, from the shortcut menu, choose Show Page Numbers to turn it on or off.

Phase 4: Edit the Titles and Captions

Depending on the theme you're using, iPhoto may offer you any of several kinds of text boxes that you can fill with titles, explanations, and captions:

- **The book title.** This box appears on the book's cover and, if you've added one, Introduction page. When you first create a book, iPhoto proposes the *album's* name as the book name, but you're welcome to change it.

  A second text box, all set with slightly smaller type formatting, appears below the title. Use it for a subtitle: the date, "A Trip Down Memory Lane," "Happy Birthday Aunt Enid," "A Little Something for the Insurance Company," or whatever.

- **The introduction.** Applying the Introduction-page design to a page produces a huge text block that you can fill with any introductory text you think the book needs.

- **Photo titles.** In some layouts—primarily the old, iPhoto 4 ones—iPhoto can display the name of each photo. (Of the new designs, only the Folio template offers such an option.) When you first create the layout, the program labels each photo with whatever its title is.

If you haven't already named each picture, you'll get only the internal iPhoto name of each one—"IMG_0030.JPG," for example. Once the book layout has been created, though, you can edit the name only in one place: directly on the book page. See Figure 10-11 for details.

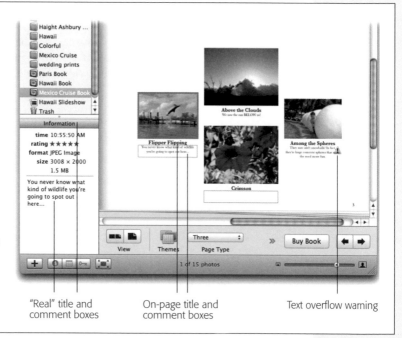

Figure 10-11:
When you first create the book layout, iPhoto inherits its initial photo name and caption text from the existing photo titles and Comments-box information. Unlike previous versions, however, iPhoto 6 doesn't link these two sources; if you change the photo's name in the Info panel, it doesn't change on the page layout. At right: A yellow, nonprinting warning sign appears if the text box is too small to display all of the comment text (or the full photo name).

"Real" title and comment boxes

On-page title and comment boxes

Text overflow warning

- **Comments.** The larger text box that appears for each photo (in some layouts) is for a caption. At the moment of the book's creation, iPhoto automatically fills in this box with any comments you've typed into the picture's Comments box at the left side of the iPhoto screen (see page 123).

  Or, to be precise, it displays the first *chunk* of that text. Most layouts don't show nearly as much text as the "real" Title or Comments box does. In these cases, iPhoto has no choice but to chop off the excess, showing only the first sentence or two. A yellow, triangular exclamation point appears next to any text box with overflow of this kind—your cue to edit down the text to fit the text box on the layout (see Figure 10-11).

Tip: If iPhoto copies the photo names and comments onto the book pages and you don't want it to, click the Settings button below the book layout. Turn off "Automatically enter photo information." This option is also available in the shortcut menu that appears whenever you Control-click a blank spot on any page.

Editing Text

In general, editing text on the photo page is straightforward:

- Click inside a text box to activate the insertion-point cursor, so you can begin typing. Zoom in on the page (using the size slider at lower right) and scroll it, if necessary, so that the type is large enough to see and edit. Click outside a text box—on another part of the page, for example—to finish the editing.

- You can select text and then use the Edit menu's Cut, Copy, and Paste commands to transfer text from box to box.

- You can also move selected text *within* a text box by dragging it and dropping it. The trick is to hold down the mouse button for a moment before dragging. Add the Option key to make a copy of the selected text instead of moving it.

- Double-click a word, or triple-click a paragraph, to neatly highlight it.

- Press Control-right arrow or Control-left arrow to make the insertion point jump to the beginning or end of the line.

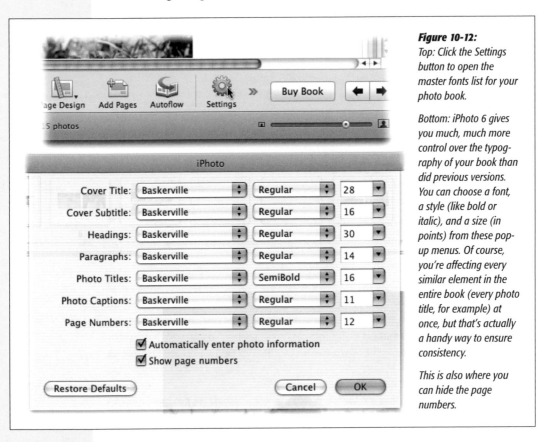

Figure 10-12:
Top: Click the Settings button to open the master fonts list for your photo book.

Bottom: iPhoto 6 gives you much, much more control over the typography of your book than did previous versions. You can choose a font, a style (like bold or italic), and a size (in points) from these pop-up menus. Of course, you're affecting every similar element in the entire book (every photo title, for example) at once, but that's actually a handy way to ensure consistency.

This is also where you can hide the page numbers.

- To make typographically proper quotation marks (curly like "this" instead of like "this"), press Option-[and Shift-Option-[, respectively. And to make a true long dash—like this, instead of two hyphens—press Shift-Option-hyphen.

Formatting Text

iPhoto offers tremendous control over the fonts, sizes, colors, and styles of the text in your book. Here's a summary of your typographical freedom:

- **Standard typefaces.** To choose the basic font for each *category* of text box—book title, photo name, caption, or whatever—throughout the entire book, click the Settings button at the bottom of the window. (If the iPhoto window is very narrow, the Settings command may be hiding in the >> menu at the lower-right corner of the window.)

UP TO SPEED

The Heartbreak of the Yellow Exclamation Point

As you work on your book design, you may encounter the dreaded yellow-triangle-exclamation-point like the one shown here. It appears everywhere you want to be: on the corresponding page thumbnail, on the page display, on the page preview (which appears when you click Preview), and so on.

If you actually try to order the book without first eliminating the yellow triangles, you even get a warning in the form of a dialog box.

Sometimes the problem is that you've tried to put too much text into a text box. So no big deal; just edit it down.

But if the triangle appears on a photo, you have a more worrisome problem: At least one of your photos doesn't have enough resolution (enough pixels) to reproduce well in the finished book. If you ignore the warning and continue with the ordering process, you're likely to be disappointed by the blotchy, grainy result in the finished book.

You may remember from Chapter 1 that the resolution of your digital camera is relatively irrelevant if you'll only be showing your pictures onscreen. It's when you try to print

them that you need all the megapixels you can get—like *now*.

The easiest solution is to shrink the photo on its page. And the easiest way to do that is to increase the number of pictures on that page. Or, if your page design has places that hold both large and small photos, you can drag the problem photo onto one of the smaller photos, swapping the large and small positions.

Decreasing a picture's size squeezes its pixels closer together, improving the dots-per-inch shortage that iPhoto is so boldly warning you about.

If even those dramatic steps don't eliminate the yellow warning emblems, try to remember if you ever cropped the photo in question. If so, your last chance is to use the Photos→Revert To Original command (page 172). Doing so will undo any cropping you did to the photo, which may have jettisoned a lot of pixels that you now need. (If Revert To Original is dimmed, then you never performed any cropping, and this last resort is worthless.)

Finally, if nothing has worked so far, your only options are to eliminate the photo from your book, or to order the book anyway.

You get the dialog box shown in Figure 10-12, where you can make your selections.

- **Font exceptions, text colors.** If you want to override the standard typeface for a certain text box, you can. Choose Edit→Fonts→Show Fonts (⌘-T); the standard Mac OS X Fonts panel appears. Here, you have complete access to all of your Mac's fonts. You can choose special text effects, shadowing, and even colors for individual text selections. Yes, the bright, multicolored result might look a little bit like it was designed by Barney the Dinosaur, but the Color option is worth keeping in mind when you're preparing books describing, say, someone's fourth birthday party.

- **Character formatting.** If you select some words and then Control-click (right-click) them, a shortcut menu appears. It offers Bold, Italic, and Underline choices, which iPhoto will apply to the highlighted text. (The Edit→Fonts menu also works, but it offers only Bold and Italic.)

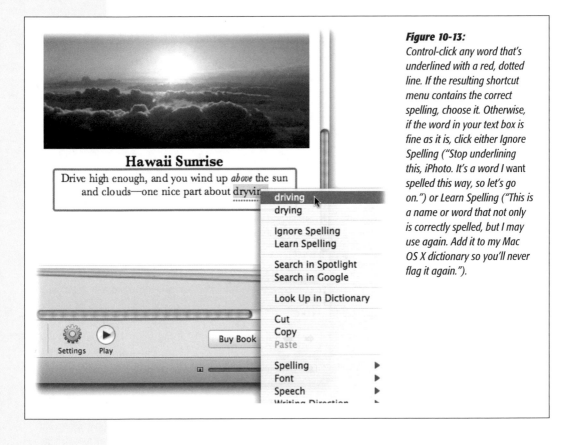

Figure 10-13:
Control-click any word that's underlined with a red, dotted line. If the resulting shortcut menu contains the correct spelling, choose it. Otherwise, if the word in your text box is fine as it is, click either Ignore Spelling ("Stop underlining this, iPhoto. It's a word I want spelled this way, so let's go on.") or Learn Spelling ("This is a name or word that not only is correctly spelled, but I may use again. Add it to my Mac OS X dictionary so you'll never flag it again.").

Tip: Can't seem to get the size, placement, or variety of type that you want? Then the heck with iPhoto and its straitjacketed text boxes—you can use whatever type you want.

All you have to do is jump into a graphics program, like Photoshop Elements, AppleWorks, or GraphicConverter. Create a graphic document that's 1350 x 1800 pixels, with a resolution of 150 dots per inch. Now fill it with text, using the graphic software's text tools. You have complete freedom of fonts and placement.

Finally, bring this graphic into iPhoto. Use it as a single "photo" on the page where you want the text to appear. It's crude and crazy, but it works!

Check Your Spelling

Taking the time to perfect your book's text is extremely important. A misspelling or typo you make here may haunt you (and amuse the book's recipient) forever.

As in a word processor, you can ask iPhoto to check your spelling in several ways:

- **Check a single word or selection.** Highlight a word, or several, and then choose Edit→Spelling→Check Spelling (⌘-semicolon). If the word is misspelled in iPhoto's opinion, a red, dotted line appears under the word. Proceed as shown in Figure 10-13.

- **Check a whole text block.** Click inside a title or comment box and then choose Edit→Spelling→Spelling (⌘-colon). The standard Mac OS X Spelling dialog box appears.

- **Check as you type.** The trouble with the spelling commands described here is that they operate on only a single, tiny text block at a time. To check your entire photo book, you must click inside each title or caption and invoke the spelling command again. There's no way to have iPhoto sweep through your entire book at once.

  Your eyes might widen in excitement, therefore, when you spot the Edit→Spelling→Check Spelling As You Type command. It makes iPhoto flag words it doesn't recognize *as you type them.*

  Sure enough, when this option is turned on, whenever you type a word not in iPhoto's dictionary, iPhoto adds a colorful dashed underline. (Technically, it underlines any word not in the *Mac OS X* dictionary, since you're actually using the standard Mac OS X spelling checker—the same one that watches over you in Mac OS X's Mail program, for example.)

  To correct a misspelling that iPhoto has found in this way, Control-click it (or right-click). A shortcut menu appears. Now proceed as shown in Figure 10-13.

Listen to Your Book

Unfortunately, even a spell checker won't find missing words, inadvertently repeated words, or awkward writing. For those situations, what you really want is for iPhoto to *read your captions aloud* to you.

No problem: Just highlight some text by dragging through it, and then Control-click (or right-click) the highlighted area. As shown in Figure 10-12, a shortcut menu appears, containing the Speech submenu. From it, you can choose Start Speaking and Stop Speaking, which makes iPhoto start and stop reading the selected text aloud. It uses whatever voice you've selected in Mac OS X's System Preferences→Speech control panel.

Phase 5: Preview the Masterpiece

Ordering a professionally bound book is, needless to say, quite a commitment. Before blowing a bunch of money on a one-shot deal, you'd be wise to proofread and inspect it from every possible angle.

Print It

As any proofreader can tell you, looking over a book on paper is a sure way to discover errors that somehow elude detection onscreen. That's why it's a smart idea to print out your own, low-tech edition of your book at home before beaming it away to Apple's bindery.

While you're in Book mode, choose File→Print. After the standard Mac OS X Print dialog box appears, fire up your printer and click Print when ready. The result may not be linen-bound and printed on acid-free paper, but it's a tantalizing preview of the real thing—and a convenient way to give the book one final look.

Slideshow It

Here's a new iPhoto 6 feature that might not seem to make much sense at first: After you're finished designing a book, you can *play* it—as a slideshow.

Just click the ▶ button at the bottom of the screen. (It's at the right end of the toolbar. If the window is too narrow to show all the icons, the Play button is probably hiding behind the >> pop-up menu.)

When you click that button, the Slideshow dialog box appears, looking exactly like it does on page 182. You can set up the usual options here, like how fast you want the "slides" to fly by, what kind of crossfade you want between them, and what musical soundtrack to play, if any.

When you finally click Play, the screen goes dark and then the cover of your book appears, full-screen and personal. It's followed by all the pages of your book, one at a time.

Viewing your book as a slideshow is primarily a proofreading technique. It presents each page at life size, or even larger than life, without the distractions of menus or other iPhoto window elements, so that you can get one last, loving look before you place the order.

But book slideshows are also kind of cool for another reason: They present a more varied look at your photos than a regular slideshow. That is, your photos appear in page groupings, with captions, groupings, and backgrounds that there'd otherwise be no way to create in a slideshow.

Turn It into a PDF File

Sooner or later, almost everyone with a personal computer encounters PDF (Portable Document Format) files. Many a software manual, Read Me file, and downloadable "white paper" come in this format. When you create a PDF document of your own, and then send it off electronically to a friend, it appears to the recipient *exactly* as it did on your screen, complete with the same fonts, colors, page design, and other elements. They get to see all of this even if they don't *have* the fonts or the software you used to create the document. PDF files open on Mac, Windows, and even Linux machines—and you can even search the text inside it.

If you suspect other people might want to have a look at your photo book before it goes to be printed—or if they'd just like to have a copy of their own—a PDF file makes a convenient package.

Here's how to create a PDF file:

Figure 10-14:
Choose a color, a quantity, and a recipient. You won't be allowed to choose a quantity or recipient, though, until you've first signed up for an Apple account, which you'll enjoy using over and over again to order books and stuff from the Apple online stores. To sign up for an account, click the Set Up Account button (not shown here, but it would appear in place of Buy Now if this were your first time).

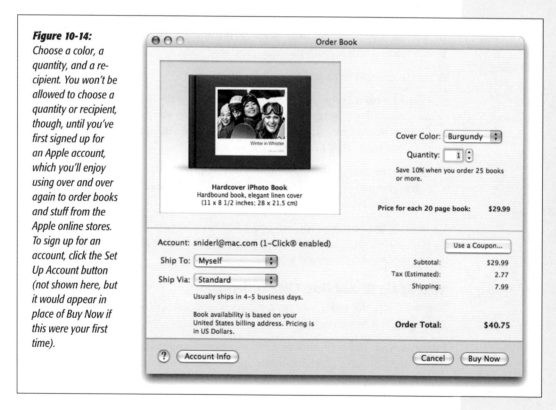

1. With your book design on the screen in front of you, choose File→Print.

   The print dialog box appears.

2. Click the Save as PDF button, if you have one, or choose "Save PDF" from the PDF pop-up button.

The Save sheet appears.

3. **Type a name for the file, choose a folder location for it, and click Save.**

    Your PDF file is ready to distribute. (Fortunately, the recipients will be able to correct the rotation within Adobe Acrobat using its View→Rotate Counterclockwise command, or within Preview using the Tools→Rotate commands.)

Phase 6: Send the Book to the Bindery

When you think your book is ready for birth, click Buy Book.

After several minutes of converting your screen design into an Internet-transmittable file, iPhoto offers you a screen like the one shown in Figure 10-14.

That is, assuming you don't get any of iPhoto's pre-publication warnings first—namely, that you haven't filled in all the default text boxes, like the title and subtitle; that some of your text boxes or photos bear the yellow-triangle low-resolution warning (see the box on page 273); that your book is "incomplete" (you didn't fill in all the gray placeholder rectangles with pictures); and so on.

At this stage, your tasks are largely administrative.

- **Choose a cover color (hardback books only).** Use the Cover Color pop-up menu to choose Black, Burgundy (red), Light Gray, or Navy (blue). The book in the illustration changes color to show you what you're getting. (If you're ordering more than one book, they must all be the same color.)

- **Inspect the charges.** If you've gone beyond the basic 10 or 20 pages, you'll see that you're about to be charged between $.30 and $1.50 per additional page, depending on the book type.

- **Indicate the quantity.** You can order additional copies of the same book. Indeed, after you've spent so much time on a gift book for someone else, you may well be tempted to order yourself a copy.

Your Apple ID and One-Click Ordering

You can't actually order a book until you've signed up for an Apple account and turned on "1-Click Ordering."

However, you may well already have an Apple account if, say, you've ever bought something from an online Apple store or the iTunes Music Store. Whether you have or not, ordering your first iPhoto book requires completing some electronic paperwork like this:

1. **In the Order Book dialog box (Figure 10-14), click Set Up Account.**

    This button appears only if you've never ordered an iPhoto book before. In any case, an Apple Account Sign-In screen appears. If you already have an Apple account, type in your Apple ID and account password here by all means. (An Apple ID is your email address; it's your .Mac address, if you have that.)

When you're finished, click Sign In. On the next screen, make sure 1-Click Ordering is turned on. Click Edit Shipping, if you like, to supply any addresses you plan to use repeatedly for shipping books and Kodak prints to. Finally, click Done. Skip to step 2.

If you've never established an Apple account before, click Create Account, and enjoy your whirlwind tour through Apple's account-signup dialog boxes. You'll be asked to provide your contact info and credit-card number, make up a password, and indicate whether you want to receive Apple junk mail. You'll also be offered the chance to set up a number of addresses for people you may want books shipped to.

You wind up right where you started: at the Order Book screen. This time, however, the controls at the bottom are "live" and operational.

2. **From the Ship To pop-up menu, choose the lucky recipient of this book.**

If it's you, choose Myself. If not, you can choose Add New Address from this pop-up menu.

Note: You can order books if you live in Europe, Japan, or North America, but Apple offers shipping only to people in your own region.

If you wind up at the 1-Click Account Summary screen following this detour, click Done.

3. **From the Ship Via pop-up menu, indicate how you want the finished book shipped.**

For U.S. orders, "Standard" shipping takes about four days and costs $8. "Express" means overnight or second-day shipping (depending on when you place the order) and costs $15. An additional book sent to the same address costs another $1 for Standard shipping, or $2 for Express.

4. **Indicate how many copies of the book you want, using the Quantity control.**

You'll see the Order Total updated.

5. **Click Buy Now.**

You've already stored your credit card information, so there's nothing to do now but wait for your Mac to upload the book itself. After a few minutes, you'll see a confirmation message.

6. **Go about your life for a few days, holding your breath until the book arrives.**

And when it does, you'll certainly be impressed. The photos are printed on Indigo digital presses (fancy, digital, four-color offset machines). The book itself is classy, it's handsome…and it smells good!

Photo Calendars

Custom-made photo books? Old hat, dude. In iPhoto 6, the big news is the other custom stuff you can order: calendars, greeting cards, and postcards. (Mugs and bumper stickers will have to wait for iPhoto 7.)

The calendars are absolutely beautiful. As shown in Figure 10-15, each is spiral bound, with a big Picture of the Month (or Pictures of the Month) above, the month grid below. You can customize each calendar with text, titles, national holidays, events imported from your own iCal calendar, and even little thumbnail photos on the date squares.

If you've ever designed an iPhoto book, designing an iPhoto calendar will give you an overwhelming sense of déjà vu. The calendar-design module is almost identical to the

Figure 10-15:
Top: All of the calendar themes are, well, designs for calendars. The differences among them have to do with font choices, photo placement, and background pattern.

Bottom: As indicated by the "Start calendar on" controls, your calendar doesn't have to start with January, and it can include any number of months up to 24 (two years).

As for "Import iCal calendars:" You can turn on the checkboxes individually for each calendar (that is, category) that you've set up in iCal: Work, Social, Home, Sports League, Casey Stuff, whatever.

book-design module, except that it's turned 90 degrees. That is, the "not yet placed" photo tray runs vertically down the side, rather than across the top.

Anyway, here's the drill.

Phase 1: Choose the Photos

Pick out pictures for the cover photo, the "picture of the month" photos, and any pictures you want to drag onto individual date squares. You can select one full album, several albums, or any group of thumbnails in the viewing area.

Phase 2: Choose the Calendar Design

Choose→New Calendar, or click the Calendar button on the iPhoto toolbar.

A dialog box appears, filled with miniature calendar designs (Figure 10-15, top). These are the calendar design *themes,* which are just like the book themes described on page 252. Once again, click a miniature to see what the finished calendar will look like. The designs differ in photo spacing, the font used for the dates, the availability of captions, and so on.

Click the theme you want, and then click Choose Theme. Now the dialog box shown at bottom in Figure 10-14 appear; here's where you can set up your calendar. For example, you can specify what period you want the calendar to cover.

The "Show national holidays" pop-up menu lets you pre-fill your calendar with important holidays. The United States dates include things like Valentine's Day, Lincoln's Birthday, and Thanksgiving; the French dates include Whit Sunday, Assumption Day, and Bastille Day (in English); and the Malaysian holidays are along the lines of Merdeka, Awal Ramadan, and Yang Di-Pertua of Sarawak's Birthday.

WORKAROUND WORKSHOP

Secrets of the Apple Book Publishing Empire

It's no secret that when you order prints of your photos via the Internet, Kodak makes the prints. But neither temptation nor torture will persuade Apple to reveal who makes the gorgeous iPhoto photo books.

It didn't take long for Mac fans on the Internet, however, to discover some astonishing similarities between the iPhoto books and the books created by a firm called MyPublisher. com. The pricing, timing, and books themselves are all identical. (When asked if it's Apple's publishing partner, MyPublisher.com says, "We don't discuss our partner relationships," which means "Yes.")

The truth is, iPhoto-generated books are more elegantly designed than the ones you build yourself at MyPublisher.

And it's certainly easier to upload books directly from iPhoto, rather than to upload photo files one at a time using your Web browser.

Still, you should know that building your books directly at MyPublisher.com offers greater design freedom than iPhoto does. You have a wider choice of cover colors and materials (even leather), you can add a glossy dust jacket, you can add borders around the pages, and you have much more flexibility over the placement of photos and text.

In fact, it's easy to get carried away with these options and produce something absolutely ghastly, which is probably why Apple chose to limit your options. This way, you simply can't go wrong.

But you knew that.

Finally, if you keep your calendar in iCal (the calendar program in your Applications folder), you can choose to have those events appear on your new photo calendar (Figure 10-15, bottom).

As a bonus, you can turn on "Show birthdays from Address Book." That's a reference to the Mac OS X address book program, which—along with names, addresses, and phone numbers—has a space to record each person's birthday. Incorporating them into your *printed* calendar means that you'll never forget a loved one's (or even liked one's) special day.

Calendar pages ⌐   ⌐ Thumbnails of unplaced photos

Figure 10-16:
There are plenty of places to click as you design a calendar or card.

Down the left side of the screen, for example, iPhoto shows the thumbnails of the pictures you've selected for inclusion—or the thumbnails of the actual calendar pages, which gives you an at-a-glance overview of your design progress.

View single pages, or two-page spreads?   How many photos on the upper page?   Captions or not?   Place remaining photos automatically   Change fonts

Tip: This isn't the only chance you'll have to make these settings. You can return to this Settings dialog box at any time—when you're moving to Malaysia, for example, and want to change the holiday listings—by clicking the Settings button at the bottom of the calendar-design window.

When you're finished setting things up, click OK; you arrive in the calendar-design module. A new icon appears in the Source list, representing the calendar you're creating; you can file it into a folder, rename it, or trash it just as you would a slideshow or a book. You're ready for the fun part: installing your photos onto the calendar pages.

Phase 3: Design the Pages

Each page "spread" of the calendar shows a month grid on the lower page (below the spiral binding), and a "photo of the month" above (Figure 10-16). On each upper page, you'll find gray placeholder rectangles where you can install your favorite photos.

You put your own pictures into those gray boxes works exactly the way you do when designing photo books. That is, you can let iPhoto fill those gray boxes automatically (by clicking the Autoflow button at the bottom of the window), or you can drag pictures onto them one at a time from the left-side waiting area.

You'll find these gray rectangles in three places:

Figure 10-17:
This palette appears when you double-click a photo you've dropped on a date square. You can use the slider to enlarge the picture within its little box; drag inside the picture to reposition it in the frame; or type a caption into the text box at the bottom.

Turn on the Caption checkbox to make it appear, and don't miss the four-way "compass" that determines where the caption appears, relative to the date square: above, below, to the left, or whatever.

- **The cover.** Choose one really good picture to grace the front. This is what the recipient (even if it's you) is going to see when first unwrapping the calendar.

- **The upper page ("picture of the month" space).** Illustrate each month with an especially appropriate photo—or more than one. Use the Layout pop-up menu to choose Two, Three, or whatever; some Themes let you place as many as seven pictures above the spiral binding.

Tip: The Layout pop-up menu has a few other surprises, too. In the Baby themes, for example, it offers an upper-page layout that contains only one tiny photo—and a lot of information about the baby's birth (time, date, gender, weight, and so on).

- **Individual date squares.** This is the part that might not have occurred to you: dragging photos onto *individual squares* of the calendar. Put people's faces on their birthday squares, for example, or vacation shots on the dates when you took them.

Tip: Once you've dropped a picture onto a calendar square, you can double-click it to open the handy editing window shown in Figure 10-17.

When you're finished editing January (or whatever), click one of the big black arrow buttons (lower right) to move on to the next month whose page you want to design.

Phase 4: Edit the Text

Once your calendar is photographically compelling, you can finish it off with titles, captions, and other text.

The cover, for example, offers both a main title and a subtitle. Click the placeholder words to select and replace them with new text of your own.

You can also double-click any date to open up a text box that you can type into (like "Robin's Graduation" or "House Foreclosure"). If the date has a photo on it, you can type into the Caption box. If not, you just get a straight-ahead text box that suffices to label that particular date square.

Tip: Once the caption box is open, you don't have to close it and re-open it for another date. Each time you click a square on the calendar, the caption box automatically changes to show its text contents. (This trick also applies to the photo box shown in Figure 10-17.)

GEM IN THE ROUGH

A Pop-Up You Might Miss

Don't miss the "pop-up icon" called Design (at the bottom of the window). It offers variations on the photo layout for each month's upper page.

In most themes, those variations don't amount to much. The Design pop-up menu usually offers only two choices: one design with a place to type a picture caption, and another without.

But in some themes, like the Paper Animals and Baby designs, the Design pop-up menu offers as many as eight different designs—different background patterns for your photos, for example.

Just as with books, you can change the font formatting—either globally (for all pages) or for just some selected text:

- To change the font globally, click the Settings button on the iPhoto toolbar. In the resulting dialog box, click the Fonts tab. Use the individual pop-up menus (for Cover Subtitle, Comments, Page Text, and so on) to specify the fonts and sizes you want. (If you decide that Apple's original font assignments were actually better than what you've come up with, click Restore Defaults.)

- To change the font for just one word (or sentence, or whatever), highlight it by dragging across it. Choose Edit→Font→Show Fonts to make the standard Mac OS X Fonts panel appear.

Phase 5: Order the Calendar

When you've said to yourself, "I'm [your name here], and I approve of this calendar," click the Buy Calendar button.

If you've left any gray boxes empty (without putting your photos into them), or if any caption placeholders are still empty, an error message appears. You won't be able to order the calendar without filling the gray boxes, although leaving captions empty is OK. (The calendar will simply print without any text there. Not even the dummy placeholder text will print.)

After a moment, your Mac connects to the Internet, and you see the Order Calendar dialog box. It looks and works identically to the Order Book screen (Figure 10-14),

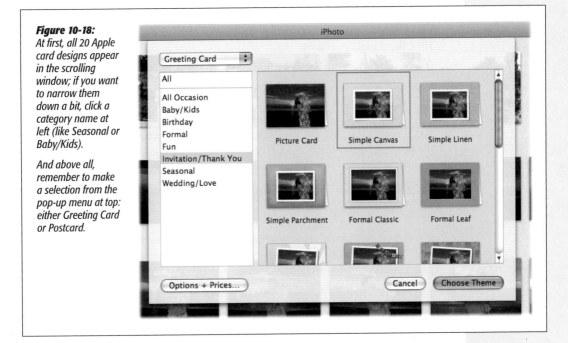

Figure 10-18:
At first, all 20 Apple card designs appear in the scrolling window; if you want to narrow them down a bit, click a category name at left (like Seasonal or Baby/Kids).

And above all, remember to make a selection from the pop-up menu at top: either Greeting Card or Postcard.

except that the pricing is a little different and you don't choose a color for the cover. (A 12-month calendar costs $20. Each additional month adds another $1.50 to the price.)

Assuming you're all signed up as a certified Apple customer (page 278), all you have to do is specify how many copies you want, where you want them shipped, and via which method (standard or expressed). Click Buy Now, and mark off the very few days on your old calendar as you want for the new one to arrive.

Greeting Cards and Postcards

Why stop at books and calendars? iPhoto 6 also offers greeting-card and postcard design modules (Figure 10-18). These items, too, are professionally printed using your own photographic material, look great, and don't cost an arm and a leg.

If you've read about how you design and order books or calendars, the description of the card-ordering process will feel like déjà vu all over again—only simpler.

1. **In your iPhoto collection, click the photo you want on the front of the card. Click the Card icon at the bottom of the window.**

   The familiar Themes dialog box appears, this time showing card designs (Figure 10-18).

Tip: If you select more than one photo in this step, you'll have the option of trying different photos on the card's front to see which you like best.

---

2. **From the pop-up menu at the top, choose either Greeting Card or Postcard. Then click the design you want.**

   iPhoto offers 20 different card-front designs: holiday-themed cards, thank you notes, baby announcements, birthday and invitation cards, and so on.

3. **Click OK.**

   You arrive in the now-familiar iPhoto page-design module, where you can adjust the photo, card background and text (Figure 10-19). You'll see two rectangles here: the inside and outside (of a greeting card) or front and back (of a postcard).

   An icon now appears in your Source list, too, representing the card in progress.

4. **Adjust the photo.**

   If you double-click the photo, you enter the picture-adjustment mode described on page 265. That is, you can drag the slider to enlarge the photo, or drag the picture to adjust its position inside the "frame."

   You can also replace the photo. If you had the foresight to choose several candidates in step 1, then a thumbnail browser appears at the top of the window. You can drag these thumbnails directly into the card's photo area to try them out and install them.

(If you didn't think ahead, all is not lost. Click the album that contains the photos you want to try as alternatives, and then drag them onto the card's icon in the Source list. When you click that icon now, you'll see the thumbnail browser containing the designated photo choices.)

Figure 10-19:
The Background pop-up menu offers a choice of color schemes (and, in some designs, patterns) for the background and interior of the card.

Greeting cards are 5 x 7 inches, come with a matching envelope, and cost $2 each (in quantities up to 24; discounts kick in at larger quantities). Postcards are 4 x 6 and cost $1.50 each. (Here again, they cost less if you order 25 or more, and even less in quantities above 50.)

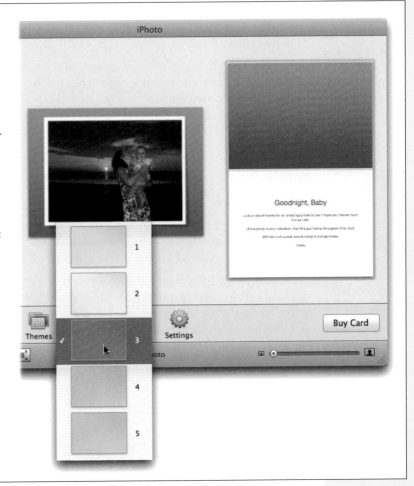

5. **Adjust the background and design.**

   The Background pop-up icon (at the bottom of the window) offers some alternative color schemes for the margins around the front-cover photo (and the corresponding accents on the inside or back of the card); see Figure 10-19.

   The contents of the Design pop-up menu, on the other hand, change depending on whether you've clicked the front of the card or the inside/back. For the front, you get alternative layouts of text and photo (like adding the option to type a caption on the front of the card, or rounding the corners of the photo). If you've clicked the back of a postcard, you get to choose a standard mailable postcard back (with lines where you can write in a name and address, for example), or a non-mailable design that looks more like the inside of a greeting card.

(The Design pop-up menu doesn't offer anything special for the insides of greeting cards.)

6. **Edit the text.**

Double-click any bit of placeholder text on the screen to open its text box for editing. (It's generally uncool to send out baby-announcement cards bearing the legend, "Insert name here.")

Tip: Don't forget that you can zoom in on any part of your card by dragging the slider at the lower-right corner of the screen.

You can also edit the type styles and fonts, exactly as described on page 270.

7. **Order the card.**

When the card looks good, click Buy Card. Your Mac goes online, and the Order Card dialog box appears. Here you'll discover that you're allowed to buy cards individually (you don't have to buy, say, 12 in a box—thanks, Apple!).

These cards are cheap enough and amazing enough that you should consider making them part of your everyday arsenal of social graces. After all, you're living in an era where very few other people can pull off such a thing—and you'll be the one who gets credited with your computer savvy and design prowess.

iPhoto Goes to the Movies

As Chapter 7 makes clear, once you select your images and choose the music to go with them, iPhoto orchestrates the production and presents it live on your Mac's screen as a slideshow.

Which is great, as long as everyone in your social circle lives within six feet of your screen.

The day will come when you want friends and family who live a little farther away to be able to see your slideshows. That's the beauty of QuickTime, a portable multimedia container built into every Mac. Even if the recipient uses a Windows PC—hey, every family has its black sheep—your photos will meet their public; QuickTime movies play just as well on HPs and Dells as they do on iMacs and PowerBooks.

The trick is to convert your well-composed iPhoto slideshow into a standalone QuickTime movie. You'll then have a file on your hard drive that you can email to other people, post on your Web page for downloading, burn onto a CD, and so on. When played on the computer or TV screen, your grateful audience will see your photos, large and luscious, accompanied by the music and effects you chose for them.

Two Kinds of Slideshows

Fortunately, iPhoto makes creating the movie as simple as creating the original show itself. You just have to know which buttons to click.

You may recall that, iPhoto 6 offers two different ways of creating a slideshow:

- **The instant slideshow.** When you click the ▶ triangle at the bottom of the iPhoto window, iPhoto interviews you briefly so that you can specify background music and a slide-to-slide transition style, and then the show begins. Every picture stays on the screen for the same amount of time, and every slide uses the same transition and same Ken Burns effect, if you've applied one.

To export an instant slideshow, you begin by clicking an *album* icon in your Source list.

- **The saved slideshow.** This technique gives you ridiculously complete control over the timing and transition effect of every individual slide in the show.

To export a saved slideshow, you begin by clicking its *slideshow icon* in the Source list.

The process of exporting these two slideshow types (instant and saved) is different, too; in fact, each approach has its own Export dialog box! This chapter covers both methods.

Instant vs. Saved Exported Files

There's no doubt that an exported *saved* slideshow is a spectacular experience. Once you've seen yours playing on a huge screen, complete with all of your stunning crossfades, panes, and zooms, you might wonder why anyone would bother with the far simpler, more primitive look that results when you export an instant slideshow.

Two words: file size.

Consider a typical 20-picture slideshow. If it's a saved slideshow, complete with fancy transitions, the resulting file weighs in at a whopping 44 megabytes when exported as a QuickTime movie. If it begins life as an instant slideshow instead, the same presentation is a svelte 3.4 megs.

Exported *instant* slideshows, therefore, are best when you intend to email the result or post it on the Web; its compact file size just shouts "portability."

Export *saved* slideshows are usually best when played back from a CD, DVD, or another hard drive. Those sophisticated motion graphics add considerable bulk to the size of the file.

You may find a difference in picture quality, too. For example, the Ken Burns effect takes its toll on the sharpness of your pictures (Figure 11-1). Overall, slideshows that you export from instant slideshows are sharper than those that begin as saved slideshows with motion graphics.

Note: Technically speaking, some of the differences in exported-slideshow quality have to do with the *codec* (compression scheme) that iPhoto uses for each type. When you export an instant slideshow, iPhoto uses the Photo-JPEG compressor; when you export a saved slideshow, it uses the MPEG-4 compressor. More on compressors later in this chapter.

Exporting an Instant Slideshow

Before you send your "slideshow movie" to hapless relatives who will have to endure downloading it over a dial-up connection, make sure it's worth watching in the first place.

Step 1: Perfect the Slideshow

As you review your presentation, place the pictures into the proper sequence, remembering that you won't be there to verbally "set up" the slideshow and comment as it plays. Ask yourself, "If I knew nothing about this subject, would this show make sense to me?"

You might decide that your presentation could use a few more descriptive images to better tell the story. If that's the case, go back through your master photo library and look for pictures of recognizable landmarks and signs. Put one or two at the beginning of the show to set the stage. For example, if your slideshow is about a vacation in Washington, D.C., then you might want to open with a picture of the Capitol, White House, or Lincoln Memorial.

Tip: If you don't have any suitable opening shots in your library, or even if you do, another option is to begin your show with a few words of text, like opening credits. To do so, create a JPEG graphic containing the text in a program like AppleWorks, Photoshop, or GraphicConverter. (Make sure this graphic matches the pixel dimensions of your slideshow, as described in the following section.) Then drag the file right into your slideshow album, placing it first in the sequence. You've got yourself an opening title screen.

Figure 11-1:
The left image is from a 640 x 480 instant slideshow exported to QuickTime; the picture at right is from a saved slideshow that's being zoomed via the Ken Burns effect. Some image quality was sacrificed for the effect, as you can see by the blurriness of the background scrub grass at right.

Your viewers may not notice the loss of sharpness, in part because the motion of the image occupies their attention. But for presentations that demand the ultimate image quality, you might want to stick with exporting from Quick slideshows—or to avoid the Ken Burns effect in saved slideshows.

Which photos make the cut

If you're used to the slideshow feature described in Chapter 7, the method for specifying which photos are exported to your QuickTime movie might throw you.

- If *one* thumbnail is selected, that's all you'll get in the finished QuickTime movie—the world's shortest slideshow. (This is the part that might throw you: An iPhoto slideshow would begin with that one selected photo and then move on from there, showing you all the rest of the photos in the album.)

- If *several* thumbnails are selected, only they make it into the slideshow movie.

- If *no* thumbnails are selected, the entire album's worth of photos wind up in the show.

When you're ready to convert your presentation to a QuickTime movie, choose File→Export. The Export Photos dialog box appears, as shown in Figure 11-2. Click the QuickTime tab, where you have some important decisions to make.

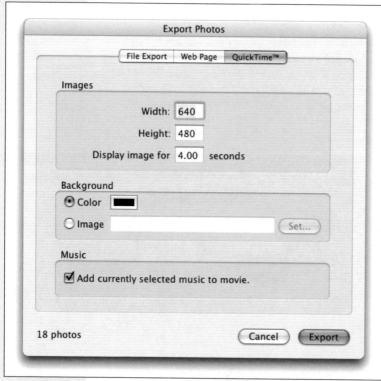

Figure 11-2:
Here's the Export dialog box with the QuickTime tab selected. This is the airlock, the womb, the last time you'll be able to affect your movie before it's born. You're free to change these dimensions, however. If the movie will be played back from a hard drive, you may want to crank up the dimensions close to the size of the screen itself: 800 x 600 is a safe bet if you're not sure. Remember, though, you have to leave some room for the QuickTime Player controls, so that your audience can start and stop the movie.

Step 2: Choose the Movie Dimensions

Specifying the width and height for your movie affects not only how big it is on the screen during playback, but also its file size, which may become an issue if you plan to email the movie to other people. iPhoto generally proposes 640 x 480 pixels. That's an ideal size: big enough for people to see some detail in the photo, but usually small enough to send, in compressed form, by email.

Proportion considerations

All of these suggestions assume, by the way, that your photos' dimensions are in a 4:3 ratio, the way they come from most cameras (see page 151). That way, they'll fit nicely into the standard QuickTime playback window.

But there's nothing to stop you from typing other numbers into the Width and Height boxes. If most of the shots are vertical, for example, you'll want to reverse the proposed dimensions so that they're 480 x 640, resulting in a taller, thinner playback window.

Size considerations

As you choose dimensions, bear in mind that they also determine the *file size* of the resulting QuickTime movie. That's not much of an issue if you plan to play the movie from a CD, DVD, or hard drive. (And in that case, you might want to generate your movie from a saved slideshow instead, as described below.) But if you plan to send the movie by email or post it on a Web page, watch out for ballooning file sizes that will slow dial-up sufferers to a crawl.

For example, an 18-slide movie with an MP3 music soundtrack would take up 3.1 MB on your hard drive (at 640 x 480 pixels)—and at least that much in your recipients' email inboxes. Scaling it down to half that size in each dimension (320 x 240) would shave off about a third, resulting in a 2.4 MB file.

You could eliminate the music soundtrack, which would shrink the movie to a mere 350 K—but who wants a silent movie?

Fortunately, there is a middle road. It involves some work in iTunes and a slight reduction in sound quality, but reducing the file size of the music track can result in substantial file shrinkage. See the box on the next page for details.

Step 3: Seconds per Photo

How many seconds do you want each picture to remain on the screen before the next one appears? You specify this number using the "Display image for ___ seconds" box in the QuickTime Export dialog box.

Step 4: Background Colors

The color or image you choose in the Background section of the dialog box will appear as the first and last frames of the export. It will also fill in the margins of the frame when a vertically oriented or oddly proportioned picture appears.

Solid colors

To specify a solid color, click the color swatch next to the Color button. The color picker described in the figure on page 233 appears.

Generally speaking, white, light gray, or black makes the best background. Black is particularly good if you've bought QuickTime Player Pro (page 297) and want to present your slideshow in full-screen mode, which turns the Mac into a virtual movie screen and makes the borders between your movie and the screen indistinguishable.

Background graphics

If you click the Image button and then the Set button next to it, you can navigate your hard drive in search of a *graphics* file to use as the slideshow background. This is where a graphics program like AppleWorks, Photoshop, or Graphic Converter comes in handy. By designing a picture there (in dimensions that match your movie) and exporting it as a JPEG file, you have complete freedom to control the kind of "movie screen" your QuickTime slideshow will have.

Step 5: Export the Movie

Having specified the dimensions, frame rate, music, and background for your movie, there's nothing left but to click the Export button in the dialog box. You'll be asked to specify a name and folder location for the movie (leaving the proposed suffix *.mov* at the end of the name), and then click Save. After a moment of computing, iPhoto returns to its main screen.

Press ⌘-H to hide iPhoto; then navigate to the folder you specified and double-click the movie to play it in QuickTime Player, the movie-playing program that comes with every Mac. When the movie opens, click the Play triangle or press the Space bar to enjoy your newly packaged slideshow (Figure 11-3).

POWER USERS' CLINIC

Musical Liposuction

If you're struggling with the size of a QuickTime movie slideshow that's too big for emailing, consider shrinking the size of the music track. By cutting its *bit rate* (a measure of its sound quality) from 192 to 128 kbps, for example, the file size for a hypothetical 320 x 240–pixel movie would shrink from 2.1 MB to 1.5 MB—and most people playing the movie over typical computer speakers wouldn't hear the difference.

This kind of surgery requires iTunes, the music-management software that comes with every Mac.

Start by choosing iTunes→Preferences. In the Preferences dialog box, click the Importing icon. From the Import Using pop-up menu, choose MP3 Encoder. Then, from the Setting pop-up menu, choose, for example, "Good Quality (128 kbps)." (A lower Custom number will result in even smaller files, although the sound quality may suffer.) Click OK to close the dialog box.

Now highlight the track you want to add to your slideshow, and then choose Advanced→Convert Selection to MP3.

iTunes converts the song into a duplicate copy that has the new, lower sample rate (quality setting). The song's name appears in your iTunes Music Library list just below the original. (You might want to rename it to differentiate it from the original, higher quality song by highlighting it and then choosing File→Get Info. Click Info in the resulting dialog box.)

Now return to iPhoto. Click the album you're going to import, click the Play Slideshow triangle below the Source list, click the Music tab, and finally select your new resampled song from the list of titles in the dialog box. Click Save Settings.

When you export the slideshow to QuickTime, you'll find that it's much more svelte, but sounds practically identical to the puffier version.

Whenever playback is stopped, you can even "walk" through the slides manually by pressing the right-arrow key twice (for the next photo) or the left-arrow key once (for the previous one).

Tip: Even Windows PC users can enjoy your QuickTime movies–if they visit *www.apple.com/quicktime/download* to download the free QuickTime Player program for Windows.

Figure 11-3:
Once you're in QuickTime Player, you can control the playback of the slideshow in a number of ways. If you don't feel like clicking and dragging onscreen controls, the arrow keys adjust the volume (up and down) or step through the photos one at a time (right and left).

Exporting a Saved Slideshow

But what if you've created a more elaborate slideshow, using the Slideshow editing mode? What if there's an Slideshow icon in your Source list at this moment, representing hours you've spent perfecting your pans, fiddling with your fades, and tweaking your timings into a work of art? This creation isn't for posting on the Web. It's designed to be savored in all its glory on a 30-inch Cinema Display. And you want to preserve every nuance when you export your masterpiece to QuickTime.

To do so, click the slideshow icon in the Source list and, once again, choose File→ Export. This time, though, the Export dialog box (Figure 11-4) asks you to make only three decisions: what you're going to name the file, where you're going to save it on your hard drive, and what its dimensions are. And even then, you're limited to three choices: 640 x 480, 320 x 240, and 240 x 180.

Make your selections, click the Export button, then go walk the dog. iPhoto will take some time to convert your Saved slideshow to a QuickTime movie.

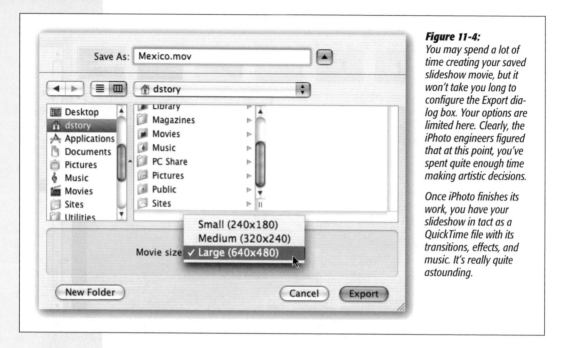

Figure 11-4:
You may spend a lot of time creating your saved slideshow movie, but it won't take you long to configure the Export dialog box. Your options are limited here. Clearly, the iPhoto engineers figured that at this point, you've spent quite enough time making artistic decisions.

Once iPhoto finishes its work, you have your slideshow in tact as a QuickTime file with its transitions, effects, and music. It's really quite astounding.

Fun with QuickTime

The free version of QuickTime Player is, well, just a player. If you're willing to pay $30, however, you can turn it into QuickTime Player Pro, which offers a few special features relevant to iPhoto movie fans.

- **Play movies in full-screen mode.** QuickTime Player Pro can play exported slideshows in full-screen mode—no menu bar, Dock, window edges, or other distracting elements. In effect, it turns your laptop screen into a portable theater.

- **Edit your flicks.** QuickTime Player Pro lets you trim off excess footage, add an additional soundtrack, or even add a text track for subtitles (captions). It's also great for combining or editing down the little movies that iPhoto downloads from your digital camera.

- **Adjust video and audio.** Only the Pro version lets you fine-tune your video and audio controls—Brightness, Treble, Bass, and so on—and then save those settings with your movie.

- **No more nagware.** Upgrading eliminates the persistent "Upgrade Now" dialog box that appears when you open the regular Player program.

If you decide that the upgrade is worthwhile, visit *www.apple.com* and click the QuickTime tab. There you'll find the links that let you upgrade your free QuickTime player to the Pro version. In exchange for $30, you'll be given a registration number that "unlocks" QuickTime's advanced features. (To input the serial number in QuickTime Player, choose QuickTime Player→Preferences→Registration, and then click the Registration button.)

Then you'll be ready for the following tricks.

Play Movies at Full Screen

If you've upgraded to QuickTime Player Pro, here's how to create a full-screen cinematic experience.

First, use a black background when you export your movie from iPhoto. That way, there will be no frame marks or distracting colors to detract from your images. Furthermore, the black bars on the sides of vertically oriented photos will blend in seamlessly with the rest of the darkened monitor, so that nobody is even aware that the photo has been rotated. Those black bars will also fill in the gap between the standard monitor shape and the nonstandard ones preferred by Apple these days (such as the screens on the extra-wide Cinema Display, the iMac, or the 15-inch laptops).

Second, export your movie in as large a size as will fit on your screen. That means dimensions of 1024 x 768, or whatever matches your monitor's current setting. (To find out, choose →System Preferences and click the Display icon.) Your images will occupy more of your Mac's display area, imparting greater impact.

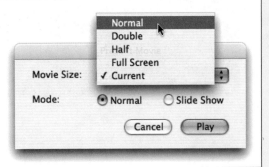

Figure 11-5:
From the Movie Size pop-up menu, choose Normal or Current. (Yes, you could choose Full Screen—but that would stretch your photos to fill the screen, often resulting in distortion.) Click Play, sit back, and enjoy.

To end a self-playing show, click the mouse; to end a show in Slideshow mode, press ⌘-period.

Once you've exported your movie, presenting it in "theater mode" is as simple as choosing Movie→Present Movie. Then set up the dialog box as shown in Figure 11-5.

Once you've created a slideshow movie, keep in mind that nothing's etched in stone—at least not if you have QuickTime Player Pro. Suppose you don't care for the empty frames of background color (or background picture) that iPhoto adds automatically at the beginning and end of your movie? Or what if, thanks to an unforeseen downsizing, a graduation, or a romantic breakup, you want to delete a photo or two from an existing movie? Using QuickTime Player Pro, you can snip unwanted photos or frames right out.

Selecting footage

Before you can cut, copy, or paste footage, QuickTime Player needs to provide a way for you to specify *what* footage you want to manipulate. Its solution: the two tiny black triangles that sprout out of the left end of the horizontal scroll bar, as shown in Figure 11-6. These are the "in" and "out" points; by dragging these triangles, you can enclose the scene you want to cut or copy.

Tip: You can gain more precise control over the selection procedure shown in Figure 11-6 by clicking one of the black triangles and then pressing the right or left arrow key to adjust the selection a frame at a time.

Or try Shift-clicking the Play button. As long as you hold down the Shift key, you continue to select footage. When you release Shift, you stop the playback; the selected passage then appears in gray on the scroll bar.

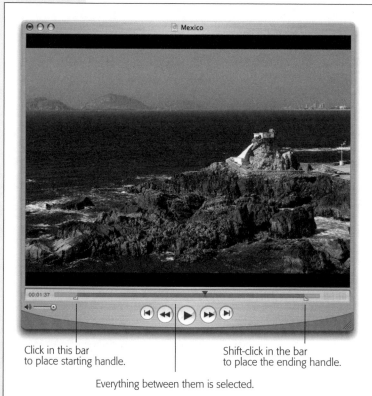

Figure 11-6:
To select a particular scene, drag the tiny black triangles apart until they enclose the material you want, or use the clicking/Shift-clicking trick shown here. As you drag or click, QuickTime Player updates the movie picture to show you where you are. The material you select is represented by a gray strip in the scroll bar.

Click in this bar
to place starting handle.

Shift-click in the bar
to place the ending handle.

Everything between them is selected.

Once you've highlighted a passage of footage, you can proceed as follows:

• Jump to the end or beginning of the selected footage by pressing Option-right arrow or -left arrow key.

• Deselect the footage by dragging the two triangles together again.

- Play only the selected passage by choosing View→Play Selection Only. (The other View menu commands, such as Loop, apply only to the selection at this point.)

- Drag the movie picture out of the Player window and onto the desktop, where it becomes a *movie clipping* that you can double-click to view.

- Cut, copy, or clear the highlighted material using the commands in the Edit menu.

Advanced Audio and Video Controls

One of the difficulties of creating multimedia productions is that there's no standard calibration for all the various computers that might play them. For example, a slideshow that your friend creates on his Dell computer might look washed-out on your Mac.

Luckily, QuickTime Player Pro offers a solution. See Figure 11-7.

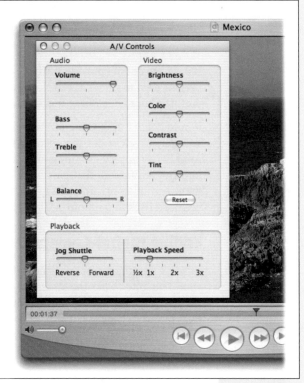

Figure 11-7:
Should you inherit movies with poor audio and video, QuickTime Player Pro gives you some useful audio and video controls to compensate.

Fortunately, you can adjust the brightness, balance, bass, or treble using these generally controls. The trick is to show and hide them by choosing Window→Show A/V Controls.

For real comedy, don't miss the Playback Speed slider, either...

Exporting Edited Movies

After you've finished working on a sound or movie, you can send it back out into the world by choosing File→Save As. At this point, you can specify a new name for your edited masterpiece. You must also choose one of these two options:

- **Save normally.** The term "normally" is a red herring. In fact, you'll almost never want to use this option, because it produces a very tiny file that contains no footage at all; it's like an alias of the movie you edited. A file that you save "normally" works only as long as the original, *unedited* movie remains on your drive. If you try to email the newly saved file, your unhappy recipient won't see anything at all.

- **Make movie self-contained.** This option produces a new QuickTime movie—the one you've just finished editing. Although it consumes more disk space, it has none of the drawbacks of a "save normally" file. This is the option you should choose.

Managing Movies Imported From Your Camera

Digital camera movies were once a novelty that few cared about. Today, though, they've become a convenient way to record video without lugging around a camcorder. Most current digicams can capture movies with standard TV-screen resolution (640 x 480 pixels), standard TV smoothness (30 frames per second), and sound. (Some, in fact, can capture movies with even higher resolution and greater frame rates.)

When you import your photos into iPhoto, the program cheerfully adds those video files to your library, denoted by a little camcorder icon and duration indicator.

But iPhoto doesn't provide any tools to edit the video, to combine it with other snippets, or even to watch it. When you double-click an imported movie, iPhoto hands it off to QuickTime Player in a separate window.

iPhoto doesn't update the movie thumbnail when you edit and save the file, either. You may have cut out the opening scene of a clip in QuickTime Player Pro—say, Aunt Betty tripping over the garden hose—but she'll still be there in your thumbnail library, even though that particular moment of video is now on the cutting-room floor. The only workaround is to save the cleaned-up version to your hard drive, then import it back into iPhoto.

Editing Digital-Camera Movies

To edit your camera-captured movies, open iMovie (the video-editing component of your iLife suite). Click the Media button and then the Photos tab, so that you can see all your iPhoto pictures—and all your iPhoto movie clips. Drag the clips you want right into your timeline. (Or, if iPhoto is running, drag the movies' thumbnails right out of iPhoto's window and into iMovie's timeline or Clips panel.)

The end.

All right, there's a *little* more to it—like learning how to *use* iMovie—but that's a different book. The point here is that you can incorporate movies from iPhoto's library in whatever iMovie project you have open, ready to edit as you would any other clips.

Tip: Want a great way to organize your camera's movies all at once? Create a new smart album as described in Chapter 5. Set it up so that the pop-up menus and text boxes in the New Smart Album dialog box say "Title" "ends with" ".mov" (or ".avi," depending on how your digital camera names its movie files). You'll always find all your movies safely collected in this self-updating smart album.

Editing Digital-Camera Movies in QuickTime Player Pro

If learning iMovie seems like overkill for some little project—if all you want to do is combine a few into one longer flick, for example—you can get by with nothing more than QuickTime Player Pro.

Suppose, for example, that you want to combine two movies called Clip A and Clip B. Open both of them by double-clicking their thumbnails in iPhoto.

Then follow along with this quick refresher that covers the basic editing techniques for this project:

- **Trim.** You can use this command to trim unwanted footage from the beginning or end of a movie clip. First, move the bottom triangles on the scrubber bar to the in and out points of the footage you want to keep, as shown in Figure 11-7. When you choose Edit→Trim to Selection, QuickTime Player eliminates the white area on the scrubber bar, retaining the gray area.

- **Select, Copy, Add.** Many digital cameras allow you to shoot only 30 seconds or a couple minutes of video at a time. So to construct your movie, you can use these commands to combine short clips into a longer presentation.

  The procedure is a lot like copying and pasting text. In the first movie—the one that will become the master, fully assembled version—click the far right triangle to move the scrubber head to the end.

  Now open the second movie. Choose Edit→ Select All to highlight the whole clip; then choose Edit→Copy. The selected video and audio is now on the clipboard.

  Return to the first movie; choose Edit→Add to Movie. (Don't choose Edit→Paste, or you'll *replace* the video in the first movie.) The copied video now appears at the end of the movie. You'll see that its duration indicator changes to reflect the added length.

- **Save As.** Choose File→Save As. Give your combined movie a new name, click "Make movie self-contained," and then click Save. (As noted earlier, don't use the regular Save command unless you intend to *replace* the original movie clip in iPhoto 6 with your edited one.) Once you've stored the new version on your hard drive, you can drag it back into iPhoto.

Tip: If your digital camera captures video at 640 x 480 pixels (that's full-screen TV size), you can add video to your exported slideshows. To do so, export an instant slideshow as described on page 291, taking care to save the result at 640 x 480 pixels. Open the exported slideshow in QuickTime Player Pro, along the desired movie clip. Using the Select, Copy, and Add commands described above, you can now create presentations beyond anything you ever expected possible from iPhoto.

Burning a QuickTime Movie CD

If your QuickTime slideshow lasts more than a minute or two, it's probably too big to send to people by email. One alternative: Burn them a CD. Here's how the process goes:

1. **Prepare your QuickTime movie.**

   Since file size isn't as much of an issue, you can make your slideshow dimensions 640 x 480, 720 x 480, 800 x 600, or any other size that will fit on the computer screen. There's no need to throttle down the music quality, either.

Tip: To make things easy for the audience (even if it's only you), you can turn on the Auto Play feature, which will make the movie play immediately after being double-clicked. (Savings: One click on the triangular Play button.)

To turn on Auto Play, start by opening the movie in QuickTime Player Pro. Choose Window→Show Movie Properties. In the Properties dialog box, click the Presentation tab, and then turn on "Automatically play movie when opened." Save the movie as usual.

---

2. **Put a blank CD in your burner.**

   A few seconds after you insert the disc, it appears on your desktop as "untitled CD." You can rename it by clicking its name and then typing away.

3. **Drag the QuickTime movie(s) onto the CD's icon.**

   These are, of course, the slideshow movies you've exported from iPhoto or the video clips from your digital camera.

4. **Click once on the CD icon and then choose File→Burn Disc.**

   A confirmation dialog box appears (Figure 11-8).

Figure 11-8:
You have one last chance to change your mind before you burn the CD. If everything's a go, then click Burn.

5. Click Burn.

The Mac saves the movies onto the CD.

When the process is complete, eject the disc. It will play equally well on Mac OS 9, Mac OS X, and Windows computers that have QuickTime Player installed.

By the way, if your Mac has Mac OS X 10.4 (Tiger) or later, another approach is to choose File→New Burn Folder from the File menu. A new folder called Burn Folder appears on your desktop. Name it anything you want, then drag your movies inside. Now open the folder and click on the Burn button in the upper-right corner. The Mac asks for a blank CD, and then walks you through the process of burning it.

Tip: If you have the software called Toast Titanium *(www.roxio.com),* an additional option awaits. You can drop the icon of your exported iPhoto slideshow movie into Toast's Video pane.

Then, if you choose the VideoCD option, Toast will burn you what's known as a *Video CD.* It's something like a low-rent, low-quality DVD. It will play on most modern DVD players, thus offering a handy way for computer-less people to watch your slideshow on TV.

Of course, if your fans have DVD players, you might have even more fun making a full-blown, commercial-style DVD for them, as described in Chapter 12. The beauty of VCD discs, though, is that you don't need a Mac with a SuperDrive (DVD burner) to create one.

Slideshow Movies on the Web

Chapter 9 offers complete details for posting individual photos on the Web. But with just a few adjustments in the instructions, you can just as easily post your slideshow movies on the Web, too, complete with music.

Preparing a Low-Bandwidth Movie for the Web (No Transitions)

You could, of course, just make a slideshow movie as described on the previous pages, and then slap it up on the Web. Unfortunately, a movie like that would involve quite a wait for your Web visitors. They would click the movie's icon to view it—and wait while the entire 3 MB movie downloads. Only then could they begin watching it.

But if you have QuickTime Player Pro, you can create movies that start playing almost immediately when Web visitors click them. Here's how to preprocess your finished slideshow movie so that it will start faster online. Open your movie in QuickTime Player Pro, and then follow these steps:

1. Choose File→Export.

The "Save exported file as" dialog box appears. Make sure that the Export pop-up menu says "Movie to QuickTime Movie," and the Use pop-up menu says Most Recent Settings.

2. Click Options.

The Movie Settings dialog box appears (Figure 11-9, top). Your job is to format the movie so that it will look good without taking a long time to download.

3. Under Video, click Settings. In the Compression Settings dialog box (Figure 11-9, bottom), choose "Photo – JPEG" from the first pop-up menu.

This format is compact and high quality, making it a good choice for slideshows.

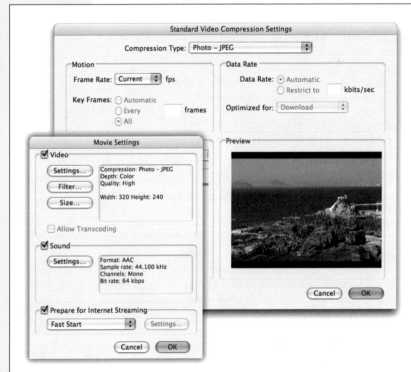

Figure 11-9:
Lower left: These settings will help you prepare your movie for Web serving. After you've tried an export or two, you can play with the adjustments to customize your slideshow even further.

Top right: These are good video settings for an exported slideshow Web movie; it will consume only 1 megabyte for a 20-slide show at 320 x 240 pixels, with music. By choosing Current for your "frames per second," you're telling QuickTime to be very frugal with the data rate. Your pictures will still look great, but you'll lose those elegant dissolve transitions. The images will simply cut from one to the next.

4. In the "Frames per second" box, select Current from the pop-up menu.

The resulting file will be small, but you'll lose the crossfades between slides, if you used them.

5. Drag the Quality slider to Medium or High, and then click OK.

You return to the Movie Settings dialog box.

6. Click the Size button. Enter 320 in the Width box and 240 in the Height box; click OK.

Use a larger size only if you're sure that your audience members all have high-speed Internet access. Note, though, that if you post your movie to a .Mac account, Apple's HomePage service will just squish it down to 320 x 240 anyway.

7. **Under Sound, click Settings. In the Sound Settings dialog box, choose AAC from the Compressor pop-up menu, and then click OK.**

The AAC Music format produces high-quality music at very small file sizes, which is just what you'd hope for in Web-played movies. (If your movie has a spoken dialog track rather than music, use the Qualcomm PureVoice codec instead.)

You return once again to the Movie Settings box. Here, confirm that the "Prepare for Internet Streaming" checkbox is turned on, and that Fast Start is selected in its pop-up menu. These settings are responsible for QuickTime's fast-playback feature, in which your viewers don't have to wait for the *entire* movie to download before playback starts. Instead, they'll only have to wait for a quarter or half of it, or whatever portion is necessary to play the entire movie uninterrupted while the latter part is still being downloaded.

8. **Click OK, then Save.**

Your slideshow takes a few minutes to export. But once the process is complete, you're ready to upload the file to your Web site.

Note: Once you've optimized and exported your slideshow in QuickTime Pro, don't use the File→Save or File→Save As command after making changes to the movie. If you do, you'll automatically turn *off* the Fast Start option you built in when you exported the movie.

It's OK to make further changes. But when you're finished, use the File→Export command again, repeating the previous steps, to preserve the movie's Web-optimized condition.

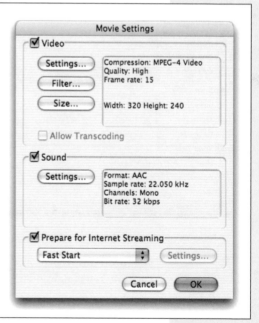

Figure 11-10:
You can preserve your cool-looking slide transitions by increasing the compressor, frame rate, and data rate for your exported movie.

These changes, of course, produce a bulkier file; for a 20-slide set, the slideshow movie file swells from 1 to 14 megabytes. Still, your audience won't mind; they have high-speed connections, and you've turned on the Fast Start option in the movie.

Preparing a High-Bandwidth Movie for the Web (With Transitions)

If you expect that your audience will have high-speed Internet connections (or if they're on your same office network), you can retain the elegant between-slide transitions that you've worked so hard to perfect. In this scenario, file size isn't so important.

The steps are the same as those outlined in the previous section, but you use a few different settings in the Options dialog box (steps 2–7). This box should look like Figure 11-10 before you click OK.

Tip: If your movie will be played back from a hard drive or CD (instead of over the Web or a network), you can be even more generous with the quality and file sizes. You can bump the frame rate (video smoothness) to 30 frames per second and the data rate to 200 or more.

Uploading to a .Mac account

If you maintain your own Web site, upload the movie as you would any graphic. Create a link to it in the same way. Your movie will start to play in your visitors' Web browsers when they click that link.

But if you have a .Mac account, posting the movie is even easier. When your movie file is ready, bring your iDisk onto the screen by choosing Go→iDisk→My iDisk in the Finder. Drag your movie file into the Movies folder, as shown in Figure 11-11.

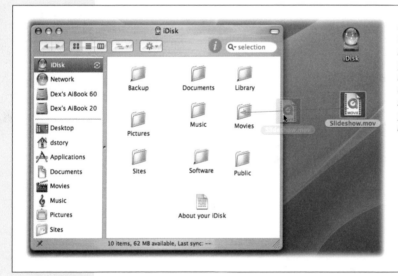

Figure 11-11:
Once you've brought your iDisk icon to the screen, drag your slideshow movie into its Movie folder. Be prepared to wait a long time for both steps; the iDisk is not what you'd call a speedy mechanism.

Now open your Web browser. Go to *www.mac.com*, sign in, and then click the Home-Page tab. You're now looking at the Web page shown at top in Figure 11-12.

1. Click the iMovie tab, and then click one of the movie templates.

Now a "big-screen" version of that template thumbnail appears.

---

2. At the top of the page, click the Edit icon.

A "Choose a file" Web page appears (Figure 11-12, bottom), featuring a tiny list of movies you've dragged into your iDisk's Movies folder. Whichever one is first in the list begins to play immediately, just to remind you of what it is.

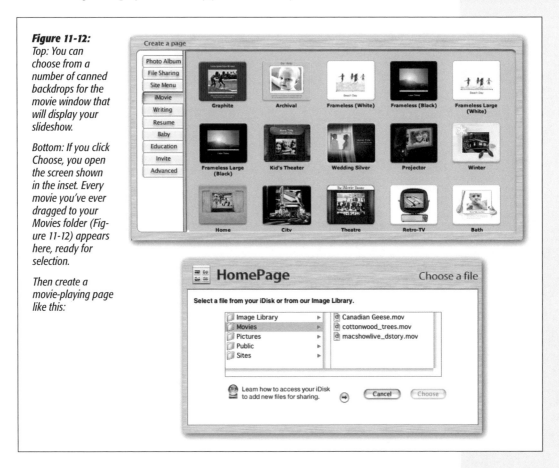

Figure 11-12:
Top: You can choose from a number of canned backdrops for the movie window that will display your slideshow.

Bottom: If you click Choose, you open the screen shown in the inset. Every movie you've ever dragged to your Movies folder (Figure 11-12) appears here, ready for selection.

Then create a movie-playing page like this:

3. Click the name of the movie you want, and then click Choose.

You return to the Edit page. Ignore the fact that your actual movie doesn't yet appear in the placeholder frame.

4. In the text boxes at the bottom of the dialog box, type a title and caption for your movie, if you like.

If you'd like a self-updating counter that shows how many people have viewed your movie, turn on the Show checkbox at the very bottom of the window.

5. Name the movie page by typing a title into the text box just above the movie, and then click Publish.

Finally, a Congratulations page appears, letting you know the Web address of the finished movie page. Note the little button that offers to email this address to your friends, family, and agent, too—a handy feature, considering that this case-sensitive address is none too easy to remember (*http://homepage.mac.com/yourname/ iMovieTheater1.html*).

You can also click the blue lettering of the address to view the movie yourself, right then and there—an almost irresistible offer.

iDVD Slideshows

et's face it. Most of the methods iPhoto gives you to show off your prize photos are geek techniques like sending them by email, posting them on a Web page, turning them into a desktop picture, and so on. All of these methods involve making your audience sit, hunched and uncomfortable, around a *computer* screen.

Now imagine seating them instead in front of the big-screen TV in the family room, turning down the lights, cranking up the surround sound, and grabbing the DVD remote to show off the latest family photos.

You can do it—if you have a DVD-burning drive. Thanks to iDVD (part of the iLife package), you can create DVD-based slideshows from your photo collection, complete with soundtracks and navigational menus and screens just like the DVDs you rent from Blockbuster.

This chapter covers the basics of how to bring your photos from iPhoto to iDVD and how to customize, preview, and burn your slideshows once you've exported them to iDVD.

The iDVD Slideshow

You don't actually need iPhoto to create a slideshow in iDVD. By itself, iDVD has all the tools you need to create interactive DVDs that include movies and soundtracks as well as slideshows.

But using iPhoto can save you a lot of time and trouble. You can use iPhoto to preview, edit, and organize all your photos into albums. Then, once your photos are arranged into neatly organized albums, one click hands them off to iDVD, which converts them into a DVD-readable format. iDVD also hooks up all the navigational links and menus needed to present the show.

Creating an iDVD Slideshow

Creating a DVD of your own photos entails choosing the photos that you've organized in iPhoto, selecting a theme, building menus, and configuring the settings that determine how your slideshow will look and operate. Finally, you can preview the entire DVD (without actually burning a disc) to test navigation, pacing, and other settings. When the whole thing looks right, you burn the final disc.

You can begin in either of two ways: from iPhoto or from iDVD. The following pages walk you through both methods.

Starting in iPhoto

By beginning your odyssey in iPhoto, you can save a few steps.

1. **Select the photos you want to turn into a slideshow.**

   You can select a freely chosen batch of individual photos (see the selection tricks on page 106) or you can click almost anything in the Source list—like an album, smart album, Last 12 Months icon, or whatever.

   If you select a slideshow icon, you'll commit the entire slideshow, complete with transition effects and music (Chapter 7), to DVD. (Once it's in iDVD, however, you won't be able to make changes to the slides or music.)

   You can even select multiple albums in the Source list at once. If you want to include your *entire* Photo Library in the slideshow, click the Photo Library icon. Either way, you can't have more than 99 photos in a slideshow.

Tip: Remember that any photos that aren't in a 4:3 aspect ratio (page 151) will wind up flanked by black bars when displayed on a standard TV set.

Figure 12-1:
If you don't see an iDVD button at the bottom of the iPhoto window, you can trigger the command by choosing Send to iDVD from the Share menu.

Or, if you'd rather install an iDVD button at the bottom of the window for quicker access, choose Share→Show in Toolbar→Send to iDVD.

3. **Choose Share→Send to iDVD (Figure 12-1).**

This is the big hand-off. iDVD opens up a default presentation window (see Figure 12-2). See how the names of your selected albums are already listed as menu items that can be "clicked" with the DVD's remote control?

Figure 12-2:
The name of each exported album appears on the main menu page. Click a name once to select it, and (after a pause) click again to edit it. Double-click a menu title quickly to open a window where you can view the included pictures and change their order.

Read on to learn how to change the menu screen's design scheme.

Technically, at this point, your slideshow is ready to meet its public. If you're looking for some instant gratification, click the ▶ button at the bottom of the window to flip iDVD into presentation mode. Then click the name of your album as it appears on the DVD menu page to begin the show. Use the iDVD remote control shown in Figure 12-7 to stop, pause, or rewind the show in progress.

To really make the finished show your own, though, you'll want to spend a few minutes adding some custom touches. See "Customizing the Show" on page 312.

Starting in iDVD

You can also begin building the show right in iDVD. To see how, click the Media button, and at the top of the panel, click Photos (see Figure 12-3). You now see a tiny iPhoto window, right there in iDVD, complete with thumbnails of your photos (and even movie clips), your Source list, and even a Search box.

Each album you drag out of the list and onto the main iDVD stage area becomes another menu name that your audience will be able to click with their remotes. (If the album won't "stick" and bounces back to the Source list, it's because either that album or that menu screen is too full. iDVD doesn't like albums that hold more than 99 photos, or menu screens with more than 12 buttons.)

Tip: You can also drag photos, or folders full of them, right off your Finder desktop and onto the main menu screen to install them there as slideshows.

Figure 12-3:
Look familiar? Yep, it's your Source list from iPhoto.

All the hard work you've done in iPhoto titling your photos and organizing them into albums pays off now, when you're designing your DVD. You can even use the search box at the bottom to find photos by name or comments.

Even your iPhoto movie clips appear here. That's handy, because you can use movie clips in iDVD in so many ways—as filler for a drop zone (page 314), as a menu background, or as even as a standalone movie on the DVD.

If you've selected some music to accompany the slideshow of that album in iPhoto, then iDVD remembers, and plays it automatically when you play the DVD slideshow.

To assign different music, double-click the name of your slideshow to reveal the Slideshow Editor window shown in Figure 12-4. Click Audio at the top of the Media pane and survey your iTunes collection. When you find a song or playlist that seems right, drag its name onto the little square Audio well, also shown in Figure 12-4. (Click the Return button to return to the menu-design page.)

Customizing the Show

iDVD provides an impressive number of options for customizing the look, feel, and sound of the slideshows you create, including its overall design scheme. That's merciful, because otherwise, every DVD you create would look like a Travel album.

1. **Choose a Theme.**

   Click the Themes button at the bottom of the iDVD window to reveal the list of ready-to-use visual themes that you can apply to your slideshow. Click a theme to apply it to your DVD's main-menu screen.

Figure 12-4:
In the Media pane, click Audio. You see your entire list of iTunes music—in fact, you even see your playlists here.

To avoid the music-ending-too-soon syndrome, you can drag an entire playlist into the little Audio well beneath the slide display. Your DVD will play one song after another according to the playlist.

2. **Add your own background graphics, if you like.**

   You can drag a photo into any theme's background. (Click Media, then Photos, and then drag a picture's thumbnail directly onto any blank area of the main menu screen.) Some let you drop a photo into more interesting, animated *regions* of the background called *drop zones,* as described in Figure 12-5.

3. **Add, remove, and reorder your pictures.**

   When you bring albums into iDVD directly from iPhoto, your photos arrive in the same sequence as they appeared within their iPhoto albums. Once you're in iDVD, however, you can change the order of these photos, remove them from the show, or add others.

   To edit a slideshow in this way, double-click its title on the DVD menu page ("Estonia" in Figure 12-2, for example).

   The slideshow editing window shown in Figure 12-6 appears. In this window, you can also set up other options, like switching between automatic and manual advancing of photos, selecting a different soundtrack, and adding navigation buttons to a slideshow.

You can rearrange the slides by dragging them (the other slides scoot aside to make room), delete selected slides by pressing the Delete key, or add more pictures to them by dragging new photos from the Media pane or the Finder.

Figure 12-5:
In this animated main-menu screen (the theme called Road Trip), the pages of the book actually flip as music plays. As for the photos on the pages: They're "drop zones," which are areas that you can fill with photos or movies of your choosing. (Click the Media button, click Photos or Movies, and drag the pictures or movies you want directly into the drop zones. And if they're moving too fast, click the little running man button to freeze them in place.)

Then, of course, there are the controls at the bottom of the window. They offer a great deal of control over the show. For example:

Slide Duration lets you specify how much time each slide spends on the screen before the next one appears: 1, 3, 5, 10 seconds, or Manual. Manual means that your audience will have to press the Next button on the remote control to change pictures.

Then there's the **Fit to Audio** option, which appears in the pop-up menu only after you've added a sound file to your slideshow. In this case, iDVD determines the timing of your slides automatically—by dividing the length of the soundtrack by the number of slides in your show. For example, if the song is 60 seconds long and the show has 20 slides, each slide will sit on the screen for three seconds.

Transition lets you specify any of several graceful transition effects—Dissolve, Cube, and so on—to govern how one slide morphs into the next. Whatever transition you specify here affects all slides in the show.

Slideshow volume, of course, governs the overall audio level.

Four more controls pop up when you click the Settings icon:

Loop slideshow makes the slideshow repeat endlessly.

Display navigation adds Previous and Next navigation arrows to the screen as your slideshow plays. Your audience can click these buttons with their remote controls to move back and forth in your slideshow.

The arrows aren't technically necessary, of course. If you set your slides to advance automatically (read on), you won't need navigation arrows. And even if you set up the slideshow for manual advance, your audience can always press the arrow buttons on their DVD remote to advance the slides. But if you think they need a visual crutch, this option is here.

Add files to DVD-ROM is an interesting one. When iDVD creates a slideshow, it scales all of your photos to 640 by 480 pixels. That's ideal for a standard television screen, which can't display any resolution higher than that.

Figure 12-6:
Changing the sequence of slides involves little more than dragging them around on this "light table." As in iPhoto, you can select multiple slides at once and then drag them en masse.

Don't miss the tiny icon at the top-right corner of the window. It switches to a list view that still lets you drag them up or down to rearrange them.

Click Return to go back to your main-menu design screen.

But if you intend to distribute your DVD to somebody who's computer savvy, you may want to give them the original, full-resolution photos. They won't see these photos when they insert the disc into a DVD player. But when they insert your DVD into their computers, they'll see a folder filled with the original, high-res photos, suitable for printing, using as Desktop wallpaper, paying you for, and so on. (In other words, you've created a disc that's both a DVD-video disc and a DVD-ROM.)

Show titles and comments means that any text you've added to your photos in iPhoto (their names or descriptions) will also appear on the screen during DVD playback. As shown in Figure 12-6, you can edit them right in iDVD.

4. **Add more slideshows, if you like.**

If you're making a "Family Photos 2006" DVD, for instance, you might create a separate slideshow called Holidays. To do that, click the + button in the main iDVD window; from the pop-up menu, choose Add Slideshow. Double-click it to open your secondary, empty menu page. Then drag albums onto it from the mini-iPhoto browser shown in Figure 12-3.

At any time, you can return to the main menu by clicking the Return button. Don't forget to rename the My Folder menu button to say, for example, "More Pix."

Previewing the DVD

Your last step before burning a disc is to test your DVD presentation to check navigation, timing, photo sequences, and so on.

1. **Click the ▶ button.**

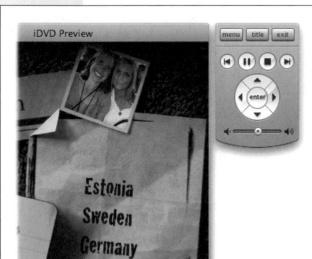

Figure 12-7
When you put iDVD in Preview mode (by clicking the Preview button) a small remote control panel appears next to the main window. It works just like your real DVD player's remote control. You can pause, rewind, or fast-forward slideshows. Clicking the Menu button takes you out of a slideshow and back to the main menu of the DVD, where you can select other slideshows or movies to view.

iDVD switches into Preview mode, which simulates how your disc will behave when inserted into a DVD player. This is a great chance to put your DVD-in-waiting through its paces before wasting an expensive blank disc.

2. **Use the iDVD remote control to click your menu buttons, stop, pause, or rewind the show in progress (Figure 12-7).**

3. **Click the Exit button on the "remote" when you're finished.**

When everything in the DVD looks good, you're ready to master your disc. Insert a blank disc in your SuperDrive and click the Burn button (just to the right of the volume slider).

Extra Credit: Self-Playing Slideshows

As you work on your DVD menu structure, iDVD builds a handy map behind the scenes. You can use it to add or delete DVD elements, and you can double-click one of the icons to open the corresponding menu, movie, or slideshow.

To view the map, just click the Map button at the bottom of the main iDVD window (Figure 12-8). The element you were working on appears with colored highlighting. (Click the Map button again to return to the menu screen you were working on.)

Figure 12-8:
The Map view is most useful when you're creating a complex DVD with nested menu screens, like one you might rent from Blockbuster.

But for slideshow purposes, its most useful feature is the AutoPlay icon. Any pictures or albums you drag onto this tile begin to play automatically when you insert the DVD into a DVD player—no remote-control fussing required.

AutoPlay icon   Map button

But the map is more than just a pretty navigational aid. It also makes possible a self-playing slideshow, one that plays automatically when the DVD is inserted, before your viewers even touch their remote controls.

Once you've got the Photos list open in the Media pane, as shown in Figure 12-8, you can also drag an entire iPhoto album onto the AutoPlay icon. Alternatively, in the Customize panel, you can click and ⌘-click just the photos you want, and then drag them en masse onto the AutoPlay icon. In fact, you can even drag photos—as a group or in a folder—right out of the Finder and onto this icon.

To control how long your still image remains on the screen, or how quickly your Autoplay slideshow plays, double-click the AutoPlay tile. You arrive at the slideshow editor shown in Figure 12-6, where you can adjust the timing, transition, and even the audio that plays behind the pictures.

If you decide to replace your autoplay material, just drag new stuff right onto it. Or, to eliminate the autoplay segment, drag it right off the Autoplay tile. It disappears in a little puff of Mac OS X cartoon smoke.

You can design a project that way for the benefit of, for example, technophobic DVD novices whose pupils dilate just contemplating using a remote control. They can just insert your autoplay-only DVD and sit back on the couch as the pictures flash by automatically.

It's even possible to create a DVD that never even *gets* to the menu screen—a DVD consisting only of autoplay material, a slideshow that repeats endlessly during, say, your cocktail reception. Just highlight the autoplay tile and then choose Advanced→Loop Slideshow. You've got yourself a self-running, self-repeating slideshow of digital photos that plays on a TV at a party or wedding reception. The DVD will loop endlessly—or at least until it occurs to someone in your audience to press the Menu or Title button on the remote. The Menu button redisplays the previous menu screen; the Title button causes a return to the main menu.

Tip: If you have trouble burning an iPhoto DVD, you're not alone. Most people have no problems, but a few run into baffling glitches like an endless pause during the burning process at "Stage 3: Encoding Assets."

If you visit the iPhoto 6 discussion area at *http://discussions.info.apple.com* and search for "iDVD slideshows," you'll discover that many people wind up solving their problems by following one of these steps. First, visit the Energy Saver panel of System Preferences and make sure that your Mac is not set to go to sleep. Second, consider buying only name-brand blank DVDs (iMation or Verbatim, for example). Third, open Disk Utility (in your Applications→Utilities folder), click your hard drive's name, and click Repair Permissions. Short of sacrificing a small mammal to the technology gods, those options are your best bets for success.

Part Four:
iPhoto Stunts

4

Screen Savers, AppleScript, & Automator

Y ou've assembled libraries of digital images, sent heart-touching moments to friends and family via email, published your recent vacation on the Web, authored a QuickTime movie or two, and even boosted the stock price of Canon and Epson single-handedly through your consumption of inkjet printer cartridges. What more could there be?

Plenty. This chapter covers iPhoto's final repertoire of photo stunts, like turning your photos into one of the best screen savers that's ever floated across a computer display, plastering one particularly delicious shot across your desktop, calling upon AppleScript to automate photo-related chores for you, and harnessing iPhoto's partnership with Automator. (This chapter's alternate title: "Miscellaneous iPhoto Stunts That Don't Fit Into Any One Category.")

Building a Custom Screen Saver

Mac OS X's screen saver feature is so good, it's pushed more than one Windows user over the edge into making the switch to Mac OS X. When this screen saver kicks in (after several minutes of inactivity on your part), your Mac's screen becomes a personal movie theater. The effect is something like a slideshow, except that the pictures don't simply appear one after another and sit there on the screen. Instead, they're much more animated. They slide gently across the screen, zooming in or zooming out, smoothly dissolving from one to the next.

Mac OS X comes equipped with a few photo collections that look great with this treatment: forests, space shots, and so on. But let the rabble use those canned screen savers. You, a digital master, can use your own photos as screen saver material.

Meet the Screen Saver

When you're ready to turn one of your own photo collections into a screen saver, fire up iPhoto. Collect the photos in an album, if they're not in one already (Chapter 5).

iPhoto takes you straight to the Desktop & Screen Saver panel of System Preferences (shown in Figure 13-1). Set up your screen saver options as described in the box on the facing page, and then close System Preferences.

Tip: Horizontal shots fill your monitor better than vertical ones—the verticals have fat black bars on either side to fill the empty space.

If your camera captures images at a 3:2 width-to-height ratio instead of 4:3, or if you have an Apple widescreen monitor (like the 15-inch PowerBook screen or the 17-inch iMac screen), there's one more step. You might want to crop the photos, or copies of them, accordingly to maximize their impact.

Figure 13-1:
In Mac OS X 10.3 and later, all of your iPhoto albums are listed in the Screen Saver panel of the Desktop & Screen Saver preferences window. Just pick the one you want to use as a screen saver, or click iPhoto Selection (in the upper part of the list) to "play" whatever pictures you've selected in iPhoto. Mac OS X turns your photos into a smooth, full-screen slideshow.

Ready to view the splendor of your very own homemade screen saver? If you have the patience of a Zen master, you can now sit there, motionless, staring at your Mac for the next half an hour or so—or as long as it takes for Mac OS X to conclude that you're no longer working and finally begin displaying your images on the screen.

Or you can just click the Test button to see the effect right now.

Tip: Your screen saver slideshows look best if your pictures are at least the same resolution as your Mac's monitor. (In most cases, if your digital camera has a resolution of 1 megapixel or better, you're all set.)

If you're not sure what your screen resolution is, go to System Preferences and click the Displays icon (or just consult the Displays mini-menu next to your menu bar clock, if it appears there).

One-Click Desktop Backdrop

iPhoto's desktop-image feature is the best way to drive home the point that photos of your children (or dog, or mother, or self) are the most beautiful in the world. You

---

Screen Saver Basics

You don't technically need a screen saver to protect your monitor from burn-in. Today's energy-efficient CRT monitors wouldn't burn an image into the screen unless you left them on continuously for two years, and flat-panel screens never burn in.

No, screen savers are about entertainment, pure and simple.

In Mac OS X, when you click a module's name in the screen saver list, you see a mini version of it playing back in the Preview screen.

You can control when your screen saver takes over your monitor. For example, the "Start screen saver" slider lets you specify when the screen saver kicks in (after what period of keyboard or mouse inactivity).

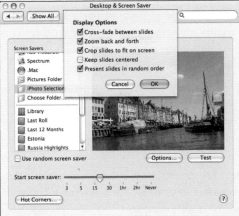

When you click the Hot Corners button, you're presented with a pane than lets you turn each corner of your monitor into a hot spot. Whenever you roll your cursor into that corner, the screen saver either turns on instantly (great when you happen to be shopping on eBay at the moment your boss walks by) or stays off permanently (for when you're reading onscreen or watching a movie). If you use Mac OS

X 10.3 or later, you can use two corners for controlling the screen saver and the other two to activate Exposé (Mac OS X's window-hiding feature).

In any case, pressing any key or clicking the mouse always removes the screen saver from your screen and takes you back to whatever you were doing.

The Options button reveals the additional settings illustrated here, some of which are very useful. Turn off "Crop slides to fit on screen," for example, if you want the Mac to show each photo, edge to edge (even if it has to use black bars to fill the rest of your monitor); otherwise, it enlarges each photo to fill the screen, often lopping off body parts in the process. (If "Crop slides" is on, you can also turn on "Keep slides centered" to prevent the Mac from panning across each photo.)

And turning off "Zoom back and forth," of course, eliminates the majestic, cinematic zooming in and out of successive photos that makes the screen saver look so darned cool.

---

pick one spectacular shot to replace the standard Mac OS X swirling blue desktop pattern. It's like refrigerator art on steroids.

Creating wallpaper in iPhoto is so easy that you could change the picture every day—and you may well want to. In iPhoto, click a thumbnail and then click the Desktop button on the bottom panel (or choose Share→Desktop). Even though the iPhoto window is probably filling your screen, the change happens instantly behind it. Your desktop is now filled with the picture you chose.

Note: If you choose *several* thumbnails or even an album, iPhoto assumes that you intend to make Mac OS X *rotate* among your selected photos, displaying a new one every few minutes on your desktop throughout the day. To confirm its understanding, Mac OS X opens up the relevant panel of System Preferences, so that you can click the Desktop tab and specify *how often* you want the photos to change.

Just three words of advice. First, choose a picture that's at least as big as your screen (1024 x 768 pixels, for example). Otherwise, Mac OS X will stretch it to fit, distorting the photo in the process. If you're *really* fussy, you can even crop the photo first to the exact measurements of the screen; in fact, the first command in iPhoto's Constrain pop-up menu (page 149) lists the exact dimensions of your screen, so you can crop the designated photo (or a copy of it) to fit precisely.

Second, horizontal shots work much better than vertical ones; iPhoto blows up vertical shots to fit the width of the screen, potentially chopping off the heads and feet of your loved ones.

Finally, if a photo doesn't precisely match the screen's proportions, note the pop-up menu shown at bottom in Figure 13-2. It lets you specify how you want the discrepancy handled. Your choices include:

- **Fill screen.** This option enlarges or reduces the image so that it fills every inch of the desktop. If the image is small, the low-resolution stretching can look awful. Conversely, if the image is large and its dimensions don't precisely match your screen's, parts get chopped off. At least this option never distorts the picture, as the "Stretch" option does (below).

- **Stretch to fill screen.** Use this option at your peril, since it makes your picture fit the screen exactly, come hell or high water. Unfortunately, larger pictures may be squished vertically or horizontally as necessary, and small pictures are drastically blown up and squished, usually with grisly-looking results.

- **Center.** This command centers the photo neatly on the screen. If the picture is larger than the screen, you see only the middle; the edges of the picture are chopped off as they extend beyond your screen.

  But if the picture is smaller than the screen, it won't fill the entire background; instead it just sits right smack in the center of the monitor at actual size. Of course, this leaves a swath of empty border all the way around your screen. As a remedy, Apple provides a color-swatch button next to the pop-up menu. When you click it, the Color Picker appears, so that you can specify the color in which to frame your little picture.

- **Tile.** This option makes your picture repeat over and over until the multiple images fill the entire monitor. (If your picture is larger than the screen, no such tiling takes place. You see only the top center chunk of the image.)

And one last thing: If public outcry demands that you return your desktop to one of the standard system backdrops, open System Preferences, click the Desktop & Screen Saver icon, click the Desktop button if necessary, choose Apple Backgrounds or Solid Colors in the list box at the left of the window, then take your pick.

Figure 13-2:
If your photo doesn't fit the screen perfectly, choose a different option from the pop-up menu in the Desktop & Screen Saver preference panel.

While you're in the Desktop & Screen Saver or Screen Effects preferences pane, you might notice that all of your iPhoto albums are listed below the collection of images that came with your Mac. You can navigate through those albums to find a new desktop image. This approach isn't as fast (or fun) as picking pictures in iPhoto, but if for some reason iPhoto isn't open on your Mac (heaven forbid!), you can take care of business right there in System Preferences.

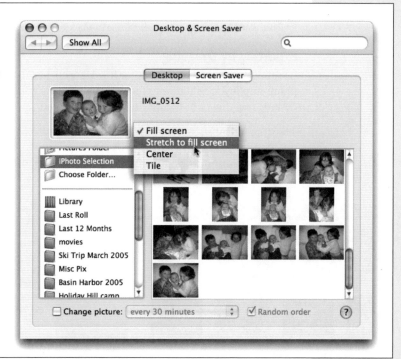

Exporting and Converting Pictures

The whole point of iPhoto is to provide a centralized location for every photo in your world. That doesn't mean that they're locked there, however; it's as easy to take pictures out of iPhoto as it is to put them in. Spinning out a photo from iPhoto can be useful in situations like these:

- You're creating a Web page outside of iPhoto and you need a photo in a certain size and format.

• You shot a bunch of 6-megapixel photos, you're running out of disk space, and you wish they were all 4-megapixel shots instead. They'd still have plenty of resolution, but not so much wasted space.

• You're going to submit some photos to a newspaper or magazine, and the publication requires TIFF-format photos, not iPhoto's standard JPEG format.

• Somebody else on your network loves one of your pictures and would like to use it as a desktop background on *that* machine.

• You want to set free a few of the photos so that you can copy them *back* onto the camera's memory card. (Some people use their digicams as much for *showing* pictures to their friends as for *taking* them.)

• You want to send a batch of pictures on a CD to someone.

Exporting by Dragging

It's amazingly easy to export photos from iPhoto: Just drag their thumbnails out of the photo viewing area and onto the desktop (or onto a folder, or into a window on the desktop), as shown in Figure 13-3. After a moment, you'll see their icons appear.

The drag-and-drop method has enormous virtue in its simplicity and speed. It does not, however, grant you much flexibility. It produces JPEG files only, at the original camera resolution, with the camera's own cryptic naming scheme.

Figure 13-3:
This technique produces full-size JPEG graphics, exactly as they appear in iPhoto. Their names, however, are not particularly user-friendly. Instead of "Persimmon Close Up," as you named it in iPhoto, a picture might wind up on the desktop named 200205040035140.jpg or IMG_5197. jpg.

Exporting by Dialog Box

To gain control over the dimensions, names, and file formats of the exported graphics, use the Export command. After selecting one picture, a group of pictures, or an album, you can invoke this command by choosing File→Export (Shift-⌘-E).

The Export Photos dialog box appears, as shown in Figure 13-4. Click the File Export tab, if necessary, and then make the following decisions:

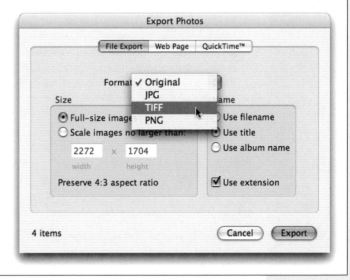

Figure 13-4:
The Export dialog box gives you control over the file format, names, and dimensions of the pictures you're about to send off from iPhoto. The number of photos you're about to export appears in the lower-left corner of the box. You can even tell iPhoto to use whatever names you gave your pictures, instead of the original, incomprehensible file names bestowed by your camera. To do so, click "Use title."

File format

You can use the Format pop-up menu to specify the file format of the graphics that you're about to export. Here are your options:

- **Original.** iPhoto exports the images in whatever format they were in when you imported them. If the picture came from a digital camera, for example, it's usually a JPEG.

  If your camera captured a RAW-format photo (page 87), though, the Original option is even more valuable. It lets you export the original RAW file so that you can, for example, work with your RAWs in a more sophisticated editor like Adobe's Camera Raw (which comes with Photoshop).

- **JPG.** This abbreviation is shorthand for JPEG, which stands for Joint Photographic Experts Group (that's the group of geeks who came up with this format). The JPEG format is, of course, the most popular format for photos on the Internet (and in iPhoto), thanks to its high image quality and small file size.

- **TIFF.** These files (whose abbreviation is short for Tagged Image File Format) are something like JPEG without the "lossy" compression. That is, they maintain every bit of quality available in the original photograph, but usually take up much more disk space (or memory-card space) as a result. TIFF is a good choice if quality is more important than portability.

• **PNG.** This relatively new format (Portable Network Graphics) was designed to replace the GIF format on the Web. (The company that came up with the algorithms behind the GIF format exercised its legal muscle…long story.)

Whereas GIF graphics generally don't make good photos because they're limited to 256 colors, PNG is a good choice for photos (except the variation called *PNG-8*, which is just as limited as GIF). The resulting files are smaller than TIFF images, yet don't exhibit any compression-related quality loss, à la JPEGs. Not all graphics programs and Web browsers recognize this relatively new format, but the big ones—including iPhoto, GraphicConverter, Photoshop, and most recent browser versions—all do.

Name options

iPhoto maintains two names for each photo: its *original file name,* as it appears in the Finder, and its *iPhoto title,* the one you may have typed in while working in the program. Click either "Use filenames" or "Use titles" to specify what names iPhoto gives the icons of the graphics you're about to export. (When you export just *one* photo, you're offered the chance to name it whatever you like.)

Your third option is "Use album name." It tells iPhoto to name your exported photos according to their album name—and sequence within that album. If an exported photo is the fourth picture in the first row of an album titled Dry Creek, iPhoto will call the exported file "Dry Creek – 04.jpg." Because *you* determine the order within an album (by dragging), this is the only option that lets you control the numbering of the exported result.

Size options

Remember that although digital camera graphics files may not always have enough resolution for prints, they generally have far *too much* resolution for displaying on the screen.

As Chapter 9 makes clear, iPhoto offers to scale them down automatically whenever you email them or transfer them to the Web. If you turn on "Scale images no larger than," and then fill in some pixel dimensions in the boxes, you can oversee the same kind of shrinkage for your exported graphics. Points of reference: 1024 x 768 is exactly the right size to completely fill a standard 15-inch monitor, and 640 x 480 is a good size for emailing (it fills up about a quarter of the screen).

Tip: You can also use this option to de-megapixelize a bunch of photos. Suppose they're all 8-megapixel photos—more than you'll ever need. Export them at, say, 2272 x 1704 pixels (about four megapixels) to a folder on your desktop called "4 Megas" (or something). Delete the originals from your Library, if you like, and then re-import the scaled-down versions by dragging that 4 Megas folder off the desktop and into the album list.

Plug-Ins and Add-Ons

On one thing, friends and foes of Apple can all agree: iPhoto is no Photoshop. iPhoto was deliberately designed to be simple and streamlined.

Yet Apple thoughtfully left the back door open. Other programmers are free to write add-ons and plug-ins—software modules that contribute additional features, lend new flexibility, and goose up the power of iPhoto.

And yet, with great power comes great complexity—in this case, power and complexity that Apple chose to omit. But at least this plug-in arrangement means that nobody can blame *Apple* for junking up iPhoto with extra features. After all, *you're* the one who installed them.

Some of the most important plug-ins and accessory programs are described in the relevant chapters of this book:

- **BetterHTMLExport** is designed to lend flexibility to the Web pages that iPhoto generates. (See page 237.)
- **Portraits & Prints** vastly expands iPhoto's printing features. It lets you create a multiple-photo layout on a single sheet of paper for printing. (See page 212.)

As the popularity of iPhoto grows, new add-ons and plug-ins will surely sprout up like roses in your macro lens. It's worthwhile to visit the Version Tracker Web site from time to time *(www.versiontracker.com/macosx)*. Search for *iPhoto*; you'll be surprised at the number of goodies just waiting for you to try.

AppleScript Tricks

AppleScript is the famous Macintosh *scripting language*—a software robot that you can program to perform certain repetitive or tedious tasks for you.

iPhoto 6 is fully *scriptable*, meaning that AppleScript gurus can manipulate it by remote control with AppleScripts that they create. (It even works with Automator, the program in Mac OS X 10.4 and later that makes programming even easier than using AppleScript. See the following section.)

But even if you're not an AppleScript programmer yourself, this is still good news, because you're perfectly welcome to exploit the ready-made, prewritten AppleScripts that other people come up with.

Preparing for AppleScript

Apple has paved the way for all kinds of AppleScript fun with its AppleScripts for iPhoto 6, which you can download from the "Missing CD" page of *www.missingmanuals.com*. You'll probably find that after decompression, this download turns into a folder called Archive on your hard drive.

Now you need some way to *run* these scripts—to trigger them—and the best way is to install Mac OS X's ingenious Script menu. Here's how you go about it:

1. **Rename the Archive folder *iPhoto Scripts*, or something equally helpful.**

   This is the folder you downloaded.

2. **Open your Applications→AppleScript folder.**

   You've just unearthed a few tools that Apple provides for AppleScript fun.

3. **Double-click the icon called AppleScript Utility. In the dialog box, turn on "Show Script Menu in menu bar." Quit AppleScript Utility.**

   Those are the steps for Mac OS X 10.4. If you have something earlier, double-click the icon called Install Script Menu instead.

   Either way, a new icon, shaped like a scroll, appears at the upper-right end of your menu bar (Figure 13-5). This, ladies and gentlemen, is the *Script menu*.

Tip: You can remove the Script menu icon by ⌘-dragging it away from the menu bar.

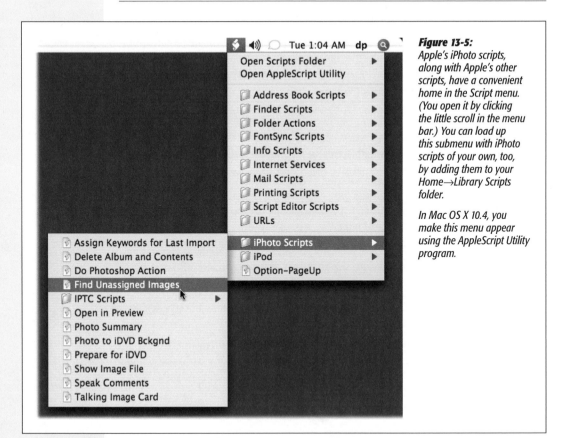

Figure 13-5:
Apple's iPhoto scripts, along with Apple's other scripts, have a convenient home in the Script menu. (You open it by clicking the little scroll in the menu bar.) You can load up this submenu with iPhoto scripts of your own, too, by adding them to your Home→Library Scripts folder.

In Mac OS X 10.4, you make this menu appear using the AppleScript Utility program.

If you open the Script menu, you'll see that it already contains a variety of interesting scripts, none of which have anything to do with iPhoto.

4. **From the Script menu, choose Open Scripts Folder.**

   A window opens; this is actually your Home→Library→Scripts folder.

5. **Drag the iPhoto Scripts folder (or whatever you named it in step 1) into the Scripts window.**

From now on, the iPhoto Scripts folder is listed at the bottom of the Scripts scroll menu, as shown in Figure 13-5. You can trigger any iPhoto script by choosing its name from the submenu.

The Scripts, One by One

Now that your downloaded scripts are easily accessible, here's what they're for.

Assign Keywords for Last Imports

This script is supposed to automate the process of assigning keywords to your last batch of imported images by presenting a Keyword dialog box, over and over again, for each photo in that batch. But it's much slower than just using the regular iPhoto Keywords feature, and a bit buggy too. You're best off ignoring this one.

Delete Album and Contents

As you know from Chapter 5, deleting an album doesn't actually delete any photos from your collection—at least not usually.

When you run this script (by choosing its name from your Scripts→iPhoto scripts menu), however, you're presented with a dialog box listing all of your albums. Select the album you want to delete, and then click OK. After asking your permission, iPhoto moves both the album *and the photos inside it* to the iPhoto Trash.

Once you choose iPhoto→Empty Trash, the album and the photos in it are *gone forever*, even from the master Photo Library. Be careful!

Do Photoshop Action

Do Photoshop Action is the mother of all iPhoto AppleScripts. It lets high-end graphics nerds run Photoshop *actions* (also known as macros—that is, canned software robots that perform repetitive processing steps) on iPhoto pictures.

In the graphic-design world, Photoshop actions automate tedious tasks like opening each photo, scaling it to a certain size and resolution, changing it to grayscale instead of full color, and then exporting it in a different graphic format. If you're not quite that high-powered a graphics professional, you can still use Photoshop to color-balance your photos and adjust their contrast—tasks that Photoshop's AutoLevels command performs with better results than iPhoto's own Enhance tool.

If you have Photoshop CS, your software is ready to go right out of the box. You don't have to download anything.

If you use Photoshop 7, though, you must take a preliminary step before you can take advantage of this powerful script: Go to *www.adobe.com/support/downloads/detail. jsp?ftpID=1535* and download the file called "Photoshop 7.0 Scripting plug-in." Run the downloaded installer by double-clicking it.

No matter which version you have, though, get ready for this AppleScript by doing two pieces of homework:

- Become familiar with actions in Photoshop. You can find the starter set by choosing Window→Actions. You have a dozen prefab actions to choose from, such as Custom RGB to Grayscale and Save As Photoshop PDF, and you can also "record" actions of your own.

- Note the name of the action you want to use. The Do Photoshop Actions Apple-Script will ask you what action you want it to apply, but you'll have to type the action's name *exactly* as it appears in Photoshop's Actions palette, including capitalization.

Now, in iPhoto, highlight a thumbnail (or several). From your Script menu, choose iPhoto Scripts→Do Photoshop Action, and then proceed as described in Figure 13-6. You've just harnessed the power of Photoshop's batch processing, right from within iPhoto.

Figure 13-6:
When you click Set Prefs (top), the script asks you to type in the name of the action you want to apply (bottom). It also lets you specify a different action set (a collection of actions in Photoshop). But unless you've created your own, Default Actions is the set you want.

Type in the precise name of the action you want, and then click Set. In the next dialog box, click Continue.

Then the AppleScript asks you where you want each modified image saved. Choose a folder location for them, or click New Folder to create a new one.

Finally, click Choose. Photoshop opens each selected iPhoto image in Photoshop, executes the action you've specified, and saves the picture into the folder you selected. Once it's finished, you can return to iPhoto for more work.

Note: If you get an error message at the end of the process telling you that, "There is no such element," you've just run up against a quirk of the script. The script attempts to open the resulting file in Preview–but if your Photoshop action contains a Close command, the file closes, and there's nothing for Preview to open.

Glitches like this are a good argument for learning to open up a script in Script Editor and make minor edits–in this case, deleting the "Open in Preview" lines of the script.

Find Unassigned Images

This command rounds up all photos that you haven't put into any album and drops them into a new album called Unassigned. You might use this script when, for example, you're burning all of your photos onto various CDs by category, and you want to make sure you're not leaving any out.

As the message tells you, this might take some time to complete, especially if you have more than 1,000 photos or so. (AppleScript will inform you along the way that it's still working.) When it's done scanning your entire library, it also lets you know how many unassigned images it discovered.

Open in Preview

This script opens an iPhoto picture in Preview, Mac OS X's graphics-viewing program. You might, at first, wonder if perhaps Apple's AppleScript team inhaled a bit too much of that new-computer smell. Why would you want to open a photo in Preview, when it's already in iPhoto, the world's greatest graphics viewer?

Actually, Preview has a few tricks up its sleeve that iPhoto doesn't know, including its ability to export graphics in a huge variety of formats (see Figure 13-7).

Figure 13-7:
In iPhoto, you're stuck with four export options: Original, JPG, TIFF, and PNG. But if you open that same image in Preview, choosing File→Export offers you twelve conversion formats.

To use this script, click a photo in iPhoto and then choose this command's name from the Script→ iPhoto Scripts menu. The photo appears in Preview a moment later.

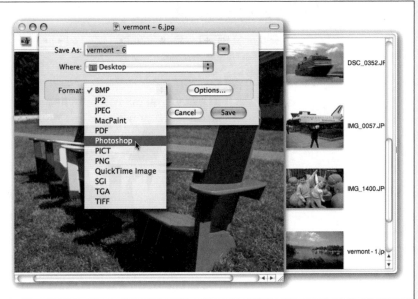

If you select *more than one* picture in iPhoto before running the script, the script offers you (via a small, misspelled dialog box) a choice: You can open the pictures either in individual windows or as a *collection* in Preview. Collections are much cooler and easier to manage; for example, once you've clicked a thumbnail in the thumbnails "drawer" (shown at right in Figure 13-7), you can move to the next or previous one by pressing the up or down arrow keys.

Photo Summary

This handy little script builds tidy, ready-to-print catalog pages of your photos, as shown in Figure 13-8.

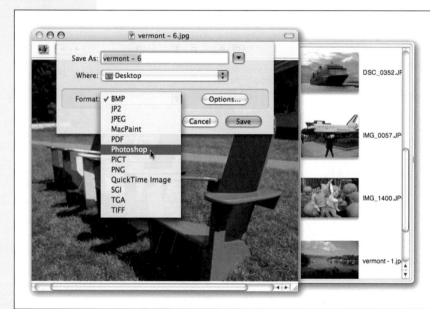

Figure 13-8:
Select the pictures you want in iPhoto and then choose this script's name from the Scripts→iPhoto Scripts submenu. You get a document in TextEdit that includes each photo's thumbnail, title, file name, width, and so on. Print or save.

Photo to iDVD Background

Once you've clicked a photo, you can use this script to turn it into the menu background for your current iDVD project. For best results, crop your picture first in iPhoto to 4:3 dimensions (see page 151), to make sure that your photo will neatly fit the TV when played on a DVD player.

Prepare for iDVD

This script is supposed to open each of the selected images in Adobe Photoshop, scale them to 640 x 480 pixels, superimpose each photo's Comment text, and then open the results in Preview as a catalog for review.

The idea is to help you prepare your photos for use in an iDVD slideshow (see Chapter 12). Unfortunately, this script isn't quite ready for prime time—it does the resizing, but doesn't actually superimpose the text as promised.

Show Image File

This script is handy whenever you're looking at a photo in iPhoto and wish you could leap instantly to the Finder icon that represents it (deep inside your iPhoto Library folder), so that you can copy it to a disk, send it across a network, or whatever. It's one of the most useful Apple scripts by far.

Tip: Once you locate the picture, don't drag it out of its folder! Doing so will hopelessly confuse iPhoto. Instead, if you want to use this photo elsewhere, *Option*-drag it out of its window. That ritual makes a copy of the original file, leaving the original safe and sound in the iPhoto Library folder.

Speak Comments

Here's a wild one that can be truly handy when you want to treat visitors (or trade-show attendees) to a slideshow of your photographic work—when you're not around to narrate.

When you choose this script's name from the Script menu→iPhoto Scripts submenu, iPhoto presents each of the selected photos, one at a time, at full iPhoto-window size and adds *spoken narration* that's based on whatever you've typed into those photos' Comments boxes. iPhoto uses whatever voice you've chosen on the Speech panel of System Preferences. It's weird, wacky, and strangely satisfying.

Talking Image Card

This one is a lot like the previous script, except that instead of performing the spoken cyber-recital out loud, it saves the result as a QuickTime movie, ready for distributing or archiving. Never let it be said that the geeks at Apple don't know how to have a good time.

To run this script, click a photo, and then choose this script's name from the Script menu→iPhoto Scripts submenu. Just in case you're not in a Victoria mood, a dialog box now offers you the chance to change the voice of the narrator—and, while you're at it, the dimensions of your movie. Click Continue when you're ready.

Finally, another dialog box lets you name the movie and choose a folder location for saving it (Figure 13-9). Click OK. AppleScript builds the movie and opens it in QuickTime. Click the Play button to let the party begin.

Figure 13-9:
You can go with the proposed voice and pixel dimension for your movie, or click Set Prefs to select your own.

Editing AppleScripts

Using the menu bar to access and use your AppleScripts is terrific if you never need to make any adjustments to the scripts.

But part of the fun is fiddling with these scripts, peering into the lines of code that compose them, and adjusting them to your own devious designs.

To open one up in Script Editor, the little AppleScript-editing program included with every Mac, just *hold down the Option key* as you choose the script's name from the Scripts→iPhoto Scripts menu.

For example, the standard Photo Summary script opens your catalog page in TextEdit, but you can change it to open in Apple's Safari Web browser.

To do that, press Option as you choose Scripts→iPhoto Scripts→Photo Summary. The script opens as a page of computer code; just change the name of the program you want to open, as shown in Figure 13-10.

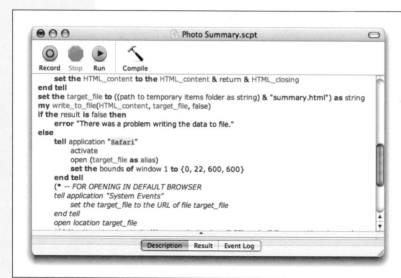

Figure 13-10:
If you change the name of the program highlighted here in yellow, you can make your catalog open in another program—Safari instead of TextEdit, for example. Posting the result on the Web may be more trouble than it's worth (you'll have to locate the image source files, copy them, then adjust the HTML code accordingly), but this exercise gives a good glimpse into the workings of AppleScript.

While you're at it, you could easily change the typeface or size in your catalog. Once again, open the script in Script Editor. Scroll down until you find this line:

```
<FONT FACE=\"Lucida Grande\" SIZE=\"1\">
```

Carefully replace the font name and size to suit your taste, like this:

```
<FONT FACE=\"Verdana\" SIZE=\"3\">
```

Note: Clearly, the size isn't represented in points, as you're probably used to. Instead, the numbers 1, 2, and 3 refer to the *relative* size system used by Web-page designers. They range from 1 (very small) to 7 (jumbo).

Now your catalog will display all the entries in Verdana type with a larger, more readable font size.

As you go, you can click Run within Script Editor to see the effects of your editing. When you're finished fiddling, use the File→Save As command, give your modified script a new, descriptive name (so that you don't overwrite the original script), and save the result onto the desktop. (From there, you'll probably want to move it into your Home→Library→Scripts→iPhoto Scripts folder.)

Automator Tricks

If you use your Mac long enough, you're bound to start repeating certain jobs over and over again. Automator, introduced in Mac OS 10.4, is a program that lets you teach your Mac what to do, step by step, by assembling a series of visual building blocks called actions. Drag actions into the right order, click a big Run button, and your Mac faithfully runs each action one at a time.

As it turns out, Automator works great with iPhoto. By following "recipes" that you find online—or the sample described here—you can add all kinds of new, time-saving features to iPhoto and your Mac.

The Lay of the Land

To open Automator, visit your Applications folder. When you open Automator, you'll see something like Figure 13-11, starring these key elements:

Library list

The Library list shows you every program on your Mac that can be controlled by Automator actions: iPhoto, Safari, TextEdit, iTunes, and so on. When you select a program, the Action list shows you every action (command) that the chosen program understands. When you find an action you want to use in your workflow, you drag it to the right into the large Workflow pane to begin building your software robot.

Action list

This list shows you the contents of whatever categories you've selected in the Library list. If, for example, you selected Safari in the Library list, the Action list would show you all the Safari actions available on your Mac. To build your own workflow, you have to drag actions *from* the Action list and into the Workflow pane. (Double-clicking an action does the same thing as dragging it.)

Workflow pane

The Workflow pane is Automator's kitchen. It's where you put your actions in whatever order you want, set any action-specific preferences, and fry them all up in a pan.

But the Workflow pane is also where you see how the information from one action gets piped into another, creating a stream of information. That's how the Workflow pane differentiates Automator from the dozens of non-visual, programming-based automation tools out there.

When you drag an action out of the Action list into the Workflow pane, any surrounding actions scoot aside to make room for it. When you let go of the mouse, the action you dragged materializes right there in the Workflow pane.

Tip: If you select an action in the Action list and press Return, Automator automatically inserts that action at the bottom of the Workflow pane.

Figure 13-10:
The process of writing an Automator program (workflow) is always the same.

First, click the name of the program you want to manipulate (in the far left column).

Then, locate the specific action you want that program to take (in the second column). You can use the Search box to help you with this.

Finally, double-click that action's name, or drag it, to place it into the far right column. Save the result as a real, double-clickable program.

Automating iPhoto

To help you get started, here's a three-step workflow (automated software sequence) that you can construct in minutes (or download, already completed, from *www.missingmanuals.com*). It addresses an age-old iPhoto limitation: The program doesn't let you import only *some* photos from your camera's memory card (or from a folder of images on your hard drive). You'll wind up with a window full of thumbnails, which you're free to choose selectively for importing into iPhoto. Neat!

Here's how to build this workflow yourself.

1. **Open Automator.**

   It's in your Applications folder.

2. **In the Library column, click Finder.**

   The Action column now displays the commands that Automator can issue to the Finder (Figure 13-10).

3. **In the Action column, double-click "Get Specified Finder Items."**

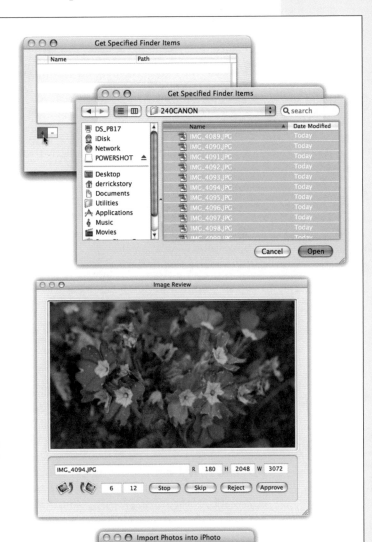

Figure 13-11:
Here's what happens when you run your completed Automator software robot.

Top left: Automator asks you for the images you're considering importing into iPhoto. Click the + button.

Second from top: Navigate to your memory card (which is either in your camera or in a card reader), or to the images on your hard drive. Select all of the photos inside by clicking the first one in the list, and then Shift-clicking the last one. (Do not select the entire card or folder; you must highlight all of the actual photo files.)

You return to the Get Specified Finder Items dialog box (top left), where your candidate photos now appear. Click Continue.

Third from top: This cool interview screen displays each picture. Click Approve ("Yes, import this one") or Reject ("No, I don't want this one") for each photo.

Bottom: You're asked to name the album that will hold the approved photos. When you click Continue, iPhoto automatically opens, imports the selected photos, and places them in the album you've just named.

It appears in the rightmost column as step 1. You've just told Automator, "Work with the icons that I'm going to specify." Now you have to specify them.

4. **Click to expand the Options flippy triangle. Turn on "Show Action When Run."**

   This means: "When this software robot does its thing, I want to be asked which files to process."

5. **In the Library column, click iPhoto. In the Action column, double-click Review Photos.**

   It flies to the right, becoming the second step of your workflow. Make sure the Approved Images box is turned on.

6. **In the Action column, double-click "Import Photos into iPhoto." When it appears in the rightmost column, click New Album.**

   Translation: "The thumbnails I select, I want imported into iPhoto, in an album."

7. **Click to expand the Options flippy triangle. Turn on "Show Action When Run." Then click "Show Selected Items," and, in the list, select New Album.**

   You've just told the workflow to put the imported pictures into a *new* album (as opposed to an existing one).

8. **Choose File→Save As. From the File Format popup menu, choose Application. Name your new workflow (something like *Import Selected Photos*), and then save your masterpiece to the desktop.**

   Ignore any error message that appears; it's a bug.

The fruit of all this labor is a new program—that *you wrote*—called Import Selected Photos. You can drag it into your Dock, leave it on the Desktop, or whatever.

From now on, whenever you double-click this new program, you'll be guided through the process of choosing the worthy photos from your memory card (or hard drive) and importing them into iPhoto! Figure 13-11 illustrates the process. No longer must you import all the photos on your memory card, wasting time and disk space.

Tip: A new, improved "Import Photos into iPhoto" action works much better than the original one that comes with iPhoto. You can download it from this book's "Missing CD" page at *www.missingmanuals.com*. (It's easy to install. Just unzip the archive and double-click the Automator icon inside. You'll now see the action listed in Automator, ready to use.)

---

iPhoto File Management

For years, true iPhoto fans experienced the heartache of iPhoto Overload—the syndrome in which the program gets too full of photos, winds up gasping for RAM, and acts as if you've slathered it with a thick coat of molasses. And for years, true iPhoto fans have adopted an array of countermeasures to keep the speed up, including splitting the Photo Library into several smaller chunks.

Now that iPhoto can manage 250,000 pictures per library, such drastic measures aren't generally necessary.

Nonetheless, learning how iPhoto manages its library files is still a worthy pursuit. It's the key to swapping Photo Libraries, burning them to CD, transferring them to other machines, and merging them together.

About iPhoto Discs

iPhoto CDs are discs (either CDs or DVDs) that you can create in iPhoto to archive your entire Photo Library—or any selected portion of it—with just a few mouse clicks.

The beauty of iPhoto's Burn command is that it exports much more than just the photos themselves to a disc. It also copies the thumbnails, titles, keywords, comments, ratings, and all the other important data about your Photo Library. Once you've burned all of this valuable information to disc, you can do all sorts of useful things:

- Make a backup of your whole Photo Library for safekeeping.

- Transfer specific photos, albums, or a whole Photo Library to another Mac without losing all your keywords, descriptions, ratings, and titles.

• Share discs with other iPhoto fans so that your friends or family can view your photo albums in their own copies of iPhoto.

• Offload photos to CD or DVD as your photo collection grows, to keep your current Photo Library at a trim, manageable size.

• Merge separate Photo Libraries (such as the one on your laptop and the one on your iMac) into a single master Photo Library.

Note: One thing an iPhoto CD is *not* good for is sharing your photos with somebody who doesn't have iPhoto! Page 344 has the details, but the bottom line is this: An iPhoto CD from iPhoto is designed *exclusively* for transferring pictures into another copy of iPhoto. (iPhoto 5 and 6 can read iPhoto 2 and 4 discs, but not vice versa.)

Burning an iPhoto CD or DVD

All you need to create an iPhoto CD is a Mac with a CD or DVD burner.

1. **Select the photos that you want to include on the disc.**

   You can hand-select some photos (page 106), click a Source list icon (album, book, or slideshow), or click the Photo Library icon to burn your whole photo collection.

   In any case, the photo-viewing area should now be showing the photos you want to save onto a disc.

2. **Choose Share→Burn.**

   A dialog box appears, prompting you to insert a blank disc. Pop in the disc; the dialog box vanishes after a few moments.

Note: If you plan to use this feature a lot, install the Burn button onto the bottom edge of the iPhoto window by choosing View→Show in Toolbar→Burn.

3. **Check the size of your selection to make sure it will fit.**

   Take a look at the Info panel at the bottom of the iPhoto window, as shown in Figure 14-1; the little graph shows you how much of the disc will be filled up. If the set of photos you want to burn is smaller than 650 or 700 megabytes (for a CD) or about 4.3 gigabytes (for a DVD), you're good to go. You can burn the whole thing to a single disc.

   If your photo collection is larger than that, however, it's not going to fit. You'll have to split your backup operation across multiple discs. Select whatever number of photo albums or individual pictures that *will* fit on a single disc, using the indicator shown in Figure 14-1 as your guide. (Also shown in the figure: the Name box, where you can name the disc you're about to burn.)

For example, you might decide to copy the 2004 folder onto one disk, the 2005 folder onto another, and so on, using the built-in year "collections" in the Source list as your source material.

After burning one disc, select the next set of photos, and burn another CD or DVD. Burn as many discs as needed to contain your entire collection of photos. If and when you ever need to restore your photos from the multiple discs, you'll be able to merge them back together into a single Photo Library using the technique described in "Merging Photo Libraries" later in this chapter.

4. **Click the Burn button.**

   As you can see in Figure 14-1, you'll either get a "not enough space" message or a "Burn Disc" message. If you get the latter, you're ready to proceed:

5. **Click the Burn button.**

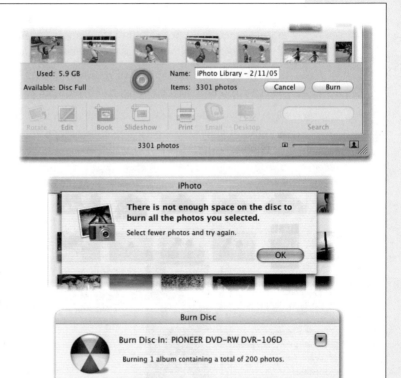

Figure 14-1:
Top: Once you've clicked Burn and inserted a blank disc, this Info panel lets you know how close you are to filling the disc. The indicator icon updates itself as you select or deselect photos and albums to show you how much free space is available on the disc.

Middle: If your photos take up more space than is available on the disc, the little disc icon turns red—and when you click Burn, you see the Disc Full message shown here.

Bottom: If all is well, however, you get this message instead. Click Burn and sit back to enjoy the fruits of your Mac's little internal laser.

First, iPhoto makes a *disk image*—a sort of pretend disc that serves as a temporary holding area for the photos that will be burned. Next, iPhoto copies the photos from your iPhoto Library folder to the disk image.

Finally, the real burning begins. When the process is done, your Mac spits out the finished CD or DVD, ready to use, bearing whatever name you gave it.

Tip: You can safely bail out of the CD-creating process at any time by clicking the Cancel button when the Progress dialog box first appears.

But don't click the Stop button once the Burning dialog box appears. At that point, your CD or DVD drive is already busy etching data onto the disc itself. Clicking Stop brings the burning to a screeching halt, leaving you with a partially burned, nonfunctioning disc.

What you get

The finished iPhoto disc contains not just your photos, but a clone of your iPhoto Library folder as well. In other words, this disc includes all the thumbnails, keywords, comments, ratings, photo album information—even the unedited original versions of your photos that iPhoto keeps secretly tucked away.

If you want to view the contents of your finished CD in iPhoto, pop the disc back into the drive. If iPhoto isn't running, your Mac opens it automatically.

Moments later, the icon for the CD appears in the Source list of the iPhoto window, as shown in Figure 14-2. If you click the disc's icon, the photos it contains appear in the photo-viewing area, just as if they were stored in your Photo Library.

You can't make changes to them, of course—that's the thing about CDs and DVDs. But you can copy them into your own albums, and make changes to the copies.

Figure 14-2:
Pop an iPhoto CD into your Mac and it appears right along with your albums in iPhoto. Click on the disc icon itself or one of the disc's album icons (as shown here) to display the photos it contains. In essence, iPhoto is giving you access to two different libraries at once—the active Photo Library on your Mac's hard drive and a second library on the CD.

When Not to Burn

The Burn command is convenient for creating quick backups, archiving portions of your Photo Library, or transferring photos to another Mac. But it's definitely *not* the best way to share your photos with Windows users, or even other Mac fans running Mac OS 9.

Think about it: Burning an iPhoto CD automatically organizes your photos into a series of numerically named subfolders inside an iPhoto Library folder, surrounded by scads of special data files like *.attr* files, *Library.cache,* and *Dir.data.* All of this makes perfect sense to iPhoto, but is mostly meaningless to anyone—or, rather, any computer—that doesn't have iPhoto. A Windows user, for example, would have to dig through folder after folder on your iPhoto CD to find and open your photos.

So if the destination of your CD or DVD isn't another iPhoto nut, *don't* use the Burn command. Instead, export the photos using the File Export or Web Page options described in Chapter 9. The pictures won't have any ratings, comments, keywords, and so on, but they'll be organized in a way that's much easier for non-iPhoto folk to navigate.

iPhoto Backups

Bad things can happen to digital photos. They can be accidentally deleted with a slip of your pinkie. They can become mysteriously corrupted and subsequently unopenable. They can get mangled by a crashed hard disk and be lost forever. Losing one-of-a-kind family photos can be extremely painful, and in some documented cases, even marriage-threatening. So if you value your digital photos, you should back them up regularly—perhaps after each major batch of new photos joins your collection.

Backing Up to CD or DVD

The quickest and most convenient way to back up your Photo Library is to archive it onto a blank CD or DVD using iPhoto's Burn command, as described on the previous pages. If anything bad ever happens to your photo collection, you'll be able to restore your Photo Library from the backup discs, with all your thumbnails, keywords, comments, and other tidbits intact.

To restore your photo collection from such a backup, see "Merging Photo Libraries" later in this chapter.

Backing Up (No CD Burner)

Even if, for some strange reason, you don't have a CD burner (and therefore can't use iPhoto's Burn command), backing up thousands of photos is a simple task for the iPhoto maven. After all, one of iPhoto's main jobs is to keep all your photos together in *one* place— one folder that's easy to copy to a backup disk of any kind.

That all-important folder is the *iPhoto Library* folder, which resides inside the Pictures folder of the Home folder that bears your name. If your user name (the short name you use to log into Mac OS X) is *Casey,* the full path to your iPhoto Library folder from your main hard drive window drive is: Users→Casey→Pictures→iPhoto Library.

As described in Chapter 4, the iPhoto Library folder contains not just your photos, but also a huge assortment of additional files, including:

• All the thumbnail images in the iPhoto window.

• The original, safety copies of photos you've edited in iPhoto.

• Various data files that keep track of your iPhoto keywords, comments, ratings, and photo albums.

To prepare for a disaster, you should back up *all* of these components.

To perform a complete backup, copy the entire iPhoto Library folder to another location. Copying it to a different hard drive—to an iPod, say, or to the hard drive of another Mac via the network—is the best solution. (Copying it to another folder on the *same* disk means you'll lose both the original iPhoto Library folder and its backup if, say, your hard drive crashes or your computer is hit by an asteroid.)

Note: Of course, you can also back up your photos by dragging their thumbnails out of the iPhoto window and into a folder or disk on your desktop, once you've dragged the iPhoto window to one side.

Unfortunately, this method doesn't preserve your keywords, comments, album organization, or any other information you've created in iPhoto. If something bad happens to your Photo Library, you'll have to import the raw photos again and reorganize them from scratch.

Managing Photo Libraries

iPhoto can comfortably manage as many as 250,000 photos in a single collection, give or take a few thousand, depending on your Mac model and how much memory it has.

But for some people, 250,000 pictures is a bit unwieldy. It makes them nervous to keep that many eggs in a single basket. They wish they could break up the library into several smaller, easier-to-manage, easier-to-back-up chunks.

If that's your situation, you can archive some of the photos to CD or DVD using the Burn command described earlier, and then *delete* the archived photos from your library to shrink it down in size. For example, you might choose to archive older photos, or albums you rarely use.

Note: Remember, archiving photos to CD using the Burn command doesn't automatically remove them from iPhoto; you have to do that part yourself. If you don't, your Photo Library won't get any smaller. Just make sure that the CD you've burned works properly before deleting your original photos from iPhoto.

iPhoto Disk Images

The one disadvantage of that offload-to-disc technique is that it takes a big hunk of your photo collection *offline*, so that you can no longer get to it easily. If you suddenly need a set of photos that you've already archived, you have to hunt down the right disc before you can see the photos. That could be a problem if you happen to be on the road in New York and need the photos you left on a CD in San Francisco.

Here's a brilliant solution to that CD-management problem: Turn your iPhoto CDs into *disk image files* on your hard drive.

Open Disk Utility (which sits in your Applications→Utilities folder); then insert the iPhoto CD or DVD you've burned. In the left pane of the Disk Utility window, click the disc's icon. (Click the CD or DVD icon bearing a plain-English name, like "iPhoto Library"—usually it's the last one listed. Don't click the icon bearing your CD burner's name, like "PIONEER DVR-103.")

Then choose File→New→Disk Image From [disk name], or click the New Image button in the toolbar at the top of the window. In the Convert Image dialog box, you can type a name for the disk image you're about to create. (You can even password-protect it by choosing AES-128 from the Encryption pop-up menu.) Choose a location for the disk image, like your Desktop, and then click Save.

You've just created a disk image file whose name ends with .dmg. It's a "virtual CD" that you can keep on your hard drive at all times. When you want to view its contents in iPhoto, double-click the .dmg icon. You'll see its contents appear in the form of a CD icon in the iPhoto album list, just as though you'd inserted the original iPhoto disc.

You can spin off numerous chunks of your iPhoto collection this way, and "mount" as many of them simultaneously as you like—a spectacular way to manage tens of thousands of photos, chunk by chunk, without having to deal with a clumsy collection of CDs.

Multiple iPhoto Libraries

There are two good reasons why you might want to consider splitting your photo collection into smaller libraries:

- iPhoto itself is faster, especially during scrolling, because there are fewer photos in it.

- You can keep different types of collections or projects separate. You might want to maintain a Home library for personal use, for example, and a Work library for images that pertain to your business. Or you can start a new library every other year.

Creating new libraries

iPhoto provides a built-in tool for creating fresh Photo Libraries and switching between several of them:

1. **Quit iPhoto.**

   You're going to do the next step in the Finder.

2. **While pressing the Option key, open iPhoto again.**

   When iPhoto starts up, it senses that you're up to something. It offers you the chance to create a new library, or to choose an existing one (Figure 14-3).

3. Click Create Library. In the following dialog box, type a name for the new library (like *iPhoto Library 2*), and click Save.

You're offered not only the chance to create a new library, but also to choose a location for it that's not your regularly scheduled Pictures folder.

When iPhoto finishes opening, all remnants of your old Photo Library are gone. You're left with a blank window, ready to import photos.

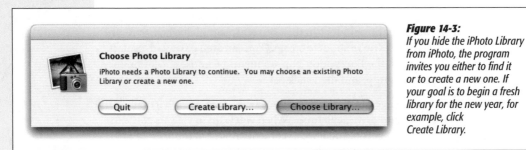

Choose Photo Library

iPhoto needs a Photo Library to continue. You may choose an existing Photo Library or create a new one.

[Quit]   [Create Library...]   [Choose Library...]

Figure 14-3:
If you hide the iPhoto Library from iPhoto, the program invites you either to find it or to create a new one. If your goal is to begin a fresh library for the new year, for example, click Create Library.

Using this technique, you can spawn as many new Photo Libraries as you need. You can archive the old libraries on CD or DVD, move them to another Mac, or just keep them somewhere on your hard drive so that you can swap any one of them back in whenever you need it.

As for *how* you swap them back in you have two options: Apple's way, and an easier way.

Swapping libraries (Apple's method)

Once you've built yourself at least two iPhoto Library folders, you can use the same Option-key trick (see step 2 above) to switch among them. When the dialog box in Figure 14-3 appears, click Choose Library, and then find and open the library folder that you want to open.

When iPhoto finishes reopening, you'll find the new set of photos in place.

Swapping libraries (automatic method)

If that Option-key business sounds a little disorienting, you're not alone. Brian Webster, a self-proclaimed computer nerd, thought the same thing—but *he* decided to do something about it. He wrote iPhoto Library Manager, a free program that streamlines the creation and swapping of iPhoto libraries. Waste no time in downloading it from the "Missing CD" page at *www.missingmanuals.com* or Brian's own site at *http://homepage.mac.com/bwebster*.

The beauty of this program is that it offers a tidy list of all your Library folders; you can switch among them with two quick clicks.

Here are a few pointers for using iPhoto Library Manager:

- The program doesn't just activate *existing* iPhoto Library folders; it can also create new Library folders for you. Just click the New Library button in the toolbar, choose a location and name for the library, and click OK (see Figure 14-4).

- You still have to quit and relaunch iPhoto for a change in libraries to take effect. Conveniently, iPhoto Library Manager includes Quit iPhoto and Relaunch iPhoto buttons in its toolbar.

Tip: You can also switch libraries using the pop-up menu from iPhoto Library Manager's Dock icon.

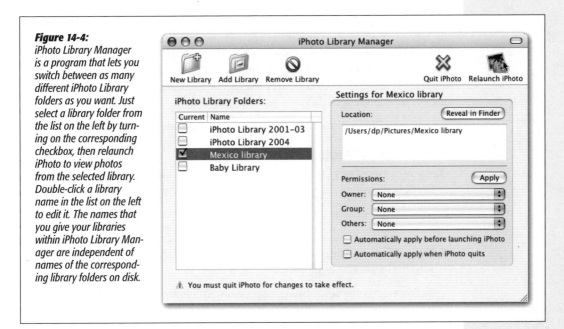

Figure 14-4:
iPhoto Library Manager is a program that lets you switch between as many different iPhoto Library folders as you want. Just select a library folder from the list on the left by turning on the corresponding checkbox, then relaunch iPhoto to view photos from the selected library. Double-click a library name in the list on the left to edit it. The names that you give your libraries within iPhoto Library Manager are independent of names of the corresponding library folders on disk.

- iPhoto Library Manager is fully AppleScriptable. If you're handy with writing AppleScript scripts (Chapter 13), you can write one that swaps your various libraries automatically with a double-click.

Merging Photo Libraries

You've just arrived home from your photo safari of deepest Kenya. You're jet-lagged and dusty, but your MacBook Pro is bursting at the seams with fresh photo meat. You can't wait to transfer the new pictures into your main Photo Library—you know, the one on your Power Macintosh Core Duo with 2 gigs of RAM and a 35-inch Apple Imax Display.

Or, less dramatically, suppose you've just upgraded to iPhoto 6. You're thrilled that you can now fit 250,000 pictures into a single library—but you still have six old iPhoto 5 Library folders containing about 10,000 pictures each.

In both cases, you have the same problem: How are you supposed to merge the libraries into a single, unified one?

How Not to Do It

You certainly can combine the *photos* of two Macs' Photo Libraries—just export
them from one (File→Export) and then import them into the other (File→Import
to Library). As a result, however, you lose all of your album organization, comments,
and keywords.

Your next instinct might be: "Hey, I know! I'll just drag the iPhoto Library folder from
computer #1 into the iPhoto window of computer #2!"

Big mistake. You'll end up importing not only the photos, but also the original versions
of any photos that you edited. You'll wind up with duplicates or triplicates of every
photo in the viewing area, in one enormous, unmanageable, uncategorized, sloshing
library. (At least iPhoto 6 is smart enough not to import all the thumbnail images,
as early iPhoto versions did.)

No, merging iPhoto libraries is slightly more complicated than that.

Method 1: Use iPhoto CDs as Intermediaries

One way to merge two Photo Libraries is to burn the second one onto an iPhoto CD
or DVD, as described earlier in this chapter.

Begin with the smaller library. (In the Kenya safari example, you'd begin with the
laptop.)

1. **Open iPhoto and burn a CD or DVD containing all the photos you want to merge
   into the larger Photo Library.**

   Follow exactly the same disc-creation steps outlined in the steps beginning on page
   342. If you want to preserve any albums you've created, select the albums, not just
   the photos themselves, when you burn the discs.

2. **Quit iPhoto. Swap iPhoto Library folders.**

   If you're trying to merge the libraries of two different Macs, skip this instruction.
   Instead, move to the second Mac at this point—the one that will serve as the final
   resting place for the photos you exported.

   If you're merging two libraries on the same Mac, swap the iPhoto Library folders
   using either of the methods described earlier in this chapter. In any case, the master,
   larger photo collection should now be before you in iPhoto.

3. **Insert the iPhoto CD you just created.**

   iPhoto opens (if it's not already running), and the iPhoto CD icon appears in the
   Source list of the iPhoto window, as shown in Figure 14-5. Albums on the disc
   appear underneath the CD icon.

4. **To copy the entire disc's contents to your current iPhoto library, drag its little CD
   icon onto your iPhoto Library icon (Figure 14-5).**

You can also drag it into an iPhoto folder icon in your Source list. You just can't
drag it onto an album or to a blank spot in the Source list.

If you don't want the entire disc's worth of pictures, you can also expand its listing
(by clicking the flippy triangle) and choose an album, or several. (You select multiple albums just as you would lists of files in the Finder: Shift-click to select several
consecutive albums, ⌘-click to select nonconsecutive albums, and so on.)

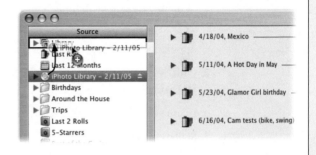

Figure 14-5:
*To merge photo libraries, drag and drop albums
from an iPhoto CD onto a blank spot in the
Source list, or onto the Photo Library icon at the
very top.*

*In this example, the contents of photo albums
named Disney World and NYC, which are stored
on the iPhoto CD, are being merged into the
main Photo Library.*

Then drag the selected albums (using any one of them as a handle) to a blank spot
at the bottom of the Source list, below all the other albums, onto a folder icon, or
onto the Photo Library icon at the very top.

In any case, this is the big moment when the "merge" happens. iPhoto switches
into Import mode and copies the selected albums from the iPhoto CD into your
main Photo Library. iPhoto also pulls in the photos' keywords, comments, ratings, and titles.

When it's all over, you won't find any new albums. You will, however, find that
your Photo Library now contains the merged pictures. (Click the Last Roll icon
to see them.)

Using this technique, you can combine the photos stored on any number of CDs into a
single library, without losing a single comment, keyword, album, or original photo.

Method 2: Share the Library with Yourself

Burning iPhoto CDs is a great way to merge two or more iPhoto Libraries, because it
leaves you with backup discs. And it's a lot simpler than what you're about to read.

Still, you use up a lot of blank discs this way, and you spend a lot of time waiting for
discs to burn.

If the Photo Libraries you want to merge are all on the same Mac—in separate accounts, for example, or just in different places—here's another method that doesn't
involve burning iPhoto CDs. Instead, it involves using the photo sharing feature
described on page 246.

To pull this off, you'll need at least two Mac OS X accounts. You'll also need iPhoto Library Manager (page 348). The steps below look long, but remember that you have to do all this only once.

For clarity, let's say that you want to merge a library called Small Batch into a bigger one called Big Library, both of which are currently in your Pictures folder.

1. **On the Accounts panel of System Preferences, click the padlock icon and, when asked, enter your account password. Click OK. Click Login Options. Turn on "Enable fast user switching." Click OK in the confirmation box.**

   This operation also requires at least one account in addition to your own. Take this opportunity to create one, if necessary. Let's call that other account Casey.

2. **Quit System Preferences. Drag the Small Batch library folder into the Macintosh HD→Users→Shared folder.**

   If you've read Chapter 9, this should sound familiar.

3. **Switch into Casey's account. Open iPhoto Library Manager. Click Add Library. Navigate to that Shared folder, click the Small Batch library, and click Open.**

   Now Small Batch is listed in the iPhoto Library Manager list.

4. **Set all three pop-up menus to "Read & Write," as shown in Figure 14-6.**

   You've just made Small Batch accessible to the Casey account.

Figure 14-6:
This method of merging your own Photo Libraries requires the assistance of the free iPhoto Library Manager. Here, you're making the library-to-be-merged accessible to the second account.

5. **Turn on the Small Batch checkbox, and then click Launch iPhoto.**

   You should now see the photos from Small Batch in Casey's copy of iPhoto.

6. **In Casey's copy of iPhoto, share the albums you'll want to merge.**

   See page 246 for details on photo sharing. Leave iPhoto running.

7. **Switch back to your own account. Open up the Big Library in iPhoto.**

   Now you're looking at the main photo collection—but after a moment, in the Source list, you'll see an icon for Casey's shared photos. (If not, choose iPhoto→Preferences, click Sharing, and turn on "Look for shared photos." Close the Preferences window.)

   Click the flippy triangle to reveal Casey's albums.

8. **Drag Casey's albums into a blank spot in your own Source list.**

   You've just copied the albums from the Small Batch library into your own Big Library. Put another way, you've just merged two iPhoto libraries without having to burn any discs!

   (And they said it couldn't be done…)

9. **Switch back into Casey's account and quit iPhoto.**

   Once you've confirmed that the photos have safely arrived in your main library, you can throw away the Small Batch folder.

Beyond iPhoto

Depending on how massive your collection of digital photos grows and how you use it, you may find yourself wanting more file-management power than iPhoto can offer. Maybe you wish you could organize 500,000 photos in a single catalog, without having to swap photo libraries or load archive CDs. Maybe you have a small network, and you'd like a system that lets a whole workgroup share a library of photos simultaneously.

To enjoy such features, you'll have to move beyond iPhoto into the world of *digital asset management,* which means spending a little money. Programs like Extensis Portfolio ($200, *www.extensis.com*), Canto Cumulus ($100, *www.canto.com*), iView MediaPro ($200, *www.iview-multimedia.com*), and Apple' own Aperture ($500) are terrific programs for someone who wants to take the next step up, as shown in Figure 14-7. (Most of these companies offer free trial versions on their Web sites.) Here are a few of the stunts these more advanced programs can do that iPhoto can't:

- Create custom fields to store any other kind of information you want about your files—dates, prices, Web addresses, and so on.

- Track graphics files stored in any location on a network, not just in a specific folder.

- Catalog not just photos, but other file types, too: PDF files, QuarkXPress and In-Design documents, QuickTime movies, sound files, PowerPoint slides, and more flavors of RAW files than iPhoto understands.

- Share a catalog of images with dozens of other people over a network.

- Customize the fonts, colors, and borders of the thumbnail view.

- Create catalogs that can be read on both Mac and Windows.

- Display previews of "offline" photo files that aren't actually on the Mac at the moment (they're on CDs or DVDs on your shelf, for example).

Some of the features in this list were obviously developed with professional users in mind, like graphic designers and studio photographers. But this kind of program is worth considering if your photo collection—and your passion for digital photography—one day outgrows iPhoto.

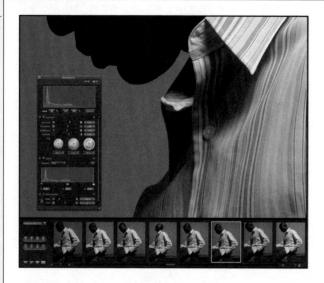

Figure 14-7:
Aperture is one of several programs that do what iPhoto does—and a lot more besides.

Here, for example, is Aperture's version of the full-screen editing mode. One key difference: when you make changes, Aperture doesn't duplicate the photo file (and use up disk space), as iPhoto does. It just remembers which changes you've applied, and can undo them in any sequence.

Bottom: iView Media can "watch" certain folders on your Mac, so that when new graphics arrive, iView catalogs them automatically.

Part Five: Appendixes

5

Troubleshooting

●Photo isn't just a Mac OS X program—it's a *Cocoa* Mac OS X program, meaning
1 that it was written exclusively for Mac OS X. As a result, it should, in theory, be
one of the most rock-solid programs under the sun.

Still, iPhoto does have its vulnerabilities. Many of these shortcomings stem from the
fact that iPhoto works under the supervision of a lot of cooks, since it must interact
with plug-ins, connect to printers, talk to Web servers, and cope with an array of file
corruptions.

If trouble strikes, keep hands and feet inside the tram at all times—and consult the
following collection of problems, solutions, questions, and answers.

The Most Important Advice In This Chapter

Apple's traditional practice is to release a new version of iPhoto (and iMovie, and
iDVD…) that's full of bugs and glitches—and then, just when public outcry reaches
fever pitch a couple of weeks later, send out a .0.1 updater that cleans up most of the
problems. That's exactly what happened with iPhoto 6.

The list of bugs in 6.0 included photocasting problems, problems viewing thumbnails
in large libraries, freezes when ordering cards, calendars and books, bogus "elements
missing" messages when opening older iDVD projects, crashes when emptying the
Trash, and more. Spare yourself the headache: update your copy to 6.0.2 (or whatever
the latest version is)!

To do that right now, choose iPhoto→Check for Updates.

Importing, Upgrading, and Opening

Getting photos into iPhoto is supposed to be one of the most effortless parts of the process. Remember, Steve Jobs promised that iPhoto would forever banish the "chain of pain" from digital photography. And yet…

"Unable to upgrade this photo library because…does not have access"

If you see the "current user does not have access" message when you open iPhoto 6 for the first time, something's gone wrong with the invisible Unix permissions that govern your library, possibly because somebody moved the iPhoto Library folder.

The steps to correct the problem are pretty straightforward, but they're lengthy. You can read them, step by step, in this Web article: *http://docs.info.apple.com/article. html?artnum=303135.*

"Unable to upgrade this photo library"

There's another reason iPhoto might not be able to upgrade your old iPhoto Library, too: There are locked files somewhere inside your iPhoto Library. If something's locked, iPhoto can't very well convert it to the version 6 format.

Trouble is, there can be hundreds of thousands of files in an iPhoto Library. How are you supposed to find the one file that's somehow gotten locked?

The quickest way is to type out a Unix command. Don't worry, it won't bite.

Open your Applications→Utilities folder, and double-click Terminal. The strange, graphics-free, all-text command console may look alien and weird, but you'll witness its power in just a moment.

Type this, exactly as it appears here: *sudo chflags -R nouchg*

—and add a space at the end (after "nouchg"). Do not press Return or Enter yet.

Now switch to the Finder. Open your Pictures folder and drag your iPhoto Library folder right *into* the Terminal window. Now the command looks something like this:

sudo chflags -R nouchg /Users/Casey/Pictures/iPhoto\ Library/

Press Return or Enter to issue the command. Mac OS X asks for your account password, to prove that you know what you're doing. Type it, press Return or Enter, and your problem should be solved.

iPhoto doesn't recognize my camera.

iPhoto generally "sees" any recent camera model, even if it's not listed on Apple's Device Compatibility page (*www.apple.com/iphoto/compatibility*). If you don't see the Import screen (Chapter 4) even though the camera most assuredly is connected, try these steps in order:

- Make sure the camera is turned on. Check the USB cable at both ends.

- Try plugging the camera into a different USB port.

- Some models don't see the computer until you switch them into a special "PC" mode, using the control knob.

- Try turning on the camera *after* connecting its USB cable to the Mac.

- Turn the camera off, then on again, while it's plugged in.

- If iPhoto absolutely won't notice its digital companion, use a memory-card reader as described on page 88.

iPhoto crashes when I try to import.

This problem is most likely to crop up when you're bringing pictures in from your hard drive or another disk. Here are the possibilities:

- The culprit is usually a single corrupted file. Try a test: Import only half the photos in the batch. If nothing bad happens, split the remaining photos in half again and import *them*. Keep going until you've isolated the offending file.

- Consider the graphics program you're using to save the files. It's conceivable that its version of JPEG or TIFF doesn't jibe perfectly with iPhoto's. (This scenario is most likely to occur right after you've upgraded either your graphics program or iPhoto itself.)

  To test this possibility, open a handful of images in a different editing program, save them, and then try the import again. If they work, then you might have a temporary compatibility problem. Check the editing program's Web site for update and troubleshooting information.

- Some JPEGs that were originally saved in Mac OS 9 won't import into iPhoto. Try opening and resaving these images in a native Mac OS X editor like Photoshop. Speaking of Photoshop, it has an excellent batch-processing tool that can automatically process mountains of images while you go grab some lunch.

Finally, a reminder, just in case you think iPhoto is acting up: iPhoto imports RAW files—but not from all camera models. For details, see page 87.

iPhoto crashes when I try to empty the Trash.

First, upgrade to iPhoto 6.0.2 or later.

Then open iPhoto while pressing ⌘ and Option; in the dialog box shown on page 365, turn on "Rebuild the photos' small thumbnails" and click Rebuild.

There are white lines through my thumbnails!

This will sound familiar: First, upgrade to iPhoto 6.0.2 or later.

Then open iPhoto while pressing ⌘ and Option; in the dialog box shown on page 365, turn on "Rebuild all of the photos" and click Rebuild.

iPhoto won't import images from my video camera.

Most modern digital camcorders can store your still images on a memory card instead of DV tape. If you're having a hard time importing these stills into iPhoto with a direct camera connection, try these tips:

- Take out the tape cassette before connecting the camcorder to your Mac.

- Try copying the files directly from the memory card to your hard drive with a memory-card reader. Once the images are on your hard drive, you should be able to import them into iPhoto.

What if I don't want iPhoto to import all the pictures from my camera?

Two possibilities. First, use the Automator program described on page 337.

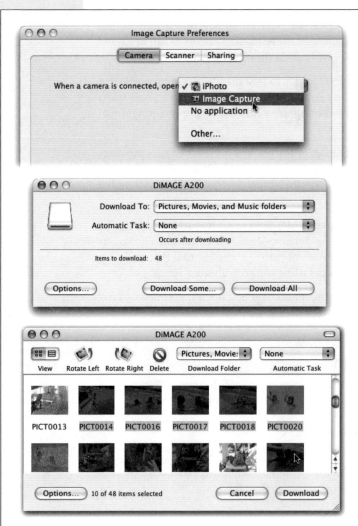

Figure A-1:
Top: First, make sure that Image Capture, not iPhoto, intercepts and downloads the photos when you connect your digital camera. To do so, open Image Capture, then choose Image Capture→Preferences.

From the Camera Preferences pop-up menu, choose Image Capture. (In fact, you could even choose another program to intervene when your camera is plugged in, by choosing Other from this menu).

Middle: This is the main Image Capture window that now appears when you plug in your camera. To download only some of the photos, click Download Some.

Bottom: This "slide sorter" window is where you can choose the individual pictures you want to download. Or, use the buttons at the top to rotate or delete selected shots from the camera. In slide sorter view, Shift-click or ⌘-click the thumbnails of the pictures you want. In list view, Shift-click or ⌘-click as though they're Finder list-view files.

From now on, Image Capture, not iPhoto, will open whenever you plug in your camera. Once the pictures are on your hard drive, copy them into iPhoto simply by dragging them (or the folder they're in) into the photo-viewing area.

Second, use Image Capture. A sort of grandfather to iPhoto, this Mac OS X program comes on every Mac. Although it doesn't perform even a hundredth of the feats that iPhoto can, it does offer one feature iPhoto lacks—*selective* importing. To make this change, use the procedure outlined in Figure A-1.

Exporting

Clearly, "Easy come, easy go" doesn't always apply to photos.

After I upgraded iPhoto to the latest version, my Export button became disabled.
This problem is usually caused by outdated plug-ins. If you have any older plug-ins, such as an outdated version of the Toast Titanium export plug-in, disable it and then relaunch iPhoto to see whether that solves the problem.

Here's how to turn your plug-ins on or off:

1. **Quit iPhoto. In the Finder, highlight the iPhoto application icon. Choose File→Get Info.**

   You may have seen the Get Info box for other files in your day, but you probably haven't seen a *Plugins* panel (Figure A-2).

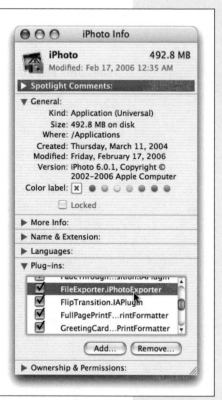

Figure A-2:
You may be surprised to discover that a number of iPhoto's "built-in" features are actually plug-ins written by Apple's programmers. Most of them are responsible for familiar printing and exporting options. Any others should be turned off in times of troubleshooting. (If you can't remember which plug-ins you've installed yourself, reinstall iPhoto.)

2. **Click the triangle to expand the Plugins panel.**

   A complete list of the plug-ins you currently have loaded appears with a checkbox next to each item.

3. **Turn off the non-Apple plug-ins that you suspect might be causing the problem.**

Now open iPhoto and test the export function. If the technology gods are smiling, the function should work now. All that's left is to figure out which *one* of the plug-ins was causing your headaches.

To find out, quit iPhoto. In the Finder, open its Get Info window again. Reinstate your plug-ins one by one, using the on/off switches depicted in Figure A-2, until you find the offending software.

Once you locate the culprit, highlight its name and then click Remove. (You may also want to check the Web site of the offending plug-in for an updated version.)

Tip: Here's another, somewhat more interesting way to remove a plug-in. Control-click (or right-click) the iPhoto icon; from the shortcut menu, choose Show Package Contents. In the resulting window, open the Contents→PlugIns folder, where each plug-in is represented by an easily removable icon.

Printing

How many things can go wrong when you print? Let us count the ways.

I can't print more than one photo per page. It seems like a waste to use a whole sheet of paper for one 4 x 6 print.
Check the following:

- Have you, in fact, selected more than one photo to print?

- Choose File→Page Setup. Make sure the paper size is US Letter (or whatever paper you've loaded). Click OK.

- Choose File→Print. From the Presets pop-up menu, choose Standard; from the Style pop-up menu, choose N-Up; then choose a number from the "Photos per page" pop-up menu. (Make sure "One photo per page" is turned off.) You'll now see all of your selected images side by side in the Preview pane. They're ready to print.

My picture doesn't fit right on 4 x 6, 5 x 7, or 8 x 10 inch paper.
Most digital cameras produce photos in a 4:3 width-to-height ratio. Unfortunately, those dimensions don't fit squarely into any of the standard print sizes.

The solution: Crop the photos first, using the appropriate print size in the Constrain pop-up menu (see page 149).

Editing and Sharing

There's not much that can go wrong here, but when it does, it *really* goes wrong.

iPhoto crashes when I double-click a thumbnail to edit it.

You probably changed a photo file's name in the Finder—in the iPhoto Library folder, behind the program's back. iPhoto hates this! Only grief can follow.

Sometimes, too, a corrupted picture file will also make iPhoto crash when you try to edit it. Use the Show Image File script described on page 335 to locate the scrambled file in the Finder. Open the file in another graphics program, use its File→Save As command to replace the corrupted picture file, and then try again in iPhoto.

My Adjust panel is missing most of its sliders!

If your Mac has only a G3 processor inside, them's the breaks. All you get is Brightness and Contrast sliders. (The rest require a G4, G5, or Intel processor.)

iPhoto won't let me use an external graphics program when I double-click a thumbnail.

Choose iPhoto→Preferences. Make sure that the Other button is selected and that a graphics program's name appears next to it. (If not, click Other, then click Set, and then choose the program you want to use.)

Also make sure that your external editing program still *exists*. You might have upgraded to a newer version of that program, one whose file name is slightly different from the version you originally specified in iPhoto.

I've messed up a photo while editing it, and now it's ruined!

Highlight the file's thumbnail and then choose Photos→Revert to Original. iPhoto restores your photo to its original state, drawing on a backup it has secretly kept.

I published a photocast, and it wiped out another one!

Strange but true: For Web compatibility reasons, iPhoto treats accented letters (é, ê, ë, and so on) as though they're all unaccented (e). It's possible, then, that you thought you were giving a photocast a different name, but because of this weirdness, you were naming it identically to your earlier photocast. The moral: Don't use accents in your album names.

General Questions

Finally, here's a handful of general—although perfectly terrifying—troubles.

iPhoto's wigging out.

If the program "unexpectedly quits," well, that's life. It happens. This is Mac OS X, though, so you can generally open the program right back up again and pick up where you left off.

If the flakiness is becoming really severe, try logging out (choose →Log Out) and logging back in again. And if the problem persists, see the data-purging steps on the next page.

I don't see my other Mac's shared photos over the network.

Chapter 9 covers network photo sharing in detail. If you're having trouble making it work, here's your checklist:

- Make sure you've turned on "Look for shared photos" in the Sharing pane of iPhoto Preferences.

- Is the Mac that's sharing the photos turned on and awake? Is iPhoto running on it, and does it have photo sharing turned on? Is it on the same network subnet (network branch)?

- Do the photo-sharing Macs have iPhoto 4 or later installed?

I can't delete a photo!

You may be trying to delete a photo right out of a smart album. That's a no-no.

There's only one workaround: Find the same photo in the Photo Library, the Last Roll icon, or the Last Months icon—and delete it from there.

All my pictures are gone!

Somebody probably moved, renamed, or fooled with your iPhoto Library folder. That's a bad, bad idea.

If it's just been moved or renamed, then find it again using your Mac's search feature (Spotlight, for example). Drag it back into your Pictures folder, if you like. In any case, the important step is to open iPhoto while pressing the Option key. When the dialog box shown on page 348 appears, show iPhoto where your library folder is now. (If that solution doesn't work, read on.)

All my pictures are still gone! (or)
My thumbnails are all gray rectangles! (or)
I'm having some other crisis!

The still-missing-pictures syndrome and the gray-rectangle thumbnails are only two of several oddities that may strike with all the infrequency—and pain—of lightning. Maybe iPhoto is trying to import phantom photos. Maybe it's stuck at the "Loading photos..." screen forever. Maybe the photos just don't look right. There's a long list, in fact, of rare but mystifying glitches that can arise.

What your copy of iPhoto needs is a big thwack upside the head, also known as a major data purge.

You may not need to perform all of the following steps. But if you follow them all, at least you'll know you did everything possible to make things right. Follow these steps in order; after each one, check to see if the problem is gone.

- **If you haven't already done so, upgrade to the very latest version of iPhoto.** For example, versions 6.0.1 and 6.0.2 fixed a host of bugs and glitches.

- **Rebuild the Photo Library.** Quit iPhoto. Then reopen it, pressing the Option and ⌘ keys as you do so.

iPhoto asks you if you're sure you want to "rebuild your Photo Library" (Figure A-3) and offers four different rebuilding techniques.

Once you click Rebuild, iPhoto works its way through each album and each photo, inspecting it for damage, repairing it if possible, and finally presenting you with your new, cleaned-up library. This can take a *very* long time, but it usually works.

Figure A-3:
These four maintenance procedures solve all kinds of iPhoto library corruptions. Sometimes you'll be instructed to use only one of the checkboxes to save time. If you're really desperate, turn on all four.

> **Rebuild Photo Library**
>
> Please choose how you would like to rebuild your iPhoto library. We recommend you make a backup of your iPhoto Library photo before proceeding.
>
> ☑ Rebuild the photos' small thumbnails
> ☐ Rebuild all of the photos' thumbnails (this may take a while)
> ☐ Rebuild the iPhoto Library database
> ☐ Recover orphaned photos in the iPhoto Library folder
>
> (Cancel) (Rebuild)

- **Repair your file permissions.** An amazing number of mysterious glitches—not just in iPhoto—arise because file *permissions* have become muddled. Permissions are a complicated subject, and refer to a complex mesh of interconnected Unix settings on every file in Mac OS X.

When something just doesn't seem to be working right, therefore, open your Applications→Utilities folder and open Disk Utility. Click your hard drive's name in the left-side list; click the First Aid tab; click Repair Disk Permissions; and then read a magazine while the Mac checks out your disk. If the program finds anything amiss, you'll see Unix shorthand messages that tell you what it fixed.

Tip: Most Mac mavens, in fact, believe in running this Repair Permissions routine after running *any kind of installer*, just to nip nascent problems in the bud. That includes both installers of new programs and of Apple's own updates.

- **Throw away the iPhoto preference file.** Here we are in the age of Mac OS X, and we're still throwing away preference files?

Absolutely. A corrupted preference file can still bewilder the program that depends on it.

Open your Home→Library→Preferences folder, where you'll find neatly labeled preference files for all of the programs you use. In this case, trash the file called com.apple.iPhoto.plist.

The next time you run iPhoto, it will build itself a brand-new preference file that, if you're lucky, lacks whatever corruption was causing your problems.

- **Import the library into itself.** If, after all of these steps, some or all of your photos are still missing, try this radical step. Create a new, empty iPhoto Library (page 348). Then drag the troubled, older Library folder right from the Finder into the empty iPhoto window. The program imports all of the graphics it finds (except the thumbnails, which you don't want anyway).

  You lose all of your keywords, film-roll names, comments, albums, folders, books, saved slideshows, and so on. And you might wind up with duplicates (the edited and unedited versions of the pictures). But if any photos were in the old library but somehow unaccounted for, they'll magically reappear.

- **Just find the pix yourself.** If none of these steps restored your missing photos, all is not lost. Unless you somehow opened your Home→Pictures folder and, while sleepwalking, manually *threw away* your iPhoto Library folder, your pictures are still there, somewhere, on your hard drive.

  Use Spotlight or the Find command to search for them, as shown in Figure A-4.

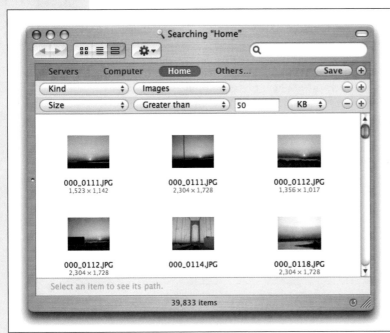

Figure A-4:
Set up a search for images (or file extensions .JPG or .JPEG), with file sizes greater than, say, 50 K (to avoid rounding up all of the little thumbnail representations; it's the actual photos you want).

The results will probably include thousands of photos to sift through. But in this desperate state, you may be grateful that you can either (a) click one to see where it's hiding, or (b) select all of them, drag them into a new, empty iPhoto Library, and begin the process of sorting out the mess.

iPhoto 6, Menu by Menu

Some people use iPhoto for years without pulling down a single menu. But unless you explore its menu commands, you're likely to miss some of the options and controls that make it a surprisingly powerful little photo manager. Especially since some commands, like Export, appear *only* in menus.

Here's a menu-by-menu look at iPhoto's commands.

iPhoto Menu

This first menu, Mac OS X's Application menu, takes on the name of whatever program happens to be running in the foreground. In iPhoto's case, that would be iPhoto.

About iPhoto
This command opens the "About" box containing the requisite Apple legalese.

There's really only one good reason to open the About iPhoto window: It's the easiest way to find out exactly which version of iPhoto you have.

iPhoto Hot Tips
Opens a page on Apple's Web site that lists a brief overview of iPhoto 6's newest features, and tricks like keyboard shortcuts.

Preferences
Opens the Preferences window (Figure B-1), which has six panels to choose from:

General

- Tell iPhoto how many months to show in the Last ___ Months album and how many rolls to show in the Last ___ Rolls album, as discussed in Chapter 5.

- Have iPhoto display the total photo count, in parentheses, next to each album in the Source list.

- Choose how you want iPhoto to open photos when you double-click them. You have four choices: Open the photo for editing in the main iPhoto window, in a *separate* window, in the new full-screen mode, or in another program (which you choose by clicking the Set button). Details appear in Chapter 5.

- Change the setting of iPhoto's Rotate button so that it spins selected photos counter-clockwise instead of clockwise.

- Choose the email program that you want iPhoto to use when emailing pictures as attachments using the Mail Photo feature.

- Specify whether or not iPhoto is allowed to check for ".01" upgrades that Apple releases via the Internet. If yes, then you'll see, from time to time, dialog boxes that invite you to download and install these updates (which usually fix bugs).

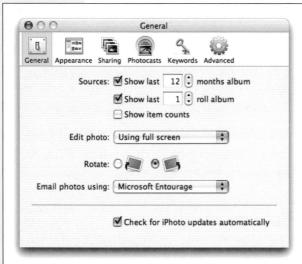

Figure B-1:
You'll probably be visiting iPhoto's Preferences window fairly regularly, so remember the keyboard shortcut that takes you here: ⌘-comma. You need to open Preferences every time you want to turn Photo Sharing on or off, for example.

Appearance

- Add a drop shadow or thin black outline frame to your thumbnails in the photo-viewing area.

- Change the background of the photo-viewing area from white to black—or any shade of gray.

- Align thumbnails to a grid in the iPhoto window.

- Superimpose a floating, dark gray label on the screen while you're scrolling, to help you figure out where you are in your vast library. (It shows the date, or rating, or name of the photos whizzing by, according to your sort criterion.)

- Choose a size (small or large) for the album titles in the Source list.

- **Use animated scrolling** refers to what happens when you press the Page Up or Page Down keys on your keyboard. When this option is on, the thumbnails slide up or down on the screen. When it's off (or when you're going too fast for iPhoto to process the animation), the window just jumps suddenly to the next screenful.

Sharing

Set up iPhoto for sharing your iPhoto Library over a home or small-office network, as described on page 246.

Photocasts

This simple panel pertains to photocasting (page 243). At the top, you choose how often you want your copy of iPhoto to check for updated versions of *other* people's photocasts. The rest of this pane simply lists the albums that *you've* broadcast; you can use the Stop Publishing to terminate the public's access to your masterpieces.

Keywords

Here's where you add or delete keywords, which you can use to tag your photos for quick retrieval later. (Page 127 has the details.) New in iPhoto 6: a pop-up menu that lets you specify what happens when you turn on more than one keyword button. iPhoto can either round up only the photos with *all* of those keywords, or the ones that match *any* of the keywords.

Advanced

A better name might be "Miscellaneous." Here we go:

- **Copy files to iPhoto Library folder when adding to library.** As noted on page 85, iPhoto 6 is willing to track your photos no matter where they are on your hard drive—in their current folder homes—without duplicating them in its own library. Here's the on-off switch.

- **Add ColorSync profile.** As you may have discovered through painful experience, computers aren't great with color. Each device you use to create and print digital images "sees" color a little bit differently, which explains why the deep amber captured by your scanner may be rendered as chalky brown on your monitor, yet come out as a fiery orange on your Epson inkjet printer. Since every gadget defines and renders color in its own way, colors are often inconsistent as a print job moves from design to proof to press.

  ColorSync attempts to sort out this mess, serving as a translator between all the different pieces of hardware in your workflow. For this to work, each device (scanner, monitor, printer, digital camera, copier, proofer, and so on) has to be calibrated with a unique *ColorSync profile*—a file that tells your Mac exactly how it defines colors.

Armed with the knowledge contained in the profiles, the ColorSync software can compensate for the various quirks of the different devices, and even the different kinds of paper they print on.

Using the ColorSync Utility program (in Applications→Utilities), you can specify which ColorSync profile each of your gadgets should use. The next step, though, is to embed a profile *right into each photo,* making all of the ColorSync tracking automatic. This feature, once relegated to the professional world, is now available right in iPhoto, thanks to this checkbox.

- **Save edited RAW file as 16-bit TIFFs.** Here's another high-end feature. As you know from page 174, iPhoto ordinarily saves RAW files as JPEG graphics once you've edited them. But many photographers object that JPEG is a compressed format that, in theory, can degrade the quality of the original photo. This option tells iPhoto to save such pictures in the TIFF format instead, which consumes far more disk space but doesn't compress the photos.

- **Use RAW files with external editor.** This means, "Open RAW photos with Adobe's RAW-file editor, as described on page 175 of this book."

Empty Trash

Purges the contents of the iPhoto Trash, permanently deleting any photos, books, slideshows, and albums in it. There's no turning back once you choose Empty Trash: Your photos are gone, and there's no Undo command. Think before you empty.

Shop for iPhoto Products

This isn't so much a command as it is a marketing ploy. It opens your Web browser and opens a page on Apple's Web site that offers to sell you digital cameras, tripods, printers, and other accessories.

Provide iPhoto Feedback

This command takes you to a Web form on Apple's site where you can register complaints, make suggestions, or gush enthusiastically about iPhoto.

Register iPhoto

This is a link to yet another Apple Web page. Registering iPhoto simply means giving Apple your contact information. There's no penalty for not registering, by the way. Apple just wants to know more about who you are, so that it can offer you exciting new waves of junk mail.

Check for Updates

As noted on the previous page, Apple occasionally patches iPhoto to make it faster or better. If you've turned off *automatic* checking, you can instruct the program manually to check in with the mother ship via the Internet.

Hide iPhoto, Hide Others, Show All

These aren't iPhoto's commands—they're Mac OS X's.

In any case, they determine which of the various programs running on your Mac are *visible* onscreen at any given moment. The Hide Others command is probably the most popular of these three. It zaps away the windows of all other programs—including the Finder—so that the iPhoto window is the only one you see.

Tip: If you know this golden Mac OS X trick, you may never need to use the Hide Others command: To switch into iPhoto from another program, hold down the Option and ⌘ keys when clicking the iPhoto icon in the Dock. Doing so simultaneously brings iPhoto to the front *and* hides all other programs you have running, producing a distraction-free view of iPhoto.

Quit iPhoto

This command closes iPhoto, no questions asked. You're not even asked to save changes, because as you've probably noticed, iPhoto doesn't even *have* a Save command. Like Filemaker Pro, 4D, and other database programs, iPhoto—itself a glorified database—continually saves changes as you add, delete, or edit photos.

File Menu

Most of the commands in the File menu involve creating new storage entities: albums, books, slideshows, and so on. This is also where you do all your printing.

New Album

Creates a new photo album in the Source list, and prompts you to name it. (You can also create an album by pressing ⌘-N or clicking the + button in the main iPhoto window.) See Chapters 5, 10, and 7, respectively.

New Album From Selection

Select some photos in the iPhoto window, then choose this command. iPhoto creates a new album, already stocked with the selected pictures.

New Smart Album

Opens a dialog box where you can set up criteria for a smart album, as described on page 117.

New Folder

This humble command is the key to one of iPhoto 6's most welcome features: the all-powerful folder. A folder is a Source-list icon that can contain other icons, like albums, book layouts, and slideshows.

Import to Library

Use this command (formerly called Import) to add photos to your iPhoto Library from your hard disk, a CD, or some other disk. Choose Add to Library, select the file or folder you want to add, then click the Import button in the Import Photos dialog box. (Apple evidently renamed this command to make clear that you're importing a *copy* of the selected photos into iPhoto's own, internal collection.) *Keyboard shortcut:* Shift-⌘-I.

Export

Yes, kids, it's the amazing peripatetic Export command—in a different menu every version of iPhoto!

Anyway, it opens the Export Images window, whose panels offer the following ways of copying photos:

- **File Export.** Makes fresh copies of your photos in the file format and size you specify. You can export photos in their existing file format or convert them to JPEG, TIFF, or PNG format. You also can set a maximum size for the photos, so that iPhoto scales down larger photos on the fly as it exports them.

- **Web Page.** Publishes selected photos as a series of HTML pages that you can post on a Web site. The finished product includes an index page with clickable thumbnails that open individual pages containing each photo. (See Chapter 9 for step-by-step instructions on using this pane to set image sizes and format the HTML pages.)

- **QuickTime.** Turns a series of photos into a self-running slideshow, saved as a QuickTime movie that you can post on the Internet, send to friends, or burn to a CD. You can set the size of the movie, pick a background color, and add music (the sound file selected for the current photos' album or slideshow) before exporting. You'll find more about going from iPhoto to QuickTime in Chapter 11.

You can save yourself a trip to the Export menu by using the keyboard shortcut Shift-⌘-E. (By the way, you may find additional tabs in the Export dialog box if you've installed iPhoto plug-in software.)

Close Window

Closes the frontmost window. Usually, you'll use this command after opening a photo into its own window for editing. If only the main iPhoto window is open, this command quits the program. *Keyboard shortcut:* ⌘-W.

Edit Smart Album

Lets you edit the criteria for an existing smart album. Select the album before choosing this command. When you click OK, iPhoto updates the smart album.

Create Film Roll

Creates a new film roll (page 100) from a batch of selected photos. Great for dividing a huge import into more manageable chunks. (Dimmed unless you've first selected some thumbnails.)

Subscribe to Photocast

Asks you for the URL (Web address) for a photocast (Internet "publishing") that somebody has initiated, so that you can enjoy their pictures in your copy of iPhoto. See page 245.

Page Setup

Opens the standard Page Setup dialog box for your printer, where you can select the paper size, orientation, and scaling of your print job.

Print

Opens iPhoto's Print dialog box, where you can print contact sheets, greeting cards, full-page photos, or groups of photos in standard sizes like 4 x 6 or 5 x 7. See Chapter 8 for details.

Edit Menu

As you would expect, the commands in the Edit menu let you edit various parts of your Photo Library, such as keywords, photo titles, and the sort order. The standard Cut, Copy, and Paste commands operate on selected text and photos as normal.

Undo

Where would this world be without Undo? In iPhoto, you even have a *multiple* Undo; using this command (and its keyboard equivalent, ⌘-Z), you can reverse your last series of actions in iPhoto, backing out of your bad decisions with no harm done (Figure B-2). How nice to know that if you go too heavy on the contrast, delete an important photo, or crop out your grandmother's earlobe, there's a quick and easy way out.

Figure B-2:
Just about any action you perform in iPhoto can be reversed with the Undo command. The menu command itself always spells out exactly what it's going to undo—Undo Add Photo to Album, Undo Cropping, and so on—so that you know which action you're backing out of. The one un-undoable action to keep in mind is emptying the iPhoto Trash. Once that's done, your trashed photos are gone for good.

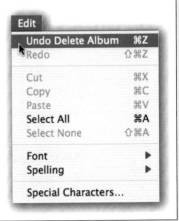

Note that the Undo command tracks your changes in each window independently. For example, suppose you're in the main iPhoto window. You enter Edit mode, where you crop a photo and rotate it. Now you double-click the photo so that it opens in its own window. Here, you fix some red-eye and adjust the contrast.

As long as you remain in the new window, you can undo the contrast and red-eye adjustments—but if you return to the main window, you'll find that the Undo command will take back only your *original* actions—the cropping and rotating.

So while iPhoto can handle multiple levels of undo, keep in mind that each window maintains its own private stash of Undos.

Redo

Redo (Shift-⌘-Z) lets you undo what you just undid. In other words, it reapplies the action you just reversed using the Undo command.

Cut, Copy, Paste

These commands work exactly the way they do in your word processor when you're editing photo titles, comments, keywords, or any other text fields. In addition, they have a few special functions when they're used in certain parts of iPhoto.

- In a photo album (not the main Photo Library), you can select photos and use Cut to remove them from the album. (This doesn't delete them from the Photo Library, only from that particular album.) To move the photos to a different album, click the album's name, or click one of its photos, and then choose Paste.

- You can assign photos from the main Photo Library to a specific album using the Copy and Paste commands. Select a file, choose Copy, click the destination photo album, and finally choose Paste.

- Cut, Copy, and Paste are all inactive when you're in Editing mode (Chapter 6).

Select All

This command (⌘-A) behaves in three different ways, depending on when you use it in iPhoto.

- It selects all thumbnails visible in the viewing area—either those in the selected album or the whole Photo Library.

- In Edit mode, with a photo opened in the main iPhoto window, the Select All command extends the cropping rectangle to the very edges of the photo.

- When you're editing photo titles, comments, keywords, or any other text fields, the Select All command selects all of the text in the field you're editing.

Select None

As you would expect, this command (called Deselect All in iPhoto 4) is the opposite of Select All. The only practical way to use this command is to employ its handy keyboard shortcut, Shift-⌘-A, to quickly deselect a group of photos without having to click the mouse.

Find

Just puts your blinking insertion point into the Search box at the bottom of the iPhoto window. Cute—real cute.

Font

Opens the standard Mac OS X Font Panel, which is of little use except when using iPhoto's book/calendar/card-designing feature (Chapter 10). You can't change the font used to display titles, comments, or keywords.

If you *are* formatting a book, calendar, or card, choose Edit→Fonts→Show Fonts (or press ⌘-T) to open the panel and make your selections.

Spelling

Use the Spelling commands to check for misspelled words within iPhoto. It's primarily useful when you're typing in the captions and photo names for books and calendars that you plan to order, as described in Chapter 10. Even then, you may find this feature a bit cumbersome (page 275).

Special Characters

Opens a palette of non-alphabet symbols for entering into text boxes.

Photos Menu

This menu's commands come in handy when you're working with one or more photos. Most of the time, you need to select the photos, using any of the methods described on page 106, before choosing from this menu.

Get Info

This command (or ⌘-I) opens the Photo Info window. Click the Photo tab in the Photo Info window to see information about a selected photo, such as its creation date and the camera model used to create it. Switch to the Exposure panel for details about the specific camera settings that were used to take the picture. (iPhoto gathers all this information by reading *EXIF* tags—snippets of data invisibly embedded in the photo files created by most of today's digital cameras.)

You can open the Photo Info window even when no photos are selected, but it won't have any info filled in. The data pops into the window as soon as you select a photo.

Tip: Once the Photo Info window is open, you can leave it open. As you click different photos, the information in the window changes instantly to reflect your selection.

Batch Change

Opens a dialog box where you can apply a new title, date, or comment to any number of selected photos. See page 122 for full details.

Rotate

You can use the two Rotate commands in the submenu—Counter Clockwise or Clockwise—to rotate selected photos in 90-degree increments, switching them from landscape to portrait orientation as needed.

However, the Rotate menu command is by far the *least* convenient way to rotate your photos. Here are some alternatives:

- Click the Rotate button below the main iPhoto window.

- Option-click the Rotate button to reverse the direction of the rotation. (You specify the "main" rotation direction by choosing iPhoto→Preferences.)

- Press ⌘-R to rotate selected photos counterclockwise, or Shift-⌘-R to rotate them clockwise.

- Control-click a photo or a thumbnail; choose Rotate from the shortcut menu.

My Rating

Lets you apply a rating of one through five stars to selected photos. See page 135 for the full story on this feature.

Duplicate

Just as in the Finder, this command creates a duplicate of whichever photo is selected and adds it to the Library. And just as in the Finder, the keyboard shortcut is ⌘-D. If you select multiple photos, iPhoto duplicates all of them.

If an album is selected (and no photos are), this command duplicates the album itself. The copy appears at the bottom of the Source list, named Album-1 (or whatever number it's up to).

Move to Trash

Moves selected photos to iPhoto's private Trash, a holding bin for files you plan to permanently delete from your Photo Library. Instead of choosing this command, you can just drag thumbnails onto the Trash icon in the Source list; Control-click selected photos and choose Move to Trash from the shortcut menu; or press ⌘-Delete. (They're not actually deleted until you choose Empty Trash.)

Revert to Original

The Revert to Original command restores edited photos to the condition they were in when you first imported them into iPhoto, reversing all the cropping, rotating, brightening, or anything else you've done (although it leaves titles, comments, and keywords undisturbed). This command is active only if you've edited the selected photo at least once.

If the Revert to Original command is dimmed out, one of these conditions is probably true:

- You don't have a photo selected.

- The photo you've selected hasn't been edited, so there's nothing to revert to.

- You edited the photo outside of iPhoto in an unauthorized way (by dragging the thumbnail to the Photoshop icon in the Dock, for example). iPhoto never had the chance to make a backup of the original version, which it needs to revert the file.

On the other hand, it's totally OK to edit photos outside of iPhoto—thereby activating the Revert to Original feature—if you do it by *double-clicking* the photo's thumbnail rather than dragging it, or by Control-clicking it and choosing "Edit in external editor" from the shortcut menu.

Restore to Photo Library

The Move to Trash command morphs into this command when you're viewing the contents of iPhoto's Trash and have at least one thumbnail selected. It moves the selected photos out of the Trash and back into your Photo Library. The shortcut is the same as the one for Move to Trash—⌘-Delete.

Share Menu

Version by version, iPhoto's menus are growing. New for iPhoto 6: the Share menu, which Apple used to offload some of the icons that had been crowding the bottom toolbar.

Email, Desktop, Order Prints...

Choosing one of these commands is exactly the same as clicking the corresponding toolbar button below the main iPhoto window. See Chapter 8 for more on printing and ordering prints; Chapter 9 for emailing, .Mac slideshows, photocasting, and Web pages; Chapter 13 for desktop pictures and screen savers; or Chapter 12 for burning slides to a DVD.

View Menu

This menu lets you change the order of your photos in the main viewing area, as well the kind of information you want displayed along with each picture (Figure B-3).

Titles, Keywords, Film Rolls, My Rating

Select any of these commands to display titles, keywords, film roll divider lines, or star ratings info in the main photo-viewing area. Titles, stars, and keywords always appear beneath each thumbnail; film rolls are denoted by horizontal lines, tiny film-roll icons, and flippy triangles.

You can turn each of these four commands on or off, in any combination, by repeatedly selecting it or by using the corresponding keyboard shortcuts: Shift-⌘-T for Titles, Shift-⌘-K for Keywords, Shift-⌘-R for Ratings, and Shift-⌘-F for Film Rolls. A checkmark next to a command shows that it's currently turned on.

Sort Photos

Determines how iPhoto sorts the photos in the viewing area. You have six options (Figure B-3):

• **by Film Roll.** Sorts the photos chronologically according to when each batch was imported into iPhoto.

- **by Date.** Arranges the photos chronologically based on the creation dates of each file.

- **by Keyword.** Sorts your photos alphabetically by the *first* keyword you've applied to each. (Photos with no keywords appear at the top of the list.)

- **by Title.** Uses the titles to sort photos alphabetically.

- **by Rating.** Arranges all of your pictures by how good they are, from best to worst—at least, if you've taken the time to apply star ratings to them (Chapter 5). Unrated photos appear at the bottom.

- **Manually.** Lets you drag your photos into any order you like. (This choice is dimmed unless you're in an album. In the main Photo Library, you must use one of the first two options.)

- **Ascending, Descending.** Reverses the sorting order, no matter which criterion you've specified above. For example, it puts oldest photos at the top rather than newest.

- **Reset Manual Sort.** What if you're in an album, you carefully drag pictures into a custom order, and then you sort the whole thing alphabetically? This command restores the manual positioning.

Figure B-3:
The View menu lets you customize how iPhoto displays and sorts thumbnails. The option to view photos by Film Roll option is dimmed out (as shown here) if you're currently viewing an album instead of your whole Photo Library. On the other hand, Manually is dimmed out if you're viewing the Library and not an album.

Show Thumbnails

Several of iPhoto's modes—editing and book/card/calendar creation, for example—feature a scrolling stream of thumbnails that lets you jump from one photo to another without exiting the editing mode. This command lets you hide or show that thumbnail browser.

Show in Toolbar

See those icons at the bottom of the main iPhoto window? Some of them are permanently installed and nonnegotiable, like Rotate, Edit, Book, and Slideshow.

The others, though, are optional in iPhoto 6. By choosing their names from the Show in Toolbar submenu, you can make them appear or disappear. (The names bearing checkmarks in the submenu are the ones that currently appear on the toolbar.)

The freedom to eliminate certain icons make a lot of sense. For one thing, some of them may not apply to you. The HomePage icon is useful only if you're a .Mac subscriber, the Send to iDVD button is helpful only if your Mac can burn DVDs, and so on. Furthermore, hiding the less useful icons leaves more room for the ones you do use (and reduces the likelihood that some of the buttons will be hidden behind the >> menu that sprouts whenever the window isn't wide enough).

Anyway, whatever functions you eliminate from the toolbar aren't gone for good. They're still available as commands right in the body of the Share menu.

Window Menu

The Window menu is filled with the standard Mac OS X window-manipulating commands.

Minimize

Collapses the frontmost iPhoto window into the Dock, in standard Mac OS X fashion. It's just as though you pressed ⌘-M or clicked the yellow Minimize button in the upper-left corner of any window.

Zoom

Zooms any iPhoto window to fill your entire screen (although it's nice enough to avoid covering up your Dock). Choosing this command is the same as clicking the green Zoom button in the upper-left corner of any iPhoto window.

If you choose the Zoom Window command (or click the Zoom button) again, the window shrinks back to its original proportions.

Bring All to Front

Every now and then, the windows of two different Mac OS X programs get shuffled together, so that one iPhoto window is sandwiched between, say, two Safari windows. This command brings all your iPhoto windows to the front so they're not being blocked by any other program's windows. (Clicking iPhoto's icon on the Dock does the same thing.)

[Window Names]

At the bottom of the Window menu, you'll see the names of all open windows. The main iPhoto window is, of course, called iPhoto, but you may also see the names of any photos you've opened for editing in separate windows.

Help Menu

You know all too well that iPhoto comes with no user manual; that's why you're reading this book! What official Apple documentation you do get appears in this menu. (Hint: It ain't much.)

iPhoto Help

This command opens Apple's Help Viewer program—eventually.

The assistance available through iPhoto Help is pretty limited, but at least you've got a searchable reference at your disposal if you forget how to do something (or lose this book).

Keyboard Shortcuts

This is just another link into the iPhoto Help system, but a particularly valuable one. It takes you to a table showing more than 50 keyboard shortcuts in iPhoto. This is one help page that's worth printing out.

Service and Support

Fires up your Web browser and opens Apple's main iPhoto support page. You may be asked to enter your Apple ID and password. (This is usually your email address plus the password you created when you registered iPhoto or another Apple product.)

Where to Go From Here

Your Mac, your trusty digital camera, and this book are all you need to *begin* enjoying the art and science of modern photography. But as your skills increase and your interests broaden, you may want to explore new techniques, add equipment, and learn from people who've become just as obsessed as you. Here's a tasty menu of online resources to help you along the way.

iPhoto and the Web

- **Apple's iPhoto support page** features the latest product information, QuickTime tutorials, FAQ (Frequently Asked Question) lists, camera and printer compatibility charts, and links to discussion forums where other iPhoto users share knowledge and lend helping hands. There's even a feedback form that goes directly to Apple. In fact, each piece of feedback is read personally by Steve Jobs. (Just a little joke there.) *www.apple.com/iphoto http://www.apple.com/support/iphoto/*

- **VersionTracker** is a massive database that tracks, and provides links to, all of the latest software for Mac OS X, including the cool iPhoto add-ons described in this book. *www.versiontracker.com*

- **O'Reilly's Mac DevCenter** features the latest Mac software techniques for power users and programmers. *www.macdevcenter.com*

Digital Photo Equipment on the Web

- **Imaging-Resource** offers equipment reviews, price comparisons, and forums, all dedicated to putting the right digital camera in your hands. *www.imaging-resource. com*

- **Digital Photography Review** is similar: It offers news, reviews, buying guides, photo galleries, and forums. It's a must-visit site for the digicam nut. *www.dpreview. com*

- **Digital Camera Resource** is just what it says: a comprehensive resource page comparing the latest in digital cameras. *www.dcresource.com*

- **Photo.net** offers industry news, galleries, shopping, travel, critique, and community sharing. *www.photo.net*

Show Your Pictures

- **Flickr.com** is the Web's most popular gallery for people's personal pictures. It's free for modest use, which is why even some Mac fans prefer it to a .Mac account. *www.flickr.com*

- **Fotki.com** is similar—it, too, is a thriving online community of photo fans who share their work online—but the free account is unlimited. Chime in with your shots, or just check out what everyone else is shooting. *www.fotki.com*

Online Instruction

- **ShortCourses.com** offers short courses in digital photography techniques and how to use current equipment. *www.shortcourses.com*

Online Printing

- **Shutterfly** is an alternative to iPhoto's built-in photo-ordering system. It's Mac OS X–friendly and highly reviewed (at least by *Macworld*). *www.shutterfly.com*

- **PhotoAccess** is another Mac OS X–friendly photo printing site that's also received high marks for quality. *www.photoaccess.com*

Pocket Guide

Digital Photography Pocket Guide by Derrick Story is a handy, on-the-go digital-photo reference that fits nicely in your camera bag or back pocket.

Index

Index

Colophon

This book was written and edited in Microsoft Word 2004 on various Macs.

The screenshots were captured with Ambrosia Software's Snapz Pro X (*www. ambrosiasw.com*) for the Mac. Adobe Photoshop CS2 *(www.adobe.com)* and Macromedia Freehand MX *(www.macromedia.com)* were called in as required for touching them up.

The full-page photos that introduce each part of this book came from iStockPhoto. com.

The book was designed and laid out in Adobe InDesign CS2 on a PowerBook G4 and a PowerMac G5. The fonts used include Formata (as the sans-serif family) and Minion (as the serif body face). To provide symbols like and ⌘, custom fonts were created using Macromedia Fontographer.

The book was then generated as an Adobe Acrobat PDF file for proofreading, indexing, and final transmission to the printing plant.